Time for Things

Time

FOR

Things

**LABOR, LEISURE, AND THE RISE
OF MASS CONSUMPTION**

Stephen D. Rosenberg

HARVARD UNIVERSITY PRESS
Cambridge, Massachusetts   London, England   2021

First printing

LIBRARY OF CONGRESS CATALOGING-IN-PUBLICATION DATA

Names: Rosenberg, Stephen D., 1966– author.
Title: Time for things : labor, leisure, and the rise of mass consumption /
    Stephen D. Rosenberg.
Description: Cambridge, Massachusetts : Harvard University Press, 2021. |
    Includes bibliographical references and index.
Identifiers: LCCN 2020016849 | ISBN 9780674979512 (cloth)
Subjects: LCSH: Welfare economics. | Consumption (Economics) | Quality of
    life. | Incentives in industry. | Quality of products.
Classification: LCC HB99.3 .R654 2021 | DDC 330.12/2—dc23
LC record available at https://lccn.loc.gov/2020016849

Contents

Time for Things

ONE

Introduction

In 1930, against the backdrop of the Depression, John Maynard Keynes wrote a short essay entitled "Economic Possibilities for Our Grandchildren" in which he cast his gaze beyond the economic ferment of his times to prognosticate about the future of capitalism.[1] Abandoning for a moment the short- and medium-run temporalities of his discipline, as well as the economist's preoccupation with scarcity and dismal trade-offs, Keynes became entranced by a much brighter vision. Economic growth would, in Keynes's view, eventually bring about an end to toil. A renaissance of human civilization would ensue, a cultural flowering reminiscent of the classical Greek ideal (or perhaps that of bohemian Bloomsbury). However, this one would not be bought at the expense of an army of slaves (or a household full of servants) but rather would be secured through exponential economic growth. Keynes's reasoning was straightforward enough. He simply took the estimated historical growth rate of capitalist economies and projected it over the following one hundred years. Assuming past rates of productivity improvement would continue unabated for the next century, the economy would, over that period, grow eightfold in per capita terms. "Mankind is solving its economic problem," Keynes proclaimed—such, he reflected, is the almost magical power of compound growth. Similarly, when Keynes looked back at the trend in work time in industrial capitalism over the previous fifty years, he saw a pattern he had no reason to believe would not continue. Increasing productivity had led to a steep and continuous decline in the length of the work week between 1870 and 1930, with working hours dropping by 30 percent in Europe and the United States. In predicting the future of capitalism, Keynes simply posited the continuation of that trend.

The conclusion Keynes drew from his brief exercise in futurology was that the productivity gains yielded by capitalism would, in the long run, inevitably lead the economy to enter into a stationary (or "steady") state, in which material wants would be satiated. Further increases in productivity would then have the effect of reducing the need for labor, radically diminishing the length of the working week. The result would be an utter transformation in the moral fabric of capitalism, returning pecuniary motive to the marginal place it held in previous eras of history and opening up new possibilities for human flourishing. Keynes predicted that in the coming era of abundance, "we shall once more value ends above means and prefer the good to the useful." To be sure, there would be a period of adjustment during which people would have to cultivate the skills and sensibility necessary for them to be able to fully enjoy their liberation. Indeed, Keynes thought that such is the cultural momentum, under capitalism, behind work for work's sake, that people might for a while voluntarily arrest the decline in work hours. He imagined people resisting working for fewer than fifteen or so hours each week, for no good reason other than to keep themselves busy. But they would certainly not choose to work more than that, for "three hours a day is quite enough to satisfy the old Adam in most of us" (Keynes 1930, p. 369). In effect, capitalism, conceived of as a system of self-exploitation and the fetishistic pursuit of monetary gain would abolish itself—or, more precisely, would evolve into something utterly different—simply by virtue of following its natural developmental trajectory. The Faustian pact made at the dawn of the modern era, having achieved its goals, was thus destined to be undone. "Purposive man," to use Keynes's phrase, would be laid to rest, having served his purpose admirably.[2]

In 2005, a group of eminent economists, including such luminaries as Robert Solow, Joseph Stiglitz, and Gary Becker, was invited to contribute essays to a book intended to evaluate Keynes's predictions about the future of capitalism (Pecchi and Piga 2008). The historical data analyzed by these economists showed that Keynes's growth projections were, if anything, on the conservative side. His predictions for growth, based on a long-run estimate of about 2 percent per year, yielded an upper bound eightfold increase in per capita wealth over the next hundred years. Fabrizio Zilibotti found, however, that in the fifty-year period between 1950 and 2000, average world economic growth was 2.9 percent per year, quadrupling per capita output.[3] Projected over one century, that rate of growth would produce a seventeenfold increase in the standard of living, twice as much as the upper bound predicted by Keynes. Most of the growth in the earlier part of the period took place in advanced capitalist economies. In Organisation for Economic Co-operation and Development (OECD) nations, between 1950 and 1970, population-weighted growth levels reached an impressive 4 percent per year.[4] And yet despite the impressive rate of per capita growth, Keynes's prediction of the dawning of a new era in which human beings would be progressively freed from necessary labor, and therefore increasingly able to pursue life-enhancing practices, was not, by the early 2000s (when the economists examined the issue), even remotely close to being realized. By the late 1940s full-time weekly working hours had stabilized at around forty across the industrial capitalist world and failed, thereafter, to fall much further, despite tremendous growth in output per hour of work in the second half of the century. Indeed, there is evidence that toward the end of the twentieth century, work time in some parts of the industrial world increased, even as productivity gains marched relentlessly onward.[5]

Economists offer a range of explanations for the failure of Keynes's prediction, some of which are close to being circular. One explanation is that work is itself a source of utility—surely that must be so, the reasoning goes, or else why would people not choose to cut their hours? Alternatively, material wants must indeed be insatiable—why else would people choose income over leisure? Other explanations offered are more substantive: consumption under conditions of affluence becomes driven by status-seeking one-upmanship, and the demand for positional goods (which index relative position in a status hierarchy) can never be exhausted; growing inequality induces a widespread fear of downward social mobility and so increases the incentive to work in order to close the income gap; higher income creates new needs, such that needs are not fixed but rather change with economic growth. These explanations surely have something to them. No one could sensibly deny that some people find some value in activities for which they happen to be paid, nor would it be wise to underestimate concerns about status and the role of conspicuous consumption in status competition. However, the explanations offered do not, for reasons set out in the next chapter, satisfactorily account for the dramatic degree to which Keynes's vision of the future failed to come to pass.[6] Indeed, the very fact that there is such disagreement between the economists on why, in the wake of growing affluence, work failed to retreat more than it did, indicates the difficulty of the puzzle.

Closely related to the question of why work hours failed to decrease more as productivity went up is the question of why consumption continued to increase so relentlessly. Productivity gains, in lieu of reduced work time, were turned into higher real income, which was used to fund more consumption. Why is consumption, like production, seemingly unbounded under capitalism? There is clearly a plausible explanation for the unending expansion of capitalist production: Capitalists try to outcompete one another by increasing productivity, seeking to turn lower costs into a bigger market share by cutting prices and expanding output. Yet it is not at all clear why effective demand should keep up with expanded output—why, in Keynes's terms, the demand for commodities should prevail over the demand for free time, even though the relative value of those commodities should, it seems, decline with growing affluence. This ongoing growth in consumption is especially puzzling given evidence that suggests that the relation between wealth and well-being is far from being a simple linear one in which added increments of wealth add increments of well-being.

The question of why and how the production and consumption of commodities should have come in modern times to so dominate human beings is a venerable one in the history of social theories of capitalism. It was posed in perhaps its most general and powerful form by Karl Marx, for whom the most fundamental contradiction in capitalism is between the degree of freedom made possible by advances in the forces of production and the form of life actually realized (and realizable) under capitalism. The capitalist system, for Marx, represented a kind of false necessity (albeit, in his more teleological moments, a developmentally necessary one) that history was destined to transcend.

From a different perspective, the question also underlies Max Weber's theory of the historical and cultural underpinnings of capitalism. For Weber, the growth dynamic of capitalism is precisely what separates it from the comparatively static economies of "traditional" societies. While Weber was interested in the spirit that drives the unremitting increases in productivity under capitalism, the other side of the equation is that which allows for the absorption of an ever-increasing volume of products (Weber [1930] 1992). Weber suggested that the methodical, rational mode of economic action and organization that underlay the ascent of modern capitalism was driven by a quest for psychological reassurance by way of the accumulation of objectified value, rendered visible as money. Money provided a metric by which success, and therefore virtue, could be measured.[7] But crucially, instrumental reason could not be monetized—therefore quantified in a general, public form, one amenable to comparative assessment—unless a ready market could be found for the things it produced. How could the productivity of capitalist A, making widgets, be compared to capitalist B, making pots, if their products were not converted through sales into money? A condition of possibility for the economy becoming a domain within which the Protestant ethic (and its secularized spiritual descendants) could express itself was thus a dynamic consumer market, capable of absorbing the ever-greater volume of products churned out by a system of production ever more regimented by instrumental reason, and converting it into a generalized, quantitative sign of value.

Bringing the concerns of Marx together with those of Weber, the question of the unbounded and irrational character of capitalist modernity was also a central concern for later generations of Marxists, most prominently those belonging to the Frankfurt School. They asked: How is it that the accumulation of wealth and refinement of technique, which should be merely a means to the end of the good life, become in effect ends unto themselves? Why, under capitalist modernity, does instrumental rationality become so systemically entrenched, unable to mature (as Keynes thought it would do) to the point of becoming (as reason suggests it should be) just a means to a higher purpose? True to their Marxian roots, the Frankfurt theorists tended to focus on cultural forms generated by the organization of the relations of production—yet they clearly also saw that without mass consumption modern industrial capitalism could not function.

The stakes in the puzzle represented by this configuration of ever-increasing production and consumption are, of course, very high given the extraordinarily urgent environmental problems of our age. Despite much talk about deindustrialization, the shift to services, and the rise of the "knowledge economy" under late capitalism, the capitalist system of production and consumption is pressing harder than ever against the limits of nature. So not only is the materialistic bias of capitalism questionable from the proximate perspective of the well-being it yields, but it in addition threatens the long-term future of the species.

This book is an extended investigation of this puzzle. My objectives are to delineate its conceptual structure, analyze its empirical basis, and build a historically grounded theory in light of which the puzzling pattern of work, productivity, and consumption becomes less puzzling. I follow the tradition, rooted equally, although in very different ways, in Marx and Weber, of doing social theory by thinking about history. While I consider general trends under capitalism in the industrial world, the empirical side of the book focuses on the United States, especially during the middle decades of the twentieth century.

My contention is that the reason why work failed to retreat in the face of relentlessly increasing productivity has much to do with the rise of practices and institutions associated with mass consumer society. Yet to adduce the supposed benefits of consumption as an adequate explanation for the failure of Keynes's prediction to come true just raises the question of why spending should have seemed more beneficial than free time. After all, it is not unreasonable to expect that as incomes increase, so the demand for leisure will also increase. Canonical economists such as Frank Knight (1921) and Arthur Pigou (1932) certainly thought as much.[8] With higher wage rates, the relative value of leisure should, according to these economists, increase, and workers should consequently feel less inclined to offer their labor.[9] The prediction that follows from this is that other things being equal, with growing affluence the supply curve of labor should become backward sloping. And yet the historical pattern under industrial capitalism between 1930 and the present day indicates not much evidence in support of that prediction. At the same time, there is evidence from late nineteenth-century America that workers in that period chose to use increasing hourly income to buy back their time—meaning that the supply curve of labor was, in the decades before the turning of the twentieth century, indeed backward sloping (Dora Costa 1998b, 2000a). So it has certainly not always been the case that increasing hourly wages has led to more consumption rather than less work. Yet after a certain point in history that is how things quite consistently went. We are thus left with some unanswered questions. What changed to make consumption as unbounded as production? Why did the value of free time apparently decline in relative terms as affluence increased? What was it about the set of institutions, practices, and moral norms associated with mass consumption that might have caused a shift in aggregate preferences away from free time and toward the accumulation of consumer goods?

I think that the answer to these questions might be found by attending to the problem of wage-labor commensuration and to the development of a form of consumption that seemingly resolves this problem. The problem of wage-labor commensuration is that the legitimacy of wage-labor exchange depends on labor being commensurable with its wage, but it is entirely unclear how the concrete activity of work *could* be commensurable with the wage, which, after all, is just an abstraction. The possibility of commensuration between wage and work rests, I argue in this book, on goods being framed and construed as stores of potential free activity. When wages are spent on goods that signify hypothetical durations of activity, wage earners receive a form of compensation that seems commensurable with the life activity they give up in labor. The actual time and freedom lost as work is compensated for by the notional free time indexed by consumer goods—and specifically, consumer durables, a category of product that became increasingly important in twentieth-century capitalism. Caught in a cycle of commensuration, wage workers were willing to take their share of rising productivity (realized as increasing hourly wages) as more consumption rather than more free time.

The commensurability of labor and wage made sense in the context of a particular understanding of the grounds on which an economic exchange can be considered fair. On this understanding, economic exchanges are fair when there is an equality between the exchanged substances. The emergence of mass consumption was closely connected to the increasing de facto legitimacy of wage-labor exchange, under this historically particular understanding of economic fairness, applied to wage labor. The fairness of wage labor exchange became possible through the establishment of an objective equivalence between labor and wage goods, as those goods came to signify free activity. This version of economic fairness was most clearly instantiated in the moral economy that underpinned the mid-century "Fordist" period of capitalism.

The Character and Scope of the Argument

The approach taken in this book is interdisciplinary, ranging across all the social sciences and diverse currents of historical research while also drawing on philosophical works. Especially in the theory sections of the book, I discuss a variety of sometimes conflicting paradigms. I ask my readers to consider approaches to social and economic phenomena with which they might be unfamiliar or perhaps might even think self-evidently wrong. The discussion turns on a dime, as it were, from neoclassical economics to Marxian accounts of capitalism, from economic anthropology to sociological theory, from political economy to behavioral psychology. At the same time, the book combines economic analysis, historical synthesis, sometimes quite speculative social theorizing, and interpretation of culture, bringing together methods and approaches that have their homes in different disciplines. But there are good reasons for tromping freely across disciplinary boundaries when considering big questions of the sort that are at the center of this book. When faced with very complex, multifaceted problems, the best approach is to regard the human sciences as a diverse tool kit, and, in order to gain some leverage on the problem, try out as many theoretical approaches and concepts as possible.

My historical analysis focuses on the United States. At the same time, I often refer to advanced capitalist society in general, especially during its postwar Golden Age era, as my unit of analysis. As noted in Chapter 2, the general puzzling pattern of work time, productivity, and consumption is present to varying degrees in every affluent capitalist society. Given its focus on the United States, I certainly would not want to claim that the evidence examined in the book provides strong inductive support for the theory across all advanced industrial capitalist societies. The aim of the book is better understood as *abductive* rather than inductive. That is, my objective is to construct a hypothesis, one that seems sufficiently plausible to be worth exploring in other contexts.[10] The analysis of patterns in US history, in addition to providing some empirical support for the argument, also serves as a heuristic for the development and exposition of the general theory.

The largely abductive aim of this book shapes the structure of the argument. It begins by drawing attention to a state of affairs that has struck many as surprising and, therefore, as standing in need of explanation. I then set out a theory of the relationship between wage-labor exchange and consumption under capitalism from which, if true, the surprising state of affairs would follow as a matter of course. I give some historical grounding to the theory, focusing on the United States, which I take to be a good case to illustrate the more general puzzle. My strategy is to show how the theory illuminates a wide range of phenomena related to work and mass consumption under capitalism. Considering the degree to which capitalism encompasses every dimension of social, cultural, and economic life, going for breadth of empirical analysis seems well advised.

The point of the empirical work is to substantiate the theory to the degree that it takes on some prima facie plausibility—providing grounds for thinking that this particular abduction might be worthy of further investigation, perhaps in delimited contexts, which might be more amenable to inductive testing. If readers conclude that the theory seems convincing in the case of US capitalism, they may go on to ponder how much light it might shed on other capitalist contexts. The empirical analysis of the United States serves as a guide to what sorts of institutions and practices to look at in ascertaining whether a similar dynamic might be at work in other places in which mass consumer capitalism developed. In other settings, there are, of course, bound to be mediating factors that complicate the picture.

In sum, the objective of this book is to construct a compelling, historically grounded theory to account for a quite general pattern in industrial capitalism. The advantage of specifying the theoretical argument on a general level is that by doing so it becomes sufficiently perspicuous and context-independent to be easily transposable to other settings. Fleshing the argument out through analysis of the United States makes the basic theoretical argument more concrete while providing some evidence for it in at least one case.

A Note on Use of Terminology:
Use Value, Use Power, Utility

Notions of use and usefulness are central to the argument of this book. Three terms are used to refer to different dimensions of usefulness: *utility*, *use value*, and *use power*. *Use value* and *utility* are common in economics and political economy, and there is a good deal of overlap between their meaning in those fields and how the terms are used in this book. Nonetheless, my deployment of the terms is in some ways idiosyncratic, so a brief account of how they are used is in order. *Use power* is an addition to the array of concepts that deal with usefulness, so it needs defining.

Utility: I use *utility* to mean the actual satisfaction realized by some state or activity. I take utility to be somewhat vague—a rough sense of how satisfying things are rather than a precise metric for satisfaction. I would not want to claim that utility is *merely* an idea—at some basic level, it has roots in real human needs and desires. But as society becomes more affluent, those needs and desires become more complex, and indeed often contradictory, which makes utility an increasingly difficult and elusive concept.

Use power: By *use power* I mean the capacity of an object to facilitate some useful activity. For example, the use power of a bicycle is its capacity to make possible the useful activity of cycling. Use power is determined by the material properties of the object as well as its symbolic associations and is conditional on the opportunities an individual has for making use of that object under specific conditions of life. For instance, the use power of a bicycle, qua resource for cycling, in the setting of a raft drifting in the middle of an ocean, is pretty much zero. However, even if the context is felicitous and the product entirely functional, that does not mean that the use power of an object will *actually* be put to use. The use power of an object is just the *potential* it offers its user to undertake some useful activity. The idea is analogous to Marx's concept of labor power. Labor power is the productive capacity workers have, which they exchange for their wage. Whether or not that capacity is made use of is contingent on various factors, primarily how effective capitalists are in extracting labor from workers during the working day. Use power is the useful activity-generating capacity workers get when they use their wages to acquire wage goods. Whether or not that capacity will be made use of depends on various contextual factors, such as the availability of time, energy, and complementary resources. The final thing that should be noted is that the use power of most objects gets depleted with use over time, because of material wear and tear. Commodity objects have a useful life—a duration of time-in-use before they become worn out and are no longer useful.

Use value: By *use value* I mean the *value ascribed* to commodities by virtue of the notional use power, or useful activity-generating potential, with which they are endowed (at times I also use the term in its more traditional Marxian sense). The difference between utility and use value is that utility is actual satisfaction, while use value is attached to the envisioned capacity of a commodity to facilitate useful activities. For a given person, the use value of a commodity depends on assessments about the extent to which its use power can be converted into actual activities, as well as the person's preferences. The use value of an object can be said to have been *realized* only through actual use, with the limits of use set by the use power of the object. As with utility, the use value of a commodity is not amenable to precise measurement but rather is a matter of rough judgment, an approximate sense of things. Indeed, precisely because different use values are qualitatively distinct, it is unclear on what basis they can be compared quantitatively.

Plan of the Book

The plan of the book follows the abductive structure of its argument. The first part of the book describes the general pattern under advanced capitalism of stagnating work time and relentlessly increasing consumption, and introduces a theory which, I suggest, offers a good explanation for the pattern. Chapters 2 and 3 explore what is puzzling about the peculiar combination of economic growth, consumption, and work time under advanced capitalism, especially in its American incarnation. In Chapter 2, I discuss the issue on a quite abstract level and consider possible explanations from different parts of the social sciences. In Chapter 3, in order to make things more empirically concrete, I analyze patterns of productivity, wages, work time, and consumption in the United States between the later nineteenth and late twentieth centuries. Chapter 4 introduces a different kind of explanation for the puzzling pattern I identify, one based on the normativity governing exchange and, specifically, on the problem of commensuration in the exchange of labor for a wage. I set out the advantages of this exchange-based explanation for the pattern of time use, work, and consumption under capitalism over other possible explanations. The first part of the book concludes with a consideration of various objections that could be raised against this wage-labor commensuration theory of mass consumption.

The second part of the book shows how various trends in US history align with the theory. I focus on two large-scale developments. The first of these, discussed in Chapter 5, is the increasing legitimacy accorded to the institution of wage labor. Wage labor began by being regarded as a deeply questionable institution, entailing coercion and loss of freedom to such an extent that it was associated with slavery but, over time, came to be seen as a potentially fair exchange relationship. This legitimization of wage labor involved the rise of an overriding concern with a conception of fair wages defined in terms of their purchasing power—the capacity of the wage to capture a set of goods, the value of which is deemed in some sense sufficient for it to count as fair compensation for the work given in exchange for the wage. The notion of measurable purchasing power in turn depended on the second trend I examine—the increasing standardization of consumer goods (as well as work and wages). Standardization had the effect of stabilizing the properties of consumer commodities, which was a prerequisite for commensuration. At the same time, the moral economy built around the notion of fair and commensurate wage-labor exchange encouraged further standardization in the sphere of consumption. Different dimensions of the standardization of consumption are discussed in Chapters 6, 7, and 8. In Chapter 9, I consider the reaction to the perceived violation of the normative order underlying the standardization of consumption, by examining the moral panic around planned obsolescence. The rise of what historian Meg Jacobs (2005) has described as a "purchasing power paradigm" in American political economy, which focused on real wages above all else, in conjunction with the standardization of consumer goods, promoted the notion that work is commensurable with its wage. And it was this commensurability of wage and work, I argue, that explains the pattern of work and consumption that emerged in the twentieth century. The book concludes with a summation of the argument and some general thoughts about the character of economic normativity under capitalism.

TWO

The Puzzle

1. The Puzzle of Productivity, Time, and Work in Advanced Industrial Capitalism

The puzzle motivating this book has two, closely related dimensions. The first concerns the relation between welfare, work, and consumption under industrial capitalism. Why, given the myriad costs imposed on individuals and on society by boundless output and consumption, and the increasingly questionable benefit of added increments of consumption once affluence has been achieved, does output nonetheless continue to expand so relentlessly? How can we explain the steady increase in consumption under conditions of affluence, while decreases in work time have slowed to a crawl? Surely there should be, as Knight asserted and Keynes simply assumed, a more even apportioning of the benefits of increased productivity between free time and higher incomes?

The second dimension of the puzzle concerns the structural dynamics of industrial capitalism. If we discard the assumption that exchange under capitalism is necessarily driven (and therefore is explained) by utility maximization—and that the capitalist economy is tugged ever in the direction of efficient equilibrium—how is it that production and consumption are, nonetheless, kept in balance to a degree that allows for the stable reproduction of the system? If consumption under industrial capitalism cannot be explained in terms of maximizing utility, how then should it be explained? What accounts for the scale and dynamic character of aggregate demand associated with mass consumption? Once the economy has been organized according to the principles of mass production, how is enough demand generated to ensure timely profit realization? The question is particularly pertinent in the case of mass production, because mass production involves heavy investment in fixed capital of a kind that tends to be very specialized. Capital-intensive production of that sort is only economically viable if output is kept close to full capacity. As mass production expanded, ever-increasing levels of aggregate demand were therefore required for profit realization. In theory, this made the economy very vulnerable to downturns in demand, either directly, by way of their effect on profit rates, or indirectly, through their influence on investment decisions. And yet, despite being a quite inflexible way to organize an economy, capitalist mass production has proven quite resilient—its output has tended to be met by an equivalent volume of effective demand.[1] How, then, was it that enough aggregate effective demand was generated to support the growth dynamic of industrial capitalism in the era of mass production? One answer is that aggregate demand was stabilized by an imbricated complex of measures and institutions, including wages policy, a corporatist industrial order, government spending, welfare provisions, and fiscal and monetary management—the elements that comprised the so-called Fordist regime of capitalist regulation. Yet all of those Fordist regulatory strategies presuppose a tendency for higher real income per hour worked (from whatever source) to be converted into more effective demand rather than less work. It is hard to see how Fordist measures to regulate the economy could have been viable without the materialistic bias—the prioritizing of commodity acquisition over less work time—that underlay mass consumption. What then was the basis of that bias? The following two chapter sections consider in more detail each side of the puzzle. I move on to a more focused, empirical analysis of the puzzle in Chapter 3, which concentrates on the case of the United States in the era of mass production.

1.1.   Consumption, Work-Time, and Well-Being

Avner Offer (2006), Tibor Scitovsky (1992), and Fred Block (1990), among many others, have made compelling arguments, on both theoretical and empirical grounds, that the notion that increasing material accumulation necessarily leads to increasing well-being is questionable. This is especially so in the case of affluent societies, because, as any basic economics textbook informs us, increasing consumption, ceteris paribus, yields diminishing marginal utility.[2] While, to be sure, not all of the axioms and theoretical postulates of economics are plausible, the idea that, other things being equal, the benefit of each additional dollar of spent income (and of the consumption that it affords) decreases as income increases seems uncontroversial. It informs the moral logic of progressive taxation, can be derived from hierarchical models of need such as A. H. Maslow's (1943), and is also implicit in the more sophisticated capabilities approach to welfare developed by Amartya Sen (1988, [1985] 1999).[3] As will be seen, there is a good amount of empirical support, based on comparative analysis of different countries, for the proposition that the welfare produced by income decreases as income increases (Easterlin 1974, 2003; Layard 2005; Offer 2006; Layard and Mayraz 2008; Kahneman and Deaton 2010). Indeed, the evidence suggests that the rate at which marginal utility of income (measured by subjective well-being) drops off is more rapid than would be the case if marginal added utility was, as predicted by utility theorists from Daniel Bernoulli onward, inversely proportional to increasing income (Layard and Mayraz 2008; Bernoulli [1738] 1954).[4]

One of the intuitions underlying the theory of the declining marginal utility of spending is that there are certain existential constants that limit the extent to which commodities can be deployed in practices in which their use value gets realized.[5] The most basic of these are limitations of time and energy, both of which are required to turn money (by way of commodities) into useful activities. All things being equal, as more commodities get accumulated, the amount of time and energy available for making use of each of them asymptotically approaches zero. A similar point holds if the pattern of ever greater commodity accumulation is considered from the perspective of attention. Inspired by the influential social scientist Herbert Simon (1971), economists have recently begun to conceive of attention as a scarce resource, on which demands are made by various aspects of the environment (Davenport and Beck 2001).[6] The thought is that human beings have finite cognitive resources, which must, like any scarce resource, be distributed over a range of competing demands. Attention can be overwhelmed by too much information, and that can lead to suboptimal outcomes.[7] Each commodity requires attention if it is to be put to use in some activity. Therefore, the larger the number of commodities a person owns, the greater the amount of attention is required from that person for their use value to be realized. Limitations of time, energy, and attention thus mean that as more goods are acquired, the constraints on realizing each of their use values become ever tighter. And yet despite these limiting existential factors, under advanced capitalism there is a seemingly endless accumulation of objects, at great cost to the environment, communities, and individuals. Not the least of these costs is the free time foregone in order to generate the income required to fund commodity accumulation.[8] How does this state of affairs come about—how does it get reproduced?

1.2. The Sources of Subjective Well-Being

The pattern of ever-increasing consumption at fixed hours of work is particularly puzzling in the light of recent research on happiness and well-being. The results of this research throw into question the assumption that the trade-off of free time for increased consumption characteristic of industrial capitalism reflects the application of a utility maximizing calculus. This is because the correlation between increasing income and improvements in subjective well-being progressively weakens after a certain standard of living has been achieved. The research on subjective well-being also indicates that happiness does not necessarily require much in the way of expenditure. At the same time, it indicates that work, for most people, is not a particularly important source of happiness, while it can be a very significant source of unhappiness.

Measuring happiness and well-being is certainly rife with conceptual and methodological, not to say philosophical, difficulties.[9] Empirical work on subjective well-being has tended to be cross-sectional and comparative rather than deeply historical, so it should be treated with caution when interpreting developmental trajectories. A more fundamental problem is that the evaluation of life has, as Amartya Sen puts it, a "complex grammar" that complicates efforts to measure well-being.[10] Human welfare has a number of qualitatively distinct dimensions, which comprise what Sen ([1985] 1999) refers to as a "constitutive plurality." Sen suggests that welfare should be thought of as a composite of goods realized along those dimensions rather than as reducible to the kind of atomic common denominator utility theorists have in mind—the economists' hypothetical "util" of satisfaction. The conceptual complexity of well-being, and the often quite subtle differences in the meaning of terms associated with it, means that the precise wording of questions about well-being influences the answers people give to them. This makes the attempt to measure well-being a rather treacherous endeavor. Nonetheless, it would be unwise to dismiss the growing body of empirical work on subjective well-being—it provides at least something to go on for those who are concerned with questions of welfare and certainly represents an advance on the expedient move economists tend to make of simply using money as a proxy for well-being.[11] While self-reports of happiness are subjective, they tend to be corroborated by reports of friends and family members, which strengthens their validity (Diener 1984). Moreover, there is evidence that reports of subjective happiness are correlated with more objective emotional markers, such as how often people smile (Eckman and Friesen 1990). There is also an increasing amount of research indicating that subjective reports of well-being are associated with various physiological measures of health, such as inflammation levels, sleep quality, and cardiovascular and immuno-logical function (Ryff, Singer, and Love 2004; Steptoe, Wardle, and Marmot 2005). The research on happiness and well-being could be plausibly inter-preted as indicating that there is indeed something contradictory about the organization of economic life under capitalist modernity. In light of what seems to promote human welfare, broadly construed, there is a significant tension between how things are arranged under industrial capitalism and how they could be arranged. The relentless drive toward economic growth that characterizes capitalism as an economic system is not easily explained just in terms of its benefits for human welfare.

The best-known finding that questions the association between wealth and human well-being is the so called Easterlin paradox, discovered by econ-omist Richard Easterlin in the early 1970s. Easterlin (1974) found, through comparative analysis, that once basic needs are met, wealth is correlated with happiness within countries at a given point in time but that richer coun-tries are not happier than less wealthy ones. Moreover, as affluent countries grew wealthier, they did not become happier. As an example, Easterlin points out that indices of happiness did not change in the United States between 1947 and 1970, even though income and wealth increased greatly over that period.[12] Following Easterlin's research, David G. Blanchflower and Andrew J. Oswald (2004) found that happiness in the United States between the mid-1970s and mid-1990s failed to increase, even as per capita income increased by close to 60 percent.[13] Research by Bruno S. Frey and Alois Stutzer (2002), examining the United States over the same period, indicates that while real income increased for nine of the ten deciles in the population, aver-age happiness only increased (and by a very slight amount) for the lowest decile. According to their data, the overall average level of happiness actually declined in the United States between the 1970s and the 1990s. Avner Offer (2006), in an overview of the literature on the relation between economic growth and happiness, concurs with Easterlin's assessment that well-being in affluent nations over time has not risen with rising income.[14]

The Easterlin paradox, it should be noted, has aroused much debate and contention. In one of the most serious challenges to Easterlin's findings, B. Stevenson and J. Wolfers (2008) argue that analysis of time series data shows that *log* GDP (which Easterlin did not consider) *is* correlated with levels of absolute happiness. Easterlin (2010) responded to Stevenson and Wolfers's study by noting that their data reveal only a short-term association between log income and happiness and adduced further longitudinal data to show that a longer-term relationship (greater than ten years) does not exist.[15] Taking up the question once more, Daniel Kahneman and Angus Deaton (2010), examining US survey data collected by Gallup, found that emotional well-being—feelings of happiness and satisfaction in the moment, as opposed to "life evaluation"—increases with income up to about $75,000 per year. Beyond that point, any further increases in income do not yield additional increases in happiness.[16]

The Kahneman and Deaton study suggests that perhaps both Easterlin's research and the Stevenson and Wolfers study are on to something. Yet, significantly, Kahneman and Deaton did not add the variable of free time to their analysis—nor indeed do many of the other studies on income and happiness. Such studies typically compare reported happiness at different levels of income but not at different levels of income in combination with different amounts of leisure.[17] The finding that emotional well-being, in a set of capitalist societies, is, on average, correlated with increasing income up to $75,000 does not imply that there are not ways of arranging life at lower levels of income, with greater amounts of free time, that produce superior levels of happiness and well-being. It would clearly be unwarranted to conclude from the Gallup data that a capitalist society in which everyone earns at least $75,000, but with all other features of capitalism in place, including its work-time regime, represents the best possible distribution of resources between income and free time. Despite the interpretive controversies around the research on the relation between income and happiness, one firm conclusion can be drawn from it for the purposes of this book: it is certainly not the case that that the empirical evidence supports the proposition that over time added increments of income necessarily increase happiness—even at a rate that is diminishing at the margin.

The research on happiness also provides some more fine-grained information about the sources of subjective well-being, in light of which the pattern of economic growth under industrial capitalism becomes yet more puzzling. Psychologists Leaf Van Boven and Tom Gilovich (2003, Van Boven 2005) found in their research that what makes people happy are experiences rather than the possession of things. Presumably some of those experiences are commodified and, therefore, demand money—but certainly not all of them are. The connection between valued experiences and the use or possession of commodities (or spending of money) is clearly a contingent rather than a necessary one. Indeed, other research on well-being suggests that it is associated with activities that can easily be pursued without much in the way of expenditure. The Gallup data on affect that Kahneman and Deaton make use of, for example, show that subjective well-being is most closely tied to a set of factors that seem to have little to do with direct consumption. These include being treated with respect, having close ties with family and friends, learning something new, exercising a skill, and having free time (Diener et al. 2010). It is not at all clear that the happiness derived from, for instance, the experience of being with friends and family is amplified in anything like a linear fashion, if at all, by the money spent during that experience.

At the same time, the research on happiness does not indicate that work itself, at least under capitalism, is prominent among its sources. While the Gallup survey data used by Kahneman and Deaton point to two sources of happiness—learning something new and exercising a skill—that are sometimes associated with work, other research indicates that it is activities outside of work that yield the most happiness. In a 2004 study, the five most highly rated sources of happiness were found to be (in descending order) intimate relationships, socializing after work, dinner, relaxing, and lunch, with everything related to work firmly at the bottom of the list. (Kahneman et al. 2004). Derek Bok (2010, p. 29), summing up findings in the empirical literature on well-being, notes that the research indicates that "almost all of the pleasurable aspects of the day take place outside of work . . . the less pleasant aspects of the day involve activities associated with one's job, including commuting."

To be sure, happiness narrowly construed, as pleasure, is not the only thing that people value—freedom, creativity, and participation in meaningful activities, which clearly are sometimes features of working life, are surely equally important components of a good life. People might then organize their priorities so as to best realize various dimensions of the good life, rather than to maximize happiness, and this could well involve committing to some amount of work time. Indeed, the importance of work in the pursuit of these values was what encouraged many women in advanced capitalist societies to enter the workforce during the middle decades of the twentieth century. The example of women suggests that when people are deprived of the possibility of work, they often want work, and not necessarily just for material purposes, for work can be a source of value and meaning independent of its financial rewards. At the same time, it is important to note that positive attitudes to waged work might to some extent reflect the valorization of paid work under capitalism as a source of agency, self-expression, and even self-possession. This raises the question of why agency and self-expression become so bound up with the activities undertaken as paid labor. For clearly work understood simply as productive activity can take place outside the cash nexus.[18] The association of paid work with personal fulfillment, in conjunction with the opportunities it offers for social life beyond the family, means that, for any given individual, paid work might well have some intrinsic value, and this probably helps keep the capitalist regime of work time in place.

And yet in the context of the labor process under industrial capitalism, those other goods—freedom, creativity, self-expression, and so on—seem very far from being realized in most working lives.[19] Labor under industrial capitalism has tended to become progressively deskilled, even given the supposed renaissance of artisanal work ushered in by the era of "flexible specialization."[20] Recent survey research conducted by Gallup indicates that in the United States only 30 percent of people feel at all engaged by their work, while the average proportion for a set of 142 countries was found to be a mere 13 percent (Gallup 2013).[21] The studies on the sources of happiness thus cast doubt on one of the explanations offered by the economists mentioned in the introduction for Keynes's failed forecast: that the twentieth-century pattern in affluent industrial societies for productivity and real income to grow much more rapidly than work time decreases can be explained by the increased satisfaction of work (Zilibotti 2010).

In sum, the research on the happiness (or lack thereof) produced by income and work under advanced capitalism certainly does not support the contention that increasing income necessarily means higher levels of subjective well-being, at least independent of the association between income and social status, which is a purely positional matter. The trend toward increasing income at fairly stable levels of labor time, which became firmly established by the middle decades of the twentieth century, is not easily explained by attributing a "happiness effect" to income and consumption sufficient to outweigh the discontents of most work under capitalism. Indeed, the empirical findings on happiness suggest that criticisms of the materialistic bias of capitalism, which have been a prominent cultural current within industrial society in the era of affluence, are not just driven by ideology but rather rest on the perception of a genuine pathology in modern capitalism. Society (to put it rather abstractly) seems significantly puzzled by its own trajectory, and this should alert us to the presence of some underlying tension or contradiction.[22] Given how persistent and pervasive has been the critique of capitalist materialism, it ought not, especially in light of the empirical findings about the relation between happiness and wealth, to be dismissed as backward-looking romanticism, aristocratic prejudice, or starry-eyed utopianism.

There are thus some sound reasons to be skeptical about the notion that the trade-off between work and consumption under industrial capitalism represents the best of all possible worlds—or even that capitalism tends over time to move in the direction of a more ideal state of affairs. To put the point in Marxian terms, under capitalism the connection among production, consumption, and *realized* use value seems from the point of view of human welfare to stand in need of explanation. The prominent French Regulation theorists Robert Boyer and Yves Saillard (2002, p. 38) define capitalism, in classic Marxist fashion, as a mode of production in which "the form of production and exchange relationship imposes the primacy of exchange value over use value and makes accumulation an imperative of the system." Political philosopher G. A. Cohen (2000, p. 303) puts the point more directly: "if the goal of production [under industrial capitalism] were use value much less use-value would be sought, produced, and consumed than is in fact sought, produced and consumed." A similar thing can be said of demand and consumption: that if the goal of consumption under industrial capitalism were *actually realized* use value, much less use value would be sought and consumed than is in fact sought and consumed. But this then raises a question. If Marxists such as Boyer and Cohen are right, and use value (in this sense meaning that which promotes real human welfare) in capitalism is sacrificed to the ultimately mindless end of the accumulation of exchange value, why should people, as workers and consumers, organize their behavior and priorities in ways that further that goal? How can we account for the role of workers and consumers in facilitating the operation of a system that seems far from having their well-being as its telos?

1.3. The Structural Version of the Puzzle

Given the questionable degree to which the trend toward increasing consumption, as opposed to reducing work, seems explicable in straightforward cost-benefit terms, a further question arises, this time on a structural level. If the bias toward consumption under industrial capitalism is not explained by utility optimization, how is it that levels of aggregate effective demand under industrial capitalism have, nonetheless, generally been sufficient to ward off structural crisis? The question is particularly relevant in the case of Fordist mass production. The Fordist order that fully emerged in the middle part of the twentieth century employed a set of regulatory policies to manage effective demand, primarily by broadening the distribution of purchasing power. But for those policies to work, a propensity to use higher incomes to increase consumption, rather than work less, had to be in place.

The question has Marxian and Keynesian versions, as well as a hybrid version represented by the social structures of accumulation (SSA) paradigm in American political economy. According to the Marxian version, most systematically developed by Paul Sweezy (1942) (and later on also by Michel Aglietta [(1977) 2000]), once mass production is in place, capitalism faces the problem of how to generate a volume of consumption commensurate with its output. Within the Marxian framework the problem is complicated by the division of the economy into Department I, which produces the means of production, and Department II, which produces consumption goods (Marx [1893] 1993). While it is possible for a while for shortfalls in effective demand in Department II to be made up for by increasing demand in Department I, most Marxists hold that in the long run the two sectors of the economy must grow together.[23] In order for balanced expansion of the economy to be possible, real wages must therefore increase at a rate sufficient to generate levels of aggregate effective demand for consumer goods capable of supporting the growth of Department I. Yet there are pressures on capitalists to reduce their wage bills as much as possible, and this leads to a tendency for imbalance between the two parts of the economy. Underconsumption in Department II then leads to overaccumulation in Department I.[24] This was especially a problem in the early decades of the twentieth century. Those decades, according to Michel Aglietta, were characterized by a contradiction between the new system of mass production and the tendency for wages to be pushed down under what he describes as the "competitive regime of regulation" that held sway in the United States and elsewhere in the capitalist

world up until the 1930s. Without measures in place to create a mass market for consumer goods, industrial capitalism in the era of mass production
would have faced an ongoing crisis of underconsumption.[25] For Aglietta the
answer to this threat was to increase hourly real wages while introducing
policies to encourage the masses to spend those wages on goods (hence sus-
taining aggregate effective demand) by way of the creation and promotion of
what he calls the "working class norm of consumption." In his view: "For the
first time in history, Fordism created a norm of working-class consumption
in which *individual ownership of commodities* governed the concrete practices of consumption" (Aglietta [1977] 2000, p. 158 [emphasis added]). This
norm allowed for the development of a "mode of consumption" that comple-
mented the Fordist "regime of accumulation" and consequently made possible the stable pattern of economic growth in the postwar decades ([1977]
2000). Developing Aglietta's theory, Robert Boyer places even more emphasis on the centrality of mass consumption to the Fordist order. Boyer (1988,
p. 11) characterizes Fordism as "a shift in consumption norms, mainly as a
result of nominal wages rising to keep pace with anticipated gains in productivity." Fordism is a system that "combines the development of consumption
norms and production norms" (Boyer and Saillard [1995] 2002, p. 39). Yet it
is not clear what processes underlay the alignment of mass consumption and
mass production under Fordism—why it was that productivity was channeled into ever increasing effective consumer demand rather than less work
time. Aglietta's only argument bearing on that question is rather mechanistic.
He suggests that the mode of consumption in the era of mass production was
in large part a functional adaptation to changes in the labor process associated with Fordism. As the labor process intensified, so workers, in an effort
to reconstitute themselves after their exertions on the job, increased their
consumption. A new "mode of consumption" thus emerged, based on private
commodity acquisition: "Individual commodity consumption is the form of
consumption that permits the most effective recuperation from physical and
nervous fatigue in a compact space of time within the day, and at a single
place, the home" (Aglietta [1977] 2000, p. 159).[26] From the perspective of the
puzzle of work time and consumption under Fordism, however, Aglietta's
explanation leads us in a circle. According to Aglietta, increasing mass consumption was required because the labor process became more intense, while
the willingness of labor to acquiesce in a high output / high income regime
ensured that the demands of work remained unrelenting. Yet if labor had

pushed more resolutely for increases in productivity to be turned into fewer work hours, then the demands of work would have been lessened, and consequently, less consumption would have been required to reproduce labor power.[27] Furthermore, arguably the most effective way for workers to restore themselves after their depletion by the labor process is rest and recreation—in other words, leisure time. If that is the case, then we are returned to the question of why increasing productivity was turned into more income rather than less work at constant income.

In a spirit similar to the regulation theorists, members of the US school of radical political economy have envisaged particular "social structures of accumulation" as securing sufficient aggregate demand in the Fordist era (Gordon, Edwards, and Reich 1982). According to these theorists, the liberal regime of accumulation that preceded the Fordist era enabled capitalists to change the distribution of income in their favor, which resulted in insufficient aggregate demand resulting in overcapacity. In response, a set of institutions developed, the purpose of which was to ensure a more even distribution of purchasing power. The SSA approach allows for more contingency than does regulation theory, giving an important role for institutional and cultural developments that are exogenous to the logic of capitalist production. Yet both SSA theory and regulation theory share a tendency to take the sources of aggregate demand as more or less given. The underlying assumption is that once the right set of supporting institutions was set up, the virtuous cycle of increasing productivity, higher real incomes, and increasing aggregate demand, which defined capitalism during its Golden Age, simply fell into place—and continued until thwarted by structural contradictions located primarily in the sphere of production. The question of why labor came to accept a compact in which wage income increased while work time remained relatively constant is not given much consideration. The demand for goods over free time is left unexamined, with the distribution of purchasing power being the only variable adduced to explain the coordination of aggregate demand with mass production. For example, Thomas Weisskopf, Samuel Bowles, and David Gordon, prominent theorists working within the SSA tradition, argue that underconsumption (inadequate aggregate demand) is caused by the excessive power of capital over labor, which enables capitalists to drive down real wages (Wiesskopf et al. 1985).[28] On this view, it is real wage levels that determine whether the demand-side cogs of industrial capitalism are sufficiently well oiled for the growth machine to grind on. For capitalism to be stable, the power of capital to suppress the wages of labor must therefore be circumscribed by things like state-sponsored collective bargaining rights and minimum wages. The implicit supposition is that aggregate demand, when backed by sufficiently high wage rates, will rise to levels capable of absorbing aggregate output.[29] Yet the fact that this has tended to happen depends on a pervasive materialism, expressed in a tendency for increasing productivity and higher wage rates to be turned into commodities rather than free time. The conditions that give rise to this materialism, which channels productivity improvements into higher demand, are not given much consideration by the regulation and SSA schools. Despite their sophistication, both the regulation and SSA approaches assume that once appropriate distributive and regulative measures are in place, demand and supply will fall into equilibrium or, at least, will be sufficiently aligned to facilitate the ongoing accumulation of surplus value.

The quasi-Keyensian version of the problem of mass consumption, as developed by Michael Piore and Charles Sabel (1986), focuses on the contribution of investment to aggregate effective demand rather than directly on consumption.[30] At the same time, because predictions about the future state of consumer demand have tremendous influence on investment, consumption remains a crucial variable in determining the stability of industrial capitalism. Piore and Sabel point out that an economy organized around mass production involves very substantial fixed capital investments in specialized machinery and argue that this presents challenges to the stability of the system. High fixed capital investments of the sort involved in mass production mean that in order to be profitable, factories must be run at or near full capacity. This makes the mass production economy very inflexible, limited in its ability to cope with sudden downturns in demand. If measures are not in place to ensure that aggregate demand is sustained at levels sufficient to support full capacity production, there will be a risk of underinvestment. Thus, Piore and Sabel interpret the Depression in broadly Keynesian fashion, as caused by a loss of nerve on the part of investors about consumer demand. This led to a self-fulfilling prophecy, as falling investment led to increasing unemployment, which had the effect of depressing aggregate demand, which in turn made the outlook for further investment even grimmer, prompting further declines in investment and more job losses, and so on, in a vicious cycle.[31]

Levels of aggregate effective demand commensurate with the growth in capacity of industrial production were secured by a series of institutional developments, stretching from the late nineteenth century to the postwar period. On what Piore and Sabel call the microeconomic side, the most important of these was the emergence of the corporation. Also important at the level of the firm was the development in the 1920s of welfare capitalism, which increased the purchasing power of wage earners.[32] On the macroeconomic side, demand was stabilized by a new, government-backed industrial relations regime, by various components of the welfare state, including minimum wages, unemployment insurance, and Keynesian fiscal and monetary policy. Of these developments, the most significant was the system of collective bargaining that emerged in the years following World War II. This system reflected a compact between labor and capital, one mediated by the state. Norms of collective bargaining in the United States in the postwar period were set by the landmark 1948 agreement between the United Automobile Workers union and General Motors, which established the principle that wage levels should be reset annually according to the formula change in productivity plus change in the consumer price index. Real wages, and therefore mass purchasing power, thus became linked to the increasing productivity of the economy. This allowed the virtuous cycle of increasing returns to scale and increasing mass consumption to take root, ushering in the postwar era of economic expansion. Importantly, Piore and Sabel note that the success of the US model led to its emulation across the advanced industrial world, as various nations developed their own versions of Fordist regulation—the American model became a kind of paradigm for the regulation of capitalist economies in the postwar era. Indeed, the United States works well as a case study for Fordism precisely because it served, at least to some degree, as a model followed by other countries in that era of capitalism.

Thus, in different ways Marxian theorists of underconsumption, those working within the regulation school, SSA theorists, and quasi-Keynesians such as Piore and Sabel see the management of aggregate demand as a central problem for twentieth-century industrial capitalism. To coordinate mass production and consumption (while ensuring adequate investment and profit realization) capitalism had to be regulated by an ultimately quite unwieldy set of institutions, policies, and practices. But once more, all of these theorists take it as given that ensuring mass purchasing power was a sufficient condition for mass consumption. The solution to the problem of aggregate demand was to widen the distribution of spending power,

primarily by increasing wages. As long as enough money could be channeled to consumers, and as long as investors remained confident that
demand would continue to be robust, all would be well. On the Marxian
model, profits could be realized, while for the Keynesians, this would ensure
that capitalists would feel confident enough about the future prospects of
the economy to invest their money, thereby securing the economy against
the danger of falling into a liquidity trap. Yet, as noted, policies devised
to increase the purchasing power of the masses, in order to stimulate the
economy, crucially presuppose that increasing income will add to aggregate demand, rather than being used to reduce work hours. Measures like
income-based tax credits, or industrial policy aimed at bolstering the power
of unions so that they can increase their wage rates, only work to stimulate the economy if the extra money put in people's hands has the effect
of increasing demand rather than reducing work hours at constant levels
of spending. However, it is not clear just why an increase in purchasing
power per unit of work-time should lead to increased aggregate consumption rather than to decreased work hours. Indeed, it was not always the case
that increasing hourly income was automatically used to increase consumption. There is, as noted in the introduction, historical evidence that wage
earners in the later nineteenth century used increasing hourly rates to cut
their work hours rather than to increase consumption (Dora Costa 2000a).
Had that pattern continued—had increasing productivity been channeled
into reducing work time at fixed levels of consumption—then the positive
feedback loop between increasing returns to scale in production, increasing
real wage income, and ever-increasing consumption would not have been
possible. The Fordist economy would then quickly have run into demand-
side difficulties of the sort that its regulatory apparatus was supposed to
prevent.[33] For capitalism in the era of mass production to be sustainable, a
stable pattern in which aggregate demand increases with increases in productivity and output was required. In order for aggregate demand to at least
roughly match the output of mass production, it was not enough simply to
raise labor's real hourly wages, for increasing wage rates could, in theory,
be used to reduce work time. Nor, for the same reason, would government
measures to provide supplemental income have been sufficient to stimulate
the required level of aggregate effective demand. Rather, the coordination of
demand and supply under industrial capitalism ultimately depended on an
inclination on the part of the population to make use of increases in hourly

wages to increase consumption rather than to reduce work time. A fundamental condition of possibility for the stability of the industrial capitalist order was, therefore, a general preference among wage earners for the accumulation of consumer commodities over more free time—or at the very least an indifference between the two alternatives, such that wage earners were amenable to an arrangement that privileged purchasing power over free time.[34]

The propensity to increase consumption rather than reduce work time is, however, not a fact of nature. Nor, at the same time, is it plausible that it appeared in 1945 ex nihilo. In this book, I explain the dynamic consumer demand that underpinned the postwar period of stable expansion of industrial capitalism as a consequence of a set of social, cultural, and institutional developments that took place roughly over the first half of the century. The most important of these—to some degree underlying all the others—was the increasing extent to which wage labor became construed as a potentially fair form of economic exchange, based on the commensurability of labor and its wage. Seeing wage labor as a potentially fair exchange of commensurable substances, affected how use value was perceived in goods and activities, imparting unto consumer commodities the characteristics of the free activity given up (through work) in exchange for the wage. The balance established between mass production and mass consumption under advanced industrial capitalism was thus made possible by the ways in which the normative ground on which wage-labor exchange became legitimate was linked to the meaning of consumer commodities.

2. Possible Explanations

In order to clear the ground for this alternative, exchange-focused account of mass consumption, in this section I briefly consider the main currents of social scientific thought about consumption and assess the degree to which they might offer a satisfactory solution to the questions under consideration: Why, under conditions of affluence, does consumer accumulation nonetheless continue unabated? Why has increasing productivity tended to be used to that end rather than to reduce work time? The currents of theory considered are neoclassical economics, behavioral economics (an increasingly influential heterodox current within economics), status theories, Marxian theories, and cultural approaches.

2.1. The Utility Maximization Explanation

Because of the prominence of economic explanations for consumer and worker behavior, it makes sense to begin with a more detailed consideration of the economic approach.[35] In the introduction, and at the beginning of this chapter, I raised some serious objections to the economic explanation for the pattern of consumption and work that developed under advanced industrial capitalism. There are, however, some responses economists could make to my criticisms.

First though, an overview of the approach might be helpful. In neoclassical economics, human behavior tends to be regarded simply as an expression of preferences, with individuals following the principle of utility maximization, posited as a very general feature underlying and organizing human action.[36] The commitment to this rational, optimizing picture of action is sometimes expressed in startlingly strong terms. "The view that consumers maximize utility is not merely a law of economics, it is a law of logic itself," comments Paul Samuelson (1976, quoted in Ainslie 2001, p. 8), presenting an axiomatic assumption in the modern economic theory of consumer behavior in a standard textbook of modern neoclassical economics. Although the content of preferences and sources of utility are usually taken to be exogenous in economic theory, once a utility function is given, the assumption is that economic action proceeds in a rational and predictable manner.[37] The economic theory of the consumer assumes that economic agents seek to optimize utility, and economists expend much creative energy demonstrating that any given instance of consumer behavior accords with this maxim. Consumer practices, from this perspective, are then most parsimoniously explained by the utility they produce for consumers. If workers, following an increase in wage rates, choose to increase their income rather than reduce their time at work, this simply indicates that the added utility for them of more consumption *must* outweigh the added utility of increasing their free time.[38]

Although the neoclassical model of human agents involves many questionable assumptions, it would be hard to deny that modern consumer practices are at least in part satisfactorily accounted for in broadly utilitarian terms. Marx was surely correct to note that for things to become commodities they must be potentially useful. That certainly seems right as we venture further down a hierarchy of needs, to those that are more basic, such as that posited by Maslow (1943). Yet, as we have seen, the utility maximizing approach, when presented as a full and satisfactory account of the pattern of work and consumption under industrial capitalism, leaves certain puzzles. First, according to economic theory itself, the marginal utility of consumption falls not just for a given product—for example, for the nth ice cream consumed—but also for the set of all things consumed.[39] If, therefore, consumers are simple maximizers, as the neoclassical model would have it, beyond a point, as productivity and hourly wages go up, we should expect the rate of consumption to begin to level off and, in place of further increases in consumption, one of two possible alternatives. Increasing productivity should either be converted into more free time (as opposed to increased output), or else the rate of saving should increase.[40] Yet actual patterns of behavior under industrial capitalism do not conform to that expectation.[41] Although there is variation across different parts of the advanced capitalist world, over the course of the twentieth century, and especially in its second half, increasing productivity in the affluent world has tended to be used to increase consumption levels.

Moreover, as noted earlier, even if levels of consumption are not at the point at which, for reasons of satiation, utility drops off steeply at the margin, if ever more commodities are accumulated at fixed or only very gradually decreasing amounts of work time, the amount of time available to make use of each commodity will decline—asymptotically approaching zero. This existential constraint on consumption, which limits the degree to which commodities can be made use of, becomes particularly salient when seen through the lens of modern consumer theory, as developed by Kelvin Lancaster (1966a, 1966b) and Gary Becker (1981). Becker and Lancaster maintain, quite sensibly, that goods are not themselves sources of utility but rather should be thought of as tools used to facilitate practices that generate utility. Consumer commodities are thus equivalent to capital equipment, by means of which the labor of consumption—the activity of making use of consumer goods—produces utility as a final output. For example, roller skates are capital equipment that facilitate the production of the utility generated by the activity of roller-skating. Becker and Lancaster thus hold that an important distinction can be made between the *potential* usefulness of an object and the utility *realized* through that object being put to use. The utility of an object only gets realized in use. From this perspective, to explain the apparent preference for higher income and more consumption in terms of maximizing utility entails that commodity objects are, on average, put to use to a degree sufficient to realize an amount of utility at least equal to the disutility of the work endured in order to obtain them. However, as we have seen, what is

puzzling about the trade-off between commodities and free time in affluent industrial societies is that ever more objects are accumulated, while the
time available for their use decreases or remains constant. If the use value
of objects is realized in activity and activity demands time, then this pattern
does not make much sense. From the point of view of modern consumer
theory, at least some aspects of the pattern of consumption under modern
capitalism therefore seem somewhat hard to explain.

One possible objection to the reasoning I follow here is that it does not take
into account that commodities can vary greatly in the amount of utility they
produce per unit of time spent using them. Becker and Lancaster could argue
that as new products emerge, the activities they facilitate become more efficient at generating utility so that the same amount of utility can be generated
in less time. As goods become more efficient in this way, consumers might
well have good reason to seek to upgrade their set of commodities, progressively retiring products as better ones become available. If higher income
makes objects yielding more utility per unit of time-in-use affordable, then
it might make sense for people to use increases in their hourly wages to raise
their incomes (in order to acquire those objects) rather than reduce work
time at constant income.[42] But while this point might be valid on a formal
level and might, indeed, account for some accumulative consumer practices,
it is unconvincing as a comprehensive explanation for the general pattern of
accumulative consumption in affluent capitalist societies. It certainly does
not account for the accumulation of multiple, functionally equivalent items
or for the acquisition of items that seem unlikely, given constraints of time,
ever to be made use of enough to justify their expense. Moreover, if it was
the case that the utility-generating productivity of consumer goods increased
at a rate sufficient to offset the decline in the time available for making use
of them, surely that should be reflected in a positive correlation between
increasing income and subjective well-being. If increasing spending at fixed
amounts of free time increases the amount of satisfaction experienced in that
time, then as income increases, so should happiness. However, as we have
seen, the evidence indicates that this is not necessarily the case in affluent
societies.

Thus, the neoclassical theory of the consumer seems unable to provide a
good explanation for accumulative consumerism, at the expense of increasing free time, under conditions of affluence. The notion that modern consumption is fully accounted for in terms of the realized utility of the things

acquired stands in some tension with some general patterns in modern capitalism, particularly in its US incarnation.

2.2. Alternatives to Utility Maximization Explanations

Social scientists outside of economics, as well as some heterodox economists, have tended to take it as given that straightforward utilitarian considerations, anchored to the functional characteristics of products, fail to account fully for modern consumption practices, and have suggested alternative explanations. These may be loosely categorized into behavioral-psychological explanations, social status explanations, cultural accounts, and various forms of Marxism.[43] In what follows I briefly consider whether these approaches (taking one or two theoretical accounts as exemplars for each) do a better job at explaining the pattern of productivity, work time, and consumption under capitalism.

2.2.1. Behavioral Economics

Recent work in psychology and behavioral economics has sought to jettison, or at least relax, some of the more unrealistic assumptions of neoclassical economics, especially those underlying the homo economicus model of the economic agent. The aim has been to develop an approach to economic behavior based on a more plausible, evidence-led theory of the human subject.[44] Behavioral theories of economic action present a very different picture of the consumer, and by extension of consumer society, than standard economic theory, one grounded in actual empirical studies of how people behave. Perhaps, therefore, behavioral economics can explain the apparent materialistic bias suggested by the pattern of work and consumption characteristic of advanced industrial capitalism.

An early, influential example of an economic approach to consumption that is informed by psychology is found in the work of Tibor Scitovsky. Working within a behavioral psychological framework, Scitovsky (1992) suggests a theory to account for the irrationalities of consumerism. For Scitovsky, commodities produce utility along two dimensions. They can be endowed with a potential to produce functional utility—for example, the capacity of a chair to yield a certain amount of sitting utility before becoming worn out. But they can also be endowed with a potential to provide various forms of stimulation for the consumer. According to Scitovsky, in affluent industrial societies the capacity of things to stimulate people typically gets exhausted before their functional capabilities wear out. Put simply, people become bored with their still functional possessions and so seek out new and more stimulating ones. The psychologist Barry Schwartz makes a similar point in his work on the discontents associated with consumer sovereignty. He comments: "When the brief period of real enthusiasm and pleasure wanes, people still have these things [consumer durables] around them—as a constant reminder that consumption isn't all it's cracked up to be, that expectations aren't met by reality" (Schwartz 2004, p. 172).

Scitovsky's theory is at first glance compelling. It certainly sheds some light on certain characteristics of capitalism, such as planned obsolescence and the rapid turnover of consumer fashions. However, the theory fails to answer the question posed at the outset of this book: Why, given the costs entailed relative to the benefits gained by accumulative consumption, do consumers not switch to less object-mediated sources of stimulation, engaging in new practices rather than acquiring new objects? Behaving thusly would seem to offer consumers a way to avoid the ennui produced by an endless cycle of commodity acquisition and disappointment. Indeed, Scitovsky himself implicitly raises this question in the solution he offers to the problem of joyless modern materialism, which is to encourage people to cultivate engaging *practices* in place of endlessly acquiring commodities that can only ever be a fleeting source of stimulation. Yet given that the solution to the problem seems somewhat obvious, why does the problem persist? If, as Schwartz and Scitovsky suggest, accumulative consumption ultimately leads to disappointment, why should people choose to be disappointed repeatedly? Surely, after a while, they should conclude from experience that the combination of high income and consumption, at the expense of more free time, does not lead to happiness and so explore a different approach—freeing up time in which to cultivate skills in place of using it to generate funds for the acquisition of things. So what is it that makes a cycle of behavior that on reflection seems self-defeating nonetheless so compelling? Scitovsky suggests that at the root of the problem lies materialist culture. But that answer only raises the question of why that culture took root and became so entrenched. As is often the case with arguments that adduce culture as an explanation, Scitovsky's account ultimately leaves some sense that the effort to explain has been prematurely ended.

A more recent current of work in behavioral economics that might explain our puzzling pattern of work and consumption challenges the assumption that people are rational in how they think about the prospective value of rewards at different points in the future. It springs from experimental findings that people are inconsistent in their intertemporal preferences, often preferring very short-term rewards to substantially higher ones with more delay while not discriminating in the same way between the same two rewards (one substantially higher than the other) with equivalent temporal spacing, only placed at later points in time. So for example, when subjects are offered a choice between $10 now and $20 in one week, they tend to choose $10 now, while when they are offered $10 in six months or $20 in six months and one week, they choose $20. George Ainslie (1992, 2001), a key figure in work on this subject, interprets this finding as indicating that people discount utility over time in a hyperbolic manner. Hyperbolic discounters discount the value of some good very steeply for short delays but at a much lower rate for long delays. The steepness of the slope of the devaluation curve at a given time in the future is roughly proportional to how far in the future that time is.

If hyperbolic discounting is commonplace, this throws into question a basic assumption within neoclassical economics—that economic agents discount utility at a time insensitive rate, such that each temporal unit of delay in consuming a good reduces the utility assigned to that good by a set percentage. This procedure yields the exponential time-utility curve. While with hyperbolic discounting, the devaluation per unit of time changes depending on the total delay, with exponential discounting, valuation falls by a constant factor per unit delay.

The exponential model certainly describes how certain economic actors reason under particular circumstances. For example, banks discount the future exponentially when they calculate interest rates.[45] However, the exponential model is less convincing as a general explanation for how people behave. Ainslie notes that the exponential time-utility discounting model does not cover apparently self-destructive and irrational behavior in which average utility over the long term is radically compromised in exchange for a short-term reward. One instance of such behavior is drug use, but there are many examples in consumer behavior, impulsive and compulsive buying for example, and perhaps also a fixation on the immediate gratification of higher wages and more spending, as opposed to increasing free time. In such cases, people apparently do not adjust utility over time delay until just before the point of consumption (or some other utility-yielding behavior), at which point expected utility spikes dramatically.[46]

Ainslie (2001), rather strongly, asserts that "people's natural discount curve is . . . specifically hyperbolic" (p. 31), suggesting further that this preference is commonplace in nature and can be explained as a product of natural selection. In line with a general tendency among behavioral economists to embrace naturalistic explanations, Ainslie interprets economic behavior as expressing a struggle in the brain between an ancient, reptilian part, impulsive and incapable of planning, and a more advanced, rational part, endowed with a capacity to reason about long-term consequences for welfare.[47] To the degree that people discount hyperbolically, so the argument goes, this reflects the influence exerted by the primordial parts of the brain. The short-term propensity for people to consume, which might not be easily explicable in terms of rational utility maximization, is then, from this perspective, a result of the residual power in humans of drives that are a legacy of their animal ancestry. These instill in them an urge to seek maximum pleasure immediately—satisfying instant, first-order desires at the expense of the well-being of their future selves.

If Ainslie's account is right, this suggests that modern, accumulative habits of consumption may simply be a consequence of a congenital human tendency toward myopic hedonism (an adaptive trait in a state of nature characterized by a profoundly uncertain future) when combined with industrial powers of production. However, while hyperbolic discounting might account for a consumerist tendency to spend rather than save, it does not explain the apparent willingness of people to push for higher wages to fund more consumption, rather than for more free time. For it is not at all clear why a hyperbolic discounter should attach more expected utility to acquiring things than to working less. Assuming that work tends to be a source of disutility, working less would seem to offer a quite immediate kind of gratification—more so perhaps than acquiring some commodity. Moreover, the model of the hyperbolic discounter still assumes that where short-term consumption involves the acquisition of commodities, it is motivated by the net utility produced by those commodities. This means that, for the hyperbolic discounter, short-term wage-funded consumption must produce a quantity of utility sufficient to compensate for the disutility of the work required in order to earn a wage. Consequently, even if people are hyperbolic discounters, there are still good reasons why we should expect them to, beyond a point, demand time over things, so that their acquisitions can be put to use sufficiently to yield their expected utility. And yet the demand for free time under conditions of affluence has been eclipsed by the demand for more consumption. Hyperbolic discounting thus fails to solve our puzzle.

In general, behavioral economics, while generating lots of experimental evidence that disrupts the assumption that homo economicus is a good model of the economic actor, is less successful at advancing plausible alternatives. The field either amounts to a list of findings that are anomalous from the perspective of standard economics, with no underlying theory, or else quickly resorts to evolutionary just-so stories, such as the one suggested by Ainslie. The theoretical limitations of behavioral economics are perhaps a result of its commitment to discovering general behavioral laws by way of experiments, in conjunction with a strong commitment to a reductive naturalistic psychologism. With this end in mind, researchers in the field tend to bracket conceivably very relevant sociohistorical factors that could account for the behavior they observe in their experiments. Moreover, because experimental subjects in behavioral economics research are typically drawn from North American or Western European capitalist societies, little is done to control for the influence of such factors. As a theoretical resource for explaining modern patterns of accumulative consumption, behavioral economics therefore has some serious shortcomings. At the same time, I will argue, in Chapter 4, that some of the experimental findings of the field, approached in a contextual fashion—that is, precisely as findings about subjects in affluent capitalist societies—support an alternative interpretation, one in line with the theory argued for in this book.

2.2.2. Social Status Explanations

Social status approaches look at consumption behavior as a means for making and challenging status distinctions (Veblen 1994; Bourdieu 1984; Sombart 1967). Increasing consumption is explained as being a result of status competition in the context of an increasingly fluid social structure. From this point of view, modern accumulative consumption is a consequence of a very long historical process in which ascribed status progressively became supplanted by achieved status (Sombart 1967). Once social identity is set less by birth and becomes more contingent on variable life outcomes, social actors become motivated to find ways to index their status by way of their consumption practices. There then ensues the kind of object-mediated symbolic competition described by Thorstein Veblen and others.

There is certainly something compelling about this argument. The status value of a good depends on its distribution across a population. As access to a given good becomes less exclusive, the status associated with it declines (Hirsch 1976).[48] Therefore, as economic growth yields greater access to goods, those higher up the hierarchy will seek to defend themselves from the encroachment of those below by "upgrading" their product set in order to symbolically reestablish social distance from them. This makes commodities into weapons in a kind of status symbol arms race, and the result of this is a very rapid turnover of products. The status interpretation of consumption also suggests an explanation for why, after basic needs have been met, higher income (and further spending) does not produce increasing satisfaction—the so-called hedonic treadmill effect (Offer 2006). If increased spending is about maintaining relative status position, then it is not surprising that it fails to produce increasing happiness.

However, the status competition approach to consumption ultimately runs into the same difficulty as the utility maximizing account. For establishing social distinctions by display of commodities is a certain kind of *use* made of commodity objects, and, as such, requires some investment of time. Conspicuous consumption must, by definition, be noticeable to have the desired effect, and display entails time spent in public, showing wares to signal status. As time available to display each status object contracts, the accumulation of more status goods yields diminishing marginal returns, and in response, we would expect people either to shift their preferences from further commodity accumulation to more free time (in which accumulated goods can be displayed) or else increased savings. To the degree that this does not happen, the puzzle remains.

Moreover, mass consumption meant that the power of goods to signal status differences probably declined, just because they became so much more commonplace. As goods increasingly come within reach of the masses, they become less effective as markers of social distinctions.[49] If the advent of mass consumption corresponded to a decrease in the capacity of things to index status, it seems unlikely that status competition can explain mass consumption. Some support for the declining significance of status-driven consumption with mass consumption is provided by the research of historian Richard Pollay (1985) on advertising content in the middle decades of the twentieth century (which I discuss in more detail in Chapter 7). While Pollay found that status is sometimes adduced in order to advertise the benefits of owning certain categories of consumer durable—especially high-end goods such, as luxury vehicles—most advertisements for products focus on their functional properties. If making, or defending against, invidious distinctions were foremost in the mind of consumers, then surely mid-century marketers would have cottoned on to that and incorporated, to a greater extent than Pollay's evidence suggests was the case, the status associations of products in their advertising campaigns. So the most common forms of mass consumption cannot easily be explained by status dynamics.

It is also worth noting that the postwar emphasis on increasing purchasing power emerged, at least in the United States, from a politics that represented a new kind of moral economy rather than being an aggregate effect of widespread concerns about status position (L. Cohen 2003; Jacobs 2005). The postwar industrial compromise—which pegged real wages to productivity and the cost of living, thereby ensuring that consumption would keep up with expanded production—was primarily a result of collective bargaining, in the context of a particular normative order. The tendency for consumption to keep pace with production reflected a general sentiment that living standards ought to progressively increase for all rather than a competition between individuals for status by way of conspicuous consumption. It is, of course, possible that each class was trying to emulate the consumption of those above it, and therefore, that collective, class-based status aspirations pushed the purchasing power agenda. But if that was the case, why was segmented marketing, which tailored products to the tastes of specific social groups, so successful? The success of segmented marketing strategies, which became prominent in the second half of the twentieth century, indicates the degree to which tastes were stratified, and stratification of tastes suggests a limit to emulative consumption. As we shall see in Chapter 5, there is evidence from social research conducted in mid-century America that the point of consumption for individuals was not to establish status distinctions, but rather was to fit in with collective standards and tastes specific to their reference groups. None of this is to say that status competition does not motivate consumption practices to any degree in the era of mass consumption. In some cases, the concern to increase real income might well in part be inspired by a felt need to keep up with the consumption of "the Joneses." But the argument that status competition provides an exhaustive explanation for the puzzling bias toward increasing income and consumption under industrial capitalism, nonetheless, remains unconvincing.[50]

2.2.3. *Cultural Approaches*

Cultural approaches to consumption tend to focus on its role in meaning-making practices. The literature exploring these practices is vast and varied. Despite this diversity, cultural accounts have in common a tendency to view (and often celebrate) consumption as an expression of agency in the making of identity. This perhaps reflects the influence of Michel de Certeau (1984), the most important theorist in this current of work, who argued that consumption is a form of potentially counterhegemonic production. According to de Certeau, consumers, by cultivating creative practices in the sphere of consumption, can disrupt the ideological configurations that support the system of production.[51] While not all cultural theorists emphasize the counterhegemonic possibilities of consumption, there is a general trend in cultural studies to focus on the role of consumption in creative projects of identity construction. As one sociologist working within this paradigm, Celia Lury (1996, p. 256), puts it: "consumer culture provides an important context for the development of novel relationships of individual self-assembly and group membership."

The cultural approach to consumption, while often interesting and useful, nonetheless has some difficulty accounting for the general pattern of materialism under affluent capitalism. Although goods are indubitably deployed to construct and express identity, as with conspicuous consumption, using them in such a fashion *requires time*. As productivity and hourly wages continued to increase under industrial capitalism, why did wage earners not push more forcefully for shorter work hours, and therefore more time in which to engage in identity making practices? Furthermore, there are clearly modes of identity construction that do not require much in the way of income, but, rather, are more time intensive. Why should people be inclined to construct identity through commodity ownership rather than the cultivation of non-commodified practices? After all, practices, insofar as they demonstrate the ability to *do* something, would seem to be a more robust source of individual identity than mere ownership of objects. Surely engaging in, and mastering, practices constitutes a firmer, more reflexively convincing basis for claiming an identity than passive displays of objects.

More generally, the pattern of consumption and work that this book takes as its puzzle is an aggregate pattern, constituted by the behavior of all consumers / wage earners. To be sure, disaggregating that pattern will reveal a patchwork of distinct practices. But interpreting local practices is quite different from explaining why, under capitalism, there is a systematic bias toward accumulating stuff, as opposed to expanding free time. Cultural approaches, in emphasizing the plurality of meaning-making practices involved in consumption, thus fail to engage with the more general issue of the pervasive materialism of consumer capitalism. They risk missing the proverbial forest for the trees.

2.2.4. Marxisms

An alternative current of theory, very much associated with Marxism, seeks to explain accumulative consumerism as an effect of the power of advertising, in particular, and of the "culture industry" more generally, to inculcate subjects with false needs via psychological mechanisms such as desublimation (Ewen 1976; Adorno and Horkheimer 1976; Marcuse 1964).[52] Given the onslaught of marketing in modern consumer societies, this explanation has some intuitive appeal. However, although it might seem plausible that marketing has some aggregate effect on general patterns of demand, studies suggest that the power of advertising to stimulate novel demand is questionable (Schudson 1986, Nelson 1975).[53] The effect of advertising seems mostly to be to redistribute given demand within a market rather than to generate new demand.[54] Moreover, construing mass consumption as simply a result of the ideological production of false needs, predominantly by way of advertising, presupposes that people are passive receptacles for marketing messages—"advertising dopes," as it were. Such a picture of the consumer is both empirically unwarranted and anthropologically suspect. At the very least, the success of marketing messages in penetrating popular consciousness should be interpreted not just as a sign of the influence of the culture industry but also as indicating something about the socioeconomic context (as well as the prevailing interpretation of that context) in which those messages are received.

Of course, the argument that the bias toward increasing consumption, as opposed to increasing free time, under advanced industrial capitalism is puzzling assumes that workers have a choice in the matter—that they could have chosen to convert productivity gains into more time (at a constant rate of consumption) rather than higher wages. But workers might well have little choice in the matter, if the compact of higher wages rather than more free time in exchange for increasing productivity is forced on them by capital (Schor 1991). If workers are *compelled* to take a higher wage rather than being given the option of a shorter working week, it seems reasonable that they would then spend the wage they receive. What good, after all, is an unspent wage? From this perspective, the bias toward consumption would simply reflect the preference of business for a stable work regime, including a regular working week, in conjunction with the fact that capital generally has more bargaining power than labor.[55] If this is correct, then turning improved productivity into increasing real wages, in order to fund more consumption, as opposed to using it to reduce work, is just a matter of wage earners making the best of conditions not of their own choosing.

While there is surely something to this view, at the same time it ignores the extent to which from the mid-twentieth century onward, workers in the industrial West entered relatively freely into corporatist arrangements with business. Unions were willing participants in the postwar compact, according to which increases in productivity would be rewarded by higher wage incomes. Furthermore, as noted earlier, wage increases can be saved as well as spent (with savings used for things like funding retirement or as a guard against unforeseen expenses). The balance of power between capitalists and labor has little direct effect on whether people choose to spend or save their discretionary income. The power of capital therefore fails to explain the surprisingly high propensity to consume (rather than save) under conditions of affluence.

To sum up, the status-centered, Marxian, cultural, and behavioral psychological interpretations of mass consumer society seem to fare little better than utility maximization as sufficient explanations for the general pattern of modern accumulative consumerism—the accumulation of ever more commodities while free time remains relatively static so that the average time available to make use of each commodity decreases. While each approach captures some dimension of mass consumption, it nonetheless remains perplexing that the improvements in productivity in increasingly affluent societies were for the most part used to increase consumption. In Chapter 4, a different kind of explanation is presented for this pattern. Before developing this alternative theory, I provide, in Chapter 3, a more detailed empirical analysis of the pattern, focusing on perhaps the paradigmatic consumer society and economy—the United States in the twentieth century.

THREE

Empirical Pattern in the United States

The last chapter presented in very general terms one of the most puzzling aspects of capitalism in the age of mass production and consumption: its characteristic combination of increasing productive power, ever growing output, and increasing consumption, at fixed or only slowly decreasing levels of work time. There is scant evidence that this combination makes much sense from the point of view of human well-being. The increasing disconnect between wealth and well-being is what Avner Offer (2006) (among many others) has described as the "paradox of affluence." The aim of this chapter is to fill out the bare-bones account introduced in Chapters 1 and 2 by analyzing large-scale developments in the economic history of the United States in the twentieth century. The United States is often taken to be the paradigmatic case of Fordist mass consumer driven capitalism and, thus, works well as a case study.

The history of the American economy between the late nineteenth and late twentieth centuries follows quite closely the general pattern outlined in the previous chapter. The economy experienced steady increases in productivity over this period. Working hours fell precipitously between the 1880s and the late 1920s, but thereafter, the rate of decrease slowed significantly and from 1940 onward further reduction in work time was very moderate indeed. As the century wore on, improvements in hourly productivity were increasingly converted into higher levels of output and (at least up until the 1980s) rising real wages at a more or less constant input of work time per full-time employee. Rising wages were for the most part funneled into increasing consumer spending, a significant part of which went to fund the acquisition of consumer durables of various sorts. Indeed, Aglietta (2008) has argued that the demand for consumer durables formed a crucial stabilizing component of the Fordist mode of regulation. Drawing on empirical work in economics and economic history, and using data from the Bureau of Labor Statistics, as well as census materials collated in *The Historical Statistics of the United States*, the present chapter examines this pattern in some detail, analyzing trends in productivity, wages, work time, and consumption over the course of the twentieth century. Getting a clear picture of these trends and their interrelations requires some auxiliary analysis of savings rates, credit, changes in retirement, life span, time spent in education, and the effect of the deployment of labor-saving devices in the domestic sphere. In order to properly contextualize developments in the twentieth century, it is also helpful to look further back in time at the history of work, so the chapter touches in passing on patterns in earlier periods.

Before pressing forward with this analysis, some attention ought to be paid to the view that there is nothing deeply puzzling about the relation between work time, hourly wages, and productivity that emerged in the United States during the twentieth century. Gary Becker (1965) sets out this position clearly in an influential paper on time allocation, written in the mid-1960s. He takes it as given that consumers are guided in their decisions by an ongoing concern to optimize utility under changing conditions. Changes in work time are, according to Becker, simply expressive of the shifting balance in consumer behavior between the income effect, where higher hourly earnings lead to increased preference for leisure time, and the substitution effect, where the added utility of higher hourly earnings leads to a preference for more work. Becker acknowledges that in the US economy, the income effect ebbs after 1940, but he simply assumes that this must have been because, for rational economic reasons, the substitution effect increased in strength.[1] Yet accounting for the change in that way involves circular reasoning. The argument has the following form: the decline in hours slowed to a creep because higher earnings yielded relatively more satisfaction. How do we know this? Because the decline in hours slowed to a creep. Becker simply takes it as self-evident that the decline in the rate of decrease in work time from 1940 onward reflects rational, optimizing choices on the part of individuals. He does not even attempt to provide historical evidence to substantiate this interpretation. My theoretical analysis sticks more closely to the rough ground of history, which seems entirely appropriate when analyzing historical trends.

The chapter is organized into a number of sections, each of which deals, in an abbreviated fashion, with a particular set of developments. The sections examine productivity, wages, work time, and consumer spending, as well as saving. At the same time as giving a brief overview of developments in each of these areas, I consider various possible explanations for the overall pattern of the set of developments taken together.

1. Productivity

Measuring productivity is a complex and technical matter, and there is much debate about methods and disagreement about exact numbers. Assessing changes in productivity over long stretches of historical time presents particular difficulties. Historical data on productivity get increasingly sketchy the further back in time we venture, and longer-term estimates of change in productivity by necessity involve creative extrapolation from often very imperfect indices. Constructing a picture of change over long periods of time usually also involves stitching together data from disparate and discontinuous archival sources. In addition, there are formidable conceptual problems with measuring productivity. While comparing quantities of material output per unit of input over time is, at least in theory, quite straightforward, it is very difficult when calculating productivity to take into account change in product quality.[2] Furthermore the productivity of economic activity that does not produce a material output—knowledge production or the provision of services for example—is extremely hard to measure.

Despite these methodological and conceptual difficulties, it is clear that over the course of the twentieth century advanced capitalist economies experienced very steady improvements in productivity, which over the long term compounded into quite dramatic economic growth. For the United States, the rate of increase of multifactor productivity per year between 1929 and 2007 has recently been estimated to have been an adjusted average of 2.17 percent (Gordon 2010).[3] The most significant increases in multifactor productivity took place between 1928 and 1950, described by economists as "one big wave" of productivity improvement (Gordon 1999). Labor output per hour increased by an average of well over 2 percent each year between 1900 and 2000, with a second big wave of improvement evident from 1940 to 1973 (Gullickson and Harper 1987). The trend of rising productivity meant that by 2007 each hour of labor produced 5.33 times more output than in 1929.[4]

There are reasons to think that the standard productivity figures substantially underestimate the real increase in productivity. The productivity figures, averaged across all economic activity, include productivity in the services sector, which economists have argued tends to be underestimated because of difficulties of measurement (Griliches 1992).[5] As the US economy matured, there was a shift in the labor force, first from agriculture to industry and subsequently from industry to services.[6] The proportion of the workforce employed in the service sector jumped from 38 percent in 1900, to 78 percent in 1999 (Fisk 2001). As the proportion of the population employed in the service sector increased over time, services took on relatively more weight in overall productivity calculations. If service sector productivity is systematically underestimated, and the service economy grew relative to other sectors as the economy developed, then it is probable that the true magnitude of the improvement in productivity over the course of the twentieth century is significantly greater than the official statistics suggest.

In addition, the standard productivity calculation fails to take into account sufficiently the additional value generated by the creation of entirely new kinds of product. When new consumer goods get invented—things like personal computers and mobile phones—sources of utility come into existence that did not previously exist. Because national income accountants have difficulty valuing this added utility, it does not get registered in standard measures of changing productivity. Economist Bradford DeLong (2002) has come up with a very rough estimate for the added value of new products, suggesting that with this added value taken into account productivity in fact increased by between 14 and 25 times over the course of the twentieth century.[7] It is not unreasonable, therefore, to conclude that the standard measures of labor and multifactor productivity should be regarded as providing a bare minimum estimate of changes in productivity. The real figures are likely to be higher, quite probably much higher.

In sum, there is little doubt that between the later nineteenth and early twentieth centuries, the economy of the United States, along with every other economy in the industrial world, experienced dramatic growth in productivity. The fact that per capita economic growth and improving productivity tended to move in tandem indicates that productivity improvements were predominantly used to increase aggregate output.

2. Wages

Of course, raw productivity figures tell us little about the distribution of the benefits conferred by per capita economic growth. Increased productivity can be realized either as higher profits or as increased hourly real wages. The general pattern for the twentieth century is that at least some part of the increase in wealth generated by productivity improvements has been captured by wage earners, although the degree to which that was the case varied over the course of the century, and also between different parts of the economy. In the United States, real wages per hour in manufacturing increased on average by 1.43 percent per annum from 1900 to 1929, by 2.35 percent from 1948 to 1973, and by 0.46 percent after 1973 (Goldin 2000). The average hourly wage in 1909 was $3.80 (in 1999 dollars). By 1999, it had risen to $13.90. However, this underestimates the real increase in compensation because it does not take into account the added value of benefits, which barely existed in the early part of the century. Benefits as a fraction of compensation continued to rise over the course of the twentieth century. By 1999, they amounted to a further $5.58 per hour. With benefits taken into account then, hourly compensation for manufacturing work in 1999 was $19.48—a fivefold increase in real terms since 1909 (Fisk 2001).[8] For all work, the average hourly wage, including benefits, was $21.16 in 2000 (Moehrle 2001).

It should be noted then that the tendency for improvements in productivity to be turned into increases in wage earnings greatly diminished toward the end of the twentieth century. Economists Lawrence Mishel and Heidi Shierholz (2011) found that between 1979 and 2009, while productivity increased by 80 percent, the hourly wage of the median American worker increased by only 10.1 percent, and most of this increase took place during the economic recovery between 1996 and 2002. From the late 1970s onward, growth in productivity and wages evidently became quite disconnected. In the last quarter of the twentieth century, the owners of capital captured the lion's share of the increase in productivity. By contrast, during the Golden Age period of American capitalism, between the Second World War and the mid-1970s, real income per annum increased at a rate quite close to increasing labor productivity—2.35 percent for wages and 2.77 percent for labor productivity.

That productivity should be linked to increasing real wages is in line with basic economic theory. In the neoclassical theory of the production function the worker is a paid a wage equivalent to her added marginal product. As the productivity of labor improves, the theory predicts that wages should increase commensurately. The argument is quite straightforward. If workers' wages are lower than their marginal product, then firms would gain by taking on additional workers, which increases demand for labor, leading to a rise in wages. If, on the other hand, workers' wages are higher than their marginal product, then the firm gains by shedding workers, increasing the supply of labor, which puts downward pressure on wages.[9] So at equilibrium, wages are set by marginal added product. In reality, of course, wage rates are determined not just by economic rationality narrowly conceived but also by a complex of sociocultural and institutional forces. Regardless of whether the theory itself is correct, however, the connection between wage levels and productivity under mid-century Fordist industrial capitalism became an institutional fact. In the postwar period, manufacturing wage levels were to a significant extent set by collective bargaining arrangements underwritten by the state (Zeitlin 1987). As the institutional and normative framework underpinning Fordism fell apart, so too did the linking of real wages to productivity.

Thus, for most of the century increasing productivity was at least to some degree turned into increasing real hourly wages. For the present inquiry, the question then arises of the extent to which increases in hourly wages were used to reduce work time as opposed to increasing real income.

3. Work Time

An increase in hourly wages, at least in theory, offers wage earners a choice between either increasing their income for the same number of hours of work, or reducing hours for the same income. It is quite possible that increases in the average household income have a ratcheting effect on the normative standard of living, with the result that wage earners become very resistant to subsequent falls in income. However, it is not clear just why an increase in hourly wages should be used to increase household income rather than to reduce time at work at constant income. There are good reasons, discussed in the previous chapter, for thinking that as income rises, the relative value placed on free time should also increase. It follows from this that at income levels above those required for basic subsistence, an increasing proportion of marginal increases in hourly wages should be used to reduce the amount of time spent at work.

In line with this expectation, work hours did indeed fall as wages increased over the course of the twentieth century. Robert Fogel notes that work hours in the United States decreased by 50 percent between 1880 and 1995 (Fogel 2000). Hours for nonfarm workers dropped from 60 per week in 1900 to

39.3 in 1990 (Lebergott 1996). Average hours per week for manufacturing workers dropped from 53 in 1900 to just over 40 at the turn of the twenty-first century.[10] The National Bureau of Labor Statistics population survey found that in 2011 the average workweek for all workers was 38.3 hours, while the workweek for those who usually work full-time was 42.4 hours (for nonagricultural work, the numbers are 38.2 and 42.3, respectively). However, most of the decline in work hours since the late nineteenth century occurred before 1940. Economic historian Robert Whaples (2001), in an overview of historical research on work time in the twentieth century, notes that, although there are a variety of series measuring the workweek over time, using inconsistent measurements, they all show more or less the same pattern, "with weekly hours falling considerably during the first third of the century and much more slowly thereafter." The length of the working week fell precipitously between 1900 and 1920, from about 60 hours to about 50 hours (a full workday).[11] It subsequently continued to fall but at a significantly reduced rate, such that between 1920 and 1929, it dropped only a further 2 hours, to 48 hours per week. William Sundstrom's (2006) analysis finds that the length of the workweek fell an average of 3.4 hours per decade from 1900 to 1950, thereafter declining only very slightly until 1980, after which it increased again to what it had been in 1950. By 1940, the full-time workweek had more or less stabilized at around 40 hours per week, and although it continued to decrease for the rest of the century, the rate of decrease became very gradual. While some recent analysts disagree with Juliet Schor's (1991) contention that work hours actually increased toward the end of the twentieth century, the evidence shows that since the Second World War, hours have not fallen by very much, if at all (Lebergott 1996).[12] Moreover, a significant number of Americans have always worked two or more jobs—according to one study, as much as 6 percent of the population (Owen 1988). This means that the average length of the workweek per job underestimates the average amount of time spent at work for each working individual.[13] There has been some increase in vacation days per year, which obviously has the effect of reducing the average amount of time spent at work each week. However, economist John Owen (1988) estimates that even when vacation is taken into account, the reduction in the working week for nonstudent males between 1950 and 1986 was a mere twenty-four minutes per week (from 39.9 to 39.5 hours). Owen makes the point that nonstudent men are a good measure of underlying trends in work time because, unlike students and women, they are less likely to have other responsibilities. A decline for that population of twenty-four minutes per week between 1950 and 1986 is very small relative to the impressive increases in productivity during those years. Over the century as a whole, there was an increase in output per hour of labor of approximately 850 percent, while during the same period the working week declined by only 30 percent. Increases in labor productivity were most significant during the "big wave" period, between 1940 and 1973 (Gordon 2010). As noted, work time did fall rapidly between 1900 and 1940, but from 1940 onward, further decline in the length of the working week was minimal, despite continued increases in productivity. Across all sectors of the economy, annual work hours in the United States declined by about 10 percent between 1950 and 2014, while in the same period productivity increased by 350 percent.[14]

The oddness of this pattern is particularly evident if we narrow our focus to manufacturing. It was the organized workers of that sector who, in the later nineteenth and early twentieth centuries, pushed for a reduction in work time, first militating for the ten-hour day and then for the eight-hour day. Examining the change in average full-time manufacturing hours per week across the entire century we see a drop from fifty-three hours in 1900 to forty-two hours in 1999—a 20 percent reduction (Fisk 2001). But once again, almost of all of this reduction in hours took place between 1900 and 1940. Between 1950 and 1999 manufacturing labor productivity increased by an average of 2.9 percent per year, for a total increase of 417 percent (Cobet and Wilson 2002). Yet over this period the length of the working week in manufacturing barely budged at all. There was thus a marked deceleration in the rate of decline of manufacturing working hours in the postwar years at the same time that there was a pronounced acceleration in both manufacturing productivity and hourly earnings.

The extent to which increasing productivity was converted into more output, rather than fewer hours, is made clear by the following calculation. As we have seen, productivity in the United States increased by at least 433 percent (5.33 times) between 1929 and 2007. In 1929, work hours averaged forty-eight per week, while by 2007 this number had fallen to about forty. If a quite moderate proportion, say 20 percent, of the increase in productivity experienced by the United States over this period had been converted into less working time, rather than higher output, then between 1929 and 2007, there would have been close to a 50 percent reduction in the length of the working week—such that by 2007 Americans would work for twenty-four hours per week, rather than close to forty. Even a very modest 10 percent conversion of increased productivity into fewer working hours over that period would have yielded a 33 percent reduction in the working week, from forty-eight hours (in 1929) to thirty-two hours.[15] If we take 1940 as a base year, rather than 1929, the results are even more striking. By 1940, the working week was just over forty hours per week. This followed the passing of the Fair Labor Standards Act of 1938, which made time-and-a-half pay compulsory for hours worked in excess of forty per week. Once hours stabilized at around forty per week in 1940, they simply failed to fall much further. Yet labor productivity increased by about 5 times between 1940 and 2007. A 20 percent conversion of increased productivity between 1940 and 2007 into fewer hours rather than more output would have reduced the workweek to twenty hours, while a 10 percent conversion would have reduced it to twenty-eight hours.

The length of the working week is, of course, only one dimension of the onerousness of labor. Other dimensions are the intensity of labor during the workday and general working conditions, both of which greatly complicate the picture. Conditions of labor in industrial capitalism in many ways improved over time, as the state increasingly stepped in to regulate things like safety in the workplace. Yet at the same time, as capitalism advanced, more effective managerial systems intensified the extraction of labor during work. Intensity of work is clearly not indicated by the length of the working day, and the extensive and intensive dimensions of labor can vary independently.

A comparison with an earlier stage of capitalism is instructive on this point. Although hours were long in the nineteenth century, social historians have provided much evidence that in the early period of capitalism, work was not clearly differentiated from nonwork. As E. P. Thompson (1967, p. 60), in his famous paper on industrial work time, noted, before the advent of the factory, artisans worked irregularly over the course of the working day, with "no great sense of conflict between labor and passing the time of day." Eric Hobsbawm (1964), in a classic overview of the topic, describes the way in which work across the capitalist world in the earlier nineteenth century was informally broken up by nonwork activities, even including frequent interruptions of the working day for drinking sessions. Labor historian David Montgomery (1980) maintains that the history of the American working classes broadly conforms to the pattern described by Hobsbawn. Herbert Gutman (1973), writing about work patterns in nineteenth and early twentieth century, concurs with Montgomery's assessment. In just one of a great many examples, Gutman quotes a cigar factory owner in 1877 complaining about his workers: "The difficulty with many cigarmakers is this. They come down to the shop in the morning, roll a few cigars and then go to the bar or saloon and play pinochle or some other game . . . working probably only two or three hours a day" (p. 558). Roy Rosenzweig (1985) describes a similar workplace culture in late nineteenth century America in his account of the transformation of work and leisure in Worcester, Massachusetts. Within this older culture of the workplace, work effort was dictated by custom and habit rather than by the exigencies of production.[16]

A large part of the improvement in productivity in modern capitalist economies has been the result of capitalists fighting against these lackadaisical work habits, exerting greater control of the labor process, in order to increase the intensity of work. For example, Joel Mokyr, examining productivity in the British economy between 1856 and 1973, notes that GDP per hour worked increased over that period by an average of 1.7 percent per year. Yet once the "quality" of labor is taken into account, adjusting for education levels and, most importantly, for increases in the intensity of effort, the increase in productivity over this period drops to 0.7 percent (Mokyr 2003). If a substantial proportion of increasing productivity is accounted for by the increasing intensity of the labor process then, as productivity advances, work per hour will tend to become more draining on the worker. Under these conditions we might expect a strengthening rather than an attenuating preference for fewer hours on the part of workers. The fact that the tendency for hours to drop diminishes in the latter two-thirds of the twentieth century then becomes even more perplexing.

One complicating factor when considering changes in productivity, wages, and hours is the impact of the entry of women into the workforce. In 1900, roughly 20 percent of women participated in paid work. By 2000, that figure had risen to 60 percent (Dora Costa 2000b). The result of this change has been an overall increase in the labor force, on one estimate accounting for a 50 percent rise in the working population aged between twenty-five and forty-four over the first four-fifths of the century (Goldin 1986). Much of the growth in female labor took the form of part-time work, particularly after 1950.[17] According to Dora Costa (2000b, p. 109), "in 1950, 23% of all working married women in couples where both spouses were between ages 25 to 39 were working fewer than 35 hours a week. By 1970 this proportion was 35% and in 1998 was still 33%." The tendency for women to work part-time hours meant that the effect of more women entering the labor force was to depress average hours worked per employee.[18] A decrease in overall average hours caused by the mobilization of women as part-time workers clearly should not be interpreted as an increase in leisure.[19] Indeed, according to Avner Offer's analysis, hours devoted to wage labor per household with children increased significantly between the late 1960s and the end of the century. On his estimation, "families with children had a combined 53 hour week working for pay in 1968, and a 64 hour working week in 2000" (Offer 2006, p. 298).[20]

Of course, if increasing female participation in the workforce was facilitated by a reduction in domestic work hours, made possible by the diffusion of labor-saving household appliances of various sorts and by the outsourcing of domestic tasks to market service providers, then even as women increased their hours of compensated work, total hours of market and nonmarket work per household might have stayed the same or even have fallen. There is some contention about whether increasing affluence, with more widespread access to appliances such as washing machines and vacuum cleaners, led to a decrease in domestic labor. Some analysts, looking at US data, argue that there is evidence that numbers of hours of housework per week have tended to go down over time (Robinson and Godbey 1999; Zilibotti 2010). However, Ruth Cowan's (1983) historical research suggests that the amount of time devoted by households to domestic labor did not fall significantly in response to the dissemination of supposedly time-saving consumer durables. According to Cowan, the effect of labor-saving domestic appliances was, rather, to increase standards for what counts as an acceptably clean and ordered household.[21] If domestic labor did not decrease very greatly over the course of the twentieth century then, as more women entered the labor force, it is quite possible that the combined average domestic and waged labor hours per household may actually have increased in the second half of the century.

Coming up with precise estimates for long-term trends in combined domestic and paid work time per household is very difficult, because reliable data are hard to come by. John Robinson and Geoffrey Godbey (1999), stitching together American time use surveys (ATUS) from 1954 to 2000, suggest that total household labor has declined.[22] But there are problems with the representativeness of the samples used in time use surveys because of low response rates. Time use studies are also problematic because it is unclear how to classify time spent in more than one activity (Hammermesh, Frazis, and Stewart 2005).[23] Also, most of the decline charted by Robinson and God-bey occurred between 1965 and 1975, with not much further movement after that period. The combination of increasing female labor force participation, along with no decisive evidence that domestic work retreated to any great degree, casts some doubt on the suggestion that total labor per household declined in the second half of the twentieth century.

Even if we believe that the patchy ATUS data indicate that total work time did modestly decrease in the final decades of the twentieth century, the decline is still small in comparison to increases in productivity. Moreover, Robinson and Godbey acknowledge that regardless of the real trend in discretionary time, there is a pervasive sense in contemporary society that people face a time bind, with ever more demands made on scarce free time. They suggest that part of the reason for this sense of time scarcity is the ongoing accumulation of commodities, which require time for their use. This interpretation implies that capitalist mass production in conjunction with mass consumption leads to an imbalance in the structure of people's lives, with too much time spent at work and not enough time to make use of the things that work produces. The obvious solution would be to channel increasing productivity into more free time rather than more production and consumption. That this has not occurred to any significant degree is precisely the puzzle under consideration in the present investigation.

Participation in part-time work is also affected by changes in education. As the number of full-time adult students increased, so too did the number of part-time workers, since many students work part-time in order to help support themselves during their studies. This has the same diluting effect on average hours across the working population as the entry of women into the labor force as part-time employees. John D. Owen's (1988) research indicates that for nonstudent men, the working week actually increased slightly in the thirty-eight-year period between 1948 and 1986, from 42.7 to 42.8 hours. Owen maintains, more generally, that any reduction in the length of the working week after 1950 can be accounted for by changes in the composition of the workforce rather than by changes of preference among the more homogenous working population prior to 1950. On Owen's (1988, p. 42 [emphasis added]) assessment: "The series for working hours of non-student men come closest to a measure of changes over time in individual work times because this group has a minimum of other types of responsibilities. *And this series has remained constant* [since 1940]."

So, over the course of the second half of the twentieth century we see an overall pattern in which productivity increases at a steady rate, while, by comparison, the working week changes very little. As the US economy entered into a period of significant and prolonged growth in productivity, with rapidly increasing real wages, it would seem, rather counterintuitively, that the relative value placed on free time—if we take this to be indicated by the ratio of the reduction in work time to the increase in real hourly wages—declined. However, that impression is based on macrolevel longitudinal trends. Economic historians have also studied the issue of work time and wages from the point of view of individual behavior, by examining how workers vary the amount they work as their hourly income varies, and how that has changed over time. As mentioned in the last chapter, Dora Costa (2000a) has shown that the supply curve of labor among late nineteenth- and early twentieth-century workers was strongly backward bending, meaning that number of hours worked was inversely correlated with hourly wages. Costa notes that her findings agree both with those of other economic historians and with observations made in that period. By the late twentieth century, however, the supply curve was no longer backward sloping. For workers in this later period, work hours do not decrease as hourly wages increase. According to Costa: "Changes in the structure of daily work hours could largely be accounted for by the relative number of daily hours workers were willing to supply. Compared to the 1890s, increases in the hourly wage no longer have a large, negative effect impact on hours worked. In fact, workers are now slightly more willing to increase their hours as their wages rise" (p. 334).[24] Costa's analysis indicates that between the late nineteenth and late twentieth centuries, a marked change took place in the relationship between wage levels and work time. Toward the end of the twentieth century, the older pattern, in which rising real wages led to a reduction in the number of hours worked, is no longer evident. By the 1970s, the relationship between wages and hours had become extremely weak, and by the late twentieth century, it had disappeared altogether—increasing hourly wages no longer affected the demand for free time.

Costa's findings are open to different interpretations. One possible explanation for them, suggested by Costa herself, is that since people typically worked many more hours in the late nineteenth century than in the late twentieth century, the relative value of free time for them would have been higher, and therefore they would have been inclined to use increases in wage rates to reduce time at work. However, wages in the late nineteenth and early twentieth century were low enough, in many cases barely affording subsistence, to cast some doubt on that explanation. Insofar as levels of absolute poverty and want were significantly higher in the late nineteenth century than in the later twentieth century, it is reasonable to expect to find a stronger preference for increased income, as opposed to more leisure, in the earlier than in the later period. Moreover, in late nineteenth- and early twentieth-century America, there was not much in the way of a welfare state. In the absence of a safety net, there would be a strong incentive to use increases in hourly wages to generate savings rather than to reduce work time.

There are also some conceptual issues with Costa's explanation. Costa presupposes that there are decreasing marginal benefits to added increments of free time, such that when time is scarce, its value is relatively high, while when it is abundant, its value is relatively low. But free time is not just another scarce economic resource. It rather has the peculiar characteristic that its marginal value very often increases as more of it becomes available. This is because many activities become more fulfilling with the acquisition of skill and experience, both of which take time. For example, the satisfaction of the ten thousandth hour spent playing a musical instrument is quite probably substantially higher than that of the tenth hour. Since many activities have this feature of increasing returns to time invested in them (as skills become perfected, friendships deepened, tastes refined, and so on), it would be wrong to assume that the value of free time necessarily declines at the margin. Furthermore, different kinds of activity take different amounts of time, so with more free time, the range of things that can be done with that time increases. The addition of the nth hour of free time might make it possible to engage in an entirely new kind of activity and so be of more value than the addition of the previous hour, which allowed only for more of the same. So while the theory of declining marginal returns makes some sense in relation to income, considered in terms of the set of goods and services afforded by a given amount of money, it is much less clear how it applies to time. Since goods and services can only be made use of in time, as income increases, the degree to which added income can actually be used to produce added utility becomes increasingly constrained by limited free time. But in what sense can the same logic be applied to time itself? It is not apparent why people should reach satiation when it comes to free time. Having time is a condition on doing anything, and there will always be a far greater number of desirable activities that *could* be undertaken in a given lifetime than *can* be undertaken—and many of those activities would require minimal funds. It seems clear, therefore, that the benefits conferred by added increments of free time do not necessarily decline at the margin.

An alternative explanation of Costa's findings, also from a standard economic perspective, is that people in the late nineteenth century chose to turn higher hourly wages into more time rather than higher consumption, because there simply weren't very many enticing consumer goods to buy. According to this explanation, when new commodities appeared, especially after the consumer durables revolution of the early twentieth century, the utility commanded by the wage increased and so, consequently, did the demand for income. Making this argument involves positing a counterfactual—that if a contemporary array of goods had been available to workers in the later nineteenth century, then the supply curve of labor would not have been backward sloping. There is something intuitively convincing about this explanation. However, against it is the thought that at low levels of income, consumption of quite basic goods, which were available yet scarce in the late nineteenth century, should yield relatively more utility than increments of consumption at higher levels of income. In addition, as mentioned earlier, the generally low wage levels and absence of a safety net in Costa's earlier period are reasons to expect that higher income would be at least as attractive to workers as less work time.

Admittedly, all of this is quite conjectural. It is ultimately very hard to know what exactly underlies the apparent difference in time / income preference that Costa discovered between the later nineteenth and later twentieth centuries. However, a more historical explanation than those thus far discussed is that there was a shift in the legitimacy of wage labor between the two periods. Attitudes to wage labor were quite hostile in the nineteenth century, with waged work often characterized as a form of bondage. It is not implausible, therefore, that the preference for less work reflected very negative attitudes toward wage labor—a resistance on the part of waged workers to the commodification of their time. Perhaps a better explanation than the one Costa suggests for the backward-sloping supply curve of late nineteenth-century labor is, therefore, that the waged workforce in that period had not yet fully internalized work-time discipline, having more in common with E. P. Thompson's (1967) agrarian and protoindustrial workers than with a fully socialized capitalist workforce. This group of workers, to a far greater extent than was the case of later generations, regarded wage labor with a great deal of ambivalence, suspicion, and not infrequently outright hostility. Wage labor was felt by a significant part of the working population to be an external imposition, often compared to slavery, to be reduced as much as possible (Glickman 1997). A good deal of research by labor historians has characterized the postbellum nineteenth century as a liminal period, stretching between the craft-centered agrarian capitalism of the earlier part of the century, and the emergent full-blown industrial capitalism of the early twentieth century (Gutman 1973; Glickman 1997; Montgomery 1987; Rosenzweig 1985). Herbert Gutman breaks the process of proletarianization into three periods: an agrarian and protoindustrial period between 1815 and 1843, a proletarianizing phase between 1843 and 1893, and a period between 1893 and 1919 that witnessed the emergence of a mature industrial working class. During the middle, transitional phase, Gutman (1973 p. 540) writes, "a profound tension existed between the older American preindustrial social structure and the modernizing institutions that accompanied the development of industrial capitalism." Over the entire period between 1815 and 1919: "That state of tension was regularly revitalized by the migration of diverse premodern native and foreign peoples into an industrializing or a fully industrialized society." Thompson, Gutman, and Hobsbawm thus present a classic Marxian narrative in which workers begin as undisciplined creatures of habit and tradition; enter the crucible of the factory, where they are subjected to the rigors and endure the trauma of industrial life; and then emerge transformed into a modern industrial proletariat. In Hobsbawm's (1964) terms, this fully formed working class had learned "the rules of the game" of capitalism. Prominent among those rules is that *time is money.* How much time is exchanged for how much money thus became the central focus of industrial struggle, pushing aside broader challenges to the institution of wage labor (Foner and Roediger 1987). According to the account given by labor historians, the waning of the struggle over hours, which had historically been framed as a matter concerning the very legitimacy of wage labor, marked the degree to which workers had become incorporated into the capitalist system (in Chapter 5, I go into a more detailed discussion of this history). To the extent that wage earners came to equate time with money, they might well have become less attuned to the difference in value between the two, and so less inclined to trade increasing income for more free time.

This corporatist account is not, however, the only one possible from a broadly Marxian perspective. A very different interpretation of the historical change Costa charts explains the apparent shift in preferences for free time in terms of class power. As noted in the previous chapter, the power relation between business and labor is unequal, and so perhaps the development of a preference for higher wages over more time was no preference at all on the part of labor but rather expressed the interests of business alone. There is probably something to this view. Juliet Schor (1991) has, as mentioned, drawn attention to the fact that workers are rarely offered the choice to take productivity-linked compensation *either* as more income *or* as fewer hours.

The problem with the class power explanation, however, is that American union membership in the middle part of the twentieth century, when the reduction in work hours more or less ground to a halt and the new corporatist industrial pact emerged, was at an all-time high.[25] This followed a period of great labor activism in the 1930s, with union membership increasing from 3.5 million in 1935 to 9 million in 1940. In the years immediately following World War II, 36 percent of all nonfarm workers belonged to a union. After the passing of the Wagner Act of 1935, which recognized the rights of workers to organize and bargain collectively, organized labor received an unprecedented degree of support from the state. To be sure, after the war there was a backlash against the pro-union policies of the 1930s, with the passage of the Taft-Harley Act of 1947. Nonetheless, collective bargaining in the postwar period became institutionalized. Moreover, even after Taft-Hartley, union membership remained high, accounting for 35 percent of private sector workers in 1954.[26] In addition, the postwar period saw close to full employment in the US economy. Low unemployment greatly bolsters the bargaining power of labor. And yet work hours stayed almost constant in the postwar era, in stark contrast to the period between 1880 and 1940 (and especially between 1880 and 1920), when work hours declined steeply, even though labor was much weaker. If workers continued to be so concerned with reducing their hours, why did they not use their relative advantage in bargaining power during the postwar years to reduce hours, as workers did in the late nineteenth and early twentieth centuries? Analysis of reported reasons for strikes shows that while shorter hours were very important between the later nineteenth century and the Second World War, the issue dramatically receded as a cause of industrial action after 1945.[27] So why, in a period in which unemployment was low and union membership at an all-time high, and in which the collective bargaining rights of labor had been recognized to a greater degree than was the case before the New Deal, did labor not press more strongly for reduced hours? After all, between 1945 and 1970, American wage earners were very successful at increasing their wages. Yet businesses are on the whole not in favor of increasing their wage bill. If business had so much power over labor, how were workers able to win such large increases in real wages in the postwar decades? In fact, wage increases were such that the rate of return to capital, as Thomas Piketty (2014) has shown, was uniquely low during the Golden Age period of capitalism. And it was declining profit rates that contributed to the rise of the neoliberal political agenda in the 1980s—one part of which was aimed precisely at curtailing the power of labor (e.g., Ronald Reagan's treatment of striking air traffic controllers in 1981).

Given the mid-century strength of labor, it is implausible that the switch from turning more productivity into fewer work hours to channeling it almost exclusively into increasing total real wages just reflected the absolute power of business to impose its preferences on labor. American workers must, at least to some extent, have consented to the new work-time regime.[28] There is some suggestive evidence to that effect in Benjamin Hunnicutt's (1996) history of W. W. Kellogg's experiment with a thirty-hour week. The experiment was introduced by management in the 1930s to address the problem of unemployment, by distributing the same amount of work to more people. Kellogg also felt that the quality of work would increase with fewer hours. After the war, however, Kellogg's management changed its position on the issue and tried to return to the forty-hour week. Some workers objected and fought to defend the six-hour day, but significantly, many did not, while some actively supported management's effort to undermine the experiment with shorter hours. Moreover, one prominent development in the second half of the twentieth century was the introduction of overtime, following the Fair Labor Standards Act of 1938. While the point of the act was to curtail work hours, working overtime subsequently became very common among workers, so much so that the system of production came to depend on it, and "working to rule" became a form of industrial action. The willingness of wage earners to work overtime suggests that there was a quite widespread preference for income over time. Evidence for the active embrace by workers of longer hours is also provided, in a later period, by the results of a 1985 Bureau of Labor Statistics survey, in which workers were asked about their preferences for work hours (Shank 1986). The survey found that 64.9 percent of workers expressed satisfaction with their current hours and pay, 27.5 percent said that they would prefer to work longer hours to increase their incomes, while only 7.5 percent wanted fewer hours with less pay. There is, then, a stark contrast between the long tradition, stretching from the 1830s to the 1930s, of American labor fighting for a shorter working week and the postwar era of collective bargaining and productivity-based wage increases (Foner and Roediger 1987; Hunnicutt 1988). The shift between the two eras cannot be accounted for simply in terms of the interests and coercive power of business.

This is not to suggest that the power of capital does not bias things in the direction of increasing output over reducing work time. As the political philosopher G. A. Cohen argues, capitalist agencies do, in effect, encourage a preference for output over free time. Cohen makes the reasonable point that under capitalism, there are no advertising campaigns promoting the desirability of more free time as an alternative to more income. As a thought experiment, he comes up with an amusing example of what an ad in such a campaign might look like (all caps are Cohen's): "WHEN YOUR UNION NEGOTIATES, MAKE IT GO FOR SHORTER HOURS, NOT MORE PAY. ELECTRIC CARVING KNIVES ARE FINE, BUT NOTHING BEATS FREEDOM" (G. A. Cohen 2000, p. 318). Cohen's argument is that the aggregate effect of advertising might be to distort people's preferences. But influencing preferences is, of course, not the same thing as brute economic coercion.

Another explanation for the changing attitude to work time suggested by Costa's data, one drawn from the perspective of developments at the very end of the twentieth century, might be along the lines of the account given by Arlie Hochschild (1997), in her ethnographic study of attitudes to work time, *The Time Bind*. Hochschild found that willingness to spend long hours at work among the professional employees she studied was connected to the increasingly fraught and work-like character of family life, in conjunction with more emotionally engaging work. Work, in effect, had become, at least for the professional classes, a welcome retreat from the stress experienced in the domestic sphere. Hochschild's findings are intriguing, but her sample is small and composed of employees working for a Fortune 500 company and, therefore, perhaps not representative of the general population. But if the part of Hochschild's account that focuses on attitudes to family life can be generalized, then the shift in preferences toward earning more income and away from free time might well reflect an underlying change in the relative satisfactions of work versus home life. As the discontents of domestic life increased, so the aversion to spending time at work decreased.[29]

There are, however, limits to this explanation, especially with respect to the long-term and large-scale trends delineated in this chapter. The domestic-discontent argument is that people choose to spend more time at work because family life has become comparatively dissatisfying. And yet (as Hochschild notes) the discontents of family life may well have much to do with the way in which the family has been affected by changes in the organization and experience of working life. The sphere of production and the domestic sphere are deeply interconnected—although, under modern capitalism, the flow of influence tends to run from the former to the latter. Reducing work time would open up possibilities for social life outside both work and home, which quite probably would have very positive effects on the quality of domestic life. Furthermore, a domestic-discontent explanation focuses on workplace and household dynamics that lead individuals to make particular decisions to commit to work time. Yet decisions about how much to work *within* a given work-time regime have a logic different from collective decisions about whether to move from a given work-time regime to a different one. Humans, to state the obvious, are profoundly social animals, and the value of free time, therefore, depends to a significant extent on the availability of other people to spend it with. If work time were to be reduced in a concerted fashion for the entire population, then the social character of nonwork time would change, since with everyone working fewer hours, greater social resources and opportunities would become available in nonwork time. The kinds of activity in nonwork time that would become available following a collective shift to less work are qualitatively different from those afforded to an isolated individual working fewer hours. To return to the music example, an isolated individual choosing to work less can spend more time playing a musical instrument. But if that person is a member of a community that collectively works less, then, in addition to the option of practicing alone, she can join with others to play music together. Moreover, the situation Hochschild describes is essentially a dichotomous one—individuals either spend more time at work or more time at home. Yet where the entire community has more free time, opportunities are expanded for spending time in social contexts that are neither work nor home. If a community opted for fewer work hours, it would thus become more possible for its members to create the kind of rich associational life imagined by communitarians. Indeed, Benjamin Hunnicutt's (1996) history of Kellogg's experiment with six-hour days shows how, after the adoption of the shorter working week, a qualitative shift took place in how people made use of their free time, with much more time given over to community activities. So while a domestic-discontent account seems to provide a plausible explanation for why, under current social conditions, at least some individuals choose to spend more time at work, it is not a good explanation for the absence, in the postwar period, of a collective politics aimed at reducing hours—one similar to the shorter hours movements of the nineteenth and early twentieth centuries.[30] The explanation is anchored to a particular configuration of work time and free time—a configuration the historical development of which this book takes as a problem in need of explanation.

In a very different vein, the failure of work time to diminish could be seen as a consequence of the widespread influence of what social psychologists would describe as an unpopular norm. One of the factors identified by Hochschild, and also by Schor, as responsible for long workdays is the valorization of work effort and the corresponding implicit stigma attached to choosing to work less. Employees feel they must put in more time on the job for fear of being labeled a "shirker" or as "work-shy." Arguably this is an example of an unpopular norm, upheld not because the majority agrees with it but, more subtly, because each individual thinks that everyone else positively supports the norm. William Macy and his collaborators, in their discussion of this type of norm, illustrate the idea by way of the story of the emperor's new clothes (Centola, Willer, and Macy 2005; Willer, Kuwabara, and Macy 2009). Each member of the crowd sees that the emperor has no clothes but, because everyone else is behaving as if the emperor is clad in fine garments, opts to behave as if what everyone else seems to be seeing is true so as to fit in with the crowd. For a community to abandon an unpopular norm, it must overcome the challenge of coordinating the communication of true preferences—or, more precisely, of "dis-coordinating" behavioral signals that misrepresent true preferences and normative commitments. If working long hours is a result of an unpopular norm of this sort, then the solution would be for every member of a community to reveal her true preferences at more or less the same time. But concerted collective action of that sort is difficult to coordinate, so once entrenched, unpopular norms can be hard to dislodge. However, while the unpopular norm explanation might give a good account of the dynamic that keeps the suboptimal work-hour norm in place once it has been established, it does not explain how or why the norm became entrenched in the first place. Nor does it account for why the organized collective effort to shift to an alternative norm—a shorter working week—that once animated large parts of American society ebbed significantly during the twentieth century.[31]

One final possible explanation that should be considered for the failure of work hours to decrease is that changes in life expectancy, and in the organization of the life course, reduced the overall proportion of lives typically spent in full-time work. Increasing life expectancy, in conjunction with the greater possibility for retirement and more time spent in full-time education, meant that as the twentieth century progressed, people typically entered the workforce later and lived for more years after the end of their working lives. Since the proportion of life spent in full-time work progressively contracted over the course of the twentieth century, workers might not have worried so much about the failure of the working week to decrease. Indeed, they might have become increasingly concerned about funding their retirements, and an obvious response would be to maximize income during their working years in order to save as much as possible.

Life expectancy increased substantially over the course of the twentieth century in the United States. In 1900, life expectancy for white males was forty-eight years and fifty-one for women. By the end of the century, it had increased to seventy-five for men and eighty for women. An increase in life expectancy of that magnitude might not have much effect on attitudes to hours at work if working life continued to the grave. However, the twentieth century saw the emergence of retirement as a new phase of life—one made possible by increased productivity. The advent of retirement reduced the number of years spent at work as a proportion of years lived. The combined effect of retirement and increases in life span led, between 1850 and 1990, to a sixfold increase in the average amount of time lived after the end of working life (Costa 1998b). Given the increased likelihood of life after the working years, it would perhaps make sense for workers to favor higher wages over more free time in order to build savings to fund retirement.[32]

However, while an increase in prospective years of life after retirement probably had some influence on attitudes to wages and work time, it is questionable whether the effect was big enough to explain the quite dramatic shift toward higher wage income, at the expense of more free time, during the working years. As discussed earlier in this chapter, in the United States at least, savings rates have been consistently low over the course of the century. This suggests that pushing for higher income, as opposed to a shorter working week, for the most part was motivated by a preference for immediate consumption, rather than by the need to save for retirement. Moreover, there is, to state the obvious, no guarantee whatsoever that a given worker will survive until retirement or for many years after retirement. And, arguably, the extent to which retirement can be enjoyed is limited by overall health, which tends to decline with age. It is not unreasonable, therefore, to suppose that wage earners would discount the value of postretirement time compared to free time when fit and healthy.[33] Economists of a psychological bent, such as Tibor Scitovsky (1992), could respond by arguing that people have a bias in favor of minimizing discomfort over maximizing enjoyment and that this influences the rate at which they discount the well-being of their future selves. Since with age comes greater exposure to discomfort, it arguably makes sense for people to adopt a strategy of forgoing enjoyment when young so that discomfort will be minimized in the future. But even if comfort is the overriding desideratum, there is little reason to think that people will act to secure the comfort of their temporally distant selves rather than maximizing their comfort in the present. As we have seen, the experimental findings of behavioral psychologists indicate that people are, to a significant extent, hyperbolic discounters, attaching much more importance to well-being in the moment than to that in even the medium-term future. This suggests that the prudent model of the economic agent is not an accurate one (Ainslie 2001). One could, in a philosophical spirit, even follow Derek Parfit (1984) in questioning whether there are any strictly rational grounds at all for supposing a continuity of identity between present and distantly future selves. The supposition that people have rational, self-interested reasons to arrange their lives to take account of the welfare of their far future selves, Parfit argues, rests on a questionable metaphysics of identity, according to which there is an essence that connects the identity of the person across the life course. Why should people sacrifice current satisfaction for future selves given that continuity of identity rests on metaphysically shaky foundations?[34]

The most powerful objection to the theory that income is preferred to free time because of a concern to fund retirement is, however, that one of its crucial empirical entailments—the prediction that workers will save at high rates when at the height of their earning potential in order to finance their post-retirement lives—fails to hold true. For the preference for income over more free time during the working years to be convincingly explained as preparation for retirement, we would have to demonstrate that the life-cycle hypothesis, developed by the economist Franco Modigliani (1970) (and Milton Friedman's [1957] related permanent income hypothesis), is supported by the empirical evidence. The life-cycle hypothesis posits that people aim to generate a constant amount of utility, through their consumption, over the entire course of their lives. According to the theory, because the marginal utility of consumption decreases, individuals, rather than spending all the money they have at any given point in time, will seek to distribute their spending over time such that it maximizes utility over their entire lives, with the result that consumption is "smoothed" across the life course. The theory predicts that people will go into debt when young and poor, save when affluent and middle aged (in order to finance their retirement), and "dissave" when old, spending down their assets. So it goes in theory, but the empirical support for the life-cycle hypothesis is not compelling.[35] Economist Angus Deaton (1992), in an overview of the empirical literature on the topic, concludes that the evidence, on balance, does not support the life-cycle hypothesis. According to Deaton, "it is certainly the case that the household data typically show no clear evidence of asset decumulation among the old." Moreover, he adds, "there are other problems earlier in the life-cycle, and although there is often some hump saving in late middle age, there is also typically a very close articulation of consumption and income over the whole of life. Survey data also show that many households possess little or no wealth, certainly not in financial assets, and many individuals have little beyond social security after they retire." Deaton concludes that "the fall in the saving rate in the US is not attributable to a redistribution of aggregate income towards the old, but comes from an increase in expenditures, particularly expenditures on *durable goods*, across all cohorts, particularly prime-age cohorts" (p. 217 [emphasis added]).[36] Deaton's overall assessment accords with that of other economists. Paul Courant, Edward Gamlich, and John Laitner (1986, pp. 278–79), for example, note that "for all its elegance and rationality the life cycle hypothesis has not tested out well." Moreover, if Modigliani's life-cycle hypothesis was correct then, as the length of time lived after retirement increased (as it did consistently during the twentieth century), there should have been a commensurate increase in the rate of saving. Yet household savings in the United States did not increase over the course of the twentieth century, despite rising income, increasing life expectancy, and the growing prospect of life after work (Maddison 1992).

In light of the failure of the life-cycle and permanent-income hypotheses to hold empirically, as well as evidence that people tend to discount the future hyperbolically, the argument that increases in life expectancy, in conjunction with the advent of retirement, account for the stagnation of the length of the working week is less than convincing.

At the other end of the life course from retirement, there was an increase, during the twentieth century, in the number of years spent in full-time education prior to entering the work force. In 1910, only 10 percent of the population completed high school. By 1940, that number had leapt to over 50 percent (Goldin 1998, 1999). High school graduation rates continued to climb until around 1960, after which they hovered at around 75 percent, declining slightly through to the end of the century. Most of the increase in the rate of graduation then took place between 1910 and 1960. Enrollment in institutions of higher education also steadily increased, from around 3 percent of the population in the first decade of the century, to 56.6 percent in 1995.[37] If increasing productivity was in part used to delay the age at which work begins, then, although it might appear as if working time stayed constant, in fact it was decreasing, as some proportion of increasing output was used to increase the amount of time spent in education. Over the course of the century, individuals entered the workforce progressively later, and this reduced the total number of hours worked over a lifetime.

This trend would go some way to explaining the pattern of work time *if* full-time education can be characterized as free time. However, that seems questionable, given that school is compulsory (at least until the later teen years) and that to a large extent the telos of schooling is work. From the point of view of the individual, time spent in full-time education might therefore seem more like a backward extension of working life than a mirror image of retirement at the other end of the life course. In the nineteenth century, workers typically began their working lives as apprentices, training "on-the-job." It makes some sense to think of the time young people spend in full-time education as somewhat analogous to an apprenticeship, as modern education is to a large extent about training for work. It would certainly be odd to categorize increasing time in education in response to the demands of the labor market as leisure time. This is not to suggest that becoming educated is not, for many individuals, an end in itself. But the main reason for the increasing time spent in full-time education prior to entering the workforce was an increase in the credentials required for work. In that sense, time spent in education should be thought of as continuous with working time rather than as a form of free time.

4. Spending and Saving

As we have seen, the history of the United States over the past century or so shows that increases in productivity have predominantly been harnessed to increase output, with some portion captured by labor, through increasing real wages. Up until the middle part of the century, increasing productivity was accompanied by a decline in the length of the working week. However, once the eight-hour day had become the norm, work time began to plateau, even as in the postwar period productivity and real hourly wages continued to rise. But what was done with this increasing wage income? It is quite hard to get a clear picture of past consumption practices, but some general trends are apparent, some of which are prima facie quite puzzling. Aggregate levels of consumer spending, as opposed to saving, are consistently high, especially in the second half of the century. Empirical analysis has shown that, not just in the United States but across capitalist economies, consumption increases proportionately with income (Thaler 1990). This goes against the view that increasing income should lead to a higher proportion of income saved (the increasing marginal propensity to save).

Bureau of Labor Statistics data show that between 1900 and 1950, average household income and consumer spending track one another almost exactly. Spending begins to lag somewhat behind income between 1950 and 2000, but it does so to a surprisingly small extent. Lizabeth Cohen (2003) notes that private consumption remained steady as a proportion of GDP, accounting for at least two-thirds of the national product. Spending in the latter half of the century absorbs a roughly constant (albeit inconsistently so—sometimes it is higher and sometimes lower) rather than a declining proportion of income (National Bureau of Labor Statistics Report 2006). In fact, with the exception of the Depression of the 1930s, levels of consumer spending remained remarkably high across the course of the century, tending to increase at least in proportion to rising income. In 1993, Americans spent over 90 percent of their incomes on consumption, and this is not untypical for the postwar period (Lebergott 1996, p. 61). In line with this pattern, the average household savings rate in the United States was fairly stable for most of the twentieth century, varying only between 6.5 percent and 8.5 percent (with the exception of a spike in savings between 1973 and 1975), before dropping to historic lows in the 2000s, when it averaged 3.5 percent (Maddison 1992).[38]

The failure of the rate of savings to increase as a proportion of income as real wages increased runs, as mentioned, in some tension with economic theory.[39] J. M. Keynes (1936) long ago posited as a "law of consumption" that as real income increases, spending will also increase, but not in proportion to increasing income, with savings making up the difference between rising real wages and consumer spending. Keynes, like many other economists, thought that the marginal propensity to consume decreases as income increases: "It is obvious that a higher absolute level of income will tend, as a rule, to widen the gap between income and consumption" and therefore "as a rule . . . a greater proportion of income [will be] saved as real income increases" (1936, p. 97).[40] The reasoning here, which is fairly intuitive, is, once more, that the marginal benefits of consumption decline as income goes up, and so, all things being equal, with higher incomes we should expect a shift from consumer spending to saving.[41] Although Keynes does not spell out the point, presumably part of his thinking was that, as real income rises, the benefit of having savings (as a kind of insurance against misfortune) increases relative to that of immediate consumption.

But as we have seen, Keynes's assumption about the marginal propensity to consume (which simply echoed the received wisdom of his discipline) is not borne out by the pattern of consumption in the United States in the twentieth century. Had increasing income been used to increase savings, then the failure of work hours to fall substantially as hourly wages rose would perhaps make more sense. Household savings offer some protection against unpredictable events, such as illness or unemployment. And as discussed in the previous section, funneling more income into savings as earnings increase might be expected against the background of the quite substantial increase in life expectancy over the course of the century, in conjunction with the emergence of the institution of retirement. Yet household saving in the United States was oddly unresponsive to the combination of increasing real wages during the working years and increased need for savings to fund retirement.

Moreover, not only did household savings rates not increase with rising real income, but the use of credit, the antithesis of savings, expanded over the course of the century. Martha Olney shows how, following World War I, the practice of installment buying spread rapidly across the economy. The beginning of the collapse of inhibitions against borrowing can be traced to the

1920s. Consumer credit as a percentage of income doubled between 1920 and 1930, from 4.5 percent to 9.5 percent, and the use of credit of various sorts continued to increase for the remainder of the century (Olney 1991). In 1933, according to Columbia sociologist Robert S. Lynd (1933, p. 862), installment purchases amounted to between 12 percent and 15 percent of total retail sales, including 60 percent of furniture sales, 50 percent of electrical household goods, 75 percent of radios sold, and 60 percent of automobile sales. Robert and Helen Lynd found ethnographic evidence of a new attitude to credit in their study of the economic life of "Middletown" (Muncie, Indiana): "People don't think anything nowadays of borrowing sums of money they'd never have thought of borrowing in the old days," Lynd was told by one of his informants (Lynd and Lynd 1929). Even during the economic downturn of the 1930s, the Lynds found that the demand for credit continued unabated. They were informed by "a discerning Middletown woman" that "most of the families I know are after the same things today that they were after before the depression, and they'll get them the same way—on credit" (Lynd and Lynd 1935, p. 203). The expansion of credit continued into the post–World War II period. Consumer credit grew elevenfold between 1945 and 1960, while credit through installment payment plans increased nineteenfold. Moreover, a new form of credit emerged in the late 1940s with the appearance of the first consumer credit cards.[42]

One of the reasons why credit took off was the failure of savings to increase in line with wages. Despite increasing productivity and wages, the static savings rate meant that for many consumers it was not possible to pay for big-ticket items without borrowing money, and so, from the later nineteenth century onward, new institutions developed to provide credit. Of course, this raises the question of why savings did not increase to fund spending on the consumer durables that were becoming increasingly available. One possible answer is that credit is a kind of saving after the fact of a purchase, such that, rather than saving first to fund a purchase, the purchase is made on credit, then money is "saved" to make payments on the debt incurred. Avner Offer (2006) has suggested that the appeal of this strategy is that it is psychologically easier to make payments on credit owed than it is to save, since failure to do the former results in very visible financial penalties.[43] Yet taking on a commitment to "save" via credit payments has definite downsides. The obvious one is the financial risk entailed by making use of credit. While wage earners accounted for only 35 percent of personal bankruptcies in 1935, by 1958 this number had increased to 85 percent, according to the National Retail Credit Association—an increase directly resulting from the expansion of consumer credit (L. Cohen 2003, p. 124). Moreover, given the rate at which new, and supposedly superior, products become available under capitalism, unless the demand for an item is quite urgent, the consumer would arguably do better by saving up for expensive items rather than using credit. By saving instead of using credit, consumers would likely have more choice when they finally get to the point of making a purchase, because, in all probability, new products would have appeared. Of course, the drawback of saving, as opposed to using credit, is that it entails forgoing immediate consumption. But it is not self-evident that avoiding the frustration of delayed gratification outweighs the benefits of saving, especially given the substantial interest typically paid with credit or installment payments.

Another explanation for the rise of credit is that it allowed rates of spending to be maintained as wages fluctuate. Credit can be used to keep spending in line with current standards, despite decreases in income. But credit can also be used in lieu of rising wages to support increasing consumption. The latter use is likely when expectations become fixed not just about current standards of consumption but also about the rate of increase of consumption. For example, the explosion of consumer credit after 1980 was partly in response to a demand for spending to continue to increase even as real wage levels stagnated—people tried to maintain the postwar pattern of continuously increasing consumption even when their purchasing power was frozen. The increasing use of credit since 1980 thus to some degree indicates a general demand for consumption to increase over time, regardless of what's happening to real wages. This suggests that the widespread expectation, established in the early postwar era, that material living standards should continuously improve, had become firmly entrenched.

But if the increasing use of credit is explained by fixed expectations about ever-increasing consumption, the question arises of why those expectations should have become so inflexible. Why should consumers, faced with stagnating real income, have chosen to use credit to maintain increasing spending levels rather than keeping their spending in line with their incomes? Why did people expose themselves to the risks associated with accumulating unnecessary debt (some debt is of course unavoidable, especially for people living paycheck to paycheck)? The answer is clearly complex, but one possible explanation that fits with the theory developed in this book is that spending is seen as just compensation received in exchange for work. If the rate of increase of real wages falls, but the perceived labor input of waged workers does not, then wage earners might well feel entitled to keep constant the rate at which their consumption increases, even if that means resorting to credit.

So, spending increased roughly in proportion to increasing real wages. But what did people spend their wages on? To a significant extent, people spent their disposable income on durable commodities. Based on Department of Commerce data, between 1925 and 1998 the value in 1998 dollars of consumer durables in the US economy increased from $32 billion to $2,418.8 billion (this excludes the value of fixed residential assets, which will be discussed later in this chapter)—a startling seventy-five-fold increase. Using a chain-quantity index measure—which better controls for variability in the purchasing power of the dollar and so gives a more reliable estimate of changes in volume of goods—output of consumer durables still increased more than twenty-one-fold between 1925 and 1998 (see table in Appendix 1). Between 1925 and 1998 the US population increased by 2.35 times (from 115,000,000 to 270,000,000) so output of consumer durables *per capita* increased thirty-two-fold, measured in constant dollars, and ninefold according to the chain-quantity index measure. Most of these goods were destined for the domestic market. According to Avner Offer's (2006, p. 178) analysis, over the postwar period in the United States, spending on durable consumer goods grew by 1.2 times as much as income, while consumption as a whole grew slightly less than did income (with income elasticity of 0.94). Economic historian Martha Olney (1991) shows that the shift in the economy toward consumer durables can be traced to the 1920s, which witnessed a "consumer durables revolution." By this Olney means a structural shift in consumer tastes towards consumer durables. Comparing the periods 1898–1916 and 1922–1929, Olney finds that spending on consumer durables went up and savings declined. Spending on durables doubled, from 3.7 percent of disposable income before the First World War to 7.2 percent afterward, while savings nearly halved, from 6.4 percent to 3.8 percent. As Olney (1990, p. 49) notes: "Such a sharp decline in personal saving rate is astounding, particularly since the 1920s were rather prosperous years and we usually expect savings rates to climb, not fall, during periods of prosperity." As we have seen, a low saving rate, in conjunction with ongoing spending on consumer durables, was to be the pattern for much of the rest of the century.[44] It continued, and indeed intensified, in the postwar era. In 1957, for example, a Federal Reserve study of patterns of credit and consumption drew attention to the shift from consumers buying services from companies that owned durable assets, to consumers acquiring durables to provide services (Garon 2012, p. 319).

Olney argues that the growing expenditure on consumer durables cannot be explained by increasing incomes in conjunction with decreases in the prices of those goods. Comparing prices in the 1920s to those of the pre–World War I era, she finds that consumer durables were actually relatively more expensive in the later period than other goods and services. So the evidence suggests that there was a real shift in demand for consumer durables in the post–World War I period. What sense are we then to make of this change in consumer behavior? Olney suggests, like Avner Offer, that we should think of the accumulation of consumer durables as a form of saving. On this interpretation, acquiring a consumer durable is an act of investment in an asset, akin to investments in fixed capital undertaken by firms. Consumers bank the utility-generating potential afforded by their artifacts for future use. Olney thus follows Becker (1981) in conceiving of households as utility-producing factories, with consumer goods as their working capital. Yet this analogy only highlights the oddness of the underlying pattern. It would be perverse for a firm to buy a piece of capital equipment and then leave it unused (or underutilized) while its value is inexorably eroded by depreciation. Also, in general it makes sense for firms and households alike to keep a good amount of capital in its fungible money form, as cash reserves, since future needs and wants cannot be easily predicted.[45] Moreover, holding capital in the form of assets incurs a penalty if, as a result of an unforeseen calamity, a firm or a household is forced to sell those assets at distress sale prices. Under specific market conditions—for example, when people expect a shortage of some good, or under conditions of very high inflation—it might be a good idea to stockpile capital goods and materials. However, although there have been intermittent periods of high inflation in the United States—for example, in the period immediately following World War II and in the 1970s—on the whole the rate at which prices have increased over the century has been fairly gradual. Nor is it the case that hoarding consumer durables can be explained by fears of future scarcity. There were shortages during the wars, which led to price controls, and distributional problems during the Depression, but apart from those periods, America has been for a majority of its citizens, and for much of the twentieth century, a "land of plenty," with low inflation and an abundance of goods. Given these historical conditions, the explanation given by Olney for the accumulation of consumer durables seems questionable.

The evidence thus indicates that consumers began in the early twentieth century to accumulate durable goods, and they did this in lieu of investing money or working fewer hours. But what kinds of goods did they acquire? Three categories immediately stand out: automobiles, houses, and appliances. The importance of car ownership in the first half of the twentieth is clear in Robert and Helen Lynd's (1929, 1937) ethnographic research. The Lynds found ample evidence of the new obsession with cars in their studies of "Middletown" (Muncie, Indiana). Time and again, the Lynds' informants speak of their obsession with owning and driving automobiles. During periods of hardship, the Lynds were informed, the very last expenditure to be cut back on is gas and other car-related expenses: "I'll never cut back on gas! . . . I'd go without a meal before I'll cut down on using a car," one informant tells them (1929, p. 63).[46] The Lynds' impression is borne out by aggregate data. Between 1916 and 1926, car sales tripled from 1.6 million to 4.3 million per year. The proportion of the population owning cars between 1910 and 1930 increased from 1 percent in 1910 to 26 percent in 1920, and by 1930, it had reached 60 percent. According to the 1929 census of distribution, Americans spent 18.08 cents of every dollar on automobiles and their upkeep—as much as on food. There are of course good practical reasons for owning a car given the progressive dispersion of urban form in modern America, with the growth of suburbs, in conjunction with a generally inadequate public transportation infrastructure. Yet this poses a chicken-and-egg question: Which came first, the taste for automobiles or the reorganization of social space such that they became necessary? I will consider the significance of automobiles as consumer durables at greater length in Chapter 5 of this book.

A second consumer durable that showed dramatic growth over the twentieth century was housing.[47] Houses are not always immediately thought of as consumer durables, because they are often regarded as investment assets. However, except for a fairly small class of speculative real estate investors, houses are, for most people, primarily consumer durables. At the beginning of the century, only 36.5 percent of Americans owned their own homes. By 1960, homeownership had spread to 62 percent of the population. The stock of rental accommodation actually shrank in the post-1945 era as Americans collectively pursued the dream of homeownership. At the same time, in the postwar period there was a huge building boom. A quarter of the housing stock in the United States after 1960 was built in the 1950s (Cohen 2003, p. 122). In part, the switch to homeownership was in response to significant federal subsidies, in the form of income tax deductions for mortgage interest and property taxes, the origins of which date back to the tax reforms of 1913 (Prasad 2012).[48] Yet even given homeowner-friendly tax policies, it is difficult to make sense of this striking trend in terms of the narrow economic benefits of homeownership. Home prices track markets more generally, so it is unclear why investing in housing makes more sense than other kinds of investment. Indeed, some studies indicate that renting and investing, as opposed to buying and paying a mortgage, is a superior strategy for wealth creation (Beracha, Skiba, and Johnson 2017). Furthermore, the United States has tended to have high levels of geographical mobility. Although we lack good time series data for geographical mobility prior to 1935, more contemporary data indicate that more than one-third of all home buyers move within five years, which is generally too soon for them to have been able to build enough equity to cover transaction costs.[49] Under those conditions renting housing would seem to make more sense than buying it. More generally, switching from renting to owning, for many, corresponds to a decline in the quality of life, as households become highly leveraged—house rich and cash poor. The strength of the preference in the United States for home buying is, therefore, quite puzzling.

At the same time as homeownership became increasingly prevalent over the course of the twentieth century, the size of the homes occupied by Americans got progressively larger. Between 1950 and 2006, the average home size in the United States doubled from around 1,200 square feet to close to 2,400 square feet. This was largely facilitated by suburbanization, which opened up cheap land for development. Yet it is tempting to interpret the growth in the size of American abodes as connected to the increasing accumulation of material durables, as larger homes were required to store and organize increasing quantities of things. Homes, seen in this light, are commodities used for the storage of other commodities.

Another category of consumer durable the demand for which took off in the early part of the century was domestic appliances. One possible explanation, touched on earlier in the chapter, for the failure of the working week to fall as wages increased, is that the commodities and services acquired with the wage had the effect of reducing necessary labor time outside work. So according to this line of reasoning, as income went up, the amount of time spent on unpaid domestic labor went down, with the net result that the amount of truly free time (left over after all necessary labor, paid and unpaid) per household increased. This explanation would seem to solve our puzzle. If increasing income at constant hours of work has the effect of reducing total household labor hours (domestic plus paid work) because the income is used to acquire domestic appliances that *save time*, then it might make sense to choose money over less paid work time so that more and better labor-saving devices can be acquired. However, it is not at all clear that the time-saving effect of commodities is sufficient to account for the degree to which increasing productivity has not been used to reduce paid work time. As discussed previously, it is questionable whether the use of new domestic appliances significantly reduced time spent on housework, as opposed to increasing standards of cleanliness and order within the household (Cowan 1983). Moreover, research on the rates of diffusion of different kinds of consumer commodities casts some doubt on the notion that the acquisition of time-saving consumer durables explains the preference for earnings over free time. Economic historians Susan Bowden and Avner Offer (1994) compared the spread of time saving and time using consumer durables in the United States and the United Kingdom during the twentieth century and found that in both societies, time-using commodities diffused significantly more rapidly than time-saving commodities. Consumers evidently directed their discretionary spending first at products whose use demanded, rather than saved, time. The prioritizing of time-using durables makes it implausible that any preference workers had for more income over fewer hours can be explained by the use of that income to acquire appliances and other products that free up more time.

The US case thus illustrates the kind of pattern that is quite typical of high industrial capitalism. After an initial period during which working hours decreased, further increases in productivity were relentlessly channeled into an expansion of output, while the rate of decrease in the length of the average working week diminished almost to zero. The pattern of trends in productivity, consumer spending, and hours of work described in this chapter is certainly hard to make sense of within the broad set of assumptions that neoclassical economists bring to their analyses. At the same time, explanations based on behavioral economics, class power, identity-making, or status-seeking, while making sense of certain aspects of the pattern that emerged in twentieth century capitalism, fail, for reasons set out in the last chapter, as full explanations for that pattern. An alternative approach, which I will take up in the next chapter, is to make sense of these trends in terms of changes in the normative framework underpinning wage-labor exchange. These affected the meaning, and especially the justification, of work under capitalism in a way that had significant consequences for attitudes toward wage goods and consumption.

Before pressing forward with the development of a theory along those lines, as an addendum to this chapter some attention should be paid to the question of whether the US pattern of productivity and work time is, in fact, atypical among capitalist societies and best explained in terms of national traits. Some analysts have suggested that the slow rate of decline in work time in the United States during the affluent postwar years reflects the cultural and historical idiosyncrasies of America, those that make it "exceptional" when compared to the rest of the capitalist world. Tibor Scitovsky (1992) and, to a lesser extent, Juliet Schor (1991) both make this kind of argument. Indeed, Scitovsky (who was by background a European aristocrat) suggests that the solution to what he regarded as a peculiarly American problem of over-work and overproduction is for Americans to emulate European practices of self-cultivation and savoir vivre. However, it is not clear how much of the difference in work hours between Europe and America is a result of a differ-ence between the two in preferences for free time, one ultimately attributable to "culture," and how much is a result of other factors. For example, during economic downturns, US firms typically shed workers. Those who remain work the same number of hours or sometimes even more, as they are forced to do some of the work of those who were made unemployed. By contrast, in Europe the response to economic downturns has, in the postwar period, been more likely to have involved a reduction of hours per worker rather than in numbers of employees. Reduced hours under those conditions clearly do not indicate a preference for leisure but rather a stronger commitment in Europe to a corporatist welfare capitalism that extends special protections to those in work (Esping-Andersen 1990). Similarly, in France the thirty-five-hour workweek was introduced in 2000 primarily as a way to address the prob-lem of structural unemployment, by redistributing work.[50] At the same time, marginal income tax rates in Europe have tended to be higher than in the United States, which decreases the incentive for working longer hours. These differences in labor market regulation, industrial policy, and taxes have the effect of depressing work hours in Europe as compared to the United States.

Taking these, and other, factors into account, Robert Gordon (2010) estimates that only one-third of the difference in work hours between the United States and Western Europe can be attributed to different preferences for leisure. The remainder Gordon considers to be "involuntary leisure," forced on European workers by conditions beyond their control.[51] This would suggest that those who have used differences in work hours between Europe and the United States as evidence of cultural differences in attitudes to work and free time have been overstating their case.

Moreover, while there are certainly differences between the work time regimes in Western Europe and the United States, the trend in both places is similar: increasing productivity has predominantly been used to increase output rather than to reduce work time. Although Western Europeans in the late twentieth century on average worked fewer hours than Americans, the difference between the two, relative to the huge increase in productivity in both regions, is not great. European productivity improved at roughly the same rate as American productivity in the postwar period, yet even taking length of vacations into account, the working week in Western Europe was longer than in the United States until at least the mid-1970s. In 1970, average hours in the fifteen countries that made up the European Union before its eastward expansion in 2004 were actually marginally higher than they were in the United States (Blanchard 2004).[52] In the mid-1970s, work hours were between 10 and 15 percent longer in Britain, France, and Germany than they were in America (Prescott 2004). It is true that by 1987, hours were 15 percent shorter in Europe than in the United States, and by 2000, the gap had increased to 23 percent (Maddison 1991; Blanchard 2004).[53] Yet since hours of work are calculated by dividing total hours worked by number of workers, the greater prevalence of part-time work in Europe distorts the picture.[54] Some of the difference in work hours toward the end of the century can be accounted for by underemployment in the EU—a consequence of the dual labor market structure created by European corporatism, which secures stable employment for some, while consigning others to permanent casual, part-time labor. Recent data from Eurostat (2017) indicate that full-time hours per week have been very similar in Europe and in the United States since 2006—around forty-one hours in Europe and forty-two hours in the United States. Furthermore, according to one study, once hours of domestic labor are taken into account, work hours in a sample of three European countries (Germany, Italy, and the Netherlands) between 1985 and 2003 were at most only 12 percent lower (at the end of that period) than in the United States (Burda, Hammermesh, and Weil 2006). Americans spent more time working in the market than Europeans, and Europeans put more time into domestic labor, while the total time Americans and Europeans gave to labor (market plus domestic) was not that different.[55] Some of the difference in market work hours between Europe and America thus reflects the tendency for domestic labor to be done in-house in Europe, while it tends to be out-sourced through the market in the United States.[56]

In sum, the contrast between leisured Europeans and workaholic Americans, to the extent that it has any empirical basis, is essentially a feature of the last quarter of the twentieth century and the years since the turn of the twenty-first century. Moreover, the glaring disparity during the twentieth century between growth in productivity on the one hand and the rate of reduction of work time on the other holds in Europe as well as in the United States, albeit to a slightly lesser extent in the years toward the end of the twentieth century.[57] More striking than any difference in work time between the United States and Western Europe is the failure of work time in both places to fall to a greater extent than it did over the course of the twentieth century. Keynes's 1930 prediction, that the industrial world would witness a radical contraction of labor time, is not much closer to being realized in Europe than it is in the United States.[58] It would seem that there is a quite general bias in capitalism toward turning improved productivity into more output rather than more free time.

FOUR

A Theory of Mass Consumption as Wage-Labor Commensuration

One way to make sense of the pattern of work and consumption described in the previous chapters is in terms of the changing experience and understanding of wage labor—in particular, by paying attention to the conditions under which wage labor came to be seen as a fundamentally legitimate form of exchange. Wage labor is, after all, the dominant feature in the organization of the economy under capitalism, engaging most of the population for much of its waking life, while consumers are almost always also wage earners. In order for wage labor to become broadly acceptable as a potentially fair economic practice, work had to be plausibly commensurable with its wage.[1] This is because commensurability is a prerequisite for a fair exchange of labor for a wage. Commensurability between labor and wage became possible in the context of an approach to commodities that unhinged their use value from the concrete contexts in which those commodities get used, so that use value becomes to a significant extent hypothetical rather than something closely tied to the practical realities of particular lives. This hypothetical understanding of object utility could help explain the seemingly perverse patterns of consumer commodity accumulation and work time that is characteristic of advanced industrial capitalism.

The early history of capitalism was characterized by a good deal of political struggle and ideological contention over wage labor as a form of exchange. The idea that free activity could legitimately be exchanged for a wage was anathema to large sections of the labor movement, and in the earlier stages of industrial capitalism, both in the United States and in Europe, wage labor was subjected to widespread criticism and condemnation.[2] As industrial capitalism advanced, however, the exchange of labor for a wage increasingly came to be accepted as part of the natural order of things. The focus of critical attention began to shift from the legitimacy of capitalism itself, and especially of the institution of wage labor, first to conditions of work, such as the length of the working week, and then to levels of compensation. Over time, wage labor became construed as a potentially fair exchange, with much effort put into thinking about the criteria by which its fairness can and should be gauged.

There have been various ways of thinking about what constitutes a fair wage, and various schemes for implementing different conceptions of fair compensation. For some economists, fair wages are just those delivered by the untrammeled operation of market forces. The marginalists, for example, held that, under free market conditions, wages reflect the value of labor's contribution to the product. Because, according to this view, wages simply measure the value labor adds to output, they are fair by definition. For some labor activists and radical political economists, by contrast, fair wages are those that capture the full value of the product, on the grounds that only labor creates value. The way in which labor has been used to calculate wage rates in practice has varied across time and place. Compensation has been figured, for example, as a rate for discrete physical actions per unit of work time or, alternatively, in terms of labor's material output, in the form of piece rates (Biernacki 1995).

What the different ways of thinking about and determining fair compensation for work under capitalism have in common, however, is a conception of fairness as objectively measurable. That is, fairness is regarded not as a matter of convention or custom but, rather, as an objective fact about an exchange, rooted in the properties of the substances being exchanged. An exchange is objectively fair, in this view, when a rational observer, without knowledge of the specifics of the set of norms governing the exchange, would judge it to be so. For example, the exchange between feudal lord and vassal, free peasant, or serf might be entirely in accordance with custom and therefore conventionally proper. A modern observer, however, would be unlikely to judge feudal exchange as fair, because of the apparent disparity in the services exchanged (not to mention the degree of coercion involved) and the apparently arbitrary nature of the underlying convention. Similarly, modern conceptions of fair economic exchange are quite different from the customary rates of pay described by historians as typical of the early industrial period (Hobsbawm 1964). This is not to say that within a customary framework, the subaltern party would necessarily consent to what would appear to modern eyes to be an unequal exchange—feudal peasants, for example, certainly expressed discontent, and not infrequently rebelled. But resistance tended to be justified in terms of the violation of other conventions and customs. For example, in late medieval and early modern England there was a counterhegemonic discourse, deployed against both feudalism and nascent capitalism, that asserted the customary rights of "free-born Englishmen."[3] Similarly, in England, enclosure was resisted on the basis of customs established "since time immemorial" and "beyond memory of any man," which gave commoners right of access to resources such as grazing lands (E. P. Thompson 1993; Wood 1997).[4]

By the later nineteenth century, the very general principle of objective fairness had become central to the understanding, both on the left and on the right, of what it is that makes an economic exchange morally acceptable.[5] Clearly however, convergence on the ideal that work should receive objectively fair compensation did not mean that there was consensus on a particular definition of fair wages. On the contrary, the inherent vagueness of the notion of a fair wage resulted in a proliferation of different interpretations of the idea. The difficulty and vagueness of the idea of fair exchange of labor for a wage was a consequence of the problem of commensuration.

If fairness is an objective fact about an exchange, determined by the ratio obtaining between the exchanged substances, then those substances must be commensurable. That is, there must be some nonarbitrary procedure for translating the quantity of goods or services flowing in one direction into the quantity of goods and services flowing in the other. If the substances being exchanged are not commensurable, then clearly it would not be possible to "objectively" judge whether that exchange is a fair one. In order for fair exchange to be possible there must, therefore, be some metric by virtue of which the exchanged substances can be seen as standing in some definite quantitative relationship to one another. Moreover, if an exchange is to be objectively fair, rather than just fair according to convention, the metric must measure some essential quality the exchanged substances have in common.[6] The notion of an objectively fair exchange, as opposed to an exchange that is fair according to convention, thus involves the presupposition that the substances being exchanged share qualities such that they are commensurable.[7]

Despite the increasing acceptance of wage-labor exchange, however, it was (and indeed remains) quite unclear on what basis the life activity given up as labor could ever be clearly commensurable with the wage. For the wage is a quantitative abstraction, while the activity of labor is qualitative. If labor activity and the wage are different in kind, therefore not obviously commensurable, on what principled grounds can they stand in a particular ratio to one another? You simply can't have a meaningful ratio between magnitudes of different kinds.[8] To be sure, the ratio of labor time to, for example, the amount of money needed to buy a car can be *described*—such that one car might equal two thousand hours of work. But describing the ratio at which things happen to exchange, at a given point in time and space, is not the same thing as establishing an objective principle of exchange, according to which a particular ratio is the correct—that is, fair—one. For an exchange to be objectively fair, some shared characteristic has to be attributed to the exchanged substances—something like utility, socially averaged labor time, or some other measure of value.

Moreover, for wage labor to be a fair exchange of commensurable substances, labor must be an alienable commodity—separable from the subject. But it is not obvious how that could be so. Indeed, a great deal of skepticism has been expressed about the proposition that labor is alienable, both in the early period of capitalism, and by thinkers such as Karl Polanyi, who argued that labor (along with money and land) can only ever be a "fictitious commodity" (Polanyi 1957). Although within capitalism, labor is de facto sold for a wage, it cannot easily be thought of as alienable, because labor is, as Marx put it, just life activity and is in that sense at one with the person. The nineteenth-century labor leader George McNeil put the point pithily: "He who sells his labor sells himself" (Stanley 1998, p. 88).

But if labor is neither obviously alienable nor self-evidently commensurable with the wage, what could a "fair wage" possibly mean? Of course, one concept of fairness in wage-labor exchange is that similar work should be similarly compensated.[9] But that norm does not make labor per se commensurable with the wage. It gives criteria for making judgements about who is being unfairly compensated *within* a reference group but does not establish whether the wages of a given group are fair relative to the work done for them. The question of whether a given wage is fair compensation for the work exchanged for it under capitalism has thus remained (and perhaps must ever remain) unresolved, an ongoing subject of debate. Finding a way to think about and represent wage labor in terms that make it into a potentially fair economic exchange became, then, a project imbued with a great deal of normative force, for workers, for the state, and for business.

The tension between the urge to find grounds on which wage labor could be fair and the seemingly insoluble problem of the incommensurability between labor and the wage points to a possible explanation for the historical pattern described over the last three chapters. The pattern, to reiterate, is the tendency for increases in productivity to be converted into higher real wages rather than more free time and for those wages to be used to accumulate a greater number of commodities than seems reasonable given constraints on their use imposed by limitations of time. That tendency begins to make more sense in the context of an ongoing effort on the part of wage earners *to make the wage commensurable with work* (such that a kind of commensuration, therefore fairness, could at least seem to be achievable). Labor becomes commensurable with the wage to the degree that wage goods come to index (to use a Marxian image) congealed durations of time-in-use—that is, free activities that *hypothetically* could be undertaken by wage earners and so serve to counterbalance the unfree activity represented by work. In accumulating commodities, and, in particular, consumer durables, consumers accumulate envisaged, or virtual, free time. The wage, which, prima facie, is not commensurable with the labor given up for it, comes to represent an exchange of roughly equivalent substances by virtue of being converted into objects that index *potential* free time. In Marxian terms, labor power is given up in exchange for the use power (we could also say "leisure power" or "activity power") indexed by accumulated commodities.

When commodities are construed as hypothetical durations of free activity, a fair trade-off between time and commodities becomes thinkable, because commodities become, in essence, stores of potential free time. To the extent that this approach to wage goods takes hold, we would expect wage workers to be at least indifferent to whether increases in productivity are realized as more free time or higher real wages. Given the tendency of businesses to prefer to turn improved productivity into increased output rather than a lower wage bill, the pattern evident in the US economy from the 1920s onward (and also, to varying degrees, elsewhere under advanced industrial capitalism) thus begins to make more sense.

Of course, as objects are accumulated with no increase in free time, it is increasingly difficult to realize their use value—time does not in reality expand as commodity objects are acquired. But once things come to index hypothetical free activity, the possibility of commensuration between labor and wage becomes plausible, insofar as the wage can be used to accumulate free-time indexing objects. By spending the wage on goods that are framed as reserves of free activity, wage earners come to have some sense of having achieved (or at least of being in the process of achieving) fair compensation for their labor.[10] Moreover, when commodities represent standing reserves of potential utility, to be drawn on in a time frame extending indefinitely into the future, it becomes easier for consumers to ignore the decreasing amount of time they have in the present in which to actually realize the use value of the commodities they own.

Thus, the use of the wage to accumulate potential free time congealed in wage goods provides wage earners with a general sense that labor can, when compensated by sufficient real wage income, be fair. And the sense that it is possible for the exchange between labor and wage, if the ratio is right, to be objectively fair, then attenuates the categorical understanding of wage earners as subjects of exploitation. The exploitation associated with wage labor changes from being an essential feature of the institution, to one contingent on the amount of purchasing power received in the form of the wage.

To be sure, certain background conditions are required for this state of affairs to take hold. The most important of these is that wage labor should not be so onerous as to strike people as abject exploitation. If work hours are endlessly increasing, or if conditions of work are dangerous, then the ability to accumulate time-indexing objects would be unlikely to seem like adequate compensation. But in the context of working conditions that are not abject, the urge to commensurate labor with its wage produces an open-ended form of consumption, as wage earners are moved to accumulate commodities that signify free time as compensation for their ongoing loss of time and freedom through labor. This accumulative mode of consumption, as noted earlier, played a crucial role in maintaining what became a quite robust dynamic equilibrium under industrial capitalism for much of the twentieth century. Increasing productivity (and aggregate output) led to rising real income, which increased aggregate effective demand (thus absorbing output), which encouraged further investment in fixed capital, which in turn then led to further increases in productivity (and output). This dynamic characterized capitalism in the relatively stable form it took during its Golden Age or Fordist incarnation (Aglietta 2000; Boyer 1990; Piore and Sabel 1986; Mandel 1999).

The materialist disposition of wage earners—expressed in their assent to an arrangement in which increased productivity was realized as more real income rather than less work—thus made possible the stability of the system of mass production. We need not, however, follow the neo-Marxist Keynesian theorists of the regulation school—or classical Marxists, such as Ernest Mandel—in positing systemic mechanisms to explain how Fordist workers became mass consumers (Aglietta 2000; Mandel 1999).[11] Nor, for that matter, need we follow the more cultural and psychoanalytic path taken by some theorists of the Frankfurt School, who saw mass consumer demand as being a result of desublimation caused by the capitalist culture industry (Marcuse 1964). Rather, the propensity to turn increased productivity into more commodities, as opposed to less work time, can be viewed as a response on the part of wage earners to the perturbing question of what underpins the legitimacy of wage labor—more specifically, to the question of what could possibly make wage-labor exchange objectively fair. Once wage earners accept that the wage *in theory* represents an exchange of commensurable substances, despite there being no conclusive, or even obvious, grounds on which to establish that a given wage is commensurate with the labor exchanged for it, there will be some impetus to convert wage rate increases (and higher productivity) into stuff—commodities—that can more readily be construed as equivalent to life activity sold as labor.

The behavior of wage earners in the sphere of consumption can, therefore, be made sense of in terms of an effort to resolve tensions underlying wage labor. These tensions were a result of the emergence of a loose consensus that working for a wage must at least potentially constitute a fair economic exchange, in the absence of any obvious objective definition of fairness—that is, one based on self-evident facts. The difficulty in arriving at a clear definition of fairness was in large part a result of the problem of the inalienability of labor and the incommensurability between labor and its wage. But wage-labor exchange, according to my argument, became plausibly fair in the context of an understanding of wage goods as reservoirs of potential free activity, and through a corresponding, accumulative mode of consumer behavior. If what wage earners get from a higher wage is a store of commodities that are at least notionally convertible into free time at some imaginable future point—in other words, something like a store of free activity—then an increase in real wages becomes qualitatively interchangeable with an increase in free time. For workers, spending the wage in order to accumulate stores of use value in effect retroactively rationalizes wage-labor exchange.

Once wage goods become understood as abstract stores of potential activity, to be turned into free activity at some indeterminate future point, and once free activity is thought about in terms strongly mediated by the use power of owned commodity objects, the decision about whether to push for more free time, rather than higher real wages, loses much of its urgency. There is no longer the kind of trade-off envisaged by some economists, whereby as income increases, so does the relative value of leisure. That trade-off would result in a backward-bending supply curve for labor, which, as we saw in the last chapter, fails to describe the empirical pattern of work time, labor productivity, and wages over the course of the twentieth century.

To be clear, the argument here does not involve a functionalist claim that in order to secure quiescent workers and sufficient aggregate demand, the capitalist system somehow induced in wage earners a tendency to think about usefulness primarily in terms of the properties of things (as opposed to thinking of it in terms of the conditions under which activities are possible). Rather, it posits a response on the part of wage earners, to make wage labor into a fair exchange by construing commodities as repositories of free activity. Given a state of affairs in which there is no alternative to wage labor, wage earners accommodate themselves to their situation by thinking about wage-labor exchange in terms that make it at least *potentially* fair. As noted, viewing commodities as indexical of free time *rationalizes* the institution of wage labor. It makes what used to be regarded as an illegitimate exchange of incommensurable substances (parts of a life for a wage) into an exchange of commensurable substances and, therefore, conceivably legitimate. The argument rests on the normative power of notions of fairness, under conditions in which there is no longer an easily imaginable practical alternative to wage labor. The concern with how to square the circle of a fair exchange of labor for a wage was, it is important to mention, present across the public sphere, and also in government bodies and business. There was a quite general tendency, once capitalism was established, to construe wage-labor exchange in terms that make it a potentially fair arrangement.

In sum, this effort to make work commensurable with its wage thus suggests a novel explanation for the demand side of capitalism's characteristic expansionary dynamic. In the introduction I posed the question: Why has aggregate demand under capitalism tended to facilitate the drive toward capital valorization in the sphere of production? If capitalism is driven to expand, how is it that aggregate demand has, on the whole, enabled that expansion? Of course, it is not always the case that there is enough short-term effective aggregate demand to forestall crisis, as was shown most dramatically in the 1930s. But why haven't economic crises occurred more often than has been the case? Why are catastrophes like the Depression periodic rather than perennial features of capitalism in the era of mass industrial production? More precisely, why, under industrial capitalism, do markets tend to clear at rates that ensure that the economy remains stable enough to allow for the reproduction of capitalism? After all, production precedes consumption, and capitalists, when making decisions about investment and output, are therefore always taking something of a leap of faith into an uncertain future.

Famously, Keynes (1936, pp. 161–62) thought that capitalist investment is impelled by irrational "animal spirits," by which he meant a "spontaneous optimism," and an irrational "urge to action rather than inaction."[12] The crucial role Keynes attributed to animal spirits followed from his belief that consumption is governed by habits that are slow to change. As he put it; "a man's habitual standard of life usually has first claim on his income, and he is apt to save the difference which discovers itself between his actual income and the expense of his habitual standard" (p. 97). The natural sluggishness of consumer demand, according to Keynes, makes the important variable in determining macroeconomic stability the degree to which capitalists feel inspired by irrational spirits to invest the difference between national income and national consumption. But clearly investment decisions in industrial capitalism are also made on a rational, inductive basis. For capitalists have good empirical grounds for believing that consumers will tend to be responsive to increases in output simply because since the inception of capitalist mass production, aggregate demand has tended to keep pace with increasing output.[13]

The willingness of capitalists to invest in industrial facilities and equipment has, then, depended not just on blind optimism, but also on what has been a quite consistent tendency for consumption to expand to absorb production. The inductive grounds on which investments are made are surely, on balance, more important to the ongoing stability of capitalism than the eruptions of exuberance Keynes had in mind. Yet it is unclear why, once affluent conditions prevail, aggregate demand should be, on the whole, strong enough to encourage investment (thereby facilitating the expansionary impulses of the system of production). Why, in Keynesian terms, should the propensity to consume be such as to facilitate the conversion of increases in productivity into increases in aggregate output? After all, Keynes himself, in his 1930 essay, argued that it is common sense that at some level of productivity, material demand would be sated, and the economy would come to rest in a stationary state. In fact, the actual historical dynamism of consumer demand, its responsiveness to increasing output under capitalism, goes against Keynes's assumptions about the habitual constraints and rational limits on consumption. It was only because under capitalism "man's habitual standard of life" had become curiously dynamic and open-ended that capitalists came to feel confident about risking their capital in productive investments. Keynes's theory thus leaves out a crucial, demand-side element in the workings of industrial capitalism.

The theory of mass consumption as wage labor commensuration argued for in this book fills that lacuna. According to the theory, the tendency of aggregate demand to keep pace with increasing output is a consequence of the moral economy underpinning the legitimacy of wage labor itself. The propensity to consume that facilitated the expansion of output under industrial capitalism reflected an urge to make the wage into something commensurable with labor. However, there is an ambiguity underlying the effort to make work commensurable with the wage through the hypothetical free time indexed by wage goods. Although free time objectified in wage goods seems qualitatively equivalent to life activity spent working, the equivalence between the two clearly does not yield a precise equation, such that n commodities = x hours of indexed free activity = x hours of work. While accumulating commodity goods might present itself as the best, or at least the most natural, way to make the wage commensurate with work, the effort to achieve commensuration is not guided by a clear and definite point at which the two are self-evidently equivalent, and a given amount of work has consequently been adequately compensated. This is because those goods can only even approximately work as commensurate compensation when they are put to use in activities, yet it is very often unclear to what degree that will be possible.

As has been noted, there are powerful constraints—such as limitations on time, energy and access to public goods—on the extent to which wage workers can actually convert accumulated commodities into free activities. These constraints, and the tensions they produce, occasionally lead to disenchantment with wage funded consumer accumulation, expressed in antimaterialistic social movements and ideologies. An alternative, and more common, response, however, is simply to move on to different products, in the belief that the problem is not constraints on free time but rather that the set of commodities the consumer happens to own at a particular time is not quite right and so needs to be changed. One effect of the difficulty of establishing just when commensuration between labor and its wage has been achieved is therefore to make consumers receptive to the flow of new products coming onto the consumer marketplace.

Moreover, because life activity and dead things are qualitatively distinct, the problem of making them commensurable remains ultimately intractable. Wage earners try to fill an ongoing deficit of freedom incurred by work by accumulating commodities that are, in themselves, just things, and so cannot possibly work as commensurate compensation. The norm by virtue of which work and wage goods are rendered commensurable is therefore inherently vague, entailing a kind of pseudocommensurability, based on only a rough sense of goods as denoting *possible* activity power.[14] The vagueness of wage-labor commensuration has three dimensions: (1) the indeterminate quantity of wage goods required to commensurate a given amount of labor; (2) the uncertainty about whether goods will actually eventually be turned into free activity, such that the commensuration is consummated; and (3) the underlying incommensurability of things and life activity. This vagueness makes the project of accumulating wage goods, in order to achieve commensuration between labor and its wage, indefinite and interminable. Thus, the pursuit of commensuration gives consumption under capitalism the same irrational, open-ended, dynamic character as the capitalist system of production.

If the commensuration theory of consumption is correct, then modern industrial capitalism, especially during its Golden Age, between the Second World War and the 1970s, was made possible by a combination of mass industrial production, organized around various forms of Fordist enterprise, the emergence of a moral economy that secured widespread acceptance of the legitimacy of the wage form on the basis of the commensurability of work and consumer commodities, and the development of a consumer economy that presented wage goods in a way that made them seem plausibly commensurable with work.[15] Had mass production developed in the absence of the latter two developments, the demand-side problems generated by mass production, identified by analysts such as Michael Piore and Charles Sabel

(1986), would have ensued. The high and stable levels of aggregate effective demand required in order for industries based on very large fixed-capital investments (the kind of enterprise characteristic of mass production) to be profitable would not have been forthcoming. The positive feedback loop between increasing returns to scale in production and increasing aggregate demand would consequently have ground to a halt.

Moreover, as noted in Chapter 2, the tendency for the working population to be at least indifferent to whether increasing productivity is turned into more free time or more wage goods formed an important background condition for the success of Keynesian macroeconomic techniques in stabilizing the economy. Where labor comes to be regarded as commensurable with the wage by virtue of the notional activity power of wage goods, increases in income will tend to be used to increase consumption rather than being used to reduce work hours. This tendency for people to spend added increments of income means that demand-side macroeconomic policies, devised to ensure that aggregate effective demand is sufficient to absorb output, are more likely to be effective. For example, fiscal policies aimed at stimulating the economy by putting more dollars in people's pockets, such as tax credits for wage earners, presuppose that those dollars will add to aggregate demand rather than being used to reduce the amount of time spent working. If increases in income were used to reduce the length of the working week at constant real income, then the whole project of macroeconomic demand management would become much less feasible. The same is true of efforts on the part of government to increase aggregate demand by way of prolabor industrial relations policies. The strategy followed, for instance, in the United States during the New Deal, to shore up demand by bolstering union power (the idea behind the Wagner Act of 1935), operated under the assumption that unions would use that power to increase their members' real wages, which would subsequently be spent, thus stimulating the economy. If union power, backed by government-sponsored collective bargaining rights, had been used to force reductions in work time at constant levels of real income, rather than to increase real income (and therefore boost aggregate demand), then that strategy would have failed.

At the same time, without the availability of mass produced, and importantly, *standardized* consumer commodities, endowed with stable properties and framed in such a way as to signify reserves of potential free activity, the exchange of labor for a wage would not have been so readily construable as a legitimate practice. For the standardized product notionally entailed a predictable duration of product use, which made it easier to envisage the accumulation of (standardized) commodities as representing an increasing store of potential free time. The creation of a certain kind of commodity—the standardized mass-produced consumer durable—understood as a material repository of free activity *in potentia*, thus made possible a form and magnitude of demand capable of supporting the system of production required for its manufacture. The moral economy that underpinned Fordism thus had both demand and supply sides—a demand for commensuration between labor and its wage, as a condition on its legitimacy, and a supply of wage goods framed in such a way as to make this commensuration seem possible.

The theory set out here is, in the first instance, an abduction—an attempt to account for a puzzling pattern by postulating a state of affairs from which that pattern would follow as a matter of course (Peirce 1903 [1997]; Frankfurt 1958). In the chapters that follow, I draw attention to some historical features of wage labor and consumer capitalism that provide some support for the theory. The empirical analysis concentrates on the United States between roughly 1900 and 1980, with particular focus on the period between 1920 and 1970. I take the US case to be an exemplar of high industrial consumer capitalism and would suggest that similar features can be found in other consumer societies, albeit in forms mediated by local conditions, particular histories, and cultural context. In the remainder of the present chapter I first note some explanative advantages, at a variety of different levels of analysis, offered by approaching consumption as a form of wage-labor commensuration. The commensuration theory of mass consumption sheds light on otherwise puzzling aspects of the economic behavior under capitalism, and on a variety of large-scale cultural, institutional, and economic developments. Second, I consider some of the more obvious objections that could be lodged against the theory and offer some responses to the objections.

1. Some Explanative Advantages of the Commensuration Theory

In this section I consider some ways in which the commensuration theory of work and consumption explains general patterns of economic behavior in modern industrial capitalist societies. This is not to claim that the theory is the only or best explanation for these patterns. However, the degree to which the theory can make sense of various features of capitalism provides some initial grounds for thinking that there might be something to it.

1.1. Explains the Rough Coincidence of the Rise of Consumer Society and the Acceptance of Wage Labor

On the most general, macrohistorical level, the theory suggests an explanation for the rough coincidence between, on the one hand, a set of large-scale changes that marked the rise of consumer society and, on the other, growing acceptance of wage labor as a fundamentally legitimate institution, by virtue of its potential to be objectively fair. The set of changes includes the increasing force of the income effect and the ebbing of the substitution effect (as increases in hourly wages were used to increase household consumption rather than decrease work time), the ascent of the modern brand, the development of new forms of credit, the consumer durables revolution, the rise to prominence, in culture and politics, of the figure of the consumer, and the growing importance in politics of the concept of purchasing power. This set of developments unfolded, in the United States, roughly between the beginning of the last quarter of the nineteenth century and the middle years of the twentieth century, and coincided with the ascent of wage labor as a legitimate form of exchange (Strasser 2004; Glickman 1997, 2009; L. Cohen 2003; Olney 1991). It seems unlikely that changes in consumption and changes in wage labor were unrelated, and yet the nature of the connection is unclear.

The obvious account of how they might be connected is that as living standards improved, allowing for the development of the mass consumer economy, the trade of labor for a wage simply became more tolerable. However, a condition can be tolerable without being thought of as being legitimate. Think, for example, of a very well-treated slave. So, improvements in living standards alone do not explain why wage labor increasingly came to be regarded as legitimate, potentially fair, and even in the nature of things. Furthermore, living standards understood in broad terms, as overall well-being, rather than narrowly, as per capita income, can improve along different dimensions. Increasing real income can improve well-being, but so, too, can decreasing subjection to work at constant levels of real income, especially under conditions of affluence, with widespread access to basic goods. The consumer economy was, as we have seen, characterized by a push for higher income, rather than working fewer hours at the same income. Potential increases in free time were sacrificed in order to secure increasing real income. This pattern suggests a materialistic bias in the uses to which improvements in labor productivity were put, one not easy to explain in utility maximizing terms.

The rough coincidence in timing between the rise of consumer society and the growing legitimacy of wage labor, however, would follow as a matter of course if mass consumption was driven by wage-labor commensuration. Wage labor gained legitimacy as consumer products increasingly came to represent decontextualized repositories of utility, indexing hypothetical free activities. At the same time, the emergence of standardized consumer goods (and indeed many of the other practices and institutions associated with the consumer society) at least in part reflected demand for a kind of product that could make the exchange between their labor and its wage commensurable and, indeed, potentially fair. Mass consumption and the growing legitimacy of wage labor were, then, mutually reinforcing developments. The various cultural and institutional forms associated with consumer society developed in reaction to the contradictions underlying wage labor exchange and, at the same time, provided a means by which those contradictions could be, if not resolved, then at least indefinitely deferred.[16]

1.2. Provides an Explanation for Materialist Consumerism

The theory of consumption as commensuration arguably gives some account of the materialism that seems to be an intrinsic part of industrial capitalism. Materialist consumerism—the felt urgency, compulsion even, to spend earnings on things—makes more sense if the point of spending is to fill a deficit (of free life activity) incurred through waged labor and made up for through commodity accumulation. Since commodities are more commensurable with labor than is money, turning a wage into things makes the exchange of work for a wage more palatable.

By contrast, the theoretical account of the materialism underpinning consumer society given by Colin Campbell, the author of the most important work of historical sociology on the topic, places much emphasis on the role of fantasy and expectation in the pursuit of commodities. Campbell (1987) attributes the modern propensity to fantasize and daydream to the development in the nineteenth century of the imaginative faculties, which were stimulated by the emergence of the novel and associated cultural forms. For Campbell, consumerism was (and is) driven by the desire of consumers to enter into a pleasurable state of imaginative anticipation, in which they become transfixed by fantasies about the practices and identities they associate with commodities they are considering acquiring but have not yet acquired. Once those commodities have been acquired by consumers, however, they become just mundane stuff, subject to prosaic existential constraints, and this produces a rude awakening, bursting the bubble of imaginative anticipation. In response, consumers seek out new objects of desire, in order to enter once more into a dream-like state of anticipation. Thus, demand becomes dynamic and restless, as consumers constantly search out new objects about which to fantasize, and yet are never satisfied once those objects are possessed.

This dialectic of desire and disappointment certainly captures some dimensions of consumerism. Yet Campbell's theory fails to account for why fantasy and hedonic expectation should fix on things as foci for imagined activities rather than the activities themselves—and why the focus should be on activities that require things rather than those that do not. For it is certainly possible to fantasize about pleasurable activities without at the same time thinking about commodities. People can ponder a ramble in nature or a swim or imagine a philosophical conversation, gossip, a flirtation, stargazing, a story, and so on—activities that demand time more than the possession of things. Moreover, even if we take a focus on things as given, Campbell's theory provides no explanation for why consumers actually acquire things, as opposed to simply bringing them to mind as objects of contemplation.[17] If, after the historical development of the imaginative faculties, what people want from commodities is to use them as foci for daydreams, seeking to remain suspended in an anticipatory state, why should they choose, once in such a state, to exit it by actually acquiring products? Why not instead become perennial browsers, connoisseurs of advertisements, experts in the art of pleasurably perusing catalogs and product descriptions? If materialistic acquisition always ends in disappointment, why doesn't that fact sink in, prompting people to stop short of acquisition of products and instead endlessly fantasize about them?

The failure to explain materialism itself is a significant lacuna in Campbell's theory, one that is filled by the commensuration theory. In Campbell's terms, object-mediated fantasies work better at achieving a desired state of anticipation than fantasizing about actual activities, because thinking directly about engaging in some practice is more likely to raise the issue of the time constraints that characterize concrete human lives. Having to confront those constraints is likely to take consumers out of their state of pleasurable contemplation. By contrast, when the fantasy is mediated by an object of consumption, attention tends to be taken up by the properties of the object, making the issue of time constraints less salient. For example, if people fantasize about a particular model of bicycle, they will tend to dwell on the powers with which that bicycle is endowed—in the case of a mountain bike, for example, perhaps its capacity to absorb shock effectively thereby enabling them to cycle in rugged and exciting places. Focusing on the activity-enabling material powers of the product—on the things they *in theory* could do with it—keeps in abeyance the disenchanting question of whether they actually have time to use the bike.

1.3. Accounts for the Different Uses of Wage Income versus Investment Income

The theory of consumption as wage-labor commensuration entails that the identity of money—primarily whether it counts as wages or something else (e.g., interest payments)—has implications for how money gets used. This basic idea accords with work in economic sociology on the nature of money as a social institution. Economic sociologists and anthropologists have observed that money is not entirely fungible but rather has a social biography that determines its action in the world. The very general idea that the way in which money is acquired affects attitudes toward it, and consequently influences how it gets used, has a good deal of empirical support in the tradition of research stemming from Viviana Zelizer's (1989, 1995) work on "special monies." Money, according to Zelizer, is not a neutral medium or empty abstraction but, rather, has an identity or aura, bestowed on it as a consequence of its provenance. For example, windfalls are regarded differently from wage earnings, while money gifts fall into still another category. The particular identity of money determines its use, and that identity is primarily a matter of the manner in which money is obtained. Where money comes from—how it is acquired—then influences whether and how it gets spent. For example, windfalls of cash, or money gifts, will tend to be spent in a more frivolous way than hard-earned wages (Zelizer 1994).

If Zelizer is right, and the provenance of money indeed determines its meaning, and consequently the uses to which it is put, then wage earnings will be treated differently from other kinds of earnings—those derived from investment, as a result of an inheritance, gambling winnings, and so on. Consonant with Zelizer's argument, the theory of consumption as wage labor commensuration posits that money received as wages is marked by its identity as compensation for labor, and that this identity influences what gets done with that money.

According to the commensuration theory, because a wage is money earned in exchange for work, the identity of money in wage form is ultimately tied to the labor given in exchange for it. When kept in the simple money form, as savings, the wage is just a number—not yet equivalent to the work given for it. In order to be reasonably construed as compensation, the wage must be converted into commodities—things endowed with use value (by virtue of their use powers), which facilitate various kinds of imagined or actual activity.

Because of the imperative to establish equivalence between work and its wage, so that the two can conceivably exchange at fair rates, money earned in exchange for labor time will be more likely to be spent on commodities and less likely to be saved or otherwise invested, than money acquired by other means. Conversely, the commensuration hypothesis entails that investment income will be more likely to be *saved* (reinvested) than wage income. This is because the return to ownership of capital is not an exchange for the labor of the capitalist but rather a kind of rent or, alternatively, as Austrian school economists would have it, compensation for delayed consumption. Either way, money as returns to capital is at least one step removed from labor, and so the issue of commensuration does not come into the picture. Income derived from ownership of capital would, therefore, according to the theory, be less likely to be turned into consumption of goods and services and more likely to be reinvested. There is at least some empirical evidence that points in this direction. As we saw in Chapter 3, in the United States, the marginal propensity to spend increasing increments of wage income was, over the course of the twentieth century, close to unity—in other words, as people's wages went up, almost all of the increase was used to fund consumption. And an empirical study by Lawrence Summers and Christopher Carroll (1987) indicates that the marginal propensity to *save* capital gains from stock market investments has, likewise, been close to unity.

Interpreting this in Marxian terms, wage-labor commensuration suggests an explanation for why, at levels of wage income above subsistence, the circuit of capital for labor is C-M-C, whereas for capital it is M-C-M′ (Marx ([1867] 1981).[18] Where wages are pegged to bare physical subsistence, C-M-C is not optional for labor, because there is simply no room for saving / investment. But once workers receive higher than subsistence levels of wages, some part of the wage could, in theory at least, be invested. This point holds even if definitions of subsistence are historically variable, because what is at issue is what gets done with the increases in income that follow improvements in productivity—whether they are spent or saved. Although Marx says that with the development of the forces of production, human beings come to discover new needs, there is no reason to expect the definition of material subsistence to automatically change as productivity and real income per hour changes. A newly discovered need, after all, could be a need for more free time. Indeed, the fact that material expectations do tend to get ratcheted ever upward is quite puzzling.[19] After all, freeing up more time allows for at least as much in the way of the discovering new needs as does increasing material output and consumption. As noted in the previous chapter, with more time, people can experiment with new practices and activities, develop new skills (or become more expert at old ones), make new friends, deepen older friendships, and so on. Following an increase in labor productivity, turned into higher hourly wages, wage earners could stick at established levels of consumption and reduce their work hours or save more. Yet, as we have seen, during the twentieth century, across the industrial capitalist world, at least up until the 1980s, real income increased with productivity, and spending levels tended to rise in line with increasing income.

The tendency for wages to be spent on wage goods at levels of income above subsistence makes sense, however, if labor (C) is exchanged for a wage (M), which wage earners then seek to turn into a form capable of justifying the initial outlay of time and effort represented by work and so, with this end in mind, transform the wage into consumer commodities (C). If we suspend for a moment Marx's abstract holism, and take capital to be the set of individual capitalists and labor to be the set of individual workers and assume, furthermore, that under fully developed industrial capitalism the two groups at least to some degree live within a common normative framework, then the difference between the two in the propensity to spend (as opposed to saving / investing) reflects the difference in the identity of the revenues flowing to each. Wage earners exchange labor (C) for a wage (M), which, in order to make it roughly equivalent to the time and effort given as work, they convert into activity-indexing consumer commodities (C). Capitalists, on the other hand, feel no equivalent compulsion to convert the returns to their capital into commodities meant for final consumption and so are more likely to reinvest that income.

Of course, interpreting the different uses of wage income and investment income as support for the commensuration theory of consumption involves a lot of suppositions. A particular problem is that investment income tends to be added at higher increments of the total income that an individual receives. The difference in how income from investment and wage income is spent might, therefore, simply reflect the marginal decline in the utility of spending as income increases.[20] That would be in line with what Keynes (1936) and other economists assume about the general propensity to consume. Still, Zelizer's research on how the uses of money are constrained by its social identity is broadly consistent with the idea that money earned in exchange for labor time will tend to be used to buy goods and services that index free activity, while money earned through investments is more likely to be reinvested.

One piece of suggestive evidence, already touched on in Chapter 3, is the surprisingly low rate of consumption of retirees in the United States. Retirees receive most of their income from either investments or social security payments and yet do not have high overall levels of income, at least compared to middle-aged wage earners (Deaton 1992). According to economic theory, retirees should be spending down their savings, while the middle-aged, who are in the phase of life when earnings are highest, should be saving. Because income is typically higher in middle than in old age, saving when middle aged is relatively less painful—so we might expect people in that stage of life to save more than when they are old. In fact, the data show that older people are more likely to save if they possibly can, while high-earning middle-aged people tend to spend all their income (Deaton 1992). The argument could be made that older people are reticent to spend their savings because they want to leave money for their children. But then we would expect higher-earning middle-aged persons to, likewise, be saving for their progeny, for a significant proportion of them face the prospect of their children needing substantial funds for things like college and down payments for cars, homes, and so on.

Perhaps this odd pattern of saving and spending across the life course is best explained by the difference between the sources of income for workers and retirees. Part of the reason why retirees spend less than middle aged people (who should, according to the theory, be saving) might be that their incomes are not construed as wage earnings. In the absence of a compulsion to spend in order to make money wages commensurate with the work given in exchange for them, maybe the urge to spend simply recedes. On this understanding, for retirees saving is not a positively directed, intentional activity but rather just the default consequence of their distance from wage labor exchange (more on this below, in section 1.7).

1.4. Explains Why the Market for Rented Goods Is Relatively Small

The commensuration theory also works well to explain why renting commodities, as opposed to buying them, is much less common than might be expected. There are good reasons to think that, under conditions in which output and real wages are increasing, but free time is not, it makes sense for consumers to rent products rather than buy them. Renting durables enables a more efficient use of resources, while also allowing consumers to change their product sets without incurring the transaction costs and loss of value through depreciation involved in selling old ones. Indeed, in recent years, a body of thought has emerged that imagines a more rational and environmentally responsible version of capitalism, partly on the basis of moving away from ownership and toward renting. This argument features prominently, for example, in *Natural Capitalism*, an influential book that sets out a manifesto for a progressive and sustainable form of capitalism (Hawken, Josin, and Josin 1999). A society-wide shift from owning objects to renting them would greatly reduce the direct cost of satisfying a given amount of demand, because output of useful products could be more closely linked to actual patterns of use. "Just-in-time" production could be precisely adjusted to meet the demand for "just-in-time" consumption, significantly reducing waste and inefficiency. Universal renting of durables would also reduce the negative externalities produced by meeting that demand. If, for example, cars were rented rather than individually owned, then far fewer cars would be required to satisfy the social demand for transportation. This decline in demand would then lead to fewer cars being produced, and that would result in less pollution.[21] In addition, mass renting of durables would help with the logistics of waste management, as rental companies are better able to efficiently recycle or dispose of obsolescent goods than are consumers.

Apart from the benefits of efficient satisfaction of social demand and waste reduction for society, renting products also offers clear advantages to individual consumers. By anchoring cost to actual use, renting circumvents the additional costs incurred by ownership. In renting an asset, consumers pay for the service they need from a given object and no more. This facilitates a lean and efficient style of consumption, in which what gets purchased is an actual duration of use, rather than a store of potential utility, some portion of which will probably never get realized. Renting goods also saves consumers time and money in repairs and maintenance; saves space, since it prevents the accumulation of unnecessary clutter; and reduces the amount of money the consumer has sunk in assets, thereby increasing their financial flexibility. Consumers who rent products, as opposed to purchasing them, also have the flexibility to satisfy a greater variety of tastes and quickly adjust to changes in their needs or desires. Moreover, since, under capitalism, the rate of obsolescence has steadily increased over time, renting products provides an easier and more affordable way to continually upgrade to the latest product model. Being able to easily change products, by renting new ones, offers particular advantages for the consumer of status goods and those used to construct identity. This is because renting status goods allows for a flexible approach to consumption, enabling consumers to rapidly change product sets in response to changes in fashion, and facilitating chameleon-like product code-switching between different sociocultural contexts. For example, the renting consumer could bring a Bentley to the Ritz for tea, a Hummer to a rap concert, a VW bus to a weekend Woodstock nostalgia event, and so on.[22] In addition, whether a product being used by a consumer to display status is actually owned or just rented is not a public fact. By strategically renting high-status items for public events, the benefits of displaying them can be obtained without having to purchase them.

There are then good reasons to expect that the rental market should be larger than the market for owning consumer goods outright, yet most consumer goods are purchased to be owned rather than rented. Why then is the market for rented consumer durables not more developed than is the case under capitalism?[23] Consider, for example, the preference for homeownership in the United States, a long-standing feature of the US economy. In the last chapter, I noted that the popularity of homeownership in the United States does not make much sense from a strictly economic point of view. High geographical mobility, a result of a far-flung and very dynamic national job market, would seem to favor renting over homeownership.[24] Despite this, the demand for homeownership is, and has been for many decades, very strong.

It is not clear that an explanation for the relatively undeveloped market for rented durables can be found on the business side. In theory at least, there is no reason why a company renting out consumer durables should not be profitable.[25] Indeed the advantages of the renting model are made clear by the degree to which firms choose to lease capital equipment such as cars, photocopiers, and computers, as opposed to purchasing them. If the rental market for consumer goods is less well developed than might be expected, this seems to be a result of insufficient demand rather than inherent problems with the underlying business model.

If, however, consumption is to a significant degree driven by wage labor commensuration, then the bias in favor of owning becomes less puzzling. The preference for ownership over renting makes sense if the point of earning more money is precisely to enable the accumulation of a store of use value, one that can realize enough free activity to make up for the time lost to work. Indeed, the goods accumulated by wage earners can index an amount of potential use time *greater* than the actual leisure time available to them. The ongoing accumulation of commodities, insofar as they represent a reservoir of potential free activity to be undertaken in the indeterminate future, makes wage-labor seem at least potentially fair, and therefore more palatable. The use value of rented items, by contrast, cannot function so easily as commensurate compensation for work, because their use is limited to the period of time for which they are rented. This means that their use value is much more obviously constrained by the amount of real time available in which to use them. The explicit temporal anchoring of rented items thus means that their usefulness must be thought about in realistic rather than in hypothetical terms and cannot be construed as extending indefinitely into the future. Of course, consumers could choose to rent durables indefinitely and so have access to them as a store of use power. But doing so would draw attention to the difference between the amount of time the items are being rented for (twenty-four hours, seven days a week) and the amount of time available to make use of them (considerably less than that). Moreover, renting goods in an ongoing manner, as reserves of use power, to be kept on hand, like a retainer, to provide services as and when needed, incurs a very visible ongoing cost—as time passes, the cost of renting goods inexorably rises. Purchasing a good to own, by contrast, involves a one-time outlay (or, in the case of buying on credit, a commitment to make a finite number of payments), after which all of the potential use power of the object can be held in reserve without further payments. This makes it easier to defer the question of whether the object is likely to see enough use to justify its expense. Although an object might not be being made use of in the present, the possibility always remains that it will eventually, at *some* point in the future, get sufficient use to justify the labor given in exchange for it—and, once the item has been purchased, the costs entailed by waiting for that point to arrive are not very visible.

Part of the appeal of owning a consumer durable is, then, the prospect of possessing a notional quantity of use value *surplus* to likely actual use, therefore indexing a surplus of free time. Indeed, the activity time indexed by a set of goods can potentially exceed the absolute amount of time remaining in a person's life, thereby perhaps suggesting that finitude has been transcended. In owning objects, possibilities seem to stretch beyond those realizable under average conditions of real use, and this makes the work-time-consumption regime typical of high industrial capitalism at least acceptable and perhaps even quite appealing.

1.5. Explains the Correlation among Saving, Spending, and Labor Decommodification across Different Capitalist Societies

Moving to a very different, much more macrohistorical and comparative, level of analysis, interpreting mass consumption as wage-labor commensuration suggests an explanation for the correlation between the degree to which labor has been *decommodified* (measured by the extent of development of the welfare state) and savings rates across the modern industrial capitalist world. It seems intuitive that capitalist nations with less developed welfare states should, in lieu of dependable social insurance, have higher savings rates than those with more developed welfare states. The larger the gaps are in a social safety net, the more reason individuals have to save money, in case they should fall on hard times. In fact, however, the countries with the weakest welfare states have the lowest saving rates. This is a surprising finding—yet one that is consistent with the commensuration theory.

In his important book, *Three Worlds of Welfare Capitalism*, Gosta Esping-Andersen (1990) categorizes capitalist societies according to the extent of decommodification of labor produced by state policies.[26] Esping-Andersen defines decommodification as the mitigation of pressure on people to sell their labor in the market. In providing alternative means of subsistence, welfare states lessen their population's dependence on the labor market, in effect, making capitalism less coercive for labor. The more dependent people are on the labor market in a given society—that is, the fewer alternatives they have for getting a living apart from selling their labor—the less decommodified labor is in that society.

Esping-Andersen uses a variety of measures to create a composite score indicating the extent to which different nations have effectively decommodified labor. He finds that countries can be grouped into three categories, characterized by particular histories of policy orientation. The three categories, in ascending order of level of decommodification, are liberal welfare states, corporatist welfare states, and social democratic welfare states. The liberal welfare states are the Anglo-Saxon nations, the corporatist states are those of continental Europe (excluding Scandinavia and including Japan), and the social democratic set comprises Scandinavia (excluding Finland), Austria, Belgium, and the Netherlands.[27]

From a standard economic viewpoint, stronger welfare states—those that to a greater extent decommodify labor—should have lower saving rates and therefore higher rates of spending. This is because the presence of a strong safety net lessens the need to save defensively. Although the correlation between saving / spending and the extent of welfare provision is not an issue that Esping-Andersen investigates, data from other sources indicate that saving rates have in fact been lowest in the liberal states—those that are the least decommodified according to Esping-Andersen. In the Euro area since 1991, for example, household saving rates have been between two and a half and three times higher than in the United States, a member of Esping-Andersen's least decommodified group, while saving in Japan (categorized as part of the corporatist group) has been between four and six times higher. Net household saving rates between 1985 and 2009 in the countries that make up Esping-Andersen's liberal group, which is the least decommodified, are consistently among the lowest in the OECD (Garon 2012). Comparing the subset of nations that are members of the OECD from each of Esping-Andersen's groups, average saving rates between 1985 and 2009 are 11.6 percent for the corporatist group, 9.6 percent for the social democratic group, and 5.6 percent for the liberal group (see Appendix 2 for table of OECD figures).[28] While the corporatist and social democratic welfare states have quite similar levels of saving, the saving rates of the liberal welfare states—those with the least in the way of a safety net—are significantly lower.[29]

Once more, this pattern is surprising, as there would seem to be more reason to save in contexts in which people are more dependent on the labor market for their economic survival. Yet it becomes less surprising when interpreted in terms of the theory of consumption as wage-labor commensuration. If the commensuration theory is correct, then the pattern would follow as a matter of course, and the grounds for surprise would be removed. The theory entails that consumer materialism—defined as the propensity to turn increasing hourly wages into increased consumption, rather than reduced work time or increased savings—should be positively correlated with the extent to which labor is commodified (or, in Esping-Andersen's terms, not decommodified). The reasoning for this goes as follows:

I.　The extent to which labor is commodified in modern industrial capitalist societies is, in part, a reflection of the degree to which wage labor is seen as a legitimate form of exchange. The less legitimacy wage labor has, the more pressure there will be on the state to provide economic support independent of labor market participation. This makes subjection of individuals to the labor market more conditional (on being able-bodied and of sound mind, on general macroeconomic conditions, etc.).

II.　According to the commensuration theory, seeing commodities as commensurable with labor contributes to the legitimacy of wage labor as a form of exchange. In order for the wage to become commensurable with the work that is given for it, it needs to be spent on commodities. Kept in money form, the wage is too abstract to facilitate commensuration.

III.　Therefore, the degree to which labor is commodified (or, in Esping-Andersen's terms, not decommodified) should, ceteris paribus, be positively correlated with rates of consumer spending and negatively correlated with saving rates. Higher rates of consumer spending should go along with more commodified labor. Capitalist nations with developed welfare states, which to some degree decommodify labor, should, therefore, have lower rates of spending and higher rates of saving.

So, where the institution of wage labor has greater legitimacy, people will tend to be more commodified (that is, subjection to the labor market will be *less conditional*). At the same time, the means by which that legitimacy is secured—the accumulative consumption of time-indexing goods—results in higher rates of spending and therefore lower savings rates. Conversely, it follows from the commensuration theory that decommodification should be inversely correlated with spending rates (and, by default, positively correlated with household saving rates). And, as we have seen, cross-referencing Esping-Andersen's empirical analysis with comparative data on rates of saving and spending reveals a pattern that provides some support for this prediction.

The connection between the rise of wage labor and the increasing propensity to spend can also be found going further back in history. If the commensuration theory is correct, then, as labor becomes more commodified (assuming this is because wage-labor exchange becomes more legitimate), so spending rates should increase. And indeed, at least according to economic historian Jan De Vries (2008), the historical process of the commodification of labor was accompanied by a greater propensity to consume.[30] However, where the labor process is to a greater extent under the control of workers, while at the same time what is being sold is the product of labor rather than labor power—as was the case in the protoindustrial phase of capitalist development—the economic exchange is somewhat different. Since, under those conditions, workers in theory retain ownership of their time, there is not the same imperative to turn increases in hourly wages into more wage goods (construed as an accumulation of congealed free time), as opposed to increases in actual free time.[31] So in earlier periods of capitalism, before the full commodification of labor power, a more balanced attitude to the trade-off between free time and money was likely to prevail.

1.6. Accounting for Certain Findings of Behavioral Economics

Changing levels of analysis once again, another way in which the theory of consumption as wage-labor commensuration sheds light on modern economic behavior is its capacity to explain some of the more perplexing experimental discoveries of behavioral economics. As mentioned in the second chapter, over the past three decades research in behavioral economics has led to experimental findings that challenge the homo economicus model of the economic agent. The rationality presupposed in that model is not easily compatible with findings like hyperbolic discounting, the endowment effect, and nontransitive preferences, which behavioral economists have suggested are widespread features of economic behavior. Behavioral economists and psychologists have tended to interpret their findings in an ahistorical fashion, as indicating general patterns in human behavior. Daniel Kahneman, one of the founders of behavioral economics, takes the various biases and heuristics discovered in the field to be psychological primitives, natural facts about the human species that, as such, are universal in scope, explicable in terms of the selective advantages they conferred in our evolutionary past. In a synthetic theoretical work, for example, Kahneman (2011) explains the disparate findings of behavioral economics through a theory of the architecture of the human brain.[32] Yet surely it is premature to leap so quickly to such a general level of explanation, without first considering the mediating influence of sociohistorical context. The experimental subjects of behavioral economics are, after all, almost always drawn from modern capitalist societies. It is not unreasonable, therefore, to interpret the discoveries of the field as reflecting the more proximate sociocultural and historical setting of the subjects on whose behavior they are based. Indeed, two prominent examples of supposedly irrational behavior discovered by behavioral economists are quite compatible with the theory of economic behavior under capitalism developed in this book.

The first of these is the so-called endowment effect. One of Kahneman's most famous experimental discoveries is the tendency for subjects to value more highly an object that is owned than the same object when it is not owned. The mere fact of possession seems to add value to an object for its owner. Kahneman and his collaborators call this the "endowment effect" (Kahneman, Knetsch, and Thaler 1990, 1991; Knetsch 1989; Thaler 1980). Within behavioral economics the commonly accepted explanation of the endowment effect is just that human beings are hardwired to feel aversion to loss. The endowment effect is interpreted as indicating a marked asymmetry between the response of subjects to prospective losses and prospective gains. In essence, people dislike losing a given valued thing much more than they like gaining the same thing. However, it is not at all clear that the theory of loss aversion does much more than offer a different way of describing the behavior it purports to explain.

The theory of consumption as labor commensuration, by contrast, suggests a substantive sociological and historical explanation for the endowment effect. The endowment effect can be explained by the tendency, in a society dominated by wage-labor exchange, for owned objects to become saturated with the sunk costs represented by the labor exchanged (and, therefore, free time given up) for the money used to acquire them. If acquiring commodities is, in part, an effort to make the wage equivalent to the free activity given up in exchange for it, and if that free activity is inalienable and qualitatively particular, then the characteristics of free life activity (sacrificed in order to work) might well get transferred to the wage goods received as compensation for its loss. Coming to own commodity objects by exchanging a wage for them then gives those objects a particular meaning by virtue of the particular bits of life exchanged for them. Wage goods, once possessed, thus become inscribed with the sacrifice represented by the work that went into acquiring them. To put it another way, if labor is indeed inalienable, then that inalienability might to some degree get transferred to the objects received in exchange for labor. Those objects then become relatively inalienable, such that their owners will be reluctant to part with them. That then gets expressed in the higher value owners place on them, compared with identical goods that are not owned—Kahneman's endowment effect.

A second important finding from behavioral economics that the theory of consumption as commensuration helps explain is the tendency, discussed in Chapter 2, for subjects to discount the utility of future rewards hyperbolically as opposed to at an exponential rate. To recap, in studies of intertemporal choice, behavioral scientists have found that subjects tend to place very high value on a reward expected in the short-term, after which its value is steeply discounted. However, the same reward, with an equivalent delay, when expected in the longer term, is discounted to a much smaller degree. In terms of consumer behavior, hyperbolic discounting implies a tendency to spend in the short term as opposed to saving strategically (to "smooth" consumption over the long term), since the utility attached to satisfying an immediate desire dwarfs the envisioned utility of satisfying more temporally distant wants. When graphed, the discount function that describes this valuation of rewards over time produces a hyperbolic curve.

Hyperbolic discounting has been a source of great puzzlement to behavioral scientists and philosophers, as it would seem to violate certain canons of rationality.[33] Rational consumers are supposed to think about the future mainly in terms of the utility cost of delayed consumption, modified by degrees of uncertainty. Economists assume that utility is discounted over time at an exponential rate, producing a discount curve that is much less bowed than a hyperbolic one. Similarly, although more distant points in time are more uncertain than closer ones, assessments of uncertainty over time should, other things being equal, be much more consistent than is suggested by the hyperbolic function that describes much economic behavior. If hyperbolic discounting simply reflects increasing degrees of uncertainty about the future, then the uncertainty attributed to the future would increase very rapidly over short intervals of time, then, oddly, flatten out over the longer term. It thus seems implausible that hyperbolic discounting has to do with the epistemic status of the future.[34]

At the same time, agents, especially institutions, do sometimes discount utility in a supposedly rational, exponential fashion. For example, when people save, the usual expectation is that interest on savings (that is, the returns for forgoing consumption) will be paid at an exponential rate. So, it would seem that humans are endowed with two discrete discount curves— one hyperbolic and the other exponential. Behavior in some contexts is best described by the exponential curve, while in others the hyperbolic curve gives a better fit.

As mentioned in chapter 2 of this book, one strategy to explain this behavioral complex, advocated by George Ainslie (1992, 2001), has been to posit multiple competing selves within the agent, corresponding to distinct neurophysiological structures in the brain, each endowed with a particular orientation toward the future, reflected in its own discount curve. The behavior of a person is then a kind of equilibrium outcome, resulting from competition between these sub-self-level actors, at what Ainslie (1992) describes as the "picoeconomic" scale. Ainslie's theory, like Kahneman's, seeks maximal scope, and is consequently very insensitive to historical context. The objective is to come up with a robust theory of human behavior, understood on the most general of levels. Yet, as noted in the discussion of Kahneman, the experimental subjects whose behavior such theories attempt to explain are invariably subjects living in, and formed by, modern capitalist societies. We might do well, therefore, to look for an explanation of their behavioral tendencies in the proximate historical context of modern capitalism.

It seems quite possible that the high value people place on spending in the short term, compared with spending over the medium or longer term, reflects a sense of urgency, in a society organized around wage-labor exchange, about converting money into use values. Money wages form the most important component of income for the vast majority of people under capitalism. Consequently, for most people, money mostly means wage earnings. The disposition to privilege short-term consumption, rather than smoothing consumption over time, might well, therefore, have at least something to do with the identity of money wages as compensation for work. If commensurate compensation for labor requires that concrete potential activity be returned to the worker in the form of commodity objects, then there will be a strong impulse to spend earnings (and possibly also make use of credit, if wages are deemed insufficient to do the job of commensuration) to acquire such objects. Accumulating money, as opposed to things, by comparison works quite poorly as commensurable compensation for labor, even where the idea is to save in order to fund later consumption. Of course, people can fantasize about what they could do with their wage rather than spending it. Contemplation of the potential use values that a money wage can afford might for some time stave off the urge to convert that wage into commodity objects, especially if wages are being saved with some particular product in mind, such as a new home or car. But the use value of money wages per se has a second-order quality about it. The usefulness of unspent money subsists in the set of use values it can in theory command, which is, in effect, a potential to command stores of potential use value. For that reason, fantasies about how money could be spent are ultimately not concrete enough to be effective in making the exchange of labor for a wage seem like a fair exchange of commensurable substances.[35] In order for a sense of commensuration to be achieved, the wage must be converted into actual stuff, endowed with use power. Wage earners will, therefore, tend to turn money wages into things, and do so sooner rather than later.

As an alternative to the quite radical theoretical move of positing multiple sub-self-level agents—biologically ingrained homunculi competing for control of the person—we can thus account for the behavioral complex described by Ainslie and others in terms of overarching institutional and normative logics within capitalism. The tendency to discount hyperbolically makes sense when seen in the context of the logic according to which wage labor is justifiable. The tendency to discount exponentially, on the other hand, expresses the rationalized, calculative dimension of modern capitalism, most famously described by Max Weber (1992, 2013). If this interpretation is correct, then rather than holding that the two kinds of discounting reflect the operation of discrete cognitive systems in the brain, we can connect each to behavioral norms associated with a particular social position. To the degree that the logics underlying each rate of discount might have some normative claim on the behavior of economic agents, we can expect to observe the behavioral inconsistencies that Ainslie interprets as evidence of the existence of multiple selves. In some contexts, for example when investing profits, the exponential style of reasoning is dominant, while in other contexts, for example when deciding what to do with money wages, the hyperbolic one prevails.

1.7. Explains Pattern of Consumption over the Life Course

The labor commensuration theory of mass consumption also works as an explanation for the distribution of consumption over the life course. As noted earlier in the chapter, and also in Chapter 3, the prediction of the life cycle hypothesis—that people will attempt to maximize utility across the life course by becoming indebted when young and poor, saving when at the height of their earning power, and then spending after retirement—is not borne out by the evidence. The actual empirical pattern is as follows: When young, people underconsume relative to the predictions of the theory, because they are resistant to borrowing. When they are old, they also underconsume, because they spend a smaller part of their income than they should do, according to the theory. When they are middle aged, at the peak of their earning power, they overconsume (that is, undersave) (Deaton 1994). The peculiar thing, therefore, is the arc of spending over the life course—which would seem to indicate irrational risk aversion in youth, irrational risk taking in middle age, and irrational risk aversion in old age.

This pattern, which economists find puzzling, fits well with the theory of consumption as wage-labor commensuration. The young are reluctant to borrow in order to spend because they are much more likely to be in full-time education or training.[36] Even if they are working, their work is more likely to have strong element of on-the-job training (as formal or informal apprenticeship) and, for that reason, is something other than a straightforward wage-labor exchange. That people spend, rather than save, when middle aged, at the height of their earning power—when they have fully settled into the workforce—can straightforwardly be accounted for by the felt impulse to make their wage equivalent to the work done for it, by converting it into commodities. Moreover, the impetus to borrow, in order to finance consumption, takes on more force when people are in full-time work and, in particular, where wage levels seem insufficient to compensate for work. The old spend less than is predicted by the life cycle hypothesis because, as suggested in the discussion earlier in this chapter about the different uses of different kinds of income, postretirement income is one step removed from wage-labor exchange. This removes the wage-labor commensuration imperative to spend for retirees, which opens up space for other attitudes to income—for example, saving it to pass it on to heirs or else being risk averse and, therefore, reluctant to spend. There are of course clearly other possible explanations for what is going on here. But the fact that the life cycle pattern of consumption fits well with the predictions of the commensuration theory provides at least some support for the theory.

1.8. Explains Waste

The theory of consumption as commensuration provides a way to make sense of the huge amounts of waste produced under industrial capitalism. Commodities require time to produce utility—yet as output and real wages increase, while the working week stays constant, the time available to make use of each thing produced tends to decline. For that reason, the actual utility realized per thing produced (as opposed to the potential use power each item contains) likewise tends to decline. The difference between the aggregate potential use value of things and the use value actualized through using them is, in effect, waste. This becomes literally so as underutilized objects drift in the direction of landfills. If commodity acquisition was informed by sensible assessments of how much time and energy is available for making use of commodities rather than by the hypothetical use value contained in commodities (as a function of their physical properties), then the production of waste itself would be self-limiting. As per capita output (and hourly income) increased beyond a certain point, there would be increasing demand for time, as opposed to things, thus reducing demand and hence working as a negative feedback mechanism. If, however, as the commensuration theory suggests, the point of consumption is not just to realize actual use value but also to accumulate notional durations of activity indexed by commodity objects, to retroactively justify the labor given in exchange for the wage, then the connection between material output and actual need is attenuated. In such circumstances, natural constraints on the production of waste get removed, with dire environmental consequences.

2. Some Possible Objections to the Commensuration Theory

The commensuration argument thus works quite well as an explanation for certain puzzling aspects of consumer behavior under capitalism. It is also consistent with macrohistorical patterns in twentieth-century industrial capitalism. There are, nonetheless, objections that can be raised against it, as well as some questions about how certain significant developments in capitalist economies fit with the theory. It is to these that I now turn. Objections and questions are posed in the heading of each subsection, followed by my responses.

2.1. Why Does Commensuration Mean That the Wage Must be Spent?

One objection to the theory could be directed at the argument that a wage needs to be spent on commodities to make it commensurable with labor—and that, consequently, workers feel compelled to convert their earnings into goods. The counterargument is that a money wage can effectively evoke a basket of potential goods even without actually being spent and so has the same power to index free activities as actually owning commodities. If this is right, then the commensuration theory gives us no reason to suppose that spending a wage will be preferred to saving it, and it therefore fails to account for the trends described in the Chapter 3. The theory would then suffer from an explanatory lacuna similar to the one I attributed to Colin Campbell's (1987) argument.

One reason for the insufficiency of the unspent money wage to work as compensation is that the status of money is uncertain. Money is evanescent, mercurial, clearly conventional, and fundamentally unstable. Worries about the uncertain status of money are reflected in disquiet about inflation, even where real wages remain unchanged or increase, and in the associated impulse to try to ground value in commodities such as gold or material assets like real estate. Indeed, I would suggest that the impulse to make value concrete, by embedding it in things, is in part animated by underlying anxieties about converting the wage into something sufficiently "real" that it can approximate labor. For wage earners, the disquieting thing about nominal inflation (where real wages keep up with prices) is that something of substance—labor and time—has been given, yet what is received in exchange—some amount of money—is unpredictable and perhaps illusory.

Moreover, as noted earlier in this chapter, the nominal wage is too abstract to function adequately as compensation for work. In buying commodities, by contrast, people come to own the set of use values embedded in them, which is far more concrete than owning a quantity of money. Possession of money in relation to use values is, as noted earlier, a second-order form of possession, in the sense that to possess money is to possess a potential to acquire potential use values. As such, money wages are removed from the concrete labor given as work. The exchange of labor for the wage is incomplete until the wage is itself spent on things that have use value.[37] However, this point raises a second, perhaps more fundamental objection to the theory.

2.2. Doesn't Converting Increased Productivity into Actual Free Time Work Better as Wage-Labor Commensuration Than Projecting Time onto Things and Then Accumulating Them?

If wage labor indeed represents lost free activity (an opportunity cost in forgone leisure, as economists would have it), and if this lost free activity is compensated for by the free activity indexed by commodity objects, why not just directly exchange increasing productivity for more actual free time rather than time in the fetish form of things? To put it simply, if products *equal* time, why not just go directly for time? Just why is there an apparent bias in favor of higher wages over more free time? If an adequate response can't be provided to this question from the perspective of the commensuration theory, then the theory is open to the charge that it merely redescribes our puzzle rather than offering a constructive solution to it.

There are a number of possible responses to this point. First, the theory minimally entails indifference between free time and increased real wages rather than a definite preference for the latter over the former. Given that businesses will tend to have a preference for turning higher productivity into increased output, because of competitive pressures and, in the case of industry, big fixed capital investments, the indifference of labor between the two possibilities will, by default, lead to the former outcome. Unless labor actively pushes for reduced work time, firms will usually use productivity improvements to try to expand their market share by cutting prices and increasing output rather than cutting overall costs at constant output.

Second, as I noted in my discussion of renting goods, the accumulation of commodities works more effectively as compensation for labor than does the reduction of work time, because it creates the illusion that existential constraints on free activity, which are ultimately set by the horizon of human finitude, can be overcome. The hypothetical activity facilitated by a commodity object is unconstrained by real limitations of time and energy. In acquiring commodities, therefore, the worker can acquire a kind of virtual surplus of free time, because wage goods can contain more potential activity than the time given up in exchange for them. This surplus of hypothetical activity time is, in theory, unbounded. By contrast, increases in productivity can only be exchanged for a definite, and quite limited, increment of actual free time—the amount by which the length of work time is reduced while keeping wage income unchanged. At the limit, where labor time is reduced to zero (as in a fully robotic economy), the free time ex-workers have is just determined by the natural duration of a human life. However, by accumulating the potential activity alienated in objects, this absolute, existential limit on free time is seemingly transcended.

Now of course, if wage earners reduce their work hours for the same wages, they are clearly getting paid more per unit of work time—and so, in theory, are receiving more congealed activity time, in the form of wage goods, for each hour of work than they were when working more hours at the same wage. But the productivity of industrial capitalism is such that the amount of hypothetical free activity indexed by the goods commanded by the hourly real wage will tend to be greater than the amount of time it takes to earn that wage. Once the distinction between empty real time and the hypothetical time signified by goods becomes elided—in order for wage labor to become an objectively fair exchange of commensurable substances—the free time indexed by turning increased productivity into higher real wages will be *greater* than that yielded by turning it into a shorter working week at constant real wages.

Third, it is easier to imagine time spent in specific activities than "empty" time. Commodities serve as useful cognitive props to focus attention on particular practices. The potential free activity contained in wage goods is, in this sense, more available to contemplation than is free activity in the abstract. That this is so might well be contingent on what Keynes (1930) saw as the withering away of traditional collective and individual practices that could be pursued relatively independently of the possession of commodities. But once the new regime of time-use and consumption took hold, recovering those kinds of practices became quite difficult.

Lastly, taking compensation for increasing productivity as increased purchasing power, rather than reduced work time, underlines the status of wage workers as free participants in a market exchange rather than subjects of coercion. Precisely because labor is not obviously alienable, in order for it to be exchanged—that is, in order for it to be *made* alienable—it needs to be "returned" in a thing-like, or alienated, form. So wage goods in effect become animated by the labor given in exchange for them, such that they come to represent durations of free activity. In acquiring those goods, the wage earner acquires the free activity subsisting in them, and in this way the wage becomes equivalent to the labor given during work. By contrast, if wage earners exchange increased productivity for less time at work, they are exchanging it for something that in theory already belongs to them—their time. That sits in some tension with the ideology of free market exchange. According to the contractual logic of "free" labor, the initial, precontractual condition is one in which the workers' time belongs exclusively to them— they then get to dispose of it as they see fit. Free workers then supposedly bring their labor power—and thus their time—to market. The presupposed antecedent state is one in which they own themselves, which entails that they own all of their time.[38] To exchange increased labor productivity for more actual free time (that is, for less time at work), however, suggests that the antecedent state is one in which the workers' time belongs to their employer, such that workers are, in effect, buying back their time. That brings the logic of wage labor uncomfortably close to that of slavery (only lacking the legal category of the slave) or indentured labor (only without the debt). In the case of slavery, all of the time of the slave is owned by the slaveholder, but slaves can, in theory at least, buy their freedom. Similarly, indentured laborers work to end their bondage. As we shall see in the next chapter, in the earlier nineteenth century, the legitimacy of wage labor was questioned, in the United States and elsewhere in the capitalist world, precisely by comparing it to slavery, while the status of the bonded laborer was generally disparaged. Wage labor became legitimate to the degree that it was construed as a free exchange of commensurable substances—that is, to the degree that it became something categorically distinguishable from slave labor or bonded labor. The only way that wage labor can be a free exchange of commensurable substances, brought to the market by independent parties, is if time is alienated in wage goods, which are given to workers in exchange for their time.[39] Indeed, as we have seen, if time is alienated in objects, it becomes possible for wage earners to gain more potential time than they have given up in work.[40]

2.3. How Do Services Fit In?

A further question about the commensuration theory is what place consumption of services has in the theory. For while the theory places great emphasis on consumer durables, advanced industrial economies have over time tended to shift in the direction of services. The three-sector developmental model of the economy, according to which economies move progressively from extraction, to manufacturing, and then to services, has proven to be an empirically very sound model of economic development. In advanced capitalist nations, the service sector has inexorably grown as a proportion of the economy. But the theory of consumption as wage-labor commensuration entails that as incomes increase, the demand for manufactured goods, not services, should expand. How, therefore, can services be made sense of in relation to the theory proposed in this chapter?

In response to this question, first it should be noted that while the proportion of GDP devoted to services has increased in every advanced industrial economy, this is in large part due to the effect that increasing productivity has on the relative cost of goods and services. Because it is difficult to increase the productivity of service sector work, as manufacturing productivity increases, the cost of goods tends to fall relative to the cost of services (Baumol and Bowden 1966). Since, over time, the relative cost of services tends to increase, it seems as if the sector is expanding. But the increase in the value of the service sector masks a material reality of massively increased output of commodities, for which there has been a ready market. As noted in chapter 3, according to a chain-quantity index measure, which best approximates actual quantity of things produced, per capita output of consumer durables increased ninefold in the United States between 1925 and 1998 (Sherby 2000). The relative shift toward services, measured in terms of GDP, is therefore evidently entirely compatible with ever-increasing production, consumption, and accumulation of material goods.[41]

Moreover, part of the apparent increase in the proportion of economy devoted to services is an accounting artifact, resulting from the commodification of activities previously carried on outside the market sphere (Gershuny and Miles 1983). For example, as eating out becomes more common, the amount of labor involved in food preparation does not necessarily increase (it might well decrease), but more people are in paid employment to provide that service. The commodification of previously uncommodified activities accounts for a significant part of the nominal increase in the value of the services sector and for the increasing proportion of the labor force employed in service provision.

Nonetheless, the increasing prominence of services cannot be entirely reduced to an accounting artifact. As capitalist economies have matured there has undoubtedly been a significant movement of labor from manufacturing to the service sector. Many of the new service sector jobs are not just the result of commodification of activities previously conducted outside the market. Rather, as productivity increased in manufacturing, industrial workers were shed and were reemployed providing quite novel services—call center work would be a prominent contemporary example. However, this development is not incompatible with the commensuration theory. The theory does not presuppose that the workforce is employed in the extractive and manufacturing sectors. The argument is that wage workers seek commensurate compensation for giving up their time and freedom, whatever sector they work within.

Moreover, the aforementioned "marketization" of services provision is arguably precisely a consequence of the time bind in affluent societies, caused by the failure of the working week to decline by much as productivity increases. The motivation for the consumption of some services—for example paying for day care for young children—is to free up more time in which to work. Outsourcing services is also a response to the demands made on individuals by the commodity objects they own. Television sets must be watched, cars driven, pots cooked with, large houses cleaned and maintained, and, underlying all of this, wages spent. The purchase of time-saving services might be driven in part by the need to shop for and maintain consumer commodities as well as to find time to make use of them.

A final thought is that there are grounds on which to wonder why the service sector, despite its growth in recent years, is not much larger than it is. Like renting goods, buying services offers a flexible form of consumption, one not requiring possession of a stockpile of goods. Moreover, because a service is consumed in real-time, at the point of purchase, it is an efficient way to satisfy some want. With services, the duration of useful activity (taking a taxi, having meals cooked, clothes washed, and so on) made use of is the same as that paid for, so nothing is wasted. But that apparent advantage becomes a constraint if the point of consumption is to achieve wage-labor commensuration. For only so many services can be consumed in a given unit of time, and so consuming services makes salient the limits imposed on consumption by the availability of time. By contrast, using money to accumulate goods can, in the context of a certain attitude to those goods, suppress the temporal horizon on consumption. As noted earlier, owning stores of potential activity power makes it possible to endlessly defer the question of whether a wage produces enough actual useful free activity to justify the labor given to obtain it—the issue gets projected into the indefinite future. So if the purpose of spending the wage is to make wage labor into a fair exchange, then spending it on commodities fulfills that purpose more effectively than spending it on services.

2.4. What about Gender?

Another possible objection to the commensuration theory of mass consumption is that it ignores gender differences in work and consumption. At least according to some accounts, in the earlier twentieth century, women formed, in the United States, a majority of consumers (L. Cohen 2003). At the same time, until relatively recently, female participation in the labor force has been significantly lower than male participation. If consumers have predominantly been women, while men have tended to be the breadwinners, that would seem to weaken the connection between consumption and work. For if nonworking female consumers are somewhat removed from the logic of wage-labor exchange, then, arguably, the force of that logic will be attenuated in the sphere of consumption.

This is a complex theoretical and empirical issue. Conceptually, it raises the question of whether, and to what extent, the household should be thought of as a composite of individuals as opposed to a corporate entity. If the household is a corporate entity, such that its members think and act in a collective manner, then the justification of the labor of the household's wage earners might well inform the consumption behavior of everyone in the household. If, on the other hand, households are composites of individuals, then, to the degree that there is a gendered division of labor that separates work and consumption, the latter will be insulated from the logic according to which the former is justified.

There is some evidence from US history that women, when contributing to the household's consumption decisions, had in mind issues of fairness and commensurability that were very much connected to wage labor. Women were at the forefront of campaigns for fair prices, as a means of preserving the purchasing power of the wage. They were also key actors in the movement to boycott non-blue-label (that is, non-union-produced) products during the early and middle years of the century (Frank 1994; Glickman 2009). This suggests that women were conscious of notions of fair exchange in consumption that were indeed articulated to conditions of production—whether workers were unionized and getting paid fair wages. And of course, in every period of industrial capitalism, large numbers of women have participated in the labor market, albeit often in part-time or temporary work.

Moreover, despite the stereotypical representation of the consumer as female, it is not clear that women, in fact, did the lion's share of household spending (as distinct from the activity of shopping). Women may have predominated in certain kinds of purchasing, for example, grocery shopping. But although provisioning corresponds to a certain stereotype of what it is to shop, there are obviously other ways for a household to spend its income, especially as that income increases. And, indeed, as general affluence rose over the course of the twentieth century, provisioning accounted for a smaller proportion of household expenditure. There is at least some evidence of a gendered division of household consumption, with women responsible for provisioning and men having more say in decisions about the acquisition of big-ticket consumer durables. Sociologist Mark Swiencicki has suggested that men's role in early consumer culture has been overlooked and underestimated. He used the 1890 census of manufacturers to assess the relative size of male versus female consumption and found that male spending levels were twice as large as female levels (Swiencicki, 1998). Furthermore, decisions to increase total wage earnings, as opposed to reducing work time, would be made by those doing the waged work, in negotiations in the workplace. Although other household members would no doubt have had some input on the issue, norms concerning the conditions under which wage labor is fair would have exerted significant influence on that decision. In sum, while the gendered division of labor and consumption within the household potentially complicates the proposition that patterns of consumption, wages, and work time reflect changes in understandings of wage labor, it is certainly not inconsistent with it.

2.5. What about the Rise of Disposable Products?

If mass consumption is about accumulating stores of use value, in order to justify wage labor, then why, in modern capitalist societies, is so much stuff thrown away? Is there not some tension between the extent to which commodities are regarded as disposable and the argument made earlier in this chapter, that people become attached (sometimes irrationally so) to the things they own because those things represent their labor? Surely things, once animated by the labor given in exchange for them, should be kept indefinitely?

Part of the answer to this question might be as prosaic as limits on storage space. According to the commensuration theory, because wage labor is a perennial fact of life, the impetus to convert the wage into potential activity stored in commodities is ongoing. If storage space does not increase to accommodate ongoing accumulation, then consumers will eventually have to discard some of their accumulated goods. But that then raises the question of why storage capacity does not keep pace with accumulation. To some extent, of course, it has done so. As we saw in Chapter 3, the average size of homes in the United States increased substantially in the postwar period. However, the degree to which living and storage space can increase is ultimately limited by the fact that the supply of land is fixed. As increasing productivity reduces the price of consumer goods, the relative cost of land, and therefore of housing, increases. This implies that the rate of accumulation of goods, as real wages increase, will be higher than the rate at which homes can grow larger. That means that even if homes increase in size (as occurred in the United States), over time they will, nonetheless, tend to fill up with goods. Periodic culling of stuff then becomes necessary to prevent domestic life from becoming increasingly impinged on, and eventually crippled, by clutter.

But it is also the case that many people in fact throw away much less stuff than might be expected, given the negative effect that excessive accumulation has on ease of life. In recent years, pathological hoarding has become a topic of great cultural fascination, reflected in reality TV shows and popular books about the condition and in the rapid spread of self-help groups (Frost and Steketee 2011). According one study, about 5 percent of the contemporary US population are compulsive hoarders, while another study found a similar percentage (4.6 percent) among contemporary Germans (Frost 2010, 2013). But hoarding tendencies are much more widespread than is suggested by focusing on a relatively small (but still quite significant) number of extreme cases. From one perspective, compulsive hoarding is just an extreme manifestation of the endowment effect—the tendency of people to become irrationally attached to the things they own—which, according to experimental research by behavioral economists, is a quite general disposition in modern capitalist societies (Kahneman, Knetsch, Thaler 1990, 1991; Knetsch 1989; Thaler 1980). Indeed, the contemporary fascination with hoarding suggests widespread recognition of the disposition underlying the pathology—which, in turn, probably reflects the degree to which hoarding tendencies are quite common in the population.[42]

The increase in throwaway consumption, however, is a product of not just the discarding of overaccumulated consumer durables but also the emergence of consumer goods that are disposable by design. For, in addition to the creation of supposedly high-quality consumer durables, the twentieth century also witnessed the appearance and rapid spread of a wide range of disposable products—razors, ballpoint pens, paper tissues (as opposed to cloth handkerchiefs), and so on. It is immediately not clear why demand for disposable goods should have taken off in the middle part of the twentieth century. Disposable products do not necessarily take up less space than more durable items; therefore, there is no reason why a consumer should own fewer disposable items than their durable equivalents—so the motivation for switching to disposables cannot be that they reduce clutter. Moreover, buying items that require frequent replacement, rather than more durable products, means devoting more time and energy to shopping. Why should consumers choose to acquire items that so frequently have to be replaced? The obvious explanation is that durable items require upkeep—straight razors, for example, must be honed, cloth diapers and handkerchiefs washed, fountain pens flushed and refilled, and so on. In addition, since regular provisioning for food occurs in any case, replacing disposables can, to a fair extent, be folded into a big weekly shop. Big shopping trips became increasingly possible with the dissemination of automobile ownership (which allowed more stuff to be transported by consumers), in conjunction with the concentration of retail space that took place with the emergence of malls and shopping centers in the postwar years (L. Cohen 2003; Longstreth 1997, 1999, 2007; Mertes 1949). In the context of these developments, using disposable items might well have been a more time-efficient option than owning and maintaining durable goods.

But if disposable artifacts are, indeed, more time efficient, then the question I raised with respect to renting objects arises. Why have things not moved more fully in the direction of a low-upkeep mode of consumerism, by making everything disposable that can possibly be disposable? Why is the market for consumer goods not entirely dominated by a combination of disposable goods and durable goods that are rented? As with rented items, the answer might be that the duration of ownership of a disposable item is closely tied to actual use. Consequently, disposable items cannot signify a quantity of free activity that *exceeds* actual free time. Of course, consumers can accumulate a very large number of disposable items, to act as a reserve of potentially useful objects. But although some consumers do engage in bulk buying and stockpiling of disposable products, that mode of accumulative consumption quite quickly runs into storage limitations. Accumulating a smaller number of more expensive durable consumer goods is a more practical way to achieve wage-labor commensuration.

A final thought is that perhaps it is significant that disposable items tend to be artifacts categorized as necessities rather than those that are associated with free activity. Clearly blowing a nose, shaving, or changing a diaper are not activities that work well to signify the negation of work. Leisure time is a residual, left over after subtracting time spent in wage work, domestic labor, and physical upkeep. It seems unlikely, therefore, that the rather mundane objects that comprise the set of disposable products can denote free activity as effectively as durable objects of discretionary consumption. Perhaps, then, the demand for disposable items is strongest for those goods that do not index free activity but rather are associated with tending to bodily functions and basic household maintenance. That might be why the market for disposable items, like that for rented goods, remains smaller than we might think should be the case under industrial capitalism. The size and shape of the market for disposable products is, however, broadly consistent with what we would expect to be the case if the commensuration theory was true. Time efficient, disposable consumption prevails, for the most part, in parts of the consumer market in which products are sold that do not denote free activity.

FIVE

Economic Fairness and the Wage Labor Background

The account set out in the last chapter, according to which modern mass consumption is at least partly explained by the imperative to make commensurate work and its wage, involved a number of broad historical assertions about wage labor. I claimed that wage labor has not always commonly been regarded as being legitimate—and, more specifically, that it has not always been thought about as an exchange of commensurable substances, such that it could be seen as at least potentially fair. It was only after a protracted period of debate and political and industrial struggle that the institution of wage labor came to be broadly accepted. I argued that the legitimacy of wage labor was secured as it became increasingly plausible to construe it as involving an exchange of commensurable substances and that this, in turn, became possible to the extent that wage goods were reframed as congealed stores of free activity. I also suggested that the background to the emergence of those grounds for the legitimacy of wage labor was the rise to prominence of the category of objective economic fairness.

In this chapter, I give some empirical support to these broad claims, focusing once more on the case of the United States. I begin by drawing on work in historical semantics to elaborate on the thoughts presented at the beginning of the last chapter about the historicity of notions about objective economic fairness. Following this, I embark on brief forays into historiographical and ethnographic analysis. The historiographical section presents an abbreviated overview of the history of the labor question in America. The point of this is to substantiate the assertion that wage labor in the United States went from being a highly questionable institution to a fundamentally legitimate one. Having given a historical sketch of the wage labor background, I go on to consider some evidence from social research conducted in the early and middle decades of the twentieth century that provides some clues about how wage workers regarded the relation between work and consumption. This research provides some support for the contention that accumulative consumption reflected an effort to make the wage commensurate with work, under a certain understanding of the commensurability of wage goods and labor.

1. The Historicity of Economic Fairness: A Note on the Historical Semantics of "Fair"

There are reasons to think that the notion that economic fairness entails an exchange of commensurable substances of roughly equal value is peculiarly modern and that, given the timing of its emergence, this idea of fairness might well have been connected to the rise of wage labor.[1] Although there were markets before the emergence of capitalism, they were quite circum-scribed, and labor markets in particular were limited in extent. Wage labor consequently had a relatively marginal place in the economy. Before the rise to dominance of market capitalism, the basis of the legitimacy of economic exchange was not that the substances changing hands were commensurable and of equal magnitude.[2] Rather, the exchange of goods and services (often between patrons and clients) in precapitalist contexts typically expressed nor-mative obligations and expectations attached to the social identity and status of the parties involved in the transaction.[3] A minimal condition (although certainly not a sufficient one) on those kinds of exchanges being legitimate was that the parties comport themselves in accordance with norms attached to their respective social positions and that the terms of the exchange con-form to customary expectations.[4] If in an exchange more was demanded or less given than custom dictated, the legitimacy of the exchange would be thrown into question.

With the growing importance of wage labor, and the broader expansion of the market economy, economic exchange became, at least in theory, a more neutral matter, in the sense that the particular social identities of the exchang-ing parties were not supposed to determine the terms of the exchange. But this did not mean that emergent, modern ideals of economic exchange were devoid of a normative dimension—a sense of the conditions under which exchanges could be deemed proper and fair. There were formal and substantive normative dimensions to modern economic exchange, both of which informed conceptions of fair wage exchange.[5] On formal grounds, economic exchanges were viewed as fair insofar as they are entered into without coercion by notionally free subjects, conceived of more or less along the lines of liberal ideology. On substantive grounds, fairness was objectively grounded in the properties of the substances being exchanged. A substantively fair exchange is one in which the exchanged substances are self-evidently of roughly equal value (however value is construed). To be sure, there were variations across different capitalist contexts in how exactly the substantive notion of fairness was worked out. As noted briefly in the previous chapter, Richard Biernacki's (1995) comparative work on the norms governing wage-labor exchange in Germany and England in the early industrial period shows how in Germany value was a function of labor time, whereas in England value was reified in the product of labor. According to Biernacki, this difference reflected distinct, culturally embedded notions about the source of value. But in both cases, there was an understanding that fairness in the exchange of work for a wage obtains where the value represented by the wage is equal to the value represented by the work given for it.

Work on historical semantics offers some evidence of the historicity of the modern notion of objectively fair economic exchange, at least in the case of the English-speaking world. According to the investigations of linguist Anna Wierzbicka (2006), it was only quite recently that the English term *fair* came to take on its contemporary ethical sense, which has connotations of equality.[6] Before the nineteenth century, *fair* meant proper adherence to an agreed-on procedure. The earliest usage of *fair* in this procedural sense is found in the expression "fair play," the first records of which date to the sixteenth century. Fair play—simply following the agreed rules of a game—captures to some degree the formal moral dimension of modern economic transactions. However, Wierzbicka notes that the meaning of *fair play* is distinct from the modern sense of *fair* as equal—the sense that is present in notions such as the "fair wage." This point becomes clear when considering the respective antonyms of *fair* (play) and *fair* (exchange of equivalents). The opposite of *fair play* was *foul play*, which means flouting the rules of a game. To play foully is to break rules, to cheat in some sense, with the assumption that the players of the game freely agreed on those rules before play began. For a player not to follow those rules thus involves reneging on an agreement, the breaking of a compact. Although the procedural sense of *fair* (the sense involved in *fair play* and *foul play*) is clearly still in common use today, that sense does not capture the contemporary, substantive, and essentially distributive notion of fairness, with its connotations of equality and, therefore, commensurability.[7] The antonym of that sense of *fair* is just *unfair*, the meaning of which is broader than *foul play*. While *unfair* can mean deviating from agreed-on rules, it can also mean substantively unequal, as in not getting a fair share of some good. It is the latter sense of *unfair* that is used to refer to *unequal* exchange, where the quantity of value given by one party is greater than the value received in return from the other party. An exchange can be judged by an observer as unfair, in the sense of being unequal, whether or not the observer knows the "rules of the game" and indeed independently of whether those rules were freely agreed on by the exchanging parties.[8] The earliest mention of *unfair* is found in the mid-eighteenth century, but Wierzbicka suggests that the modern meaning of the word did not fully emerge until well into the nineteenth century. The emergence of *fair* as meaning equal thus, significantly, coincided with the rise of industrial capitalism and wage labor.

To complicate matters further, before the nineteenth century the word *fair* primarily had an aesthetic, rather than an ethical, meaning. As a noun, the word could mean beautiful, agreeable, clear and distinct, smooth, even, free of irregularities, well-proportioned, and in balance. The word could be used as a verb, to mean to smooth, to make even, to beautify. It was perhaps as much by virtue of the aesthetic meanings of *fair* as it was of the procedural sense associated with *fair play*, that the word came to be extended to economic matters to mean substantively equal exchange. For the aesthetic sense of *fair* can more readily capture the idea of commensuration implicit in fair / equal exchange than can the narrowly procedural *fair play*. This is because the notions of balance and symmetry involved in the aesthetic meaning of *fair* entail a kind of commensurability. For something to be symmetrically arranged, proportional, or well balanced, clearly it must have some property—weight, for example, or area, or shape, or shade—in terms of which it can be seen, or otherwise sensed, as proportional, in balance, or symmetrical. In order to judge, for example, whether a figure is symmetrical, it must be possible to compare the area and shape of different parts of that figure. Similarly, in order to gauge whether a symmetrical object is well balanced, the distribution of its weight around its axis of symmetry—how the weight on the one side compares to that on the other—must be discerned. An objectively fair exchange is one in which exchanged goods or services are in balance, while to be in balance they must be commensurable. The aesthetic sense of *fair*, as balanced and well-proportioned, thus gets at that concept of fair exchange. In addition, the aesthetic meaning of *fair*, when extended to denote substantively equal exchange, suggests that whether or not an exchange is objectively fair is something that can be perceived in the objective form of the exchange—in the degree to which the substances being exchanged are *self-evidently* balanced and in proportion. The aesthetic denotations of *fair* thus work well to convey the idea that legitimate economic exchanges are characterized by equal exchange of commensurable substances—an idea deeply embedded in market justifications of wage labor.

The increasing normative force of the idea of objectively fair economic exchange set up a tension in wage labor. Wage labor had by the later nineteenth century become, to a large extent, simply a fact of life. Perhaps it was acknowledgment of that de facto situation that led to the growing influence of the politics of purchasing power, which accepted the broad parameters of the capitalist system, yet sought better terms of exchange between labor and capital. The legitimacy of wage labor hinged on the degree to which labor was regarded as alienable, and wages were seen as commensurable with work. But seeing labor as an alienable thing, commensurable with the wage given in exchange for it, was in tension with customary understandings of work. Moreover, as emphasized in the last chapter, it was entirely unclear how labor—the activity of a person—could be alienable or in what terms it could be seen as commensurable with a wage and, therefore, what criterion should determine a fair exchange of labor for a wage. So while the general idea that wage labor can be fairly compensated had taken root by the late nineteenth century, there remained, in part as a result of the persistence of older understandings of work, deep conceptual problems with putting that idea into practice. In the next section, I briefly consider how these tensions were worked out in the case of the United States.

2. A Brief Note on the History of the Legitimacy of Wage Labor in the United States

The story of the ascent of wage labor is not just about its spread as economic practice but also about its growing acceptance—the increasing tendency for it to be taken for granted, a quasi-naturalized institution. There is broad consensus among American labor historians, and indeed historians of other parts of the capitalist world, that wage labor in the early period of capitalism was regarded with a great deal of suspicion and that its legitimacy was, at best, questionable.[9] In antebellum America, the economic dependence entailed by being a waged laborer was seen as undermining the condition of individual autonomy that, according to the Republican ideology that held sway at the time, was a prerequisite for virtuous citizenship. During the first half of the nineteenth century, according to Sean Wilentz (1984), the American labor movement was more or less united in holding that labor is not a marketable commodity and so should not be treated as such. Eric Foner (1995) has similarly drawn attention to the degree to which antebellum America was marked by widespread hostility to wage labor, even as the ideology of "free labor" became increasingly influential. Foner argues that, as wage labor increasingly became the dominant economic relationship, "the ideal of the autonomous small producer reemerged . . . as a full-fledged critique of early capitalism and its inexorable transformation of free labor into a commodity" (p. xvii).

The spread of wage labor in the United States, and indeed elsewhere in the capitalist world, was a gradual and complex process, the result of incremental moves on the part of business and labor away from customary arrangements that determined pay and work conditions and toward more explicit contracts.[10] Amy Stanley (1998) has charted the cultural, intellectual, and legal complexities of the early history of wage labor in the United States. She shows how in the first half of the nineteenth century, contracts were predominantly informal and tended to serve the interests of employers, at least with respect to who controlled the labor process. In taking a job, a worker was presumed to have consented to all rules imposed by the employer, even those unstated in the contract itself. It was not uncommon for piece rates to be decided by foremen and subcontractors on an ad hoc basis, on terms that rarely favored the worker. Early labor struggles were often directed at making contracts more explicit, as well as at establishing the principle of collective bargaining. According to Stanley, it was "[labor's] efforts [that] altered the wage contracts from an oral promise full of ambiguities to a precisely worded written document" (p. 68). The picture drawn by Stanley broadly accords with Eric Hobsbawm's (1964) sweeping account of the history of industrial relations across the capitalist world during the nineteenth century, in which he shows how the proletariat became increasingly savvy in its dealings with employers. But Stanley argues that the more explicit written contracts that emerged in the wake of older customary arrangements, while having some advantages for employees, at the same time struck many workers as uncomfortably close to a form of bondage. While, in Hobsbawm's terms, American workers had, by the later decades of the nineteenth century, learned to play "the [capitalist] rules of the game," they nonetheless remained deeply ambivalent about those rules.[11] In Stanley's nuanced argument, wage labor embodied a contradiction. On the one hand, a wage-labor contract is notionally freely entered into by the worker, but at the same time, it legally inscribes a relation of domination and subordination. This contradiction was expressed in contract law. According to what Stanley (1998, p. 83 [emphasis added]) describes as the "modern definition," set out in an 1886 "plain statement" on labor law, a "hireling" is: "one who, *by reason of contract* . . . becomes subject to the authority and control of another in some trade." Wage labor amounted, therefore, to a kind of voluntary bondage.

The status of wage labor was made more problematic in the United States by its entanglement with the question of slavery. Slavery complicated the issue of wage labor during the nineteenth century because of apparent similarities in their underlying logics. Both arrangements involved, to varying degrees and in different ways, coercion and the sale of labor. Lawrence Glickman (1997, p. 157), summing up a generation of research by labor historians, concludes that "most antebellum workers placed wage labor with slavery along a continuum of bondage." Indeed, for much of the nineteenth century, a very common way to condemn wage labor was to refer to it as "wage slavery." The association of wage labor and slavery was not just a rhetorical ploy but a central animating idea in the labor movement, both in the United States and elsewhere.[12] The call to reduce hours in the postbellum period, for instance, was very much couched in the language of emancipation, reminiscent of the rhetoric used in the campaign against slavery. Ira Steward, eulogized on his death by American Federation of Labor leaders as "the most important American contributor to labor thought," saw the fight for shorter hours as entirely continuous with the abolitionist cause (Roediger 1986).

The question of the legitimacy of wage labor thus turned to a significant extent on the degree to which it was viewed as being different in kind from slavery. Stanley (1998, p. 88) sums up the debate about the relation between slavery and wage labor as follows: "The crux of the disagreement concerned the meaning of emancipating all men to sell their own labor—whether this transformation established self-ownership or self-dispossession, contract freedom or wage slavery." The answer to that question, in turn, depended on whether labor could be reasonably construed as an alienable commodity, just like any other: "The legitimacy of commerce lay in the legal equality of employers and workers and the likeness of labor to other commodities" (p. 76). As long as wage labor was conceived of as different in kind from the commodities afforded by the wage, it remained overshadowed by the question of whether it could, even in theory, be fairly compensated. For how can inalienable life activity be in any sense fairly exchanged for a wage and the lifeless things it commands? This question threatened to undermine the legitimacy of the wage-labor exchange.

The comparison between wage labor and slavery was not just a feature of radical labor ideology and politics, confined to the margins of thought about the problems and dilemmas of early industrial society. Rather, during the nineteenth century, there was very widespread disquiet about the moral status of wage labor, which was felt well beyond the laboring classes. Wage labor was generally thought of as presenting an intellectual and moral problem, one that aroused debate among politicians, political economists, and in legal circles. The moral complexity of wage labor was acknowledged in 1883 congressional hearings on the matter, which, according to Stanley (1998, p. 84), "registered the wider concerns of public debate" about the "enduring ambiguities of the wage contract in free society," at the core of which lay the question of whether labor should be treated as just another commodity. As a legal matter, the question was eventually settled by the Supreme Court in 1923, in the Adkins vs. Children's Hospital case (concerning the constitutionality of a minimum wage law). According to the ruling; "In principle there can be no difference between the case of selling labor and the case of selling goods" (Holmes 2010, p. 173). How much a worker should receive for her labor was thus taken to be a matter equivalent to how much a merchant could get for her wares. In both cases, the market alone should decide. That was necessary for this point to be spelled out in a ruling by the highest court in the land indicates the extent to which it was a matter of contention in the United States during the nineteenth and early twentieth centuries.[13]

Beginning in the years following the end of the Civil War, the mind-set described by the historians of antebellum labor began to change. The focus of American labor shifted from a critique of wage labor and struggles over the length of the working day to increasing the purchasing power of the wage. Labor was not initially unified behind this change of agenda, and, particularly between the late nineteenth century and World War I, radicals and moderates competed for working class support. Howard Kimeldorf, in his analysis of turn of the century labor activism, sees the different mottos of the American Federation of Labor (AFL) and the Industrial Workers of the World (IWW) as expressing the main contending ideologies within organized labor. The AFL adopted for its motto "a fair day's wage for a fair day's work," while the more revolutionary IWW chose "abolish the wage system" (Kimeldorf 1999). The IWW emerged to fill the vacuum left by the AFL's move toward a more corporatist vision of industrial politics. According to Kimeldorf: "By the time of the IWW's formation in 1905, the AFL had come firmly to embrace American values and institutions, including its system of capitalism, which Gompers, the former Marxist radical turned pragmatist, endorsed as 'the best yet devised'" (p. 2). Kimeldorf sees the first twenty years of the century as a critical turning point, as the radical agendas of the Knights of Labor and the IWW came to be replaced by the workplace-focused syndicalism of the AFL. According to his account, there was a real ideological struggle between the ALF and the IWW, the outcome of which was not a forgone conclusion. But by the end of the First World War, the AFL and its moderate agenda were clearly in the ascendant. The post–World War I era saw the beginnings of welfare capitalism and corporatism, setting the stage for the coalescing of the Fordist regime in the years following the Second World War.

By the third decade of the twentieth century Selig Perlman (1928) was confidently characterizing American labor as, above all else, wage conscious. For Perlman, and other members of the industrial relations school founded by John Commons, the struggle of labor was not over the fundamental legitimacy of wage labor but rather about how well labor is compensated for its labor. While the projection back in time of Perlman's picture of American labor has been challenged, as has the associated argument that American workers are, for deep cultural and historical reasons, essentially conservative, it is certainly true that by the middle decades of the twentieth century, the legitimacy of wage labor per se (as opposed to particular wage contracts and labor practices) had become largely uncontested. Over the first half of the twentieth century there was thus a reorientation of the politics of labor from a more radical agenda, which questioned the capitalist social order, to a reformist one, presupposing an increasingly corporatist model of industrial relations.

Labor's pursuit of purchasing power, as opposed to pushing for a broader and more political agenda that challenged capitalism itself, corresponded to the waning of the struggle to reduce the length of the working week. In the period following the Civil War the industrial struggles about work time were animated by ambivalence about wage labor because of its close association with bondage. The effort by labor to limit the length of the working day was conceived of as being part of a broader movement to overthrow, or at least contain, "wage slavery." In 1866, the General Congress of Labor resolved in a meeting in Baltimore that "the first and great necessity of the present is to free the labor of this country from capitalist slavery, is the passing of a law by which eight hours shall be the normal working day in the states of the American union." (Toph 1898, p. 131). Limiting hours at work would, according to this reasoning, limit the extent of the subjection of workers to wage slavery, since work under capitalism and wage slavery essentially amounted to the same thing. The call to reduce the length of the working week powerfully galvanized workers and was closely associated with the May Day demonstrations of the 1880s. In 1872 over 100,000 workers went on strike in New York City in support of an eight-hour limit to the working day at a time when, according to the 1870 census, the number of people working in manufacturing in the city was 144,285. As with the broader question of wage labor, the concern to shorten the working day was shared by a many in society. William Bliss (1897, p. 1,230), minister, investigator for the Bureau of Labor, and editor of the *Encyclopedia of Social Reform*, wrote, "Today almost all economists and social reformers favor a shorter day, the only questions being how rapidly it can be introduced, and in what ways."

The issue of the length of the working week continued to have some presence on the agenda of organized labor until World War II. In the 1930s, for example, against the backdrop of mass unemployment, work time was still a living issue for unions.[14] But over the first half of the twentieth century, the importance of the issue of work time gradually waned (as the concern with increasing purchasing power waxed). And, as historian Benjamin Hunnicut (1984, 1998) has noted, the effort to limit hours at work, somewhat mysteriously, almost vanished in the second half of the century. There were occasional local upwellings of support for shorter hours. For example, sociologist Jonathan Cutler (2004) shows how in the 1950s and 1960s members of UAW local 600 branch pushed, against the will of the union's leadership, for shorter hours. But in the postwar period, there was nothing like the huge national shorter hours movement of the late nineteenth-century.[15] Of course, in part the issue of work time became less pressing because, as we saw in Chapter 3, hours fell significantly between 1880 and 1920. Yet, as I noted in that chapter, it is not at all clear why, as productivity improved, and hourly income continued to increase, working hours did not continue to decline at an equivalent rate.

The ebbing of older concerns about wage labor being tantamount to a form of bondage coincided with the emergence of mass consumption—a correlation which, according to the argument of this book, is not without significance. The change in focus of the labor movement from work time to purchasing power was not an isolated phenomenon, but rather was part of a broader reorientation of politics away from production and toward consumption. Lizabeth Cohen has noted that in the late nineteenth century, the public good was thought about primarily in terms of the health of production. But, beginning in the Progressive era, the interests and welfare of the consumer came increasingly to represent the public good. By the early 1930s, FDR could declare without risk of stirring controversy: "we are at the threshold of a fundamental change in our popular economic thought [such] that in the future we are going to think less about the producer and more about the consumer" (L. Cohen 2003, p. 24). The rights of wage earners were, in line with this, increasingly tied to their emerging identity as consumers.

As alternatives to wage labor increasingly vanished, the picture of wage labor as a form of bondage began to fade, and in its place, there emerged not so much a set of arguments as a largely unspoken assumption that a wage could, at the right level, be fairly exchanged for a given quantity of work. Indeed, historian Glickman (1997) notes that as the general concept of wage slavery declined, an alternative metaphor involving slavery appeared—the "wage slave." The term *wage slave* referred to a person who toils for low levels of compensation—who works, that is, without, being given a commensurate amount of purchasing power in return for her labor. For wage laborers to have a status akin to that of slaves, thus, became contingent on the buying power of their wages.

The increasing acceptance among workers of wage labor as a de facto reality was in part a response to the consolidation of the power of business and to a state that was increasingly hostile to labor. Howard Kimeldorf (1999) and Kim Voss (1993) have shown in their studies of late nineteenth- and early twentieth-century labor activism that there were also considerable organizational impediments to carrying out a more radical agenda. These difficulties added to the impetus to accept wage labor as, more or less, a fact of life. As Glickman (1997, pg. 2) puts it: "In the period between the Civil War and World War One workers learned to accept wages and to identify themselves as wage earners because they had no alternative." But this did not mean that their conception of what made wage labor legitimate was the same as that of liberal political economists. Part of how workers came to conceive of wage labor as a justifiable institution was by a consumerist reorientation of class consciousness. The toil of work became justifiable in terms of the supposed fruits of consumption, measured by the concept of purchasing power.

There were efforts to fix fair compensation in absolute terms, pegged to a specified set of goods. For example, AFL leader Samuel Gompers argued that wages should be set at levels capable of supporting an "American standard of living," which he defined as "the neat convenient well fitted bathroom . . . food in good quantity and quality, presentable clothes, a comfortably furnished home," a wage "sufficient to maintain an average-sized family." (Shergold 1982, p. 90).[16] This absolute conception of fair wages is somewhat similar to feudal norms of economic exchange, according to which the landed elite was obligated to provide basic security for their serfs in exchange for services rendered. At the same time, the absolute conception of fair compensation for work reflected a presupposition that labor can be fairly compensated by wage goods and that the two are therefore commensurable. Conceptions of a fair wage in absolute terms, however, could not deal with the very dynamic situation created by rapidly increasing productivity. For organized labor also made the argument that increasing productivity should, on grounds of fairness, be rewarded by increasing real wages. As noted in the last chapter, anchoring fair wages to a fixed basket of goods makes it unclear on what moral grounds labor can press for higher wages in exchange for its contribution to increasing productivity. The absolute version of a fair wage, set out by Gompers and others in the early twentieth century, is, then, better conceptualized as specifying minimal standards of living that any wage should secure. It provided necessary, but not sufficient, conditions that must be met in order for a wage to qualify as being fair and decent. It did not provide general criteria for determining whether the exchange of a given wage for a given amount of labor is fair. In the second half of the twentieth century, the absolute conception of fair wages became supplemented by a more dynamic notion, which linked increases in productivity to increases in the purchasing power of the wage. The background to this was the development of a mass consumer economy focused on standardized consumer goods.[17]

By the second half of the twentieth century, the concept of purchasing power, against the background of mass consumption, had come to provide grounds for the legitimacy of wage labor, which for much of the nineteenth century had been a subject of considerable controversy. As long as wage labor was conceived of as entailing a loss for the worker that was incapable of being compensated, an irrevocable diminishing of her humanity, it remained a deeply questionable practice. The legitimacy of wage labor was secured to the degree that it came to be thought of as, in theory, capable of being commensurately compensated by a sufficient quantity of consumer goods. The fact that the development of the institutional, cultural, and social forms associated with consumer society coincided with the gradual acceptance of wage labor as a legitimate form of exchange was, as noted in the previous chapter, not coincidental.

What is not clear, however, is how exactly consumption could make what had previously seemed tantamount to a form of slavery or bondage into something fair and acceptable. At least part of the answer to this question is that consumer commodities became reframed as increasingly standardized quantities of use power—free time and activity frozen in the form of commodities. This change was both reflected in and facilitated by the emergence of a new kind of product, as mass-produced, standardized modern consumer durables became available.

3. The Meaning of Consumption in the Shadow of Wage Work—Some Evidence from Mid-Twentieth-Century Social Research

I characterized the theoretical argument made in the last chapter as an abduction—a conjecture that posits a state of affairs to account for a surprising empirical pattern. The existence of that state of affairs would remove the grounds on which the pattern strikes us as surprising. If the point of consumption is to achieve commensurate compensation for labor, then the tendency for consumption to increase with increases in productivity would follow naturally, as a matter of course. But are there more direct indications that mass consumption was motivated to a significant extent by wage-labor commensuration? What evidence do we have about attitudes toward the connection between work, wage, and consumption among wage earners in the period that saw the emergence of welfare capitalism and the purchasing power paradigm—the period roughly spanning the 1920s to the 1950s?

Uncovering the attitudes of wage earners toward the relation among work, wages, and consumption is a difficult endeavor. It involves the reconstruction of popular mentalities buried in the past from often fragmentary and indirect evidence deposited in the archive. Disinterring past attitudes to work, spending, and saving demands intense social historical investigation of a kind that, for practical reasons, is most easily undertaken in empirically quite delimited contexts. For that reason, social histories that investigate the work-life nexus often take the form of local studies or microhistories. One example is Roy Rosenzweig's (1985) detailed historical investigation of work and leisure in Worcester, Massachusetts, between 1870 and 1920. The present book, however, has objectives different from those of local histories such as Rosenzweig's. Its aim is to develop a general theory of the relation between wage labor and mass consumption under industrial capitalism, based in the first instance on abductive inferences made from large-scale historical patterns and trends. Finding evidence that is, on the one hand, rich enough to use to reconstruct attitudes to the relationship between work and consumption and, on the other, representative of wage earners under industrial capitalism is, to say the least, challenging.

There are, nonetheless, some historical sources that present suggestive evidence about the relation between understandings of work and the meaning of consumption. In particular mid-century qualitative research on wage earners provides at least some sense of the ways in which wage labor was justified, during the first half of the twentieth century, in terms of the accumulation of consumer commodities. To be sure, ethnographies written in the past should be approached with caution, because the interpretations they contain are inevitably refracted through the commitments and biases of their authors. Nonetheless, they provide at least something for us to go on. In the remainder of this chapter, I examine a number of studies of industrial wage workers conducted between the 1920s and the 1950s that touch on the interrelated meanings of work, wages, commodities, and leisure. In particular, I consider the evidence presented in sociological investigations by Robert Straughton Lynd and Helen Lynd in the 1920s and early 1930s and by Eli Chinoy, Robert Guest, and Bennet Berger in the 1950s. The Lynds' analysis of work, consumption, and leisure in *Middletown* and *Middletown In Transition* provides some suggestive, albeit often oblique, evidence about the relationship between the meaning of work and consumption. The ethnography of autoworkers in Lansing, Michigan, conducted in the 1950s by the industrial sociologist Ely Chinoy (1955), is especially informative because Chinoy was specifically interested in how wage earners justified their labor, to themselves and to others. Research on autoworkers by Richard Guest (1954) and Bennet Berger ([1961] 1970), also conducted in the 1950s, helpfully supplements Chinoy's study. Of course, these ethnographies are very far from being based on a representative population sample for the United States, let alone for industrial capitalism in general. Both the Lynds and Chinoy investigated very particular contexts—a small, Midwest nonunion town in the Lynds' studies and unionized autoworkers in a small midwestern factory town in Chinoy's case. Nonetheless, what these studies lack in breadth they make up for in depth. Moreover, the research on postwar autoworkers by Chinoy, Guest, and Berger focuses on a group of workers who, following the UAW's landmark 1948 collective bargaining agreement with GM, had tremendous influence on wage setting and industrial relations in the economy at large (Piore and Sabel 1986; Katz 1985). How autoworkers in this period understood the meaning of their work, and its relationship to their wages and to the consumption afforded by those wages, reflected, but also informed general conceptions of wage and work standards.[18] To reiterate, however, the objective of this brief survey is just to provide some evidence in light of which the notion that mass consumption is in part explained by wage-labor commensuration becomes at least plausible. It goes without saying, therefore, that my discussion amounts to an opening note, rather than the last word, on the topic.

3.1 Wages, Work, and Consumption in Mid-Century America

Early on in the Lynds' (1929, p. 52) first study of Middletown, they offer a synthetic overview of the moral economy connecting work and money to the life of the town: "The whole complex of doing day after day fortuitously assigned things, chiefly at the behest of other people, has in the main to be strained through a pecuniary sieve before it achieves vital meaning. This helps account for the importance of money in Middletown, and, as an outcome of this dislocation of energy expenditure from so *many* of the dynamic aspects of living, we are likely to find compensatory adjustments in other regions of the city's life." They make a related point in their second study, *Middletown In*

Transition, published almost a decade later, describing the "master formula" at play in Middletown (and by extension in American industrial capitalism more generally) as "Work = money; money buys leisure. Non-work = loss of opportunity to make money, and therefore loss of opportunity to buy leisure." They continue, "It is thus that pecuniary culture transmutes even leisure into its own terms" (Lynd and Lynd 1937 p. 294). The Lynds are drawing attention here to the commodification of all dimensions of life, but especially of leisure, in a town in which most people got their living by selling their labor. As social life became increasingly mediated by money transactions, a process at the root of which lay the growing importance in all aspects of life of the wage relation, so the meaning of everything became "strained through a pecuniary sieve." The point about the commodification of life, how leisure became mediated by money, seems clear enough and very much in tune with standard criticisms of capitalism. Yet what is peculiar and interesting in the Lynds' account is the suggestion that this "pecuniary straining" was not a source of disenchantment but rather a means by which an otherwise quite alienating form of life, and especially work, became imbued with "vital meaning." What might it mean for the wage to endow deadening work with "vital meaning"? A wage taken in nominal terms is just a number, perhaps functioning like points in a game. But while accumulating money in this nominal sense might serve as a measure of relative success for the archetypal Weberian capitalist, something so abstract would hardly seem sufficient to imbue alienated wage work with vital meaning. And how could money in its nominal form secure the idea of fair compensation for work? Money construed as an end-in-itself is surely much too abstract and anemic to make up for the real deficits—of freedom, time, self-ownership, and so on—incurred through subjection to the labor process.[19]

Assuming that the Lynds were on to something in their analysis—that the filtering of deadening wage labor through a "pecuniary sieve" did indeed somehow redeem the otherwise deeply alienating activity of labor—surely this effect must be explained by the use of money to buy wage goods, in conjunction with the particular meaning taken on by those goods in the notionally free sphere of consumption. I suggested in the last chapter that in order for the equivalence between work and wage to be established, and some semblance of moral balance restored to wage-labor exchange, the wage must be converted into goods, framed as congealed reserves of potential activity. If that is right, then the flow of influence that the Lynds describe in their analysis of leisure, from the wage / money economy to the form of life of the community, travels in both directions. While wage labor leads to the commodification of various aspects of life, at the same time, deadening labor becomes retroactively reanimated through the conversion of wage money into objects seemingly endowed with a vital power. Consumption, when directed at the possession of empowering objects, thus projects an animating meaning back on work.

3.2. The Automobile as the Ultimate Consumer Commodity

For the workers of Middletown, the commodity that seemed more than any other to justify the alienating activity of labor—endowing work after the fact with "vital meaning"—was the automobile. As mentioned in Chapter 2, the diffusion of the automobile in Middletown was rapid and dramatic, affecting all aspects of social life. "In 1890 Middletown was a 'horse culture,'" the Lynds report, but "by 1920, Middletown had become a horse-power culture. By 1923, there were 2 cars for every 3 families. The ownership of automobiles substitutes, in many cases, for saving (and sometimes even for food and clothing). It is not uncommon to mortgage a home to buy a car" (p. 254). Even in the 1920s, before the era of interstates and large-scale suburbanization, people seemed almost irrational in the importance they attached to cars. "We'd rather go without clothes than give up the car," one informant, a mother of nine children, told the Lynds (1929, p. 255). Most cars were purchased using finance, with car payments, according to the Lynds' calculations, amounting to 25 percent of the average wage earned by working people.[20] Yet cars were very much conceived of as objects of discretionary consumption. The Lynds note that one of the chief leisure time activities of Middletown workers was to go for a drive and that vehicles were more objects of pleasure than utilitarian tools. One gets the impression that the Lynds' wage workers to a significant extent worked in order to be able to drive—or at least that the activity of driving to some degree justified the labor sold for a wage.

In *Middletown in Transition*, the Lynds' second study, they observe that the obsession with automobiles continued into the 1930s, even against the backdrop of the Depression: "Car ownership in Middletown was one of the most depression proof elements of the city's life in the years following 1929—far less vulnerable, apparently, than marriages, divorces, new babies, clothing, jewelry, and most other things, both small and large." The Lynds note that "the passenger registrations in Middletown's entire county not only registered scarcely any loss in the early years of the depression, but both in numbers and in ratio to population, stood in each of the years 1932–35 above the 1929 level" (1937, pp. 266–67). While the purchase of new cars declined, suggesting that hard economic times in the 1930s prompted people to hang on to their cars for longer, at the same time, gasoline sales dropped only 4 percent during the toughest years of the Depression, indicating that patterns of car usage did not change much. A union organizer interviewed by the Lynds claimed that it was because of their obsession with automobiles that workers in the town proved so hard to unionize. "It's easy to see why our workers don't think very much about joining unions," he remarked, continuing, "So long as they [the workers] have a car and can borrow or steal a gallon of gas, they'll ride around and pay no attention to labor organization; and if they can't get gas, they're busy trying to figure out some way to get it. . . . The automobile always comes first" (1937, p. 26).

According to the Lynds, the automobile had come to symbolize "living, having a good time, the thing which keeps you working"—which is why the worker "clings" to it with such "tenacity" (1937, p. 245). Evidence of the importance of car ownership as rationalization for work can also be found in Eli Chinoy's postwar investigation of autoworkers. In research conducted two decades or so after the Middletown studies, Chinoy found, much as the Lynds had, that the automobile had a central place in anchoring people to their jobs. One worker, reflecting on the reasons for his having been stuck in his factory job for so long, commented: "It's my own fault. I was going to work here for a year after I graduated from high school, then be a printer's apprentice. . . . But then I bought a car, and that was my downfall. I couldn't afford to leave if I was going to have a car" (Chinoy 1955, p. 124).

Why should the car have had such significance for the Lynds' wage earning informants? Why was owning and driving an automobile so important? At one point the Lynds mention that part of the appeal of motor cars was the opportunity driving offered families for spending time together. Yet presumably a family stroll would be just as, if not more, effective in that regard. Of course, cars could, and sometimes did, serve as positional goods, signifying the purchasing power, and associated status, of their owners. But the power of automobiles to signify status does not by itself seem sufficient to account for the obsession with them. Presumably any one of many expensive goods could serve as a sign of the wealth required to buy them—why the singular focus on cars rather than, for example, jewelry or some other commodity? A simple needs-based explanation also seems less than convincing, as the Lynds' eth-nographic work was done in a small town in the 1920s and early 1930s, before the postwar era of suburban sprawl and "mallification," which made driv-ing increasingly necessary on practical grounds. As noted earlier, the Lynds' informants categorized automobiles as a luxury rather than a necessity.

Perhaps part of the explanation is that cars seemed uniquely to represent freedom and that exercising agency is what "living"—as opposed to the get-ting of a living, by working—means. The Lynds draw attention to a line in an automobile advertisement, "Hit the Trail to Better Times," suggesting that this slogan indicates that the car was powerfully symbolic of agency, expressed in peoples' capacity to transform their life circumstances (1929, p. 256). This was (and still is) very much in line with the tendency for car advertisements never just to show automobiles doing quotidian things but rather to depict vehicles driven on endless open roads through dramatic landscapes, headed to destinations that could change at the whim of the person behind the wheel. Cars represented the antithesis of work, converting the wage into a thing with an almost mythical association with freedom. The automobile was thus well suited to serve as compensation for work, a counterbalance to the loss of freedom represented by having to sell labor for a wage. However, that interpretation leads back to the same question: Why exactly did automobiles have that kind of symbolic force?

One possible answer lies in the way in which the automobile could, more than any other commodity, function as a kind of extension of the worker's embodied will. The pleasure in driving was the sense of expanded agency, the capacity for the will to transcend the limitations of the body. The deficit of agency experienced in wage work—the diminishing of the will that fol-lowed the subordination of the body to capital—perhaps seemed compen-sated for by the extended powers acquired through the ownership of cars. If that is right, then automobiles did not just index the status associated with the money required to buy them, but also a kind of augmented individual agency, facilitated by their technical capacities. In this sense, the motor-car pointed to itself as much as to its owner, its power and panache working as a potent symbol of freedom and transcendence. The workers of Middletown drove primarily not for instrumental purposes but just for the sheer joy of it—for the sense of empowerment imparted by driving. The pleasure of pos-sessing a car was, however, not just realized in the moment, during the activ-ity of driving, but derived also from "pride of ownership"—from the feeling of possessing an object endowed with the powers that cars are endowed with. In owning a motor car, workers possessed a store of use power, of hypothetical possibility, of a kind that extended their natural capabilities in a fashion that, to some extent, made up for their diminishment at work.[21] Car ownership in this way worked supremely well as commensurable compensation for the loss of free activity represented by wage work.

3.3. "Getting a Living" and "Getting Ahead"

A very important topic in the Lynds' analysis, one that comes up repeatedly, is attitudes to the business of "getting a living." The phrase itself is telling, in that it suggests a separation between the business of living and the business of working—work is a means for living rather than a part of living. The Lynds tell us that for their working informants, "living" is something that occurs in their leisure time. Given limited social mobility, it is not surprising that, according to the Lynds, Middletown's wage earning class attached much more importance to direct leisure than to occupational attainment. Members of Middletown's "business class," on the other hand, saw the point of work not as simply "getting a living" but as "getting ahead," which meant social advancement.

Two decades after the second Middletown study, Eli Chinoy (1955) paints a somewhat different picture of his working-class informants. For Chinoy's autoworkers, the key concept was not "getting a living" but, like the business class of Middletown, "getting ahead." On Chinoy's interpretation, the importance of "getting ahead" for the autoworkers he studied indicated that they had embraced some version of what he calls the "American dream"—a vague vision of life as defined by opportunity, agency, self-making, and progress. But, significantly, for Chinoy's autoworkers "getting ahead" did not mean occupational mobility but rather the accumulation of material commodities—what Chinoy describes as "a quantitative increase in things within the reach of everyone" (p. 134). Unlike the workers of Middletown, Chinoy's autoworkers were unionized. The union was seen primarily as a means for increasing purchasing power, in order to fund more commodity accumulation. While the labor organizers interviewed by the Lynds saw workers' preoccupation with material objects as a distraction from the kind of class consciousness that would inspire them to join unions, Chinoy's workers embraced labor politics precisely because they saw their union as an effective means to the end of higher wages and increasing material accumulation. This change in attitude fits with Meg Jacobs's (2005) history of the ascent of the politics of purchasing power in the postwar period.[22]

Defining "getting ahead" as material accumulation rather than occupational mobility made sense in a context in which there were limited opportunities for advancement at work. Autoworkers in the 1950s were under no illusions about the constraints of their class position. The different groups of workers interviewed in the 1950s by Chinoy—and, in separate studies, by Guest, and Berger—all expressed pessimism about their chances of upward occupational mobility. In research, conducted in the mid-1950s, on attitudes of autoworkers, Richard Guest found that while workers aspired to improve their jobs, at the same time they had little faith that it would happen. Some 60.7 percent of young workers and 81.5 percent of older workers rated their chances of occupational mobility as "poor or no chance" (Guest 1954, p. 158). Indeed, Guest concludes his article by commenting on the degree to which the findings of his survey echo those of Chinoy's ethnographic study. Guest's workers, like Chinoy's, were in general quite negative about their jobs and bleakly realistic about their chances for upward occupational mobility. Chinoy notes that workers often mentioned their long-term plans to escape the factory and go into business, yet he observes that these plans typically did not lead to action. Bennet Berger's ethnography of a suburban community of autoworkers in the late 1950s, like Guest's research, also echoes Chinoy's findings on attitudes to social mobility. Berger found that the workers he interviewed were very much resigned to spending their lives in the factory. Of his interviewees, 94 percent reported that they thought of their jobs as "permanent," and only 3 percent reported "keeping their eyes open for something better" (Berger [1961] 1970, p. 16).

Like the workers described by the Lynds, Chinoy's informants tended to find meaning not in their work but in their leisure time activities. One thing shared by Chinoy's workers and those of the Middletown studies is a sense of profound alienation from their work. "The things I like about my job are quitting time, pay day, days off, and vacations," lamented one of Chinoy's (1955, p. 85) informants. Another informant, whose opinion, according to Chinoy, was quite representative of those of the workers he spoke with, commented that his satisfactions came from "the things I do when I get home" (p. 132).[23] "Their main interests lie in the things they do in their leisure hours" notes Chinoy (p. 115). Yet, unlike the Lynds' workers, those interviewed by Chinoy associated the idea of "getting ahead" with the project of using the wage to accumulate commodities. On Chinoy's assessment, "advancement has come to mean the progressive accumulation of things as well as the increasing capacity to consume." As one worker interviewed by Chinoy explained: "A lot of people think getting ahead means getting to be a millionaire. Not for me though. If I can just increase the value of my possessions as the years go by instead of just breaking even or falling behind, if I can keep adding possessions and property, . . . I'll figure I got ahead quite a bit" (p. 126). Similarly, another worker averred, "We're all working for one purpose—to get ahead," continuing, "I don't think a person should be satisfied. My next step is a nice modern home of my own. That's what I mean by bettering yourself—or getting ahead" (p. 126). The definition of getting ahead was, then, to a large extent couched in terms of the accumulation of material possessions. Chinoy summarized the attitude as follows: "If one manages to buy a new car, if each year sees a major addition to the household—a washing machine, a refrigerator, a new living room suite, now probably a television set—then one is getting ahead" (p. 126).

Chinoy (1955, p. 126) saw this attitude as indicating a tension between the constraints of class and the valorization of ambition and social mobility: "American culture encourages men to seek both occupational advancement and the acquisition of material possessions. But workers who respond to both of these admonitions use the second to rationalize their failure to achieve the first." His interpretation is thus essentially psychological: "Workers . . . try to maintain the illusion of persisting ambition by extending the meaning of advancement to include the acquisition of personal possessions" (p. 130). According to Chinoy: "In order to convince themselves that they are getting ahead and that they are not without ambition, workers apply to the ends they pursue the vocabulary of the tradition of opportunity. They extend the meaning of ambition to include the search for security, the pursuit of small goals in the factory, and the constant accumulation of personal possessions" (p. 124). Despite expressing deep dissatisfaction with their jobs, Chinoy's informants regarded them as basically acceptable to the degree that, in exchange for their alienated labor, they were able to accumulate consumer commodities.

But what might it mean to "get ahead" by way of the accumulation of commodities? One interpretation would be that "getting ahead" was about status competition by way of conspicuous consumption. On this understanding, the urge to "get ahead" is a more competitive version of the imperative to "keep up" with the Joneses. What workers sought, perhaps preemptively, to "get ahead" of were their friends, workmates, and neighbors. Yet a status-focused interpretation of the acquisition of commodities seems odd, because the setting of Chinoy's study was a community in which occupational status was relatively fixed. While a few autoworkers harbored dreams of eventually going into business for themselves in some capacity, most felt that all they could hope for was social mobility for their children. In contexts in which everyone is stuck in more or less the same kind of job, the only thing conspicuous consumption is going to index is likelihood of being in debt.

Of course, a person's occupational status is not necessarily public knowledge. Perhaps, therefore, workers acquired goods in order to use them to project higher status than they actually had. However, status display of that sort only works in certain kinds of settings. In their Middletown studies, the Lynds offer the very general Veblenesque speculation that as cities grow in size, so conspicuous consumption becomes more important. This is because increasing anonymity entails that "personal means of placing oneself in the group, involving considerations of the kind of person one is, yield to more quickly determinable, shorthand symbols, namely what one owns" (Lynd and Lynd 1929, p. 467).[24] But the informants in Chinoy's and in the Lynds' studies inhabited relatively small towns (Lansing was smaller than Muncie, but both had populations of less than 100,000) with fairly cohesive communities, one major employer, and social and spatial segregation along class lines. In that kind of setting, it is likely that people would have a good sense of what others do for a living, making it difficult to successfully "fake" high status through ostentatious display of goods. Moreover, none of the workers interviewed in the Lynd and Chinoy studies say anything to indicate that the motivation for accumulating commodities is to shore up or improve their status position. To be sure, informants would perhaps not care to admit as much, even if it was true. Yet Chinoy emphasizes the marked degree to which his autoworkers had low self-esteem and were in general quite self-deprecating and resigned to their station in life. As noted, the industrial workers he interviewed felt very much fixed in their status and saw only very limited opportunities for social mobility. While they spoke of "getting ahead" to describe the accumulation of goods, there is no suggestion that they felt that accumulating things would improve their status in any deep and meaningful sense. It does not, therefore, seem likely that the point of the preoccupation with material accumulation that Chinoy draws our attention to was simply to gain position in the status hierarchy.

In addition, research in the 1950s by the sociologist William H. Whyte presents some evidence that a new mode of consumption was emerging in the 1950s, the point of which was precisely *not* to stand out from neighbors but rather to conform to the appropriate group standard. Whyte (1954) claimed, in his work on social life in the suburbs, to have discovered a tendency toward *inconspicuous* consumption. This style of consumption reflected a desire to fit in with prevailing consumption norms rather than one-upmanship. Supporting Whyte's analysis, David Riesman and Howard Roseborough (1955) note the extent to which, by the mid-1950s, consumption was organized into "standard packages," the contents of which varied by social class. According to Riesman and Roseborough, for most people consumption was about acquiring a set of material objects that conforms to the standard package appropriate to their class rather than making a symbolic claim to a status higher than others in their reference group. Of course, class standards for consumption were dynamic rather than fixed. As real income increased for a social stratum, new commodities would be added to its standard set. In line with this collective, class-organized picture of consumption, Chinoy notes that unions were seen as a means for gaining access for the entire group of workers to an improved set of consumer commodities. The objective was the collective advancement of all workers represented by the union. "Getting ahead," then, could mean at least two different things. For individuals, it could mean acquiring the set of goods that comprises the standard package for their class. But it could also mean a whole group increasing its wages so that its standard package of wage goods could be upgraded. As an aside, one precondition for standard packages of consumption goods is that products themselves are *standardized*—a point I will explore at greater length in the next chapter.

An alternative interpretation of what it means to "get ahead," already touched on in this chapter, is that it was understood in intergenerational terms, as the accumulation of capital that could then be used to support upward mobility in workers' offspring. There is evidence in these studies that to some degree this was the case. Chinoy's informants, as do the Lynds', tell him of their desire to not have their children enter the factory. Similarly, the autoworkers interviewed by Berger mention their ambitions for their children to attend college. But, as we have seen, aggregate spending and saving patterns in the United States do not lend strong support to that interpretation. If the motivation to "get ahead" was to ensure intergenerational mobility, then surely savings rates would be higher than they in fact were in the United States over the course of the twentieth century. Moreover, the ethos expressed by Chinoy's workers was much more "work to spend" than "work to save."

The materialist aspirations underlying the preoccupation with "getting ahead" are consistent with the theory developed in this book. As we saw in Chapter 3, by the 1950s, work hours per week had become fairly stable—year-on-year, they were dropping little, if at all. At the same time real wages and spending were steadily increasing, with a good proportion of the spending directed toward consumer durables. What "getting ahead" via commodity accumulation might have meant for wage workers in that context was improving the ratio between subjection to labor and ownership of goods that represented the opposite of labor. If goods roughly translate into congealed free activity time, then, as workers acquire more of them, the amount of free time stored in their accumulated wage goods increases relative to the time given up as work. "Getting ahead," seen this way, means accumulating an ever-greater surplus of potential use power, stored in wage goods, over the ongoing loss of time to work. Even at low levels of income, this kind of accumulation could seemingly progressively diminish the difference between the loss of time to work and the activity time represented by the goods afforded by the wage.

Chinoy and the Lynds describe worlds within which the accumulation of consumer commodities justifies, or at least rationalizes, otherwise alienating work. For Chinoy's autoworkers, the accumulation of commodities, to a significant extent, defines what it is to "get ahead." This would suggest that the exchange of labor for a wage had become acceptable by virtue of the increasing purchasing power of that wage. As long as the purchasing power of the wage allowed workers feel that they were making "progress" by increasing the quantity and improving the quality of the commodities they own, the underlying exchange was at least arguably legitimate and potentially fair. This certainly does not mean that work was enjoyable. There is, as noted, plenty of evidence of alienation among workers in Chinoy's and in the Lynds' ethnographies. Yet the attitude of wage workers in both cases is one of resignation. Wage labor, by comparison with earlier periods, had become a quasi-naturalized "fact of life," one that was tolerable to the extent that it allowed for material "progress," by way of commodity acquisition. This is in stark contrast to the attitudes to wage labor described by labor historians of the nineteenth and early twentieth centuries—which, as described earlier in this chapter, called into question the very legitimacy of wage labor as an institution. The data on nineteenth-century wage earners analyzed by Dora Costa suggest that "getting ahead," for them, meant using increases in wages to progressively reduce the temporal duration of their subjection to work (Dora Costa 2000a). It seems likely that what those earlier wage earners had sought to "get ahead" of was a capitalist system that would extract as much labor power from them, and therefore as much of their time and energy, as possible.

SIX

Standardization of Consumption, Work, and Wages

In Chapter 4, I suggested that if consumer objects had been thought about in a more contextual, practice-centered fashion, then wage earners would have pushed harder for increasing productivity to be realized as more free time rather than focusing primarily on higher real income. I went on to argue that the apparent absence of strong consideration of the contextual conditions on commodity use makes more sense when seen in relation to the emergence of a particular understanding of wage labor. On this understanding, the wage relation is potentially fair, and therefore fundamentally legitimate, only insofar as it represents an exchange of commensurable substances. However, it is not at all obvious on what grounds the life activity sold as labor and the wage received in return, are commensurable. Indeed, as discussed in the last chapter, for much of the nineteenth century the popular criticism of wage labor was that it involves the sale of something that is essentially inalienable and for that reason has something in common with slavery. I suggested that the wage is rendered commensurable with labor by virtue of an interpretation of consumer commodities as congealed quantities of potential utility (use power), imagined as durations of free activity. As wage labor took on increasing legitimacy through this particular mechanism of commensurability, wage earners became primed to view the use value of commodity objects in a relatively decontextualized manner. Objects of consumption began to index durations of hypothetical free activity, with the question of the availability of time to actually realize their use value pushed into the background. Thus the availability of "congealed time" in the form of consumer durables obscured the question of real free time.

Change in understandings of wage labor is, however, only one side of the picture. The other side, which is the topic of the present chapter and the two that follow, concerns the ways in which commodities were presented to the consumer. Beginning in the early decades of the twentieth century, a set of developments took place that had the effect of reframing objects of consumption, focusing attention on the commodity-in-itself, as opposed to the commodity-in-use. These developments both reflected and at the same time fed into the tendency for utility to be thought of primarily as a property of objects rather than as a product of real practices, in the course of which objects are actually put to use. The set of developments were quite large in scale. They include the stabilization of the physical properties of products so that products became more uniform, the rise of product brands, changes in the legal (and underlying moral) framing of the entitlement of consumers to useful products, and the emergence and institutionalization of consumer product testing. These developments took place against the background of the rapid standardization of the economy—a complex and multifaceted process that became a subject of intense discussion, especially during the first three decades of the twentieth century. It was the standardization of consumer products (as well as work and the wage) that made it possible to think of the wage as commensurable with the time and effort given up in exchange for it. Standardization in part reflected the coalescing of a new moral economy under industrial capitalism, in which wage-labor exchange was rendered fair by virtue of the purchasing power of the wage over consumer commodities that signified stores of potential activity.

Standardization is typically taken to refer to efforts to coordinate production in an industrial economy, with the objective of reducing the costs of production. Although originating in the sphere of production, however, standardization also came to have a significant impact on consumption, with implications for the meaning of consumer goods. It was standardized goods that drove the early mass consumer market—the model T Ford being the paradigmatic example. In addition to standardized consumer products, standardization in the sphere of consumption was manifested in the development of consumer brands, which indexed regular and predictable product characteristics, and the emergence of warranties for consumer durables, which signaled commitments on the part of firms to ensure that goods would perform as advertised. Those who promoted standardization often described its benefits in terms of higher-quality and more reliable consumer products. This was reflected in the early years of the twentieth century in the emphasis marketing campaigns put on the mechanical properties of products. The standardized commodity was supposed to be a transparent and stable container of utility, even as the increasing technological complexity of consumer goods rendered them ever more black-box like. As goods themselves became standardized, so too did the means of their distribution, as the chain store model of retail spread rapidly across the economy in the later nineteenth and early twentieth centuries.

Standardization also came to influence consumption through the regulation and testing of consumer goods. Systematic product testing has its origins in the work of early corporate laboratories. Independent testing was first conducted by state agencies such as the National Bureau of Standards, the Bureau of Chemistry, and the Federal Drug Administration, followed by various nongovernmental consumer advocacy organizations. The results of product testing eventually became regular content in a wide range of periodicals and other kinds of media, coming to perform a watchdog function, by working to ensure that manufactured products lived up to acceptable levels of functionality. Somewhat orthogonal to these developments were fundamental changes in the legal regulation of consumer transactions, with a gradual shift, over a period of about a century, in the locus of risk bearing from consumer to producer. These legal developments established contractual entitlements for consumers, in the form of the implied warranty, to what was considered fair and reasonable amounts of use value from the commodities they purchased.

In concert, these developments had the effect of presenting consumer goods as congealed quantities of potential utility, to which consumers were viewed as being entitled. Yet the exact nature of the entitlement is unclear. It did not follow automatically from the general ethical precepts that developed with markets—or from the noncontractual moral framework within which market contract became possible—because the strong version of consumer entitlement emerged only in the twentieth century. That was much later than the emergence of market society itself, which is typically dated to the eighteenth century in England, and the early nineteenth century in the United States (Polanyi 1957; Stanley 1998; Larson 2009). Indeed, for much of the nineteenth century the legal principle governing market transactions in the

United States was *caveat emptor*, meaning that the consumer was responsible for ascertaining whether products would perform in a satisfactory manner (Hamilton 1931). So the growing influence of the principle that consumers have a strong moral entitlement to "fair" quantities of use value from the goods they purchased has to have a more historically proximate explanation.

I would suggest that the explanation has to do with the grounds on which wage labor became acceptable as a legitimate form of exchange. In the context of the moral economy of wage-labor exchange, consumers were seen as being entitled to fair quantities of use value in the commodities they acquired. The assumption was that consumers deserve decent products in exchange for their hard-earned wages. Reflecting this moral imperative, the state was increasingly viewed as responsible for ensuring fair exchange in the consumer marketplace. The right of consumers to high-quality, functional goods was a natural extension of the right of wage earners to fair levels of compensation. On the one hand, commodities, viewed as stores of potential free activity, made the wage—the purchasing power of which was measured in quantities of these commodities—more easily commensurable with labor. At the same time, the urge, on the part of wage earners and capitalists alike, to make wage labor thinkable as a potentially fair exchange of equivalent substances contributed to a tendency for commodities to be represented so as to facilitate this—that is, as standard quantities of potential utility. The sense of consumer entitlement that emerged around the turn of the twentieth century has then much to do with the increasing influence of the idea of wage labor as a fair form of exchange that was outlined in the last chapter. Wage labor became legitimate insofar as the purchasing power of the wage became stable and quantifiable, such that it could represent a capacity to capture a set of use values potentially sufficient to compensate workers for their loss of free life activity to labor. Standardized products, which were promoted on the basis of their predictable qualities, and the quantity, transparency, and robustness of their useful powers, provided a means by which purchasing power became more easily imaginable, and in this way provided a kind of material-cultural substrate for the legitimacy of wage labor in the era of mass production.

The remainder of this chapter consists of a general discussion of standardization, primarily as it became manifested in the sphere of consumption. The purpose of this discussion is twofold. First it sets up the context in which the more particular features of standardization that I go on to analyze— the development of brands, commercial warranties, the emergence of the implied warranty, and consumer product testing—should be interpreted. Second it draws attention to the fact that standardization, especially where it concerned commodities meant for final consumption, was understood in moral as well as technical terms. As noted, the moral dimension of standardization has to do with the increasing sense that consumers deserve clear and fair quantities of use value from the commodities they received in exchange for their earnings. In making this argument, I draw extensively on the discussions that took place about standardization in the first three decades of the twentieth century while also analyzing institutional developments accompanying the shift to standardized goods. Following this general account of standardization, Chapters 7 and 8 go on to examine certain aspects of standardization in more detail. These include the rapid expansion of brands as signs of standardized consumer products, the emergence of the standardized commercial warranty, and the regulation of standardized products by way of consumer product testing.

1. Varieties of Standardization

Standardization, in economic terms, primarily refers to various efforts to rationalize the economy, encompassing both production and consumption.[1] In the secondary literature, three kinds of standardization are identified, as are three methods whereby standardization is implemented. The three general categories are standardization of product performance, standardization of measurement, and standardization to ensure compatibility between parts. The modes of implementation of standardization are de facto, where standards evolve spontaneously; de jure, which is standardization imposed by government regulation; and voluntary consensus, where various interested parties come together to agree on standards (Tate 2001; Russell 2008). The major agencies implementing or promoting standardization have been the state, business, professional organizations, the judiciary, unions, and various social movements, especially the consumer movement.

While standards of various sorts are probably, as sociologist Lawrence Busch (2011) has suggested, as old as culture itself, the concept of standardization has fairly recent origins.[2] The earliest recorded appearance of the term *standardize*, according to the Oxford English Dictionary, is in 1873, used in relation to chemical solutions. Similarly, *standardization* was first used, in 1896, in the context of pharmaceuticals. The first recorded use of the either term to denote economic rationalization occurred in 1901 (the year in which the Bureau of Standards was created).[3] Over the next three decades there was a veritable explosion of discourse about standards and standardization. If the number of newspaper titles in which the term appears is any indication of the topicality and urgency of the issue, the most intense period of discussion about standardization clearly took place in the first half of the century, especially between 1910 and 1930.[4] Talk about the issue subsided in the postwar era, although in the 1990s it increased again with discussions about standards in information and communications technology. In the first half of the century, the term is most commonly used in accord with its social scientific sense, to refer to the standardization of economic production. However, across the whole century the word has a multitude of meanings, used variously to refer to the rationalization of wages, to a tendency toward aesthetic conformity, and often as a vague term to denote a principle diametrically opposed to individuality and creativity.[5]

The rise of the concept of standardization coincided with the tail end of the second industrial revolution—the electrification and mechanization of the American economy, which took place roughly between 1880 and 1920. Common standards were needed in order to efficiently apply the new technologies that emerged in that era to industrialized mass production.[6] But although standardization is often associated with modernization, it was not, as economists have tended to suggest, an automatic consequence of market-led economic development. Standardization was a project as much as a developmental process, championed with great enthusiasm by its advocates, and actively promoted by a set of actors who arguably constituted a movement of sorts. It was led by crusading engineers, technocratic-minded politicians, and consumer activists, as well as by business figures—and indeed many of its most prominent promoters, people such as Herbert Hoover, Frederick J. Schlink, and Arthur Kallet, were several of those things at once.

Some sense of the fervor with which people took up the cause of standardization is indicated by a sign hanging over the door in 1910 of the superintendent of equipment of the Brooklyn Rapid Transit Co. building, which served as a mission statement for the department: "Early to bed and early to Rise / Work like hell—to standardize."[7] In response to criticisms of the standardization movement in 1923, Albert W. Whitney, chairman of the American Engineering Standards Committee, issued a robust defense. Standardization, he proclaimed, lies "at the bottom of both natural evolution and of civilization" and amounts to "essentially only the selection of the best among a mass of the inferior." It "not only opens the way to a fuller material life, but it is a condition which makes the spiritual life possible."[8] So pervasive was this new gospel of standardization that some commentators felt the need to deflate its claims: "Standardization is not by any means the new and revolutionary thing that efficiency engineers and scientific managers would have you believe. Standardization is in fact as old as the hills," we are told in a short piece in the *Chicago Defender*, which went on to cite as examples of premodern standardized products buggy wheels, circus rings, and ladders.[9]

The most intense period of concern about standardization, during which the term became common currency in discussions about the workings of the economy, was the first three decades of the twentieth century. During those years, the passion for standardization was directed toward all parts of the economy, from raw materials to manufactured goods, styles of construction, regulations, and measures and weights. Urgent calls were made for the standardization of a vast range of materials, products, and services, including public utilities, freight cars, trucks, automobiles, traffic control systems, munitions, currency, education, color charts, textiles, all manner of produce, credit arrangements, real estate agent qualifications, worker's accident compensation rates, tennis balls, golf balls, bowling balls, the list goes on and on. There were even appeals for the standardization of methods of evangelizing. Reverend A. N. Archibald of Lowell, Massachusetts, surveying in 1918 what he took to be the dismal state of the national evangelical mission, concluded that the essence of the problem was a deficit of standardized method.[10] "There can be no success in this [spiritual] war without standardization," he pronounced, continuing: "If the fight is to be won swiftly, definitely, and completely, evangelism and its methods must be standardized."[11] In the early decades of the century standardization was frequently identified as an element of the zeitgeist: "This is an age of the standardization of everything" announced a piece in the *San Francisco Chronicle*, an opinion frequently echoed in newspapers and periodicals.[12] In the first *Yearbook* issued by the American Engineering Standards Committee in 1927, standardization was breathlessly described as "the outstanding note of this century," reaching "the remotest details of our industrial regime" and making use of "all sources of scientific knowledge and [affecting] every phase of design, production, and utilization" (quoted in Cochrane 1966, p. 256).[13] Indeed such was the enthusiasm for standardization in this period that it became a target for humorous comment. The

Los Angeles Times, for example, ran a piece in 1930 in response to standard specifications issued by the National Bureau of Standards, the federal organization responsible for overseeing standardization, for mop sticks: "Recently the Bureau devised an instrument to measure the energy required to fold a sample of fabric, the energy recovered when the sample is allowed to unfold. Describing how this device is used, *Textile Maintenance Notes* reports that 'the energy lost when a sample is folded is dissipated in producing a crease in the fabric. This energy loss . . . may be taken as a measure of the wrinkle ability of the fabric.'" The piece goes on to make the droll observation that similar thinking could be applied to "the powder ability of nutmegs . . . the eraser ability of rubbers," asking "are there any standards for shoelace tips, key rings or soup ladles? If not, why not?"[14] This piece of satire draws attention to the way in which consumer commodities were standardized, in essence, to the degree that they came to be measurable as precise quantities of stored usefulness; for although standardization began as a diffuse project to rationalize production, it soon came to encompass consumption.

Opinion about the trend toward standardization of the economy was far from being uniformly positive. There were dissenting voices, together forming a rather consistent current of opinion that bemoaned the alienating character of a standardized world. Some expressed the fear that standardization would slow or even halt the march of industrial progress by ossifying techniques of production and product design. "It has never been my experience that 'standardization' means the cessation of active improvement" commented one industry spokesperson, trying to allay this fear.[15] Others were concerned that standardization would result in the death of competition and the rise of monopolies (Hoyt 1919). A more typical complaint was that with standardization comes monotonous uniformity, the collapsing of all that is unique and interesting into bland repetition—a bleak vision of industrial society that resonates with Chaplin's in "Modern Times."[16] The worry that standardized production would lead to a standardization of values was very much in line with theories later developed by the members of the Frankfurt School: "The effort of the reformers seems to be to standardize the world. To standardize its commerce, its morals, its religion and everything else," complained one commentator.[17] Another voiced fears that standardization would soon creep into creative literature, with the effect of expunging the "creative" from literature.[18] Concern was also expressed that standardization would somehow debase the "art" of politics.[19] Standardization of things would, according to this critical current of opinion, inexorably leads to standardization of people.[20] Thus, perhaps reflecting a more general dichotomy in discourses about modernity, there were two opposed visions of standardization, one that pictured it as an essentially progressive force, the other that saw in it a threat to human values. Opinion about standardization was sufficiently divided that one commentator opined: "If the controversy about standardization keeps up, there will soon develop a pro and anti-standardization party in this country."[21]

Despite the variety of things and processes to which the term got applied, historians and social scientists have tended to interpret standardization primarily in terms of the logic of production in an industrial capitalist economy. The classic case study of industrial standardization is Alfred Chandler's (1977) account of the agreement on a standard gauge for railroad tracks in the nineteenth century. Chandler sees standardization as the means whereby technical economies of scale and scope were realized in a developing industrial economy. The increasingly complex division of labor after industrialization meant that there was pressure on firms and public organizations to agree to implement common standards for products and parts. Standardization provided a solution to coordination problems in integrated, technologically sophisticated national economies.[22]

But while standardization was certainly driven to a large extent by technical considerations of the kind described by Chandler, I want to approach the topic from a different angle, by emphasizing the significance of standardization in an emerging Fordist moral economy, at the core of which lay the relationship between wage labor and consumer entitlements. Standardization certainly served to increase the efficiency of industrial production, but at the same time, it entailed the stabilization of the properties of consumer commodities. The professed motivation for standardizing product properties was not just to make production more efficient but also to improve the quality, and especially the durability, of consumer products. The engineer's focus on product function thus came to inform the way in which consumer products were regarded more generally. Standardization thus concerned consumption as well as production. And the project of standardizing consumption was bound up in an emerging moral economy concerning the entitlement of wage-earning consumers to a fair share of the use values churned out by industrial production.

The importance of the perspective and interests of consumers in standardization is indicated by the fact that, when making decisions about product standards, the National Bureau of Standards (at least in theory) gave equal weight to input from consumers and industry.[23] The purpose of standardization, for the bureau, was to give "better value" to the consumer while also making the properties of products more transparent in the marketplace. So, while standardization was, to be sure, one part about the rationalization of production, it was also about endowing mass-produced consumer commodities with stable quantities of use value. Stabilizing the use value of commodities had the effect of reinforcing the moral economy underlying the wage relation, by facilitating what Meg Jacobs (2005) calls the "purchasing power paradigm." For Jacobs, the commitment to increasing the purchasing power of wage workers—a commitment that was shared by organized labor, the state, and to a significant extent industry also—defined the political economy of the great compromise that began to emerge in America in the 1930s and continued into the Golden Age years of the postwar period. Yet this focus on the purchasing power of the wage could only make sense if the quality of wage goods was reasonably stable and invariant. As mentioned earlier, this is because in order for purchasing power to be meaningfully measurable, the properties (and hence quality) of consumer goods must be held at least relatively constant. Standardized consumer goods were therefore an important element in what the political economists of the regulation school have described as the Fordist regime of accumulation (Aglietta [1977] 2000; Boyer 1990; Boyer and Saillard 2002).

The main forms of standardization over the first forty years of the twentieth century were standardization of production, standardization of products, standardization of measures, and standardization of wages. In the following sections, I give a brief overview of the issues at stake in each of these areas during those years. My objective is to give some sense of the overall shape of the preoccupation with standardization.

2. Standardization of Production

Standardized production was typically seen as a particular phase of industrial development, one that heralded the arrival of a brave new future. It was opposed to simple "manufacturing," the older approach to production, which the standardized approach was supposedly set to supersede. While with manufacturing, at least in its archetypical form, most of the parts of a product would be made in one factory, standardization involved the distribution of its production over an entire industry. This would be facilitated by increasingly complex forms of industrial organization, which could coordinate the production process across different factories and enterprises.[24] More generally, standardization entailed a regimentation of the economy around the principle of maximizing efficiency. In order to achieve deep efficiencies, standardization had to be extended from the sphere of production proper to distribution and consumption.

In 1925, the secretary of the American Standards Association, P. G. Agnew, gave a retrospective assessment of the accomplishments of the standardization movement over the previous two decades.[25] He noted that there had been a broad reorganization of American society around standardized systems, especially in production, where, alluding to Taylorism, standardized techniques had gone a long way toward eliminating "unnecessary motions." Looking forward at a bright future, Agnew predicted that further standardization "will make for efficiency and economy in production, distribution, and consumption."[26] Similar sentiments were expressed by other prominent industry figures. For example, Bernard Gherardi, vice-president of AT&T, in his retirement address chose to speak about the great progress made toward standardization since 1918.[27]

Standardization of production in the early twentieth century was most closely associated with the automobile industry. Inspired by the success of the standardization of railroads in the nineteenth century, auto manufacturers began very early on in the history of the car industry to create intercompany technical standards. These efforts, which were spear-headed by a combination of engineers and forward-looking industrialists, began in earnest around 1910. By the 1920s, other American manufacturing industries realized the usefulness of shared standards and embarked on similar standardizing projects (G. Thompson 1954).

Engineers were not just at the cutting edge of the standardization of the auto industry but also leaders of the broader standardization movement. They were to be found at the helm of standardizing projects in various state bodies and consumer organizations, as well as in a variety of industries. Their disparate efforts were brought together under the auspices of the American Engineering Standards Committee (AESC), founded in 1918, which actively worked to persuade businessmen of the benefits of standardization.[28] The AESC included nine engineering societies, seven government departments, and nineteen industry organizations, which met regularly with the aim of hammering out standards for all aspects of the economy.[29] The mission of the organization was to advance standardization against the often inefficient and chaotic ferment of the free market. The standardizing activities of engineers and their associations did not go unnoticed—in the popular press engineers were singled out for praise for their efforts to improve the economy.[30]

While standardization was supposed to bring some order to the chaos produced by unregulated competition, the standardizing work of engineers was also seen as a preferable alternative to state regulation.[31] The role of professional engineering organizations was to encourage voluntary standardization, as opposed to top-down standards imposed by government. Pioneering engineer and entrepreneur George Westinghouse, addressing a meeting of engineers from different national associations, including the American Society of Mechanical Engineers, the Boston Society of Civil Engineers, and the American Institute of Electrical Engineers, proclaimed: "By a combined effort of all the engineering societies, with the financial support of all manufacturers . . . it seems to me that such a bureau [of standardization] could be established and could work a reform of incalculable value in our present practice and thus forestall government activity in the same direction."[32] As Westinghouse's comments indicate, to an extent the voluntary movement toward shared standards on the part of business was motivated by a desire to preempt rulings by the National Bureau of Standards. In the vanguard of the effort to advance voluntary standardization was the Society of Automotive Engineers (SAE), which was founded in 1905. The standardization work of the SAE was widely known and, like that of other crusading engineering organizations, not infrequently extolled. An article in the Boston Globe described the SAE in the following glowing terms: "Its work is of interest not merely to the technician but to the layman who demands efficiency, safety and comfort in the use of his motor car, but who has little idea how largely these desired qualities are the fruit of vast research and labor."[33] Similarly, a piece in the New York Times to mark the twenty-fifth anniversary of the SAE depicted those who led the organization as the unsung heroes of the rise of the industry, saving the American consumer huge amounts of money as a result of production of standards for auto parts while conducting vitally important research on automobiles.[34]

The appeal of standardized production was then not just that it resonated with the efficiency-driven engineering mind-set. Standardization was also supposed to secure concrete material benefits for consumers. The 1930 *Year Book of American Standards,* for example, promised that standardization would offer great benefits to the "ultimate consumer."[35] At the same time, the interests of the consumer were seen as being in alignment with the broader goal of economic efficiency. J. N. Willya, maker of the Overland automobile, emphasized the advantages to consumers of standardized mass production: "Quantity of production gives quality of product. It also offers a fixed and definite dollar value to the consumer, much greater dollar for dollar than do the small operations of the concern that tries to accomplish big things on a small scale" [and all this is a result of the fact that] "standardization is absolute."[36] Harry Lord, of the Lord Auto Company made similar arguments about the new era of standardization, commenting that; "The automobile world is fast awakening to the importance of standardization. In standardization two great principles are involved. First, the elimination of useless and needless variations from the normal. In lessening the field of certainties, logically you enhance the opportunities for maximum efficiency. Second is the selection and combination into a single product of all that is most useful and best adapted to its purpose. . . . The motor vehicle industry [following an early period of disorder and chaos brought about by] countless crass attempts at individualism . . . is entering into the Utopian stage of standardization." Reduction of waste, improvements in efficiency, and the perfecting of products were seen as complementary consequences of standardization, distinct virtuous dimensions of the same process.

Various organs of the state were fully in support of the project to standardize the economy. In addition to the ongoing special work of the Bureau of Standards, standardization was more generally actively promoted by the Department of Commerce, especially in the early 1920s, under Herbert Hoover.[37] An engineer by training and a leading light of the efficiency movement, as Secretary of Commerce Hoover enthusiastically advocated "the elimination of waste in industry through standardization."[38] With this objective in mind, he created, in 1922, the Division of Simplified Practice, as a department within the Bureau of Standards. According to Hoover, the division was to be "the medium through which producers, distributers, and consumers could agree upon simplification of production by reducing the number of sizes and models of products" (quoted in Noble 1977, p. 81). From the point of view of the state, the benefits of standardization were increasing efficiency, improved and cheaper products for consumers, and greater economic stability. E. T. Pickard, chief of the textile division of the Department of Commerce, speaking at an industry meeting, affirmed with great enthusiasm the advantages of standardization for industry while also noting its broader importance for national wellbeing: "Standardization, simplification and the elimination of waste, when confined to reasonable measures and operations, may be interpreted in terms of national welfare. . . . They lead to stabilization of trade and industry and equilibrium of employment. The resulting economies of production and distribution enhance the purchasing powers of the consuming public, thus enabling them to enjoy a progressively higher standard of living."[39] The *New York Times* in 1919 published an article making a similar point, suggesting that the vicissitudes of industrial capitalism could be tamed by the mindful application of a standardized approach to production: "Debt to standardization: It Has Brought Order Out of Chaos in the Machinery World," ran the headline.[40] Thus, even before the era of Keynesian macroeconomic policy, standardized production, which entailed a coordinated economy, was seen as a means whereby economic stability could be maintained. The perspective of the Commerce Department was not, however, always shared by other government organizations. There was some suspicion that standardization of commodities would lead to monopoly. Indeed, rumors circulated in 1931 that the Federal Trade Commission would rule against guidelines for voluntary standardization drawn up by industry in collaboration with the Commerce Department (the FTC later denied that these rumors were true).[41]

In general, however, commentators placed great emphasis on the benefits of standardized production for product quality. "US auto manufacturing is distinguished by standardized production techniques" observed one journalist, continuing, "Europeans often think this results from a 'quantity technique,' but in fact it is all about quality control."[42] There were in fact real advancements in that area during the interwar years. Modern quality control techniques were invented in the 1930s by A. Shewhart, who, while working for AT&T, developed the first systematic manufacturing product inspection regime, employing statistical sampling of product characteristics to ensure that basic design parameters were being met (Busch 2011, pp. 126–29). The ultimate benefit of standardized production was supposed to be the improved quality offered by standardized products as well as cost savings to the consumer.

3. Standardization of Products

Standardized techniques of production thus yielded standardized products, and standardization was most often justified by the supposedly superior characteristics of those products. For some, the benefits of standardized products were continuous with those of standardized production—uniform products would make society as a whole more efficient. Herbert Hoover, for example, felt that the standard of living for the American people would be raised if they could be persuaded to buy a smaller range of more standardized products. He consequently advocated a great "elimination of styles" of consumer goods in order to increase the overall efficiency of the economy and improve living standards.[43] As president, Hoover continued to advocate strongly for standardization, defending the practice in trenchant terms during a 1931 radio talk: "Critics talk about the evils of standardization. Well standardization helps individualism; the standardization of bathtubs and radios, motor cars and a thousand other things actually built up individualism by increasing the horizon of the individual; by adding to his chances, his comforts and his opportunities."[44] P. G. Agnew, secretary of the American Standards Association, made explicit the connection between the standardization of commodities and raising the living standards of the population to middle-class levels. Standardized products, endowed with substantial and precisely measured amounts of utility, would, according to Agnew, facilitate a felicitous embourgeoisement of the population. Agnew consequently urged that all products be made to conform to national specifications, averring that "such a regulation would constitute a major advance in national economy."[45] The National Bureau of Standards certainly made a heroic effort to comply with Agnew's wishes. In 1931, it published a ten-volume encyclopedia of product specifications, while offering a certification program for manufacturers whose products were in compliance with the specifications.[46] Lyman Briggs (1934, p. 154), director of the NBS, claimed that the advantage of specification standards for consumers was that they "established quality as a basis for competition among manufacturers." The Bureau of Home Economics, a division of the Department of Agriculture established in 1923, with responsibility for "homemaking," went even further, pushing specifically for government imposed specifications for consumer commodities (Lynd 1933, p. 884). By the late 1930s, the Federal Trade Commission was actively promoting what it described as "permissive standards" for goods—those arrived at and policed by associations of producers—as part of its effort to establish fair trade practices.[47]

Part of the motivation behind pinning down products through the creation of standard specifications was the felt need to bring some stability to what was becoming a very dynamic marketplace for consumer products, especially durables. The idea was that standard specifications for goods, made accessible to the public through certification and labeling, would bring some clarity to what had become a confusing flux of consumer products. Economist Charles Wyland (1937) reports that in 1928 the US consumer market offered around 1,000 brands of canned peach, 2,500 brands of perfume, and 10,000 brands of wheat flour. In the late 1920s, sewing machine needles came in nine diameters and varied in length by as little as one-thirty-second of an inch (Chase and Schlink 1927, p. 174)). Robert S. Lynd noted in 1934 that "in a single city the size of Milwaukee, the consumer must choose from among 250 kinds of toothbrushes, 100 kinds of washing machines, 160 kinds of fountain pens, 50 kinds of motor oil and so on through the long list of things he must buy," while a department store like Macy's offered 350,000 "possible choices" (p. 6). Standardization would, so its advocates argued, incrementally reduce this chaotic plenitude of products to a more manageable selection of choices. But the justification for standard specifications for commodities to which most weight was given was that standards would establish minimum acceptable quality levels for products.[48]

While the National Bureau of Standards cooperated with the American Standards Association (ASA), which represented industry, in creating standards, it was not clear that both organizations were on the same page when it came to protecting the public interest. When in 1933 the Department of Commerce suggested for budgetary reasons that the functions of the Division of Simplification be outsourced to the ASA, the response from the standards community was sufficiently negative that the Commerce Department was moved to reconsider the matter. "There can be no substitute for standards promulgated by or under Federal auspices," commented Dr. F. M. Williams, chairman of the Home Economic Association's Committee of Consumer Standards.[49] Robert Lynd, who was a prominent member of the Consumers Advisory Board, which had been set up by Roosevelt as part of the National Recovery Administration, went even further. He wrote a well-publicized report (the 'Lynd Report') in which he suggested that both the ASA and the NBS were too beholden to business (Agnew 1934).

The greater efficiency with which standardized goods could be produced, of course, meant cheaper product prices, and much was made of the savings passed on to consumers. According to one estimate, given by the Society of Automotive Engineers, the standardization of parts and the pooling of patents by 1930 were in combination responsible for reducing the cost of automobiles by 30 percent.[50] However, the advantage of standardized products was not just a matter of their cheapness. In addition, standardized products were, as we have seen, represented as being more reliable, more uniform in quality, and more transparent in function. The idiosyncratic and therefore often unpredictable products of the prestandardized era were to be replaced by standardized products with stable and regular properties. The point of standardization, as early consumer activists Stuart Chase and Frederick Schlink put it, was to set standards for consumer goods, which would ensure "performing excellence" in products, while forcing "persistently inferior types off the market altogether."[51]

The connection between standardization and product quality was clearly laid out by H. M. Leland, general manager of Cadillac: "You may call me rabid if you like on the subject of standardization, but sooner or later, every man who buys a touring car will insist on this qualification before every other . . . why should the buyer of an automobile not be entitled to the same degree of mechanical certainty that is guaranteed to the buyer of a sewing machine or typewriter?"[52] The durability of standardized goods was an ongoing theme for Leland, who declared two years later: "We are actually face to face, today, with motor cars which will last the ordinary lifetime of the average owner— or at any rate, grow old in his service; or in the service of subsequent purchasers. It is all a question of standardization. All over the country there are cars in service which are as sound and as efficient as the day they were built eight years ago. These cars endure because they possess a peculiar element of vitality which results, to put it crudely, from the perfection with which one part fits into its component part; and the harmony of operation that exists between all the parts which constitute the car as a whole. . . . The greater [the] degree of standardization, the lesser the degree of friction, the longer the life."[53] Especially in the auto industry, standardization of products was primarily represented as being about increasing durability—standardizing parts would ensure longer lasting, more durable vehicles.[54]

The greater durability of the standardized automobile was to be accompanied by improved reliability. Journalist F. E. Moskovics, writing in 1910, drew attention to the reliability of standardized cars.[55] A publicity spokesman for car maker Abbott-Detroit similarly emphasized the reliability of the standardized automobile, among other qualities: "The man who puts his money in a new Abbott-Detroit gets the only standardized mid-priced car in America. He gets a car that can be relied upon to do more than its daily work on account of the standardization of every individual part in the machine. He gets a car that we stand behind—that will deliver and operate above specified rating—that the manufacturer will guarantee for one year."[56] The application of standardization to improve product quality was seen as a response to consumer demand. According to a 1910 editorial in the *Chicago Tribune*, "The era of standardization has arrived, for it is clearly apparent that the designers have come to a realization of the needs of the users of automobiles and are endeavoring to give the people what they want."[57]

A further advantage of standardized products was that they ensured parity of quality across samples of a given product. For example, an official spokesperson for Maxwell, a car manufacturer, argued that standardization brings uniformity of product quality, which is essential from the point of view of fairness for consumers. For, he claimed, it is "only fair to consumers to make cars uniform, so that two cars bought by different customers do not vary in quality."[58] Interpreting this reasoning in terms that resonate with the theory argued for in Chapter 4, fairness obtains when the purchasing power represented by a given wage (and therefore by a given quantity of labor), measured by the objective use value endowing properties of wage goods, is invariant. Arbitrary difference in product quality violates this condition, insofar as it results in arbitrary differences in the purchasing power of identical wages. Invariance in the quality of standardized products was interpreted as having the added benefit of reducing risk for the consumer. Frank Hughes, sales manager of the Greer-Robbins Company, Chrysler distributers for Southern California, commented in 1927 that "standardized quality at one step eliminates 'purchaser's risk,' ends the buyers doubts and fears as to quality. . . . This is because . . . cars are built to the same quality standards, and must pass the same inspections in relation to the tasks they are asked to perform."[59]

As noted, the paradigmatic standardized consumer good, the most prominent representative of the new class of products fabricated by modern techniques of manufacturing, was the automobile. Commentators were sometimes quite absurd in their breathless enthusiasm for the standardized automobile. Homer McKee, auto advertising executive, marketing guru, and enthusiastic exponent of standardization, in trying to convey the great virtues of the standardized motor car, was moved to deploy his most lyrical voice (and most purple prose): "Thus it came about that the strength of the oak, the speed of the winds, the soft pad-footed stealth of the panther, the tirelessness of the seasons, and the beauty of the vines that cling were gathered together by the great Brain and the great Hand and put into a single thing which should be the all-powerful servant of man. And they called that thing—the Motor Car."[60] Even as early as 1910, commentators noted how widespread standardization was in car design and manufacture. Journalist Earle C. Anthony, attending an early automobile show in LA, found that, "The most striking feature of the exhibit . . . was standardization of models. All of the manufacturers are working toward an ideal car, which is sure to come. Then we will have embodied in one car all the good features of many."[61] The degree to which early automobiles were commonly seen as standardized products suggests that Henry Ford's vision of the standardized car, characterized by business historians Richard Tedlow and Thomas McCraw (1998) as unique and even quirky, was in fact continuous with quite widespread conceptions about how automobiles and other mass-produced consumer durables should be built. The ideal characteristics of the standardized industrial product—reliable, durable, free of waste and excess, efficient—reflected a general understanding of the desiderata in the industrial design of early mass consumer goods. This conception of what industrial products should be informed the early consumer testing organizations, Consumers' Research and Consumers Union. As economist Edith Ayres (1934, p. 161) noted, these organizations: "By emphasizing the engineering point of view in consumption [sought to encourage] a change in consumers' values away from standardization on the basis of appearance and towards standardization on the basis of physical function."

At the same time, the standardization of products began, by the early 1930s, to become a target for some criticism, on the grounds that it slowed or halted progress in product design. Charles Kettering, vice-president in charge of research at General Motors, questioned whether product standardization over the decade preceding 1931 had been an altogether good thing, suggesting that it had contributed to industrial stagnation. In part this reflected the emergence of a new approach to design at General Motors, to counter Ford's success with the model T. Kettering's comments were motivated by GM's move away from Ford's hyperstandardized approach and the beginnings of its segmented marketing strategy.[62]

Still, even after the inception of GM's segmented approach to marketing and product design, the standardization of commodities remained a powerful normative ideal. The normative force in the early part of the twentieth century behind the notion that goods *should be* standardized is indicated by expressions of anxiety about products *not* being sufficiently standardized. Calls for standards for products had an air of urgency about them and carried something of a moral charge. In 1910, for example, women were encouraged by activist Ida M. Tarbell to organize to pressure government to set standards for fabrics: "The primary trouble here is, of course, that we have in this country no standards for textiles," Tarbell wrote.[63] Tarbell's concerns were shared by the American Home Economics Association (AHEA), which actively campaigned for the standardization of textiles and clothing (Mack 1934). The issue for the AHEA was the need to provide consumers with clear information about products. The following decade, a legislative bill intended to correct the situation described by Tarbell, by standardizing the measurement and manufacture of cotton duck, was presented to the state assembly in California. Andrew Swanfeldt, chairman of the Southern California Tent and Awning Manufacturer's Association, who was responsible for the proposed new law, commented that "the bill, as proposed is badly needed as it regulates a commodity in which there has been a great deal of jugglery in the past and should be standardized so that the consumer, regardless of where he buys his cotton materials, will receive absolutely the same weight, construction, and width."[64] Part of what lay behind the calls for standardized consumer products was a desire to make wage goods in the marketplace maximally legible to consumers.

The era of the rise of standardized goods was accompanied by a standardization of the regulation and measurement of those goods. Part of the drive toward regulative convergence was the need to coordinate state laws in an increasingly integrated national economy. One area of particular concern was the need to coordinate the regulation of road traffic across the country, and significant progress was made in the 1910s and 1920s toward "standardizing" (such was the terminology) laws covering motor vehicles across state lines.[65] These early moves toward standardizing local and state regulations in order to better integrate the nation were to continue through the first half of the twentieth century. In the economic realm, they culminated in the passing of the Uniform Commercial Code in 1952, a comprehensive piece of legislation intended to harmonize disparate state laws covering commerce. As we shall see in the following chapter, the Uniform Commercial Code, significantly, also extended the implied product warranty to every state in the nation, marking a significant move away from the principle of caveat emptor.

Much of the work in standardizing product measurements was carried out by the National Bureau of Standards. The bureau introduced a wide range of standardized measures, from the creation in 1909 of an international standard for candlepower as a measure of luminosity to the development of "color meters" to established "objective" standards for colors.[66] Although arguably some of the activities of the bureau simply expressed a technocratic fetish for precision (which was sometimes ridiculed), standardization of measurement was justified primarily in terms of the protection of the interests of the consumer.[67] Indeed, standardizing weights and measures was seen as merely the first step toward standardization of product quality. T. N. Carver, marketing expert, giving voice to this view, saw the two forms of standardization, of quantity and of quality, as being of a piece. According to him, in both cases "economy of effort" is achieved by reducing transaction costs incurred by consumers having to carefully inspect goods prior to purchasing them. Standardization would eliminate that effort by institutionalizing quality assessment for the consumer. Time saved in shopping would then be time made available for increasing production and for increasing the "velocity of trade" (Carver 1917).

The idea that standardization of measurements had the benefit of making things clear and explicit for consumers was also embraced by engineers working in the manufacturing sector. Coker F. Clarkson, secretary and general manager of the Society for Automotive Engineers, wrote in 1908 of the benefits to the buying public of the standardization project pursued by the Association of Licensed Automobile Manufacturers. In particular, he drew attention to the development of horsepower as a measurement of car engines: "The primary purpose of the formula is to give light to the public as to the motors rated high, as offering big value, and those rated modestly."[68] Likewise industry observers argued that truck payload capacity measurements should be standardized so as to make comparison across different models as easy as possible for consumers.[69]

In the 1920s the Bureau of Standards joined forces with the Department of Agriculture to bring greater transparency and consistency to the marketplace by standardizing scales used to weigh produce.[70] In its efforts to standardize measures the bureau often worked in close consultation with business and professional associations.[71] But business figures were often independent advocates for the development of standardized product measures. Samuel W. Reyburn, president of the department store chain Lord and Taylor, addressing the eleventh annual meeting of the Textile Color Association, gave a speech in 1926 entitled "On the Importance of Color and Color Standardization to Retail," in which he argued that regularizing color categories would benefit both merchants and the general public.[72] Similarly Michael Schaap, president of Bloomingdale's, at a 1935 meeting of the Housewares Club of New York, called for greater standardization of household products and advocated the use of standardized color cards for products.[73] In 1927, Macy's, the department store chain, went as far as to establish its own bureau of standards, complete with laboratory testing facilities, in order to provide precise product information for its customers. The idea was that "responsible retailers" should ensure that their customers are furnished with as much information as possible about how products would behave in use.[74] Macy's example was followed by other big department stores, including Hearn Inc., which created an in-house bureau of standards in 1937. The Hearn bureau introduced a "quality assurance" tag indicating the fabric content of garments—an innovation that mirrored the National Bureau of Standards' certification labels. The new tag was applauded by consumer groups.[75] The value of commercial product testing, measuring, and certification was in part seen in its deterring fraud on the part of manufacturers, but it also served the goal of maximizing product transparency for the consumer. Consumers were not, however, just passive bystanders to moves by business and government to make knowledge about products easier to obtain. Ephraim Freedman, head of Macy's standardization bureau noted in 1937 that customers were becoming increasingly insistent about having their goods described in terms of "reliable standards." Given the pressure from consumers, according to Freedman, "the retailer for his own protection must continue to refuse to buy blind, as he refuses to sell blind."[76]

4. Standardization of Wages and Purchasing Power

As well as production and product properties, standardization was also applied to work and wages. That the standardization of work should go hand in hand with the standardization of production and of products is not at all surprising. Standardized production, after all, entailed a regularized labor process, along broadly Taylorist lines, while standardized products also meant standardizing the skills required to make and service those products. The "standardization" of wages, however, was a more complex and contentious matter. What after all, might it mean to standardize a wage? The answer is not obvious. Different conceptions of the logic according to which wages ought to be standardized were advanced by different interested parties—business, labor unions, and the state.

The best-known early experiment with standardized wages is surely Ford's decision in 1914 to pay his automobile factory workers five dollars per day. The logic of standardization in that case was that wages should be set at levels that would permit workers to afford the mass-produced commodities they made while also encouraging quiescence and greater intensity of effort in the labor force (Raff 1988; Meyer 1981; Gartman 1986).[77] Although Ford's experiment was relatively short-lived, it indicated the establishment of a normative connection among production, product, work, and wage. Standardized production, yielding a standardized product, was linked to standardized pay, with the value of the wage measured by its purchasing power over the goods produced by the labor given in exchange for it. In advocating the five dollars a day Ford also showed some understanding of the importance of mass buying power in an era of industrialized mass production. For this reason, Ford's policy is often seen as presaging the postwar era of industrial capitalism, with its technocratic management of demand and supply (Aglietta 2000).

Ford's version of standardized wages was, however, not the only one in the early twentieth century. The labor movement called for "standardized wages" in order to improve the conditions of its members. Labor leader Samuel Gompers, for example, speaking to the Senate in 1918, made an impassioned plea for the "standardization of wages."[78] To some extent labor activists used the term *standardized wages* in ways that made it interchangeable with other terms frequently used in this period—*family wage, fair wage, American wage.* All these terms were intended to mean higher real wages. Indeed, it is surely no coincidence that calls by unions for the standardization of wages took place at the same time as the question of the American standard of living became a central concern for American labor. Yet the term was often used in a more particular sense to mean rationalizing wages in an upward direction, by increasing the pay of all workers within a given category to match that of the highest-paid worker in that category.[79] In that sense it meant something distinct from calls for a more general increase in real wages. For some political economists and management scientists, standardization of pay, in the sense of making wages uniform for a given category of worker, stood in some tension with the standardization of inspection methods used to assess the product of labor (Dunaway 1916). Their suggestion was that piece rates should be adopted, only adjusted to take account of the quality of a worker's output. For once standardized inspection regimes were introduced, new means became available for differentiating the quality of work done by different workers in the same job. The introduction of systematic assessment of product quality would thus facilitate more accurate assessments of quality of work, which should, according to this line of reasoning, then be reflected in compensation. In a spirit somewhat like Ford's, progressive technocrats, who supported the welfare capitalism that many in the 1920s viewed as the key to resolving industrial strife, approached the issue of standardization from the angle of work conditions, as opposed to pay. The argument was that for a given wage, conditions of work ought to be standardized. Doing so would have the beneficial effect of "steadying labor," thus ensuring that employers would get "a fair return in work for the wage they pay, from a non-shifting, contented, and physically fit working force" (Erskine and Roach 1917, p. 82).

The difference in notions about how wages should be standardized came into particularly sharp focus in a series of industrial actions by East Coast railroad workers in support of standardized wages, which took place over the first two decades of the twentieth century. This protracted industrial struggle turned on the issue of whether and how wages should be standardized, and the public relations battle waged by the two sides took the form of a debate about the logic according to which standardization of wages should proceed.[80] For the rail unions, standardized pay meant the same nominal wage for the same position, with standards set by the highest-paid worker in a category. For example, in 1909, just after the campaign for standardized wages had been launched, rail unions demanded the "standardization" of conductors' pay on all railroads east of the Mississippi.[81] Standardization of wages, for the unions, also meant uniform pay scales across geographical areas. In 1910 unions called for the ending of wage differences across different regions of Pennsylvania, in the name of standardizing wages.[82] The railroad companies and their sympathizers, however, had a different conception of the logic that should underlie the standardization of pay. For them, standardized pay meant equivalent real buying power (that is, the same real wage) for equivalent labor inputs. Since the cost of living varied considerably across different localities, and because the intensity of at least some kinds of railroad work depended on how busy on average things were, the railroad companies argued that wage scales ought to be flexible, to take into account the particulars of local situations.[83] What the railroad workers meant by "standardized wages" was essentially uniform nominal wages for equivalent jobs (by adjusting all wages to match the highest ones in the category), whereas what their employers understood by the term was equivalent wage purchasing power for equivalent intensities of labor power. The issue of which logic should determine the standardization of pay scales of railway workers proved to be an ongoing source of contention, as employers claimed the union version would produce unsustainable increases in costs and was in any case irrational given differences in the cost of living across the country.

The views of Judge Anderson, former member of the Interstate Commerce Commission and of the Massachusetts Public Service Commission, and a figure broadly sympathetic to the railroad companies, are typical of those who argued against nominal (and upward) wage standardization from a business perspective. Anderson complained that the railroad union's concept of wage standardization was an "utterly unsound and unjust standardization," denouncing as "absurd" the "scheme of paying the same wages all over the country, regardless of living conditions and of the work required." He condemned the "artificial standardization of wages on a mere money basis, that is, regardless of money purchasing power in various sections and of the quality and quantity of service," noting, furthermore, the difference between the workload of an employee toiling in a busy city station and one working in a quiet rural station. Anderson ended his comments on the matter by urging "in the interest of the workingmen themselves" the abandonment of the standardization of wages.[84]

In the public relations battle, the railroads repeatedly suggested that the union's version of standardized wages would threaten the economic well-being of railroad companies.[85] Having ceded some ground on the issue of wage standardization to the unions before the First World War, the railroad companies launched a counterattack in the postwar period, arguing that standardized wages put the whole industry in peril.[86] This point echoed an analysis of the initial wave of strikes, of 1909, by economist William J. Cunningham. Following the first big push by unions for standardized wages, Cunningham published an article, in 1910, in which he argued that standardization, far from ending inequalities, permitted them to remain, and even led to their accentuation. On the political right, some commentators, pursuing an antilabor agenda, came up with a harsh, probusiness version of standardized wages, a rhetorical counter to the union version. R. A. Gill-Smith, writing in the *Wall Street Journal,* suggested that wage rates be standardized around a "*maximum* rate . . . fixed by law." "This," he said "would not only put a stop sometime to increasing costs of living, but would go far to regulate most labor troubles. This would prove a boon to labor itself, as it would put in operation there the law of the survival of the fittest, whereby good and bad workmen would each receive their due reward."[87] The state eventually intervened in the 1909 dispute, to impose what it took to be a balanced approach to standardized wages. The Erdman Act of 1898 had given the federal government powers to take an active role in the arbitration of interstate industrial disputes involving the railroads. In the 1909 dispute between railroad workers and their employers, the Federal Railway Labor Board initially enforced the standardization of wages at the behest of unions, on terms they found agreeable.

The federal government stepped in to support standardization of wages in other industries also. A fact-finding commission was set up under the Harding administration, to investigate conditions in the coal industry. The main objective of the commission was "ascertaining and standardizing the cost of living for mine workers and their living conditions and standardizing as far as is practicable the amount of work a man shall perform for a reasonable wage."[88] This formulation suggests that the commission was trying to strike a middle path between the positions of business and labor. On the one hand the recommendation was that the content of work at a given wage should be "standardized" in order to limit the capricious intensification of the labor process by ruthless businesses. On the other, the report suggested, in line with arguments made by business, that real purchasing power, rather than nominal rates, should be considered in deciding how to standardize wages.

By the late 1930s, with the inception of the New Deal state, standardized wages had increasingly come to mean those decided upon as a result of state regulated arbitration between labor and business, setting in place one of the elements of the Fordist compromise that was to fully coalesce in the postwar era. As with government efforts to impose product standards, moves on the part of the state to impose a top-down standardization of wages prompted calls from industry figures for action to preempt government intervention.

W. W. Finlay of the Wright Aeronautical Corporation, addressing a 1938 conference sponsored by the American Management Association, urged companies to move voluntarily toward adopting a "scientific" basis for wages, lest the government intervene to do it for them.[89] Ironically, by the late 1930s Henry Ford, great advocate of standardized production and standardized products, had turned vehemently against the state and union sponsored project to standardize wages and promote state mediated collective bargaining agreements. Ford characterized this project as tantamount to an effort to impose a "wage dictatorship," at the root of which lay the machinations of nefarious "financiers."[90]

Standardized pay was also one of the demands made by early campaigners for women's rights. One activist in 1920 was reported as issuing the following cross-partisan rallying call in support of standardizing wages for men and women working for the federal government: "Through the women of the Democratic and Republican committees the women voters of the country are urged to take up the cause of the standardization on an equality with men of the wages of women in the federal services."[91] Some calls to standardize women's work, however, meant ensuring that the work was appropriate for their gender. During the First World War, for example, some concern was expressed about the kind of work women were being called on to do. In 1918, Miss Goldmark, a representative of the Consumer's League of New York, called for the work of female railroad employees to be "standardized" according to the supposed characteristics of their sex. She expressed particular concern that women workers were doing hard physical labor.[92]

In addition to campaigns for standardized pay as a means of combatting inequality, the project of standardizing wages was also adopted as a bureaucratic measure by government. Throughout the early decades of the twentieth century, particularly at the level of local government, standardization bureaus were set up to rationalize pay scales. These bureaus were staffed by "wage and salary standardization experts." Los Angeles began in 1916 to classify all city employees according to standardized criteria, with the aim of making its pay scales more rational by adopting a standard salary schedule.[93] The city established its own bureau of standards in 1917 to manage the task of standardizing pay scales for salaried workers, and the policy was extended to cover wage workers in 1918.[94] Similar efforts were undertaken in the early twentieth century by New York City, San Francisco, and Detroit, as well as Massachusetts and New York State. As in the case of the railroad dispute, the meaning of standardized government pay became a matter of some contention. Part of the issue was concern on the part of salaried workers that they would be placed in the same category as wage earners. They were worried about being classified in a downward social direction.[95] But a more significant concern for public sector workers was that the underlying agenda local government had in standardizing wages and salaries was cutting costs and that this would inevitably result in a downward standardization of pay. In New York State, for example, standardization measures were introduced in response to calls for a $1,500,000 reduction in the state payroll.[96] The New York City Bureau of Standardization set itself the task of cutting the city's annual wage bill by $20,000,000 by standardizing the wages of eighty thousand workers.[97] With such objectives in mind, standards were typically set by the lowest-paid worker in a given category rather than the highest-paid worker, an approach that was naturally very unpopular with government workers. At the same time, public criticism was leveled at bureaus of standardization for failing to successfully cut pay, and indeed for adding significant new costs to local government. The New York City Bureau of Standardization was estimated to cost the city $100,000 per year.[98] While standardization of public sector pay was primarily advocated on the basis of cutting costs, it was also seen as a means to eliminate irrational and often unfair variations in pay for workers. A city auditor in San Francisco in 1918 complained about the "manifest injustice" of differences in pay for similar work, and advocated "standardization [of salaries] for all [city] departments."[99] Massachusetts, likewise, justified standardization of state pay by asserting that it would eliminate inequalities between people doing the same work. Similar claims were made (almost twenty years later) by the city government of Detroit.[100]

In discussions and disputes about the standardization of wages, all sides deployed the rhetoric of fairness. A standardized wage meant a wage that fairly reflected the work done for it, however that was interpreted by various actors in specific cases. Standardized wages were also supposed to be transparent, making the criteria linking wage and work as clear and open as possible. In that sense, the standardized wage was close to the standardized product, representing a stable quantity of use value. In both cases standardization supposedly brought clarity and stability to things that seemed at risk of being opaque and arbitrary. Moreover, standardized wages and salaries, insofar as they came to be understood in terms of real "purchasing power," rather than in nominal terms, drew attention to the wage goods in terms of which that power was gauged. With wages rationalized on the one hand, and wage goods stabilized on the other, the notion that wage labor could constitute a fair exchange of equivalents became more plausible.

The idea that wages should be standardized, and that product properties should be fixed for a given good, was presupposed in the formula that governed industrial relations in the years following the Second World War, which formed a central pillar of economic regulation in the Fordist era. As mentioned earlier in this book, according to that formula, first established by the 1948 agreement between the United Auto Workers (UAW) and General Motors, yearly changes in pay were determined by a combination of increases in productivity and changes in the consumer price index (Piore and Sabel 1986; H. Katz 1985). The principle became generalized in the economy at large, with even nonunion workers, public sector workers, and management taking their lead from pay negotiations of the big industrial unions, most prominently the UAW. In one form or another, it was adopted across the advanced capitalist world in the postwar era. The formula directly linked mass purchasing power to the increasing capacity of industrial production, thus ensuring some degree of coordination between production and consumption in the industrial economy. It formalized and institutionalized a dynamic conception of fair wages that was quite different from earlier notions, which were anchored to absolute standards of living. Yet the governing formula in postwar industrial relations was also a result of the growing consensus, which emerged in the first half of the twentieth century, that wage levels ought to be determined by an objectively reasonable procedure. The linking of wage levels to changes in the cost of living only made sense once product properties became standardized. For changes in real prices can only work as an index of purchasing power, and thus as an independent gauge of the value of a wage, if the properties of wage goods—the basis of their value—can be held constant.

Standardization of products and of labor was a prerequisite for generalized commensuration in economic exchange—for commensuration between categories of object or action. This is because the question of the ratio at which things of a given type should be exchanged for other categories of object can only be addressed once things (and perhaps also actions, if we consider services) within categories are made uniform, such that each thing can be easily recognized as a token of its type. If individual instances of a given category of thing were to vary too wildly, then the category itself would become unstable, threatening to become an arbitrary set of singular things rather than a set logically anchored by the (sufficiently) uniform predicates of its elements. Where the things in question are commodities, that instability would lead to higher transaction costs in commerce. For high variation in product quality would mean that goods would have to be carefully inspected, with prices adjusted for units where deviations from the ideal standard version of each kind of good are found. And where careful inspection proves difficult, this would lead to the kind of problem of marketplace uncertainty (potentially leading to market failure) that economist George Akerlof describes in his famous account of the market for lemons (Akerlof 1970). Perhaps, therefore, one of the limiting conditions on the extent of the development of the market economy is the degree to which categories of object become standardized. Rather than thinking about what sociologist Lucien Karpik (2010) calls economic singularities—singular products and services that have unique properties, such as works of art—as anomalous phenomena, in need of special explanation, we might instead think about how it came to be the case that, in general, individual goods are *not* singularities but rather have become tokens of supposedly uniform types.[101] This would raise at least two questions. What social, cultural, and technological conditions are required for the creation of stable, uniform types of product? And what effect did the organization of the economy around the exchange of this kind of product have on economic and social behavior? The answer to both questions, I suspect, would involve the moral economy around wage-labor commensuration.

The insistent emphasis on the material characteristics of the standardized consumer product entailed a narrowing of the meaning of use value to the physical properties of commodities. In directing attention to the material substrate of use value, standardization displaced use from the concrete social context of actual practice and, as it were, placed it in the things themselves. The pressing questions became; how functional, durable, and reliable are consumer commodities, and how many can be commanded by a given wage? The utility of commodities thus became unhinged from the total ecology of practice within which objects actually become useful. Once use value became primarily a property of things—while things became reserves of utility, stores of potential activity—wage labor was much easier to imagine as an exchange of commensurable substances and hence as potentially fair. Wage labor, which had become a necessary fact of life under capitalism, one imposed largely through economic coercion, was thereby turned into a conceivably legitimate institution. Thus, the reframing of commodities as standard quantities of use value relieved some of the central tensions in labor under capitalism and facilitated the incorporation of previously recalcitrant wage earners into the capitalist growth machine.

SEVEN

Standardizing Utility: Brands and Commercial and Legal Warranties

In this chapter, I turn from a broad interpretive overview of standardization to focus in more detail on a number of developments. These developments were very much connected to standardization and were particularly important for the status of the standardized commodity as a repository of abstract utility. They include the ascent of the modern branded product, the evolution of standardized commercial warranties, and changes in warranty law. In Chapter 8, I go on to examine the emergence of consumer product testing as an important institution within consumer capitalism—and, specifically, as a means by which standards in consumer goods were policed.

1. Branding of Standardized Products

On the commercial and marketing side, standardization was manifested as the proliferation of branded goods. Brands, understood in a very loose fashion as names attached to manufactured artifacts produced in high volume, have a long history, with archaeological evidence suggesting that they existed as far back as ancient Babylonia (Moore and Reid 2008). They can certainly be found at the dawn of the industrial age, with the appearance in England during the eighteenth century of brand names associated with commercial manufacturing enterprises such as Wedgwood Pottery (McKendrick 1984). However, it was not until the twentieth century that branded goods became the default products in the consumer marketplace, such that unbranded products became, ironically, the marked category.

The consensus among business historians is that the modern era of brands commenced around 1870 (Strasser 1989; Low and Fullerton 1994). Brands had existed in America in the earlier nineteenth century but were for the most part restricted to two kinds of commodity—patent medicine and tobacco. From the later nineteenth century onward, however, branded goods spread throughout the marketplace and into all product categories.

The spread of branded, mass-produced goods was dependent on developments in production, distribution, and commercial law. Standardized mass production made it possible for consumer goods to be much more consistent in quality, which allowed brand names to be anchored to uniform products. On the most basic level, brand names operate by indexing regularity in the properties of the goods they are attached to—it is difficult to imagine brands working in that way if individual samples of branded products were to vary too wildly. For that reason, the standardization of product specifications was a prerequisite for the rise to dominance of the modern branded commodity. Advances in packaging technologies and new printing techniques made it easy to produce striking labels on which brand names could be displayed. The expansion of transportation along with the appearance in the later nineteenth century of department stores and chain stores as vital nodes in new distribution networks, gave producers unprecedented access to national markets (Chandler 1977). Access to these national markets made possible new economies of scale, which made it worthwhile for manufacturers to invest in brand recognition. Brand recognition was facilitated by the growth of print media, which greatly expanded opportunities for advertising. Lastly, changes in trademark law in the late nineteenth century made it much easier for brand names to be protected.[1]

With these material and structural conditions in place, the branded consumer commodity soon became commonplace in the market. According to Robert Lynd, writing in the early 1930s, the value attached to businesses with recognized brand names had in the space of just a few years increased from five times annual earnings to sixteen times annual earnings (Lynd 1933, pp. 875–76).[2] George Burton Hotchkiss, chairman of the department of advertising at New York University, reminisced in 1925 about a time when, to the astonishment of all, a brand name for baking powder was valued at $5,000,000—"a million dollars a letter," as he put it. Yet Hotchkiss observed that such valuations had, at the time of his writing, become quite unexceptional, commenting that, evidently, "we have become accustomed to the idea that the name of a product (or a person) can acquire monetary value through the process of becoming favorably known to the public."[3] The increasing value attached to brand names was accompanied by their rapid proliferation. By 1934, over half a million trademarks had been registered in Washington as identifying brands. The marketing trade journal *Printer's Ink* in the mid-1930s counted over five thousand "commodity slogans" associated with brands (Wilcox 1934). As brands became increasingly pervasive, so did awareness of them among consumers. Research in the 1920s revealed that brand-name recognition had become widespread, with one study showing that 100 percent of its sample (of three hundred men) were able to name brands for each of the category of goods they were asked about and another showing that 90 percent of Chicago grocers claimed that at least three quarters of their customers asked for products by brand name (Strasser 1989 p. 52). The annual consumer survey conducted by the *Milwaukee Journal* in 1930 indicated the extent to which everyday consumer purchasing decisions were brand-led. Of the households surveyed, 71 percent bought coffee by brand, 78 percent bought soap by brand, 87 percent bought soups by brand, and 81 percent bought butter by brand, with similar numbers for most other staples. By the middle part of the twentieth century, branded commodities were firmly in place at the center of the consumer economy.

The analysis of brands in the contemporary social scientific literature, at least outside economics, has tended to focus on their narrative power and semiotic salience. Approached in this way, brands are primarily vehicles for potted ideologies, or else, more neutrally construed, operate as signifiers, able to be appropriated piecemeal in an ad hoc manner by consumers and incorporated into idiosyncratic composite narratives or configurations of signs expressive of particular social identities (Baudrillard 1996; Lury 2004; Twitchell 2004). While, to be sure, modern brands work in those ways, brands also have a more general and abstract meaning, and this was particularly so during the first half of the twentieth century. What early brands indexed, before anything else, was a commitment on the part of the companies they represented to provide goods endowed with stable quantities of use value. In that sense, attaching a brand name to a product was a kind of speech act—an implicit promise—that established certain expectations and obligations between seller and buyer. As Susan Strasser (2004, pp. 30–31 [emphasis added]) puts it in her history of the emergence of the mass market in America: "by marking [that is, branding] their products, manufacturers *took responsibility for them."* That responsibility was, specifically, to make sure that products measured up to statements made about them on labels and in marketing campaigns, and more generally, to ensure that products conformed to broad expectations about standardized commodities.

According to one interpretation, the quality assurance implicit in the act of branding a product was continuous with the best practices of craft production. Margaret Dana, writer of the "Before You Buy" column in the *Los Angeles Times*, opined that the branded commodity harkens back to an artisanal age, when craftsmen would sign the product of their skilled labor with a mark that "became, in effect, his word of honor that anything bearing that brand or name would be a product made by that craftsman, to the same high standard. The same thing is true today, even in our mass production economy." Yet, she adds, the modern branded commodity comes with the extra assurance of having been subjected to rigorous objective tests, through which the manufacturer "offers proof [of quality]. This is where official standards of performance and accepted tests back up the brand name which really means something."[4] The meaning of a brand name, on this view, is ultimately rooted in the underlying physical properties of the object it names, the quality of which is assured by standardized techniques of production.[5]

For consumer advocates, the grounding of the meaning of brand names in the material characteristics of the products they are attached to entailed that any change in product characteristics should be signaled by a change in name. This view was set out explicitly in a 1949 editorial statement in "Consumer Research Bulletin": "It is CR's view that every product should correspond to a particular composition or design; that each change of design characteristics should be accompanied by a change of name."[6] This idea ran in tension with the logic of the "family brand," an approach initiated by companies such as Heinz, Standard oil, and National Biscuit, in which a range of products would be placed under one brand name (Silbur 1983). The idea that names should stand in a one-to-one correspondence with particular products suggests a kind of nominalist approach to brands, one that contrasts interestingly with marketing talk about the "essence" of a brand name, construed as some only vaguely definable quality carried by a large set of different products.

The primordial sense of brands as signals of quality is hinted at by the fact that early on in its history, the term *brand name* was interchangeable with the term *quality name*.[7] And in the first half of the twentieth century brand consciousness was commonly equated with attaching importance to product quality.[8] Technocrats and analysts of consumption in this period saw brands as a means to ensure the quality of consumer goods. *Materials for the Household,* a consumer advice publication put out in 1917 by the National Bureau of Standards, advised consumers to buy branded goods, on the grounds that they provide "some safeguard as to stability of quality" (Cochrane 1966, p. 137). Economist Clair Wilcox, writing in 1934, maintained that the rise of brands led to "uniformity and standardization," while the considerable expense involved in marketing a brand gave companies an incentive to "keep quality high." Likewise, Robert Lynd (1933, p. 876) in his contribution to *Recent Social Trends*—Hoover's comprehensive report on the state of American society—averred that "national brands unquestionably make for greater uniformity of quality." The association of branded products with quality was reflected in attitudes among retailers. According to a survey conducted by the marketing and research division of the Wholesale Dry Goods Institute in 1945, "most retailers believe they are in a stronger competitive position stocking nationally advertised brands on a quality and style basis than they would be if they emphasized unbranded goods on a price basis."[9] Sears officials noted, in 1938, the dramatic success of its branded products: "The merchandise bearing our own brand names is meeting with a steadily increasing demand on the part of the buying public. These branded articles are made by manufacturers of other nationally known products, who make our branded merchandise according to Sears' own specifications for quality and style. . . . The purpose of these brands is to ensure the customer quality at real savings, and every one is backed by Sears' own guarantee and by the guarantee of a reliable maker."[10] The answer to the question the Sears official was responding to—"what's in a [brand] name?"—was thus quality and dependability.

The importance of brand names as indexes of product quality was a major theme in the battle in the marketplace between "private" brands and "national" brands, which took place in the 1930s and 1940s. Private brands were in-house brand names created by large-scale retailers, such as chain stores and mail order companies. Products labeled with private brands tended to be cheaper than national brand-name goods, and during the Depression years of the 1930s, they began to make inroads into retail markets. At the same time, the point of private brands, like national brands, was to reassure consumers that the goods they were attached to were in general reliable and of good quality. Although the retail companies that owned the private brands did not manufacture the goods they sold, the quality of the goods was supposed to be safeguarded by rigorous inspections performed before they were placed on the store floor. Faced with increasing competition from private brands, the national brands fought back, using the argument that their names were a surer guarantee of product quality. They even tried to persuade chain stores, many of which had their own private brands, of the unique value of national branded goods. At the 1931 annual conference of the Western Chain Grocers Association, H. H. Lestico, speaking on behalf of national brands, argued that chain stores should give up their private brands and instead stock nationally advertised goods. The argument he made was that the cost of advertising campaigns on a national scale ensured that the products being advertised would be uniform and of high quality. In Lestico's words: "The national advertiser protects the millions invested in his label with rigid and scientific uniformity, which satisfies the exacting demands of your customers' expectancy."[11] Because private brands, by contrast, did not engage in expensive national advertising campaigns, the suggestion was that they were less motivated to make good on their quality assurances.

The cause of branded goods was represented by the National Brand Names Association, which organized campaigns to promote the general idea that nationally branded products denote quality and reliability. In the late 1940s, for example, the organization conducted a publicity campaign on behalf of its members, under the slogan "Buy the known brand." The idea was to persuade the public that established national name brands would guarantee the quality of the products sold under their name to a degree that private brands, maligned as "no-name" brands, and unbranded goods never could.[12] Despite the rapid growth of private brands during the Depression, in the affluent postwar years, the national brands bounced back. Marketing research, conducted in 1947, and reported on in *Business Week*, showed some evidence that consumers preferred products sold under national brands even where these were significantly more expensive, and with no obvious difference in quality. A marketing experiment was conducted in a department store in which identical beds were sold either as "Simmons," a well-known national brand, or as "Dreamland," a private brand associated with the store. Consumers chose the national brand item at a ratio of 15:1. In follow-up research, the price of the Dreamland mattress was reduced so that it was 12 percent cheaper than the Simmons—yet customers still chose the national-branded item over the private-branded one at a ratio of 8:1.[13] The writer of the Business Week article covering the research predicted that private brands were doomed to a marginal place in the market, and that "the basic distinction will shortly be between manufacturers' and distributers' national brands, rather than between national and private brands" (p. 66). By the 1950s, the retail market had become increasingly segmented, with private brands remaining a significant presence on the low-end side, while national brands dominated the middle and high-end parts of the market. The issue was perceived quality versus price, for, as one analyst commented, "the buyer [of national-branded goods] felt sure that he was getting a standard quality when he bought a nationally advertised, nationally distributed item."[14] The problem for private brands was that the goods sold under their name were not manufactured by the retailers who owned the brand name. This meant that the "quality assurance" they offered seemed removed from the actual production of the goods, which made it less believable.

Above and beyond the particular cultural associations with a given brand, brands were thus received as signaling devices about product quality.[15] Viewed in this way, the proliferation of brands, from the later nineteenth century onward, can be understood as one dimension of a more general concern to standardize product quality. The point of a brand was to indicate a standard set of properties that consumers could reasonably expect in the products labeled with the brand.[16] And indeed, the arguments made by manufacturers in favor of branded goods were similar to those they made in favor of standardized goods. W. W. Wachtel, chairman of the executive committee of the Brand Names Foundation, speaking in 1951 on the importance of trademark protection, argued that, as a result of the quality commitments entailed by branding a product, "brand-name products will always resist the pressure of higher costs and material shortages, and are the last products upon which prices are increased or qualities lowered."[17] In the middle of the twentieth century, to brand a good was thus to indicate that it was a standardized product, notionally endowed with predictable and stable use value. And those goods were acquired using buying power that was safeguarded by inflation-resistant, productivity-linked standardized wages.

The emphasis on the mechanical properties of consumer objects was reflected in the content of advertising in the mass consumer market. The growth of consumer brands was accompanied by a massive expansion of advertising aimed at spreading brand name recognition. Between 1890 and 1929 advertising expenditure increased tenfold, from $360 million to $3,426 million, and thereafter continued to swallow an ever greater part of GDP (Bureau of the Census 1960, p. 526). By 1998, total expenditure on advertising amounted to $201,594 million.[18] According to cultural historian Jackson Lears, over the course of the first half of the twentieth century, this marketing onslaught emphasized the narrow functional and material properties of commodities. In Lears's account, this reflected a growing demand for "a kernel of hardness" or "actuality" in product information—a demand that came to inform the medium as well as the message of advertising. Lears suggests that the very rapid rise to prominence of the photograph as the dominant representational medium in visual advertisements can be explained by the belief that photography delivers an unmediated picture of reality. Photographs in advertisements thus disclosed the "actuality" of consumer products. In the catalog for a 1930 exhibition of advertising photography, quoted by Lears to illustrate this conception, photographs are described as promising: "*sincerity* in displaying [a] product [as well as] drama in portraying its virtues" (Lears 1994, p. 324, emphasis added).

Richard Pollay's (1985) quantitative study of 2,000 print advertisements between 1900 and 1980 broadly supports Lears's contention that ads focused on the material qualities of goods. Pollay's analysis reveals what he takes to be a perplexing tendency, especially from the 1950s onward, for advertisements to emphasize the attributes of products, as opposed to the benefits that would accrue to the consumer following the consumption of the good. As the emphasis in advertising shifted toward product attributes, Pollay notes that the presence of humans in ads decreased, pushed to the margins by the things themselves.[19] Moreover, advertising pitches based on status associations with products were, according to Pollay's data, less common than might be supposed. Pollay found that by the 1950, only 10 percent of ads appealed to status, while 27 percent emphasized technological prowess and 31 percent focused on newness.[20] Even in the earlier part of the century, when the product-anchored utilitarian dimension was more muted, two-thirds of ads used what Pollay describes as a "straight pitch," presenting "assertions where logical induction and deduction would lead to product preference" (p. 30). Pollay's findings echo those of other research. A 1935 study of advertising content found that 85 percent of its sample of 2,500 magazine advertisements focused on product quality, as opposed to status or newness (Reid 1938).

The growth of brands qua signals of consistency of product quality was a response on the part of business to the growing influence of the normative expectation that products should be endowed with stable and predictable amounts of use value. For the brand to work as an incentive to buy a consumer good, it had to indicate, or at least suggest, the presence in the commodity of an acceptable level of quality. From this perspective, modern brands can thus be read as helping stabilize the notional purchasing power of the wage, by indexing definite qualities and durability in wage goods. In this way, brands contributed to the conditions under which labor could be commensurable with its wage.

2. Standard Commercial Warranties

The idea that brands basically functioned as signaling devices, indicating the presence in commodities of acceptable quantities of potential utility, gains some support from the fact that modern branded products were typically accompanied by standardized commercial warranties. If attaching a brand to a commodity is, as suggested above, akin to a speech act performed by a company to the effect that it is taking responsibility for ensuring that its products can be relied on to be of a certain standard quality, then the commercial warranty put that commitment in writing—formalizing that responsibility.

Modern warranties can take one of two forms; they can be implied warranties, enforced by law, or voluntary commercial, "express" warranties. The implied warranty (about which more will be said in the next section of the chapter) is a legal obligation on the part of those who sell goods to ensure that those goods are reasonably functional. The implied warranty emerged quite recently and has become the default legal warranty attached to all commercial goods. It stipulates that products should be "fit for purpose," and therefore "merchantable." Express warranties, by contrast, are statements voluntarily made by the makers of goods about how those goods will perform in use. Typically, express warranties guarantee that goods will perform in the intended manner for some specified period of time.

Express warranties have a two-sided legal character. On the one hand, they are used by companies to unilaterally limit their legal obligations, by making explicit statements about the performance parameters of their products.[21] The standardized commercial warranties that began to appear in the twentieth century were in part a response to changes in liability law that made manufacturers more accountable for mishaps resulting from the use of their products. One of the functions of the commercial warranty was, then, to specify written contractual limits to the liability of the manufacturer. At the same time, companies were legally obliged to make good on any statement about their products that they made in an express warranty.[22] So if a warranty made claims about quality and durability that went beyond the legal minimum standard for "merchantable" or "serviceable" goods, the manufacturer had to ensure that its goods lived up to those claims.

Commercial warranties operated to reinforce brands, serving to signal that a good has superior attributes, and to indicate that a manufacturer stands behind its products. One marketing innovation in the early part of the century was the creation of the "lifetime" warranty. The earliest newspaper advertisements for products with such a warranty appeared in the 1920s.[23] The lifetime warranty was to some degree a slippery marketing ruse, since the meaning of "lifetime" could be the lifetime of the original owner, an indefinite commitment over the lifetime of all owners, some specified period of time (typically twenty or twenty-five years) thought lengthy enough to qualify as a "lifetime," or, somewhat tautologically, the lifetime of the product itself, whatever that happens to be. Which of these applied in a given warranty was often left deliberately vague, or else was hidden in small print. At the same time, for some manufacturers standing behind their "lifetime" warranties was an important marketing strategy. Sheaffer Pens, for example, was renowned for the level of support it provided for its "lifetime" product line, which was introduced in 1924 and was signified by the presence of a white dot on the pen cap. Sheaffer's 1924 advertising campaign for its new line of pens promised that they would be "unconditionally guaranteed for a lifetime." The company had a very good reputation for addressing any issues consumers had with their products, regardless of how old the products were.[24] Parker Pens, Sheaffer's main competitor, also warrantied many of its pens for the lifetime of the original owner.

It is tempting to think that offering lifetime warranties was an attractive marketing strategy for these companies because pens are more likely to get lost than break, in effect limiting the costs entailed by the obligation to repair or replace broken pens. However, the robustness of the warranty offered by these companies was reflected in the durability of the products covered by it. Both Sheaffer and Parker made serious efforts to ensure that their products were maximally durable, insisting, for example, on manufacturing tolerances far more stringent than is typical of most contemporary consumer products. Sheaffer's whole marketing strategy was based on creating a reputation for producing uncompromisingly high-quality, durable pens.[25] The principle followed in production was the opposite of planned obsolescence (a topic discussed at length in chapter nine of this book). The objective was to make products that would indeed last for a lifetime rather than for as many years as on average a pen would be owned before it was lost. The durability of perhaps the most famous pen in mid-century America, the Parker 51, for example, was such that it quickly approached the point of saturating its market, prompting the company to turn toward a segmented marketing strategy for the line.[26] So at least in some cases "lifetime" warranties were anchored to products engineered to last for much longer than average durations of actual use. In those cases, durability was a significant selling point, and good warranty support was an important part of marketing and public relations.[27] More typically, however, warranties specified conditions of "normal usage," the violation of which would result in the voiding of the warranty.

The standard commercial warranty provided engineers with a target level of durability to aim for in the products they designed. For instance, during a 1912 meeting of auto manufacturers on standardization, the discussion about how to standardize motor trucks went hand in hand with decisions about what form the standard guarantee for those trucks should take.[28] Standardization was then a matter not just of rationalizing techniques of production but also of setting parameters of use for commodity objects, with implications for the conditions specified in the contract between purchaser and manufacturer. The notion of "normal use" was very much connected to standardization, in that some conception of typical, or "standard," patterns of use was involved in the design of a standardized product. In that sense, warranties presuppose a standardization of practices.

Express warranties draw attention to the physical constraints that limit the duration of usefulness of consumer artifacts. Warranties, in effect, stipulate a minimum amount of use consumers can expect from the products they acquire, quantified as a temporal duration of use under "normal" conditions. In acquiring a bicycle with a five-year warranty, for example, the consumer notionally acquires at least five years of "normal" use from the item. When commodities are framed in this way, the social and political question of whether life in general is arranged such as to enable the item to actually be used for that duration of time drops into the background. The focus is on the physical, use-endowing features of the artifact, and the moral and legal obligation of manufacturers to "stand behind" their products. Warranties anchored use to the decontextualized mechanical attributes of the commodity, which both reflected, and in turn promoted, an understanding of the value of wage goods, and by extension of the wage, in terms of potential rather than actual or probable usefulness.

3. From Caveat Emptor to the Implied Product Warranty

The development of commercial warranties did not take place in a legal vacuum. For the twentieth century witnessed fundamental changes in laws covering consumer transactions and product liability, and these changes formed the backdrop to evolving commercial practice. In broad terms, the changes can be characterized as an overturning of the legal principle of caveat emptor (let the buyer beware), with moves, albeit not uncontested ones, toward its replacement by the opposite principle, caveat venditor (let the seller beware). President Roosevelt, in an address to Congress on March 29, 1933, referred to the new principle. Arguing for the need to regulate the market for securities, Roosevelt noted that "this proposal adds to the ancient rule of *caveat emptor* the further doctrine: Let the seller beware."[29] The new mood was echoed in retail trade magazines. The pronouncement was made in a piece published in 1931 in *The Chain Store Magazine* that "truly, the old maxim, 'Let the customer beware,' should be changed to 'Let the merchant beware.'"[30]

According to the principle of caveat emptor, the buyer takes on the burden of risk inherent in any commercial transaction. If goods are faulty in any way, this must be discovered by the purchaser *before* purchasing the item. The only exception to this rule is where the buyer can prove that the seller deliberately concealed functionally significant flaws in the purchased product, in which case the buyer has a legal right to a refund. But the seller has no legal obligation to guarantee that the goods she sells are "fit for purpose." Caveat emptor entailed that all consumer transactions are by default covered by an implicit "sold as-is" clause.

Although it had some precedent in Roman law, in the Anglo-Saxon legal tradition caveat emptor first emerged in the sixteenth century. It remained, in the English-speaking world, the dominant legal principle covering marketplace transactions through the nineteenth century. In the United States, it was first clearly established as a legal principle in 1817, in the case of *Laidlaw v. Organ*. Legal scholar Walton Hamilton (1931), in his still definitive history of the subject, suggests that the doctrine of caveat emptor was even more influential in nineteenth-century America than it was in Victorian England.[31] In the early twentieth century, however, thinking about commercial law in the US began to change. The turning point is marked by the Uniform Sales Act of 1906, which was loosely based on the British Sale of Goods Act of 1893, and first established the principle of the implied warranty. According to the principle of the implied warranty, the default legal assumption in commercial transactions is that a good should be fit for a specific purpose. Where goods are found to be not fit for their purpose, the consumer has legal recourse. To avoid legal obligations entailed by the implied warranty, the default assumption of fitness for purpose must be explicitly nullified by a statement on the part of the vendor to the effect that goods are sold "as is," at which point the balance of risk in the transaction switches to the buyer.[32] The implied warranty thus effectively reversed the situation obtaining under the principle of caveat emptor. It took some time for the implied warranty to be accepted throughout the United States. The Uniform Sales Acts encountered significant resistance from the states, especially those in the South, and by 1947, more than forty years after the 1906 act, only 34 states had adopted it. In 1952 a more comprehensive piece of legislation, the Uniform Commercial Code, superseded the Uniform Sales Act, and was promptly passed into law in every state. The Uniform Commercial Code reaffirmed the legal principle of the implied warranty.

Nathan Isaacs, a professor of business law at Harvard, writing in 1934, characterized the 1906 provisions for implied warranties as "liberal." They included "implied contracts of correspondence with description, conformity to sample, fitness for particular purpose, and compliance with trade usages and customs" (Isaacs 1934, p. 181). Assessing the impact of the principle of the implied warranty, Isaacs writes: "The setting up of a standardized contract of sales by statute, from which deviation is possible only by making clear provisions to the contrary, is a mighty force in this busy world to bring about *even-handed* bargains" (p. 181 [emphasis added]). This characterization raises the question of what criteria must be met in order for a given exchange to qualify as "even-handed." To be sure, even-handedness meant the elimination of egregious asymmetries of information between seller and buyer—the 1906 legislation addressed that issue by making it incumbent on the seller not only to not actively conceal flaws, but also to point out those that might not be apparent to the prospective buyer. Yet the notion of "fitness for purpose" suggests something more substantive than just securing transparency in the marketplace, for purpose implies use and use entails practices extended in time. In order for a product to be fit for its purpose it must be able to perform its function for a "reasonable" number of uses, and therefore for some approximate duration of time. If a product, say a bicycle, were to break after having been ridden for only five days, it would not be judged as having been "fit for purpose." To specify that goods must be fit for purpose then entailed that consumers have the right to some duration of use from them (most states specified that a "reasonable" duration of effective usefulness for consumer durables under the implied warranty is four years). The legal concept of "fitness for purpose" was, therefore, connected to the norm that goods should contain some objectively reasonable quantity of abstract use power (measured as a duration of time in use) while also suggesting a standardization of the uses of things—use "under normal circumstances."

The development of commercial law is certainly a deeply complex matter, subject to diverse cultural, professional, political, legal, and social influences. In relation to the argument of the present book, however, the significant point is that the drift of commercial law over the course of the twentieth century was in the direction of affirming the right of the consumer to some *quantity* of usefulness from purchased products. The rise of the implied warranty indicates that fairness in exchange had shifted from being primarily a formal matter of free assent to a contract to being a matter of a roughly equal exchange of substances. Fair market exchange obtains where the quantity of usefulness notionally represented by the money exchanged for a commodity (in turn indexing the value of the labor given in exchange for the wage) is met by reasonably equivalent quantities of usefulness in the commodity.

The legal notion that consumers have a right to useful objects through market exchange was, like all rights, grounded in a broader normative order. The entitlement of consumers to wage goods containing a reasonable duration of use power flowed, I would suggest, from the moral economy underpinning wage labor itself. As we have seen, historians have suggested that the moral economy of mid-twentieth century American capitalism coalesced around the concept of "purchasing power," the ongoing increase of which constituted a "fair exchange" for labor's contribution to increasing productivity. The effort to secure the use value of consumer commodities, by legal, commercial, and political means, expressed the imperatives of that moral economy while also providing it with vital institutional and ideological support.

The increasing concern with securing by law the right of consumers to a "fair" quantity of use value (that is, a reasonable duration of hypothetically realizable use value) from the products they purchase dovetailed with the regulations to standardize consumer products. Ensuring that consumers would get a fair exchange in the marketplace became a growing preoccupation for government regulators. According to business historian Richard Tedlow's analysis, between 1914 and 1938 the Federal Trade Commission's advertising regulation policy shifted from concern with competition to care for consumers—with care conceived of as making sure that consumers get a "fair deal." The change in the FTC's regulatory practice is significant in that fairness was construed as something more substantive than getting products at market rates, determined by free competition (Tedlow 1981). At the same time, by the middle of the century securing a fair deal for the consumer was not just a matter of abstract justice—ensuring that each consumer gets her "money's worth" or that deals are "fair and square." For consumer rights had, in addition, an important social and political dimension. In accounts of the origins of strict product liability, for example, legal scholars have noted that over the course of the twentieth century, judges increasingly took into consideration the social consequences of their legal decisions, rather than just considering matters of causation and fault and the relative interests of the plaintiff and defendant in the case at hand (Hackney 1995). Social consequences often meant consequences for the interests of consumers, who were regarded as a vitally important social constituency.

Taking into account the social implications of legal decisions suggests the dominance of practical, social reasoning over formal rational concerns—or, in terms of philosophical ethics, of a broadly consequentialist position (one concerned with consequences, most usually for aggregate welfare) over a deontological stance (one concerned with rights and duties). However, the consequentialist perspective, in this case, was connected to an interpretation of the grounds on which the social order could be construed as being legitimate. If a practice was seen as being unfair, the social consequences might be destructive to the sociopolitical order, and the legal system took that into account. The duty of a right-thinking, socially minded, consequentialist judge was, therefore, to render decisions that would uphold the delicate moral equilibrium on which social order and political legitimacy depended.

In this sense, the legal concern to protect consumers was continuous with that of the broader sociological jurisprudence movement, which was influential in the early and middle decades of the century. Led by prominent legal thinker Roscoe Pound (1911a, 1911b, 1912), sociological jurisprudence advocated a pragmatic, consequentialist approach to legal reasoning.

The preoccupation with safeguarding consumer rights, and protecting consumer interests, indicates the growing influence of the concept of the consumer citizen (L. Cohen 2003). The importance in the twentieth-century political imaginary of consumers was reflected in the creation of a number of government bodies with specific concern for consumer interests. During the Depression years, these included, among others, the Consumer's Counsel Division of the Agricultural Adjustment Administration and the Consumer's Advisory Board of the National Recovery Administration. The Office of Price Administration, which had a central role in running the consumer economy during the Second World War, was also perceived as advocating for consumer interests.[33] In the postwar years, the concern to represent consumer interests continued at the highest political levels. Calls for consumer protection, which had been relatively muted since the reforms of the Progressive era, became commonplace from the 1950s onward, as did demands for cabinet-level representation for consumers (Glickman 2009). John F. Kennedy went so far in 1962 as to float the idea of a consumer's bill of rights.[34] The emergence of the implied product warranty was thus not an isolated legal development but rather part of a constellation of institutional developments the point of which was to ensure that consumers were fairly treated in the marketplace—with fairness understood as obtaining where consumers receive a fair amount of use value in exchange for their wages.

Upholding consumer rights was important for the legitimacy of capitalism, especially in the era of mass production, because through those rights, a connection was forged between wage labor and fundamental tenets of capitalist ideology. Consumer rights are an extension of rights attached to self-ownership, which can ultimately be traced to the possessive individualism that constitutes the deep normative ground for capitalism—articulated by liberal thinkers from Locke onward (MacPherson 1962). The moral force behind substantive (as opposed to formal) consumer rights is grounded in the right to commensurate compensation for having sold one's (alienated) labor. For wage earners to have consumer rights is precisely to underline the fact that they are something other than slaves, despite the quite significant degree of economic coercion involved in the commodification of labor. As a free seller of labor, the wage laborer is entitled not just to arbitrary nominal compensation, set by the capricious workings of the labor market, but to substantive compensation in the form of a certain quantity of real buying power—which in turn is measured by the notional use power contained in commodities. As the legal and commercial developments discussed in this chapter safeguarded the use value of consumer commodities, so wage labor itself became more imaginable as an exchange of commensurable substances.

EIGHT

Product Testing and Product Regularization

Standardized production, as we have seen, produced standardized consumer goods—which, at least in theory, were supposed to be reliable, durable, and endowed with predictable characteristics. Such was the ideal, often indexed by a brand and sometimes backed by a commercial warranty. In practice, however, the consumer durables churned out by the system of industrial mass production not infrequently failed to live up to expectations.[1] Although product specification standards were stipulated by various industry and government bodies, enforcement of standards was spotty at best. Where products were found to be faulty, commercial warranties could not necessarily be relied on to make things right, while taking matters to court involved a serious commitment of time and money. One consequence of the standardization of consumer products, was, therefore, a movement to regulate and test final products, to ensure that they measured up to acceptable standards (however exactly those were defined). Consumer product testing, particularly in the period after the Second World War, was to develop into a basic institution of consumer capitalism. The rapid expansion of consumer product testing in the second half of the twentieth century indicates a growing concern with the material properties of commodities. And as attention focused on the material properties of commodities, so the issue of the context in which things are put to use fell into the background. The preoccupation with the material properties of commodities suggests a shift in thinking about utility from being primarily a function of the conjunction, within particular lives, of potentially useful things and actual activities to being primarily a matter of the things themselves, taken in isolation.[2]

Systematic third-party consumer product testing by nongovernment organizations first emerged in the United States in the 1930s, with testing laboratories set up by Consumers' Research and its rival, Consumers Union (CU). Over the following decades consumer testing became widespread, with results reported in the publications of consumer organizations, in periodicals devoted to particular products or hobbies and in mainstream newspapers and magazines. Even as early as 1955, 5 to 10 percent of America's purchasing units, according to one estimate, were directly influenced by recommendations made by CU's publication, *Consumer Reports (CR)* (N. D. Katz 1977; Sargent 1958). This figure probably greatly underestimates the extent of the influence of product testing, as test results informed the reputation of products and brands even for consumers with no direct knowledge of the results.

In the postwar period, business began to take increasing note of the activity of consumer testing organizations, especially Consumers Union. According to Jean Whitehall, managing editor at CU, this was because businesses realized that "adjustments of a product based on CU comments were beneficial to sales" (N. D. Katz 1977, p. 314). Manufacturers also began to refer to *Consumer Reports* test results in their marketing campaigns. The change in attitude of business to *CR* was in response to the broader dissemination of consumer consciousness in the postwar era, as the ideas and concerns of the consumer movement became more mainstream. Historians have noted that in the postwar period, workers were supportive of the consumer movement, seeing the campaign to secure quality in consumer goods as a natural extension of labor's postwar objective of increasing real income (Creighton 1976; L. Cohen 2003). Consumer product testing quickly became a common practice, spreading well beyond consumer advocacy organizations and government labs into all corners of the public sphere.

Given how widespread product testing has become, there is a surprising paucity of scholarship about the subject. The research that has been done has approached the topic from the angle of production. In the literature, consumer product testing is broadly portrayed as an expression and extension of the rationalizing principles developed in early twentieth-century mass production, associated with Taylorism (N. D. Katz 1977; Noble 1977; Silbur 1983; L. Cohen 2003; Glickman 2009). On this understanding, consumer product testing, like much else in capitalist modernity, reflects an unending quest for ever more optimized technique. Testing was just one more manifestation of rationalization, subsumed under the broader drive for efficiency, where ultimately efficiency is thought about from the point of view of the economy as a whole—efficient production and efficient consumption working together to minimize the aggregate waste generated by the economy.

That interpretation certainly captures one dimension of the ascent of product testing, for testing was indeed connected to the broader project to make production more rational and scientific. A lineage can be traced between the early efforts to test consumer products and the activities of testing laboratories established by corporations such as American Telegraph and Telephone, General Electric, Dupont and Westinghouse.[3] The function of these corporate labs, in addition to developing new products, was to establish standards for materials used in production and to test batches of the materials purchased by the company to ensure that those standards were met. This was similar to the idea behind early consumer product testing by Consumers Union and Consumers' Research, which was to set standards for consumer goods and police those standards by way of an ongoing program of product testing.

As with standardized production, the origins of product testing lay in the passionate work of proselytizing efficiency engineers, who were inspired by a rationalist vision of optimized production. The efficiency movement had a significant presence in civil society over the first three decades of the twentieth century. It encompassed the home economics movement, which emerged at the turn of the twentieth century, and assimilated the household (and therefore mass consumption) to its grand vision of optimized economic efficiency. The Home Economics Association (HEA), founded in 1908, took an active role in creating and promoting standards for household products such as sheets and blankets (Ayres 1934). The point of standards, as seen in Chapter 6, was to safeguard the use value of consumer commodities. Home economist Rosalind Cook (1927) gave a succinct statement of this perspective: "It is a commonly conceded fact that service value is an important factor in practically every product we buy. In certain cases we speak of quality as durability, and in others as work value; some speak of it as economic value; but whatever term we may use in describing the quality, we recognize it as fundamental and inherent in the product itself. How can we assure ourselves that such a quality exists in the product and the degree in which it is present? The answer seems to be through the use of established measurements which have the accuracy and authority of a standard . . . standard specifications assure the purchaser of a measured amount of the factors which make for durability or service quality." The HEA's mission was to educate the wider public about the meaning and value of the work of enlightened experts in establishing standards for consumer goods. Max Getz, chairman of the Committee on Ultimate Consumer Goods of the American Standards Association, writing in the *Journal of Home Economics*, described the work of home economists as filling an "urgent need among consumers for more examples, ideals, rules, for more types, models, or examples for comparison, yes even for more 'tests,' . . . [for] standards [are a] language that must be taught" (Getz 1940, pp. 520–21). But standards without systematic testing would be ineffectual. As early as 1910, the women's magazine *Good Housekeeping*, under the influence of the home economics movement, established a research institute that featured a model kitchen and testing station for household devices, along with a "domestic science laboratory."[4] The "Good Housekeeping Research Institute" bestowed the magazine's "seal of approval" on goods that passed its tests, which was backed by a two-year limited warranty. For home economists, promoting consumer product testing and standardized specifications was a part of its broader pedagogical agenda, which was to make consumers "conscious of the characteristics of consumer goods."[5] The idea was for consumption to be a field of technical knowledge, which would be disseminated to the public. Homes, in this vision, would eventually come to be managed by expert home makers, "household engineers," who would practice a "science of ultimate consumption" (Goldstein 1997).[6]

The general quest for economic efficiency and standardization was, as we have seen, also a project of the state. Beginning in the early twentieth century, government agencies were created to ensure quality control for government purchases.[7] Early consumer activists were inspired by, and drew attention to, the effort on the part of the federal government to establish standards for the products they procured. Stuart Chase and Frederick Schlink, pioneers of the consumer movement, opined, in 1925, that "there are billions to be won if the consumer—both ultimate and intermediate . . . can follow the example of the federal government in purchasing material."[8] The National Bureau of Standards (NBS), in addition to its work establishing standards (discussed in Chapter 6), developed an elaborate testing program to ensure that those standards were met. Other government agencies, such as the Bureau of Chemistry and the Bureau of Home Economics, did likewise, building their own testing laboratories. While in-house laboratories and standards divisions were developed by various governmental agencies, it was, however, only the National Bureau of Standards (NBS) that had a program to conduct systematic testing specifically of consumer products.

Even before independent consumer organizations began testing products, the NBS had been engaged in similar activities. Early testing conducted by the bureau was meant primarily for engineers and product specialists working in industry and so focused on industrial materials and processes rather than consumer products. But this early orientation toward industry was seen within the bureau as a shortcoming, precisely because it excluded the end user of industrial products—the consumer. As a corrective, in 1915 the bureau began to publish circulars written expressly for the general public. The first of these, circular no. 55, focused on appliances and was entitled *Measurements for the Household*. It enumerated its purposes in the introduction as: "(1) to give information as to units, methods, and instruments of measurement useful in household activities (2) to describe the available means of assuring correct quantity in articles bought by weight and measure, and (3) to give other facts of interest which would awaken an appreciation of the role of measurement in daily life" (National Bureau of Standards (1915), p. 7). The publication proved much more popular with the public than had been expected. While the usual print runs for circulars were two hundred to three hundred, demand for circular no. 55 was such that ten thousand copies were printed within three months of publication. By 1917, thirty-three thousand copies had been sold. *Measurements for Households* was followed, in 1917, by NBS circular no. 70, a 259-page manual entitled *Materials for the Household*. The pamphlet described its aim as "practical," listing its objectives as follows: "(1) to stimulate the interest in household materials (2) to explain the nature of their desirable properties (3) to aid in their intelligent selection (4) to promote their effective use and preservation" (p. 9). Fifteen thousand copies of *Measurements for Households* were sold in the year of its publication. The goal of both circulars, according to the bureau, was "to make scientific results available for those with little or no technical training" (quoted in Cochrane 1966, p. 137). Circular nos. 55 and 70 would become templates for the pioneering consumer movement publications *Consumer Bulletin* and *Consumer Reports*. Indeed, Schlink and Chase argued that there was a need for an organization equivalent to the NBS, able to perform "impartial tests" in order to enforce "impartial standards," only entirely devoted to the testing of consumer products. For, they complained, unlike items purchased by the government, "the great bulk of the things which we consumers buy are never reviewed by any impartial testing body."[9]

According to Rexmond Cochrane (1966, p. 138), author of the official history of the National Bureau of Standards, these early efforts to promote a scientific approach to consumption decisions "made so great an impression on the public that for years the Bureau was identified in the public mind with the testing of household materials and appliances and besieged with correspondence requesting personal help with home problems." The bureau's tentative effort in the 1920s and 1930s to provide scientific, test-based guides to consumer products for the buying public was to a large extent in response to increasing demand for such information. Consumer product testing had always been one of the bureau's areas of activity, but over time, the demand for that service increased. George K. Burgess, director of the bureau, estimated that between 1922 and 1927, the number of tests undertaken for consumers and producers doubled. By 1924, the volume of requests from consumers for bureau product tests of radios, as well as requests for information about tests of radios conducted by the bureau, had grown so large that an announcement was made that further requests would not be considered.[10] Yet in the 1930s, the Bureau of Standards was still being overwhelmed by inquiries from the general public about the relative merits of various commodities. Public demand for the testing of consumer goods presented the bureau with something of a problem, for while it was committed to disseminating objective information about products, the information it produced tended to be rather technical and, therefore, not expressed in terms easily understood by laypersons. Moreover, while the bureau was responsive to public demands for consumer product testing, its primary role was to support industry. Given this role, some consumer activists expressed skepticism about the degree to which the National Bureau of Standards could adequately represent consumer interests as opposed to the interests of business (McConnell 1934).

There were occasional bills proposed in Congress to expand the NBS's testing of consumer goods, but these encountered resistance because of the expense involved (Briggs 1934). But even in the absence of consistent political support, the amount of consumer product testing by the bureau, often in collaboration with industry and consumer groups, increased substantially in the 1920s and 1930s. By 1927, thirty-six American industries had established their own testing facilities, jointly operated with the bureau.[11] In the later 1920s, the bureau launched its specification program, in which it worked with manufacturers and consumers to define acceptable parameters for a vast range of products. In 1928, it set up a special Commercial Standards Unit, to deal with what one commentator described as "the pitfall of the consumer and the bane of the conscientious manufacturer . . . the maker of inferior goods."[12] The unit tested consumer products to ensure they met minimum quality specifications. As noted in Chapter 6, the bureau also offered to certify products that met specifications so that manufacturers could indicate this to consumers. By 1931, it had received fifteen thousand requests for certification, along with thirty thousand notifications from manufacturers indicating that they were "willing-to-certify."[13] Manufacturers wanted certification so that they could display "certified" labels to reassure consumers about the quality of the products they sold. The new labels worked, to use historian Norman Silbur's (1983) words, as a "certificate of character issued to an inanimate object" and spread rapidly through the marketplace, especially for consumer durables. By 1934, for example, three quarters of all gas burning appliances bore labels indicating that they met "nationally recognized specifications" (Agnew 1934, p. 61). Certification was in a way quite analogous to early branding. In both cases the point was to pin down products, ensure their quality, and remove uncertainty from the marketplace.

In addition to policing established standards, the Bureau of Standards conducted some research on how to improve consumer products. This work received a good amount of positive publicity and was commended and given support by various organizations. In 1924, for example, the American Automobile Association (a service member organization founded in 1902, known more commonly by its acronym, AAA) urged Congress to increase funding of the automative section of the Bureau of Standards. The AAA argued that the research activities of the bureau were "of greater value to automobile owners of the country than any other activity of government on behalf of motorists."[14] In particular, the AAA cited work done by the bureau that had doubled the life of brake linings, at no additional expense to the consumer.[15] In the same year, perhaps to promote its activities, the Bureau of Standards conducted well-publicized tests of golf balls, using a purpose-built machine, in order to encourage the golfing industry to adopt a standardized ball. According to one newspaper report, the bureau's golf ball testing machine "demonstrated that whereas [prestandardized] balls left the tee with a velocity of 156 feet a second, the new balls of standard manufacture had a speed of nearly 175 feet a second."[16]

The promotion of product standards and testing by the state, and by engineers working in industry, had, as mentioned, a good deal of influence on the consumer movement. Many of the important figures in the consumer movement who advocated a systematic program of product testing had backgrounds in engineering and sympathized with the ethics and aesthetics of the standardization movement. Schlink, one of the founders of Consumers' Research, was a trained engineer, as were many other influential figures in the movement. Schlink was also a former employee of the Bureau of Standards, and so was Arthur Kallet, cofounder along with Schlink of Consumers' Research. Chase, a key figure in Consumers Union (which broke away from Consumers' Research in 1936) and author of *Your Money's Worth*, one of the founding texts of the consumers' movement, had a background in accountancy. Under these figures, CU and Consumer's Research preached a gospel of efficient consumption. Influenced by Thorstein Veblen's ideas, the early consumer testing organizations criticized status-driven consumerism and espoused a narrowly utilitarian approach to consumption. Consumers were to be taught to be skeptical of the claims made by corporations about their brands and encouraged to spend their income in a maximally efficient fashion. In addition, the state was tasked with protecting consumer interests and promoting this rational approach to consumption (Schlink 1934).

Given the prominence of zealous members of the efficiency movement in early consumer testing organizations, it is tempting to see the diffusion of testing as being a result of the efforts of an enlightened reforming elite to educate the public about how to consume in a rational manner. It would be wrong, however, to interpret the rise of consumer testing solely in a "top-down" fashion, as the work of a vanguard of reformers, or of an increasingly technocratic state. For such an approach gives little sense of why product testing became so popular with the public and increasingly so as the century wore on. Moreover, how consumer product testing began (and who its pioneering figures were) did not determine the meanings it took on and what it subsequently became. While product testing might in its early years have been closely associated with reformist politics and the efficiency movement, it evolved into something quite different. The growth of consumer product testing was not just a manifestation of a grand historical process of technocratic rationalization. Rather, it also reflects changes in thinking about the locus of utility and in general attitudes toward commodities that took place in the context of the growing legitimacy of wage labor as a form of exchange.

One way to track the development of consumer product testing over the course of the twentieth century is by examining the evolution of the most popular and influential publication devoted to the testing of consumer products, *Consumer Reports*, along with its parent organization, Consumers Union. Both were very much at the center of the development of product testing as a mainstream, institutionalized practice in the postwar period. As the NBS consumer circulars became templates for *CR*, so *CR* became a model for product testing in other publications. Of course, interpreting the content of product testing, as it shifted over time, as indicative of changing consumer attitudes toward commodities raises the question of just how representative *CR* was of views among the great buying public. But Consumers Union was, from the end of the Second World War onward, increasingly concerned with expanding its membership and so tried to be finely attuned to the public mood. As CU moved from being an advocacy organization with an attached publication to being primarily the publisher of a magazine, attracting a sustainable subscriber base became a matter of great importance (N. D. Katz 1977).[17] The organization consequently became very sensitive to *CR* reader preferences and began to employ market research to better tailor consumer product testing to the interests and tastes of the public. The history of *Consumer Reports* and Consumers Union, then, to a fair degree does reflect broader changes in the orientation of consumer capitalism. The general trend evident over the history of the organization, and its increasingly popular magazine, was toward greater focus on the scientific testing of consumer durables, with less attention given to the political and social context of consumption and production.

1. Historical Trends in Consumer Product Testing in *Consumer Reports*

1.1. Rapid Expansion

The growth in the number of *CR* subscribers, especially in the postwar period, was dramatic. In 1946 the magazine had 80,000 subscribers. By 1949, the number had increased to 250,000; by 1950, to 400,000; and in 1957, there were close to 1,000,000 subscribers (N. D. Katz 1977, p. 308). In the early postwar years, *CR* became commonly available in public libraries, so the number of consumers consulting the magazine was certainly much greater than the number of subscribers. Moreover, as noted earlier, test results published in the magazine undoubtedly spread further afield by word of mouth. The influence of *CR* on consumer purchasing decisions was considerable. Its editor, Robert Brady, writing in *CR* in 1955, estimated that between 5 percent and 10 percent of "buying units" in the country were influenced by *CR*—a figure that Brady thought greatly underestimated the true extent of *CR*'s influence on consumer decisions.[18] Following the success of *CR*, other periodicals began to introduce product testing, and testing of consumer goods soon became common across the public sphere.

1.2. Depoliticization

As *Consumer Reports* expanded, it rapidly shed the political agenda it had been committed to in the 1930s. Early issues of the magazine had paid considerable attention to the working conditions under which consumer commodities were produced. Each issue featured a report on conditions of work in particular parts of the consumer goods industry. Readers were encouraged to assess products both from the standpoint of the consumer and from that of the workers who made the products. This reflected Consumers Union's explicit political and ethical objective to make connections between the concerns of consumers and those of workers, a goal which was clearly set out in the first issue of the magazine, published in May 1936. The justification given for this goal was that consumers are always at the same time also workers—and so it made no sense for consumer organizations to restrict their concerns to consumer interests alone. This point was made repeatedly in the magazine during its early years, becoming something of a mantra. For example, an editorial in July 1936 complained of the widespread tendency to fall "into the old confusion of treating consumers and workers as separate beings."[19] Helping consumers was taken to mean improving their material conditions as workers, following the logic that "the only way in which any organization can aid them materially as consumers is by helping them in their struggle as workers to get an honest wage."[20] At the same time, the editors of *CR* noted that "fighting for higher wages is not enough. Workers must fight also for fair prices and good quality in the products they buy."[21] Consumer and worker were thus seen as two sides of the same coin, both subject to the exploitative tendencies of the business class in America.

The prewar consumer movement thus took a holistic approach to assessing the welfare produced by industrial capitalism, considering the conditions under which goods were manufactured, as well as the properties of the goods themselves. In the postwar period, this holistic, political perspective was gradually replaced by a much narrower concern with testing—with an emphasis on the objective material characteristics of consumer products. The change in *CR* was reflective of a shift in the wider consumer movement in the middle part of the century. The 1950s witnessed what historian Gary Cross (2000, p. 135) characterizes as a "narrowing of scope of the consumer movement" as it came to focus solely on the "pricing and attributes of goods." Most significantly, in the late 1940s *Consumer Reports* ceased reporting on working conditions. In the postwar period, its parent organization, Consumers Union, took on a more technocratic perspective and became much less critical of the general contours of industrial capitalism.

The decrease in the attention given to the working conditions under which consumer goods are produced in part reflected the changed political environment in postwar America. Against the backdrop of McCarthyism, CU leaders were very eager not to be seen as tarnished by the brush of communism. Yet after the McCarthy witch hunts had receded into historical memory, there was no return to the more explicitly political agenda of the 1930s. A more politicized version of consumer activism did emerge in the 1960s, with Ralph Nader's campaign against corporate negligence in product design and manufacture. But the environment- and health-and-safety-centered agenda of Nader's new incarnation of the consumer movement was quite different from the concerns about labor that had animated the movement in the 1930s.

The change in orientation of *CR*, away from politics, to some degree reflected the changing socioeconomic profile of its subscribers. In the early years after the war, the expansion of CU's membership was predominantly middle class, and these new members were not very interested in labor issues of the sort that preoccupied consumer activists in the prewar period. Yet it would be wrong to take the middle-class perspective of CU in the postwar period as reason to think that the organization no longer had any relevance to the concerns of labor. For, as seen in earlier chapters, those concerns shifted in the postwar era. Although self-identified consumer activists tended to be middle class, consumer consciousness became incorporated into the labor movement. This was reflected in the reorganization of labor politics around the concept of purchasing power, which brought together labor and consumer interests.[22] Meg Jacobs (2005) and Lizabeth Cohen (2003), among others, have argued that over the course of the twentieth century the identity represented by "consumer" became universal in a way that transcended differences of class. But the universality of consumer identity (and of the supposed interests of the consumer) was itself an indirect consequence of mass participation in the labor market, against the backdrop of widespread acceptance of the legitimacy of wage-labor exchange and emergent corporatism in industrial relations. To a significant extent, the American public converged in the postwar decades on an acceptance of what could be described as an affluent compact. In exchange for working hard and accepting the broad parameters of American political economy, wage earners would be ensured decent and improving living standards. That this exchange appeared to be self-evidently reasonable and fair depended, in part, on a particular understanding of what consumer commodities are and how they relate to use—one in which use became to some degree abstracted from concrete, socially embedded practice, instead becoming a hypothetical function of the narrowly material use powers of products. The growing prominence of this understanding is evinced by the changing history of Consumers Union and *Consumer Reports*. The approach to consumer products expressed and promoted by CU, and by the broader practice of product testing, played an important role in relieving some of the attendant tensions of the contradictions of labor under capitalism, if not fully resolving them.

1.3 Changes in the Set of Objects Tested and in the Guide to Testing

A significant percentage of the products tested by consumer organizations in the prewar era were perishables. Increasingly in the postwar era, however, testing shifted to consumer durables. The obvious explanation for this is that as incomes increased, consumer durables came to form an increasingly important part of household consumption. Indeed, the relatively greater amount of attention paid to testing perishables and other nondurable goods in the early issues of *CR* could be interpreted as just a reflection of the dismal economic conditions of the 1930s. However, *Consumer Reports* in its early years, as noted, very much catered to a middle-class readership, which was therefore relatively insulated from the economic ravages of the Depression. Moreover, the great era of expansion of the market for consumer durables—the so-called consumer durables revolution—took place roughly between 1910 and 1940 (Olney 1990, 1998). Even against the background of deteriorating economic conditions in the 1930s, demand for consumer durables remained high, and continued to increase. And if we compare the post-Depression period to later periods, the same trend is evident. For example, in the 1947 *Consumer Reports Buyers Guide*, the annual compendium of test results, out of 373 pages, 75 were devoted to food, and a further 136 pages were taken up by pharmaceuticals and personal care products, leaving only 129 pages of tests of durable goods. By comparison, in the 1985 *Buyer's Guide* 375 out of a total of 385 pages were devoted to tests of consumer durables.

As suggested, to some extent this change in the kind of objects tested can be explained by changes in the consumer product mix. As real incomes increased, which they did steadily in the postwar period, the market for consumer durables expanded, and so durables became more prominent in household purchasing decisions. Since consumer durables are typically expensive, and tend to be complex artifacts, expert advice and test results would be comparatively more important for purchasing decisions about them.[23] There were also organizational factors involved in the predominance of cheap goods over durables in testing by CU in the 1930s. In its early years, Consumers Union and Consumers' Research operated on shoe-string budgets, and so could not afford to buy many consumer durables to test. These explanations go some way toward accounting for the difference between the kinds of products tested pre- and postwar in *Consumer Reports*. At the same time, the increasing preoccupation, in the postwar period, with scientifically interrogating durable goods in order to disclose their useful powers (or lack thereof), is consistent with the theory that mass consumption was driven by wage-labor commensuration. For if wages are fairly exchanged by virtue of the use power contained in wage goods, then getting clear about just how much use power they contain becomes very important. Durable goods, construed as repositories of potential free activity, are uniquely able to make the wage commensurable with the labor given in exchange for it. This means that it is particularly important for worker / consumers to gain information about them—which would explain the increasing prevalence of durable products in consumer testing.

Another change in *CR* testing over the course of its history is in the size and content of the guide to how tests should be interpreted and used. In 1947, the "how to" section took up six pages and included a guide to shopping judiciously, as well as a statement about the objectivity of the testing procedures. By 1987 that section had been cut to just three pages, containing a description of the layout of the book, an account of the reasoning underlying the decisions made by the organization about what items to test, a note on how to interpret symbols used in product assessment, and a statement about the objectivity of the organization. The shrinking size of the guide section, which in the 1930s and 1940s had included advice about how to get the best price for a given good, indicates a change in focus from the practice of shopping, with the emphasis on promoting prudence in the marketplace, to the characteristics of the goods themselves.

1.4. The Rise of Scientific Testing and Quasi-Quantitative Ratings

From its beginnings, CU was eager to use scientific testing to pin down the properties of consumer goods. Consumers Union had always emphasized the scientific nature of its work, describing itself as above all else "a technical organization." The first issue of *Consumer Reports* set out its primary goal as follows: "The main effort of its staff, and the main use of its funds will be to conduct research and tests on consumer goods," with the aim of "giving technical aid" to the consumer. Products were to be systematically rated based on "laboratory tests." At the same time, it was acknowledged that both objective and subjective criteria are important in establishing the quality of a given product, and there was some recognition of the limitations of scientific testing. An editorial preface to an early issue admitted that while for example, "stockings may be carefully tested in the laboratory . . . experts are far from being in agreement as to the value of such tests in determining how well a pair of stockings will wear."[24] Nonetheless, the mission of the organization was, as far as possible, to promote consumption decisions made on a purely "technical" basis, and the organization was eager to assure the buying public of the rigor of its methods. The introduction to the yearly guide published by the organization set out the mission of the organization in the following terms: "The technical staff gives its assurance to members of Consumers Union . . . that it will exercise greatest care in testing and judging products, in checking data, and in preparing ratings . . ." [with the objective of substituting] ". . . the best technical knowledge that can be made available for haphazard guessing; and it does give the consumer the satisfaction of having his buying choices determined by technical tests rather than by the cleverness of an advertising copy writer or the ingenuity of a manufacturer in making a shoddy product look like a good one."

Over time this emphasis on the technical, scientific side of product testing intensified. The concern to conduct rigorous scientific testing led CU to make increasing investments in sophisticated laboratories and testing facilities, and between 1944 and 1954, the laboratory space at CU underwent a massive expansion. The scientific prowess and technological sophistication of CU increasingly became the major selling point of its publication, *Consumer Reports*. As the century wore on an increasing amount of space in *Consumer Reports* was given over to elaborate descriptions of testing procedures, in order to indicate their rigor and objectivity. Greater prominence was also given to the scientific credentials of those doing the testing. Also evident over this period is a move from loose assessment of objects as imagined under conditions of daily use, to subjection of tested items to extreme conditions, to chart the ultimate limits of their useful properties. In pushing products to their breaking point, testing moved away from the conditions under which products would likely get used, to focus instead on probing their physical limits. A further change in *CR*'s testing objectives between the pre- and postwar periods was a shift in emphasis from protecting the public from dangerous products, to making fine distinctions between acceptable ones—distinctions which, for an average user, would often be of little practical consequence.[25]

While objectivity and scientific precision were the guiding principles in product testing, the early ratings system was purely qualitative. In the prewar era of testing, products were placed in one of three qualitative categories: "acceptable," "also acceptable," and "not acceptable." These later became "best buy," "acceptable," and "not acceptable." The assessment system was explained in early issues of *CR* as follows: "The ratings are determined by both quality and price. If Brand A wears half as long but costs only a quarter as much as Brand B, then Brand A will get the higher rating." "Best buy" therefore is not the highest-quality product, but the one that gives "best value (in use terms) for money." The postwar period, however, witnessed a gradual shift from qualitative assessments toward the use of quantitative product ratings. An important change in this direction took place in the 1970s, when *CR* adopted "Harvey Balls," a system of ideograms to represent product quality developed by (and named after) business consultant Harvey Poppel. *CR*'s lead was followed by many other publications, and Poppel's ideograms became widespread in the 1970s. With the use of Harvey Balls product test reports started giving, in effect, quasi-quantitative assessments of qualitative characteristics. As shown in Figure 8.1, degrees of quality are signified by each symbol, with quality increasing progressively in each row as we move from right to left. Quality is denoted by the proportion of a circle that is shaded. There are different versions of the system—the one adopted

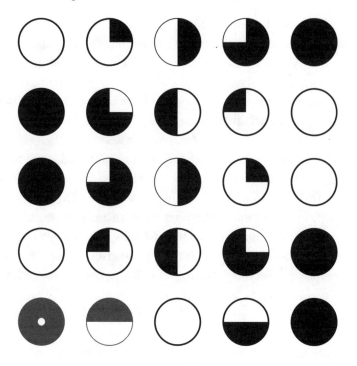

Fig 8.1: Harvey Balls. mintsauce/openclipart.org/CC0 1.0

by *CR* is displayed in the lowest row in the figure. In *CR*'s system, two colors are used. The more red (represented here as gray) there is in the circle, the higher the quality of the product; conversely, the more black there is in the circle, the lower the product quality. The empty middle circle represents "average" quality.

The thing to note here is that this system of ideograms, although in one way presenting an ordinal ranking of quality, is graphically suggestive of proportional relations between what appear to be the *quantities of quality* represented by each circle. For example, in the system shown in the second row above, the fully shaded circle represents the highest-quality rating, while the empty circle represents the lowest-quality rating. This mode of graphic representation implies that as the circle becomes more completely shaded, quality proportionately increases. The *CR* system, shown in the bottom row, is more complex in that, as noted, two shading colors are used, red and black, with red denoting degrees of above average quality and black denoting degrees of below average quality. Yet still, an intuitive interpretation of the almost fully filled in red circle is that it represents roughly twice as much quality as the half-filled circle—which in turn contains twice the quality of the empty middle circle. And likewise, the half-filled black circle represents twice as much quality as the fully filled in black circle. The semiotics of Harvey Balls thus suggest a translation of qualitative assessments into quasi-quantitative ratings. The use of the same quasi-quantitative system of ideograms to rate a very wide range of consumer products implies that there is a metric by virtue of which qualitatively quite distinct items (for example, cars and stereos) can be rendered commensurable. Such a metric suggests the existence of a kind of universal unit of quality, which makes possible a comparison between proverbial apples and oranges. Later in its history, *Consumer Reports* shifted from the sole use of ideograms, to joint use of ideograms and a numerical product score for each qualitative dimension of tested items, along with an aggregate score for each item. In effect, this turned qualitative assessments directly into quantitative scores. This trend in the representation of product test results became quite general over the course of the last third of the twentieth century, with widespread use in the media of quasi- or fully quantitative scales to represent degrees of product quality.

The increasing prevalence of quantitative measures of quality is suggestive for the argument of this book. For it indicates the growing influence of a form of thinking that reduces the use value of disparate kinds of product to a general, measurable, abstract unit of quality. Consumer products when construed as quantities of quality roughly map onto the wage, taken as a quantitative valuation of the qualitative activity given as labor. As wage labor quantified the qualitatively specific life activity given as work, so the qualitatively particular use values commanded by the wage became construed in quantitative terms. The conceptualization of quality in terms of quantity made more plausible the commensurability of labor and its wage, by virtue of the purchasing power of the wage over goods invested with units of quality.

2. Interpretation

How should the rise of consumer product testing be interpreted? In part, testing was a response to the increasing opacity of commodities. This opacity was, to some degree, a consequence of the advanced division of labor, which broke up work into increasingly specialized activities, and thereby disconnected individual labor from the finished product.[26] The increasing technological complexity of consumer products also contributed to the estrangement between product and user. Consumer durables, in particular, became sets of propositions about functional capacities, sold to consumers as promises, attached to artifacts that were increasingly becoming black boxes. Product testing then involved interrogating those promises by opening these black boxes—a project of reverse engineering instigated, appropriately enough, by engineers.

Seen in this way, the popularity of third-party product testing could be interpreted as simply reflecting an entirely reasonable ongoing effort on the part of households to gain information on the basis of which to direct consumption in a maximally efficient fashion. Product testing, on this understanding, performs essentially the same function for households as it does for business and the state. Businesses and state organizations test in order to monitor the quality of the goods and materials they procure, to ensure that resources have been used in an efficient manner. Likewise, for households, testing provides information to assist them in making rational decisions about resource allocation.

But drawing this parallel between households and firms raises a question: What output does the household seek to maximize? One account of what it is that buying units are trying to maximize could be derived from economist Alfred Marshall's (2013) concept of the *consumer surplus*. The consumer surplus is the difference between what a buyer would have been prepared to pay for a good, and the actual price of the good.[27] In textbook economics, the aggregate consumer surplus for a given good is represented by the area below the demand curve and above the point of price equilibrium. Consumers whose demand lies in that area would have paid more for the good than its equilibrium price, so when they buy at that price, they, as it were, pocket the difference (measured in virtual money terms). Another way of putting this is that their subjective valuation of the good is higher than the objective price it sells at—its market price. A household can be construed as attempting to maximize its total consumer surplus over the basket of goods that it purchases, and the degree to which it is spending efficiently can in theory be measured by the size of its consumer surplus. Testing then gives households information they can use to come up with accurate valuations of goods. However, the consumer surplus interpretation assumes to an implausible degree that consumers know with some precision what their subjective money valuation of a good is, and, further, that this maps onto its utility for them.

An alternative account of what households seek to maximize could be taken from modern consumer theory. As we saw in Chapter 2, two prominent economists who, in their respective theories of the household production function, have come up with a theoretical answer to this question are Kelvin Lancaster (1966a, 1966b) and Gary Becker (1981). To recapitulate, Becker and Lancaster hold that households can be thought of as factories, using consumer products to generate utility, much as firms use capital goods to produce commodities. Within this framework, households use product testing to gain information they can use to develop a purchasing strategy that will maximize the utility they produce. Indeed, Lancaster (1966b, p. 18), makes reference to the product testing activities of Consumers Union in his 1966 essay on technologies of consumption, noting that CU's testing performs the function of providing information about the utility generating power of commodities, on the basis of which households can make efficient purchasing decisions.

Although this explanation initially seems straightforward, on reflection an immediate problem arises. The firm can calculate the degree to which a given set of expenditures is an efficient one by comparing money costs of production to the realized or projected money value of output. However, it is not clear how a household can make equivalent calculations about utility. For that to be possible, the quality of experience of household members would have to be quantified so that the relative benefits of different allocations of household resources could be systematically compared. In addition, the total utility of expenditure would have to be compared to the disutility of the work done to generate household revenue. Yet without being able to use money as a proxy for quality of experience (the expedient move economists tend to make), it is not at all apparent how those kinds of calculations could be carried out. Efficiency calculations require a degree of precision that is possible where the objective is to maximize money revenues, because money is a public, therefore observable metric. But such calculations are much trickier where the object of maximization is construed in terms of the vague, essentially psychological, concept of utility.[28]

More concretely, as I noted in Chapter 2, even if we accept Becker's picture of households as utility factories, his theory, when placed in the context of actual historical patterns, runs up against the empirical time / work / income puzzle. For if we assume, with Becker, that household decisions can be, and indeed are, directed by the goal of maximizing actual utility, with consumer goods working as capital equipment in the production of this final output, how can we account for the consistent tendency, identified in earlier chapters, for households to turn increasing hourly income into more capital goods rather than more time in which to use them? Following Becker's reasoning, if consumer goods are household analogues to a firm's capital goods, then units of leisure time are analogues to units of labor time. Labor and capital combine in producing an output, whether goods or utility. It makes no obvious sense, therefore, for the household, following an increase in hourly wage income, to use all of the extra income to buy capital (utility-generating) goods rather than allocating some of it to increase the amount of labor (free time) available to make use of added capital goods to produce utility. For a household to spend all its available income on consumer commodities while not increasing time available to make use of those commodities is equivalent to a firm purchasing capital equipment without hiring the labor required to put it to work. The result is that the equipment is left idle—hardly an efficient outcome from any perspective (what firm would be happy with investing in capital that subsequently languishes unutilized?).

Of course, under any given regime of work time and income, it seems reasonable that households would use information from product tests to direct spending so as to generate as much utility as possible. But seeing product testing as just a reasonable guide to rational consumer decision-making, under the particular regime of consumption and work-time that developed in the mid-twentieth century, takes the institution of product testing, and all that it represents, to be exogenous to that regime. However, the institution of product testing was not independent of that regime, but, rather, reflected an attitude toward commodities that to some degree explains its emergence. This is because product testing emphasized the physical properties of consumer objects and did so in a quasi-scientific and quantitative manner. The fit between a given product and the conditions of life within which the product would typically get used, was not a matter that was given much consideration by consumer product testing organizations such as CU. The rapid growth of product testing then indicates that increasing importance was attached to specifying and measuring the potential utility inhering in the physical properties of commodities—which in turn indicates the growing influence of a narrow and hypothetical conception of use value, in light of which a money wage became more easily imaginable as commensurable with the labor given in exchange for it. In this sense, product testing has a significance similar to the developments described in the previous chapter—the rise of branded consumer goods, commercial warranties, and the emergence of the implied warranty. The effect of these developments was to stabilize and standardize the use value of wage goods while encouraging a tendency to think about matters of utility and usefulness in terms of the properties of objects rather than situated practices.

To sum up this chapter, and the two that went before, standardization, where it concerned consumer goods, was as much a moral as a technical matter. The moral dimension of standardization subsisted in the value attached to the production of "honest" commodities—those imbued with solid and durable qualities, indexed by trustworthy signs (brands and product certifications), underwritten by commercial warranties, to some degree safeguarded by the regulation of the state and courts, and policed by testing activities in the public sphere. There was a clear sense in which people, as wage earners and consumers (or rather, as wage workers who consume), were, to an increasing extent over the course of the century, seen as being entitled to products that met those ideals. But this entitlement did not entail a right to a form of life within which accumulated commodities could actually be made use of in practice. Rather, the emphasis was on the properties of the things themselves, and particularly on the duration of useful activity they contain *in potentia*. In the next chapter, I consider the moral reaction to cases (imagined or real) in which the entitlement to fair, standard durations of use power in products was thought to have been violated by manufacturers.

NINE

Moral Panic about Utility: Planned Obsolescence

Over the last three chapters, I considered a number of institutions and practices, closely associated with consumer capitalism, that are suggestive of a shift in the locus of utility from the total context of use to the material properties of things. These included the development of warranty law, specifically the change from express to implied product warranties, the growth of consumer product testing, increasing state regulation of products, and the emergence of the brand as an index of standardized product characteristics. All these developments can be interpreted in terms of an effort to fix or stabilize the notional use power contained in things. In the present chapter, I narrow my focus, turning to the debates and discussions about planned obsolescence that took place in the middle part of the twentieth century. The worries expressed about planned obsolescence amounted to, if not quite a moral panic, then at the very least a sign of significant moral disquiet, which reveals something about the normative grounding of exchange relationships in the capitalist economy of the so-called Golden Age of industrial capitalism (roughly spanning the years between 1945 and 1975). In particular, the concern about planned obsolescence indicates something about the nature and location of use value within a broad moral economy connecting labor, the wage, and consumer commodities. If the institutions and practices described in the last three chapters can be interpreted as indicating normative expectations about the quantity and quality of usefulness contained in wage goods, the situation under consideration in this chapter is one in which those norms were perceived to have been violated—in which the use value of consumer commodities was thought to have been intentionally limited or degraded by practices of so-called planned obsolescence on the part of industry.

Planned obsolescence has a complex history, the shape of which depends on the makeup of the set of practices and ideas to which the term is taken to refer. Concerns about planned obsolescence are from one perspective continuous with perennial worries about uncertain product quality. Product adulteration, for example, was an ongoing issue in America throughout the nineteenth century.[1] Adulteration was a central concern within an older moral economy and was framed in terms of rights to subsistence in a custom-bound setting, the classic account of which is given by E. P. Thompson (1993). Food safety was certainly a matter of concern into the modern era of consumer activism. In the United States, worries about product contamination animated the consumer movement in its first phase, during the Progressive era, which culminated in the creation of the Food and Drug Administration in 1906. However, adulteration and contamination most often involve perishables rather than durable goods, so those worries were less applicable to the kinds of goods produced by the nascent system of industrial manufacturing. If planned obsolescence is taken to mean preemptive changes in product design reflecting awareness, on the part of producers, of the mercurial character of taste, then the practice dates at least as far back as the eighteenth century (McKendrick, Brewer, and Plumb 1984). Indeed, the modern dialectic between shifting tastes and changing design probably goes back as far as the ending of sumptuary laws at the waning of the middle ages—and insofar as we have plenty of archaeological evidence of changing styles in artifacts manufactured for exchange, conceivably all the way back to the early beginnings of commodity production. The understanding of something like planned obsolescence as a necessary consequence of the industrial economy, on the other hand, can be found in the nineteenth century. For example, Charles Babbage (1832), the influential engineer and mathematician, argued that the rate of industrial technological progress was such as to guarantee that manufactured products would rapidly be superseded by newer, improved versions, rendering them obsolete.

Despite these conceptual precursors, the actual term *planned obsolescence* first appears in the 1930s, in the decade after General Motors introduced the marketing strategy with which the term was later to become synonymous. It was in the middle years of the twentieth century, however, that the term became a lightning rod for criticisms of industrial capitalism. The term began to gain notoriety following its promotion in the 1950s by the influential industrial designer Brook Stevens, dubbed "the crown prince of planned obsolescence" (Slade 2006). In a brochure published in 1953, Stevens defined planned obsolescence as "instilling in the buyer the desire to own something a little newer, a little better, and a little sooner than is necessary" (Adamson 2003, p. 129). He later set out the place of the doctrine in the role of the industrial designer: "Our task is to induce the public to buy or to possess something that is always new, and thus to promote the industries to go on with production" (Heskett 2003, p. 4). The crystallization of the moral controversy around planned obsolescence can be dated in particular to the publication in 1960 of Vance Packard's best-seller, *The Waste Makers*. Reflecting the timing of Packard's polemic, *The Barnhart Dictionary of New English Since 1963* (1973) registers *planned obsolescence* as an important new phrase in the language in the early 1960s. During that decade, the issues surrounding planned obsolescence came into sharp focus and were broadly thematized and discussed with some urgency across the public sphere. In the 1960s, planned obsolescence became part of the stock list of complaints about capitalism. It was, for example, listed as one of the chief ills of capitalism in the 1962 Port Huron statement, issued by the Society for Democratic Students. The statement condemned: "The tendency to over-production, to gluts of surplus commodities," claiming that the system "encourages 'market research' techniques to deliberately create pseudo-needs in consumers—we learn to buy 'smart' things, regardless of their utility—and introduces wasteful 'planned obsolescence' as a permanent feature of business strategy" (SDS 1964, pp. 15–16). C. Wright Mills (2008, p. 177) made a similar point in his essay "The Man in the Middle," written in 1958: "Continuous and expanding production requires continuous and expanding consumption, so consumption must be speeded up by all the tactics and frauds of marketing. Moreover, existing commodities must be worn out more quickly for as the market is saturated, the economy becomes increasingly dependent upon what is called replacement. It is then that obsolescence comes to be planned and its cycle deliberately shortened." Assessments of this sort could be folded into the current of twentieth-century American social thought critical of the emergent industrial order, which included the writings of such figures as Thorstein Veblen, Vance Packard, Kenneth Burke, J. K. Galbraith, Marshall McLuhan, and Stuart Chase (Brick 2006; Horowitz 1994). However, the concern over planned obsolescence extended well beyond a narrow circle of public intellectuals. In the middle years of the century it became commonplace in discussions about the operation of the industrial economy.

A central part of the argument of this book is that a precondition for the development and stabilization of mass consumer capitalism was that the use value of commodities became construed narrowly in terms of their material properties, with little consideration given to the broader contextual conditions required for their use. It was by virtue of use values being construed in this way that the wage relation could be represented as an exchange of commensurable substances. The mid-century concern about planned obsolescence reflects this preoccupation with fixing use, and especially a duration of use, in commodity objects. The moral force behind the negative reaction to planned obsolescence is at least in part plausibly explained by an underlying concern, implicit in the wage compact, with a just and fair exchange of use values.

1. Different Versions of Planned Obsolescence

What did people mean in mid-century America when they made use of the term *planned obsolescence*? Commentators writing at the time identified three kinds of planned obsolescence, which I will call material obsolescence, style obsolescence, and technical obsolescence.

Material planned obsolescence, the most straightforward of the three, is obsolescence caused by breakage. The product becomes obsolete because it has become physically compromised to the point that it is no longer able to perform the function it is meant to perform.

Style obsolescence, also referred to as "psychological obsolescence," has a more subjective character. The product is able to function properly but is obsolescent because it is no longer the latest model of its kind. Not being "up to date" produces an impetus in consumers (the nature of which is unclear) to substitute a newer version of the product for an older one. The paradigmatic example of this is the obsolescence of older automobile models caused by yearly changes in model style (a practice begun by General Motors in the 1920s).

Technical obsolescence is obsolescence resulting from a change in the context of use that affects the use value of a product. The product retains its physical integrity, and indeed possibly also its psychological appeal, but is no longer compatible with other objects required for its proper functioning. This kind of obsolescence often follows changes in industry standards. An example would be an outdated computer, which can no longer perform certain tasks because current software requires more powerful hardware, while the older software that the machine can run is no longer supported.

In discursive practice there is much semantic slippage between the different forms of obsolescence, and it is often unclear exactly what form is at issue in a given discussion. There are also liminal cases that fall between the different kinds of obsolescence. For example, cases in which a product retains its functionality yet comes to be thought of as obsolescent because newer versions appear that are technically superior fall between style and technical obsolescence. While the "obsolete" product is still entirely functional, at the same time because it is technically inferior to newer versions, it becomes regarded as obsolete by comparison.

2. What Is Puzzling about the Concern over Planned Obsolescence?

Before pressing forward with a finer-grained analysis of the mid-century controversy around planned obsolescence, some consideration ought to be given to a possible objection to the notion that there is much of interest in the topic. Surely, the objection goes, the concern about planned obsolescence simply reflects an entirely understandable preoccupation on the part of consumers with getting value for money, in combination with a sensibly suspicious stance toward big business and its underlying motives. If this commonsense intuition is correct, what then is so puzzling about the mid-century worries about planned obsolescence?

There are at least two reasons for thinking that the preoccupation with planned obsolescence was not just a straightforward matter of rational consumers practicing due diligence by interrogating the design of industrial products. First, the degree of concern over planned material obsolescence is surprisingly high, given that the evidence for widespread implementation of the practice was slim to nonexistent. As we shall see later in the chapter, in the early 1970s the Federal Trade Commission investigated material obsolescence and found no evidence that the practice was at all common. Moreover, it is unclear what criterion should be used to determine whether egregious material obsolescence is present in a given product. If material obsolescence means that an object breaks before its time, what then determines its time? What is it that establishes a reasonable duration of use for a consumer durable? In the discussions about planned material obsolescence (so-called death dates), the answer to that question remains obscure.

Furthermore, according to basic economic theory, under competitive market conditions costs of production and price tend to converge, so if cheaper, less durable materials get used in a product, this should result in cheaper prices. That implies that under broadly competitive conditions consumers on the whole get what they pay for and so have no obvious cause for feeling cheated when their products fail. It seems plausible that material obsolescence in its most heinous imagined form, scrimping on materials and workmanship while keeping prices high, is, therefore, only possible under monopoly conditions (Bulow 1986). Yet for economic and legal reasons—competitive pressures in the capitalist economy on the one hand and antitrust laws on the other—monopolies (and oligopolies) are not easy to establish or maintain. So it would seem that the most objectionable form of material obsolescence—low quality at high prices—was quite unlikely to have been a widespread feature of the mid-century economy.

Of course, even in the absence of monopoly conditions, with price and product characteristics set by the market, it could still be the case that consumers would prefer their products to be significantly more durable than is typically the case. Yet that would be puzzling given the rate at which—for reasons connected to style and technical obsolescence—consumers replace commodities. What sense would it make to add to costs, and therefore price, by designing products to be more durable than the likely duration of ownership? If, for example, consumers on average replace their cars every three years (as was the case in the 1960s), why should they object if manufacturers design them not to last for much longer than that, as long as that gets reflected in the price? Surely material durability should be determined by the predicted average length and intensity of product use? Indeed, an alternative way of understanding planned material obsolescence is as the application of "value engineering," According to the principle of value engineering, which was pioneered by General Electric during the Second World War with the aim of maximizing the efficiency of wartime production, probable patterns of product use should be taken into account in designing product durability. The idea is to engineer a level of durability in products that fits the expected average duration and intensity of their use, with some added margin for safety. Within this paradigm, products not designed with their likely use in mind risk being inefficient by virtue of being "overengineered"—a condition in which a product's material durability is higher than it needs to be. The product then tends to outlast its actual useful life. Insofar as a gratuitous surplus of durability increases cost with no added benefit in use, this counts as waste.[2] From the perspective of value engineering, therefore, to reject planned material obsolescence risks the wasteful use of productive resources in overengineered products.[3]

Style obsolescence, of the sort most commonly identified with yearly model changes in the automobile industry, is a more obviously real phenomenon than material obsolescence. It is not clear, however, in what sense any reneging on contractual or moral obligations on the part of business is involved in this form of obsolescence. If consumers choose to trade in last year's model of some commodity for the latest version, in what sense are producers to blame? And yet a good deal of criticism was directed at the practice of frequent model changes. Even as sober a body as the Federal Reserve Bank of Philadelphia, in a study analyzing depreciation in the auto market, came to the conclusion that style obsolescence has deleterious economic effects.[4] The view expressed in the study was that the depreciation caused by planned obsolescence of style (as opposed to substantive changes in function) is in some sense a "false" depreciation, resulting in unnecessary waste. The study, which was cited by Vance Packard (1960, p. 88), estimated that frequent model changes were causing automobiles to depreciate "twice as fast as they reasonably should." A normative distinction was being made here between genuine material reasons for depreciation and style-related reasons that are somehow illegitimate. But within what moral framework is style, or "psychological," obsolescence objectionable, and loss of value for aesthetic reasons an "unreasonable" kind of depreciation? Again, the answer is not obvious.[5]

Technical obsolescence might have been a more genuine concern. If products are rendered useless because they have become incompatible with an infrastructure required for their use that is continuously being upgraded, then consumers might have good reason to feel hard done by. Yet prior to the explosive development in the later twentieth century of consumer products incorporating information technology, with software standards linked to rapidly evolving hardware, obsolescence of this kind was not very common. In the mid-century discourse about planned obsolescence, concerns about technical obsolescence are, in any case, not strongly expressed. The moral panic about the issue focused primarily on material and style obsolescence.

Concerns about obsolescence thus seem underdetermined by the economic facts of the matter, given the unlikeliness of widespread material obsolescence, the obscurity of the reasons for regarding style obsolescence as problematic, and the fact that technical obsolescence was not a common fact of product life until later on in the twentieth century (by which time the intense concern about planned obsolescence had largely subsided). How then can we account for the force of mid-century fears and suspicions about planned obsolescence?

In the remainder of this chapter, I try to answer this question by analyzing talk about planned obsolescence in the middle part of the last century. My objective is to tease out the issues at stake in the discussion and its underlying assumptions. With this aim in mind, I chart the changing terms of the controversy around planned obsolescence, as it unfolded in the public sphere from the first appearance of the concept in the 1930s, through to its articulation to nascent concerns about the environment in the early 1970s. The focus of the chapter is on how the controversy illuminates normative notions about use and exchange in the context of the Fordist moral economy that emerged by the middle decades of the twentieth century.

3. Tracking Moral Panics and Disturbances

It is perhaps a sociological truism that not every element of a culture that has normative force is spelled out explicitly as a norm. Even where norms are made somewhat explicit, for example in law, it is often the case that the account given of the norm is rather thin—the norm is articulated as a rule without elaboration of the underlying system of values within which the rule makes sense. Moreover, the relative importance of a norm, and its influence on behavior, cannot be inferred just from formal statements of the norm. Some rules can be broken with relative impunity. Others, when transgressed, induce extremely powerful reactions. For these reasons, in order to give a full account of a norm, it is often necessary to elicit a "thick" account of it, by way of various forms of ethnographic investigation. What can we do, however, when we are interested in the normative dimension of a past that is accessible only as refracted through the materials of archives—when, therefore, it is impossible to develop a deeper understanding of the norms underlying actions and reactions by questioning, or just directly observing, living subjects? To get a fuller picture of past norms we must go beyond just attending to formal statements about norms, such as those found in law, and develop more oblique interpretive approaches. One strategy is to analyze the shape and intensity of the response where norms are thought to have been transgressed. The historical analyst pays particular attention to the way in which things get talked out in expressions of outrage, then makes abductions about the moral background within which that talk makes sense.

In order to track the discussions around planned obsolescence, and the shape of the moral disturbance created by fears about the practice, I analyzed newspaper articles in which the term appeared in a set of major regional and national newspapers in the United States, paying particular attention to the period between 1932 (when the term first appeared) and 1975. I take the mid-1970s to roughly mark the end of the Golden Age era of capitalism (Marglin and Schor 1991). The set of newspapers includes the *New York Times, Chicago Tribune, Baltimore Sun Times, Los Angeles Times, Wall Street Journal, Washington Post, Chicago Sun Times, New York Post, Pittsburgh Courier, New York Amsterdam Times, Los Angeles Sentinel,* and *Atlanta Daily World.* In these publications between 1930 and 1975 there were 469 pieces in which the term *planned obsolescence* appeared. In addition, I analyzed especially influential magazine articles and books about planned obsolescence—for example, Vance Packard's seminal discussion of the topic, and pieces by prominent figures such as J. K. Galbraith, Marshal McLuhan, and Viktor Papanek. I also looked at discussions about planned obsolescence in the business and finance literature, in professional and trade journals, and tracked the concept in the academic and para-academic literature, especially in economics. Lastly, I examined company reports about planned obsolescence as a marketing strategy, or as an objective in product development, and looked at advertisements that invoked planned obsolescence. As well as following discussions about planned obsolescence, I tracked cognate terms, such as *death dating, psychological obsolescence, dynamic obsolescence,* and *progressive obsolescence.*

I treat this quite diverse collection of sources as a reasonably representative sample of discourse about planned obsolescence. In consulting this material, I had two objectives: first, to reconstruct the array of issues at stake in the idea of planned obsolescence and, second, to note how concern about the issue ebbed, flowed, and changed in nature over time.

4. Overview of General Trends

Some sense of the waxing and waning of the concern about planned obsolescence over the course of the twentieth century is given by breaking down the number of articles in which the term appears by decade in a sample of four major national dailies: the *New York Times, Chicago Tribune, Washington Post,* and *Wall Street Journal.* The numbers are as follows:

1930–1939: 3
1940–1949: 1
1950–1959: 13
1960–1969: 165
1970–1979: 107
1980–1989: 86
1990–1999: 120
2000–2009: 113

The peak decade for articles discussing planned obsolescence was the 1960s, after which the term drops away somewhat, until the 1990s, which show an increase over the preceding decade.[6] This pattern reflects the heightened concern about planned obsolescence in the late 1950s and 1960s, the ebbing of the issue in the later 1970s and 1980s, and then, toward the end of the century, the increasing importance of a new context of application for the concept, with the rapid growth of the information technology industry.

Insofar as the term *planned obsolescence* has a presence in the 1930s (and it does not to any significant degree), it is in relation to debates and discussions about the role of underconsumption in producing, or prolonging, the Depression. The term first appears in print in the work of businessman Bernard London, whose pamphlet *How to End the Depression by Means of Planned Obsolescence* was published in 1932. The nature and scope of London's argument is quite explicit in its title. London advocated using planned obsolescence to increase consumer demand by reducing the length of ownership of things. The benefit of this would be that it would provide much-needed stimulus for the depressed economy. This use of *planned obsolescence* was similar to an earlier term, *progressive obsolescence,* which was used by the American home economist Christine Frederick in her influential 1929 book, *Selling Mrs. Consumer.*[7] Like Charles Babbage a century earlier, Frederick (1929, p. 81) saw progressive obsolescence as a natural and necessary byproduct of the onward march of technology and industrial society: "The machine and power era makes it not only possible but vital to apply in the home the doctrine of creative waste." Frederick defined *progressive obsolescence* as :"1) A state of mind which is highly suggestible and open;

eager and willing to take hold of anything new either in the shape of a new invention or new designs or styles or ways of living. 2) A readiness to 'scrap' or lay aside an article before its natural life is completed, in order to make way for the newer and better thing. 3) A willingness to apply a very large share of one's income, even if it pinches savings, to the acquisition of the new goods or services or way of living" (p. 246). Although Frederick wrote her book before the Depression had taken hold, she, like London, argued that, for the sake of economic stability, consumption should be regimented according to the requirements of the Taylorist system of mass production.[8]

In the postwar period, however the term *planned obsolescence* takes on a very marked negative moral charge. Perhaps significantly, Vance Packard makes no mention at all of London's positive account of planned obsolescence in his influential 1960 book on the topic. Packard's primary target was rather the industrial designer Brook Stevens, who, in the early 1950s, advocated planned obsolescence as vital for the health of business and the economy at large.

In the middle years of the century, planned obsolescence was typically regarded as problematic because the practice supposedly short-changed the consumer. Businesses were seen as reneging on their obligations to the consumer by cutting short the duration of potential useful activity facilitated by commodities they sold to the public, either by engineered "death dates" or by inducing psychological dissatisfaction. From the early 1970s onward, however, concerns about planned obsolescence took an environmental turn. The practice was condemned on the grounds that it produces pollution and waste, with adverse effects on the environment. At the same time, in the last quarter of the century the perceived locus of the problem to some extent shifted from nefarious business practice to misguided or unthinking consumers.

Planned obsolescence has continued to have a significant presence in public discourse up until the present day. However, the negative moral aura carried by the term dissipated to a significant extent toward the end of the twentieth century. The term became more neutral and descriptive, used in particular in reference to increasing technical obsolescence associated with information technology, which tends to be narrated as a quasi-natural process. By the century's end planned obsolescence came to be viewed much as Babbage and Frederick saw it, as a normal corollary of technical progress.

I would suggest that the waxing and waning of concerns about planned obsolescence reflects tectonic changes in capitalism. The evolving discourse about planned obsolescence, as mentioned earlier, tracks the decline of capitalism's Golden Age corporatist form, in which a stable arrangement between labor and business ensured that increases in labor productivity would be reflected in increasing real wages (Glyn 2006). Arguably the environmental critique was able to take center stage discussions about product obsolescence in part because the moral framework undergirding Golden Age corporatism had receded somewhat. In that framework, labor, productivity, wages, and consumption had been brought together in a moral economy hinged on the fair exchange of equivalents. I will return to this line of interpretation in the discussion at the end of the chapter.

5. Planned Obsolescence and Business Practices

The actual business practice most closely associated with twentieth century planned obsolescence was General Motor's annual automobile model changes. GM's policy began in the 1920s, as a competitive strategy to outflank Ford, which had committed itself to a very different philosophy of design. Ford's approach to industrial production was to build standardized and quite undifferentiated cars, with an emphasis on value and durability. Not only would the five-dollar-per-day wage policy, instituted in 1914, ensure that Ford workers could afford to purchase the products they made, but the products themselves would also be constructed in such a way as to provide what was considered to be a very respectable duration of use for their owners. A rough equivalence between work and the wage was thereby established, with standardized production-line labor exchanged for standardized wages that could be converted into standardized consumer commodities that indexed predictable durations of free activity under standard conditions of use. This suggested a reasonable, rather than a capricious or exploitative, circuit of use value, with the use value represented by work exchanged for working consumer products that at least notionally represented a roughly equivalent amount of use value. In this sense, Ford's approach was very much in accord with the moral framework of industrial corporatism.

Although the sense in this arrangement seemed self-evident to Henry Ford, Alfred P. Sloan, president of General Motors, suspected that certain social and psychological forces could be mobilized to outflank Ford's business strategy. The yearly model changes Sloan introduced, and the associated marketing campaigns, took advantage of a complex and imbricated set of structural conditions, psychological dynamics, and cultural concerns, including segmentation of social identity along lines of gender and class, status anxiety, and neophilia. The marketing strategy proved to be quite successful, eventually forcing Ford to give up its single-minded focus on function and durability in favor of GM's strategy of planned obsolescence. In 1932, Ford introduced yearly model changes.

6. Packard's Polemic and Its Echoes

While the modern practice of style obsolescence in industrial design was closely associated with GM's annual model change, it was, as noted earlier, Vance Packard's polemical journalism of the late 1950s that popularized the term *planned obsolescence*. In *The Waste Makers*, published in 1960, Packard argued that planned obsolescence represents a conspiracy on the part of business to short-change consumers by making products less durable than they could be, or by encouraging consumer behavior that would in effect reduce use-value per dollar spent, thereby reducing the quantity of use value afforded by the wage (its purchasing power). This was accomplished, Packard suggested, by designing products with "death dates" and by manipulating consumers into buying items because they had features that were superficially novel, but functionally redundant.

The argument was not without precursors. One of Packard's main inspirations (according to Packard himself) was a journalistic piece, published in 1930, but written just before the Wall Street crash of 1929, by literary critic Kenneth Burke. Burke (1930, 1956) did not use the term *planned obsolescence* in his essay, but the ideas expounded (partly tongue in cheek) therein are very similar to those later developed by Packard.[9] The economist Paul M. Gregory likewise presented ideas similar to Packard's in a 1947 paper entitled "A Theory of Purposeful Obsolescence," published in the *Southern Journal of Economics*. Like Packard, Gregory delineated the different forms of obsolescence and suggested that planned obsolescence is dictated by the logic of industrial capitalism. Perhaps taking his cue from the timing of Ford's adoption of style obsolescence, Gregory argued that prior to 1930, model changes had indicated real product improvements but that after that year, changes in design were no longer driven by improvements in function but rather were a marketing ploy. He explained the change as a consequence of demand saturation, which led to the need to generate "false needs" for product replacement in the consuming public.[10] The argument received some notice outside narrowly academic circles, becoming the subject of a *Washington Post* article in 1948. The article focused on Gregory's suggestion that model changes were no longer a response on the part of manufacturers to actual changes in taste but rather were driven by the need for industry to "make room for new models."[11]

The term *planned obsolescence* has some presence elsewhere in the academic and para-academic literature of the earlier 1950s. Marshall McLuhan, in *The Mechanical Bride*, characterized the nihilism of consumer society as "born of the social conditions of rapid turnover, planned obsolescence, and systematic change for its own sake" (McLuhan 1951, p. 13). *Challenge*, a periodical covering economic affairs, published a piece by economist Lawrence A. Abbott (1957) about "a new trick-of-the-trade: 'planned obsolescence.'" In it, he explored the thought that "planned obsolescence can be real or psychologically induced," with the former being a result of substantive progress, while the latter implying merely superficial changes in product form. Abbott's summary of the dilemma consumers face when confronted by the specter of planned obsolescence is typical of mid-century concerns expressed about the practice: "Here is a real problem for consumers. Does obsolescence measure benefits in real goods or does it indicate the presence of waste and inefficiency? To put the matter bluntly, are we, as consumers, getting our money's worth, or is business pulling one over on us?" (p. 33).

It was, however, through Packard's book that the concept became a lightning rod for popular worries about the workings of the industrial economy. Packard's prominence as a critic in mid-century America should not be underestimated. His polemics against industrial and commercial practices evidently hit a nerve with the public at large. Indeed, a lengthy 1964 *Chicago Tribune* portrait of the journalist went under the title "Vance Packard: Specialist in Touching Raw Nerves!"[12] Between 1957 and 1960, he published three books, all of which made the *New York Times* best-seller list—*The Hidden Persuaders* (1957), *The Status Seekers* (1959), and *The Waste Makers* (1960). *The Waste Makers* stayed on the best-seller list for six weeks and quickly became the main reference point for discussions about the issues surrounding product obsolescence. Business ethicist Joseph Guiltinan (2009, p. 19), reminiscing in 2009 about the early stages of his career, writes, "when I first started teaching marketing [in the 1960s], Vance Packard's criticisms of planned obsolescence were widely discussed by students and faculty. The prevailing view was that it was unethical to design products that would wear out 'prematurely' (i.e. have useful lives that were well below consumer expectations) particularly if they were costly to replace." The ethics underlying GM's strategy of style obsolescence, one of Packard's targets, were also frequently questioned in the 1960s. Even business leaders in the car industry expressed qualms about the practice. For example, in response to the suggestion by a US auto executive, hired to help revive the fortunes of trouble British car manufacturer British Motor Holdings (BMC), that American practices of planned obsolescence should be introduced to the UK market, UK executives responded that such an approach would be "unfair to customers."[13]

Packard was tapping into a broad current of concern about product quality and sales tactics, which had been building for some time, and became crystallized in fears about planned obsolescence. Even before the publication of *The Waste Makers*, these fears had become widespread enough that in 1959 an article appeared in the *Harvard Business Review* on the topic of how business should respond to them.[14] The editors introduced the piece by noting that "business has been subjected to a barrage of criticism about one of its characteristic practices, planned obsolescence."[15] Evidently there was concern in the business community about the popular sentiment gathering around the issue. A representative expression of the kind of criticism that gave rise to this concern is given by Irwin Frost, writing as the "Voice of Youth" in the *Chicago Tribune*: "One of the greatest evils in industrial society is that of planned obsolescence." Irwin announces, "This . . . maneuver of most manufacturers to squeeze the sponge of the customer's pocketbook dry is the least excusable. Products are quietly but definitely fabricated to wear out, break or become useless in a relatively short span of time."[16] In an attempt, in 1958, to give a more balanced assessment of planned obsolescence, Charles Neal, economic pundit for the *Los Angeles Times*, weighed the pros and cons of the practice. Echoing London's argument, Neal saw an upside to the practice in its stimulating effect on production. For Neal the considerably weightier downside, however, was its negative impact on families with limited budgets, and the risk of "overproduction."[17] Fear of planned obsolescence was cited as one of the motivations households had for consulting the publications of testing organization such as Consumers Union.[18]

The broad impact of concerns about planned obsolescence is indicated by the thematization of the topic across a number of different cultural forms. In 1962 a radio program was devoted to the issue, under the title "Consumer

GRIN AND BEAR IT   By Lichty

"Sure, I agree it's got a great new transmission, improved torque, flashing getaway . . . but saleswise I think the planned obsolescence is too sluggish."

Fig. 9.1: Grin & Bear It, © 1962 North America Syndicate Inc.

Problems: Planned Obsolescence."[19] By the early 1960s, the idea of planned obsolescence had become prominent enough to be a subject for a number of newspaper cartoons, such as the one in Figure 9.1, from the *Washington Post*.

In 1968, a play was staged in Los Angeles, taking comic aim at "horsepower addicts," while in the process dealing with issues of intergenerational difference. The play explored the idea that planned obsolescence separates the young from their elders. In it a youth informs us that "planned obsolescence has penetrated into the heart of the people. For us of this generation, nothing lasts, not even love." One reviewer, writing in the *Los Angeles Times*, wryly opined that; "the play is one that would be unlikely to enjoy a long run in Detroit but Angelenos will find it an interesting trip."[20] A *Chicago Tribune* piece pleading for the preservation of an old Chicago federal building makes a similar association between planned obsolescence and the aesthetics and values of the younger generation, explaining the urge to trash the old building as a product of: "the cult of newness, youth, and planned obsolescence."[21]

In the 1970s, the concept still had enough cultural currency to be thematized in a popular board game, *Beat Detroit*, put out by Dynamic Games. In the game players move cars around a board while avoiding hidden traps set by the auto industry. The goal is for players to get sufficient use value out of their vehicles to justify their purchase price, thereby "beating" the auto industry. The game concept was introduced as being "based on an elemental fact of American life: most automobiles disintegrate before they can be paid for (in economic language that's known as planned obsolescence)."[22] This description was evoking concerns about a practice thought to be widespread in the auto industry. A poll of consumers conducted by the Louis Harris organization in 1972 for *Life* magazine found that a large majority thought that the auto industry was interested in "planned obsolescence rather than long term use," with 75 percent registering "a negative rating on the industry's ability to give a good value for money."[23]

The suspicion that planned obsolescence was at play in industrial design extended well beyond the confines of Detroit and the automobile industry. "Nowhere is the curse of American planned obsolescence more infuriating than in the toy department," we are informed in a review of a guide to shopping by mail.[24] The opinion put forth in an article about hi-fi is quite typical in its assessment of the pervasiveness of planned obsolescence: "Planned obsolescence and shoddy workmanship seem to be a fact of life one must learn to live with when buying and using most consumer goods."[25] The accusation of planning obsolescence was even leveled (albeit with a certain amount of levity) at luminaries of the economics profession. In a review of the latest edition of Paul Samuelson's hugely successful textbook, *Economics*, Robert F. Mathieson slyly noted that "by keeping his discussion of problems contemporary he can come out with a new text every three years. Planned obsolescence at its best."[26] The term became extended to refer to the social, political, and even biological domains. One natural extension of the concept of planned obsolescence was to describe what happens to workers made unemployed by technological change. Such change effected "the planned obsolescence of a . . . career."[27] In this case, the term was used to evoke a pervasive anxiety about the rate of change in the modern economy and the ability of its workforce to keep up. The term was also used to describe the plight of other categories of person one way or another threatened with being made redundant by change. In 1960, the *Los Angeles Times* ran a series on the "housewife dilemma," about the fate of stay-at-home mothers after their children begin school, which begins by posing the question: "Must today's home-maker be a victim of planned obsolescence?"[28] Planned obsolescence was also used to rhetorical effect to characterize attitudes toward the elderly as well as to describe the biological process of aging. An article entitled "Can We Control Aging" begins by noting that "the aging process has been likened to planned obsolescence—in that every cell in the body is programmed to die."[29] The term cropped up everywhere.

But most commonly, planned obsolescence was seen, in the spirit of Packard, as one part of a concerted strategy on the part of big business to exploit the consumer. The set of nefarious practices that made up this strategy, listed in a *Washington Post* article from 1964, include; "declining product standards, phony retail list prices, planned obsolescence, hidden credit card charges, fraudulent packaging, misleading advertising and labeling." The accusatory title of the article (addressed to the reader), "It is partly your fault," clearly accords some measure of blame to consumers, for being complicit in their exploitation by business. But the argument of the piece is not that consumers are guilty of weakness of will for letting themselves be exploited but rather that by abandoning the project of organized consumer resistance, individual consumers had become isolated and had thereby rendered themselves vulnerable to business manipulation.[30]

There was some conjecture that the notional conspiracy to impose planned obsolescence on an unsuspecting consuming public explained how product guarantees work. A common suggestion was that the material failure of a consumer durable was timed to occur just after the expiration of its guarantee. A comment in one newspaper article notes that "it's pretty well established, at least in the minds of suspicious persons, that household appliances and automobile accessories have an uncanny way of expiring the day after the guarantee runs out. In fact, it's a little awesome to contemplate the know-how obviously required to achieve this built-in mortality. The economists call it planned obsolescence. The idea behind it is that when a washing machine conks out the owner will have to buy another."[31] Similarly, a *Washington Post* piece on planned obsolescence, from 1969, quotes a housewife voicing suspicions about engineered "death dates" in her appliances. "I am beginning to believe in the charge of 'planned obsolescence' that has been directed at the manufacturers of appliances, particularly kitchen equipment," she declared, noting that her appliances failed "apparently on schedule" and that the cost of repair makes replacement seem the more attractive option.[32] It was perhaps partly in response to the popular suspicion that product warranties measure product lifespan that some manufacturers began to offer "lifetime" warranties, which, as discussed in Chapter 7, became increasingly common in the middle decades of the century.[33]

Warranties were also regarded as suspect on the somewhat different grounds that they were a means of protecting companies that practiced planned obsolescence, by foreclosing the possibility of legal recourse for frustrated consumers. An article entitled "Falling Apart Is the Name of the Game" begins with a typical indictment of the supposedly widespread practice of planned obsolescence: "Modern manufacturers are constantly coming up with new and better ways to make what we buy fall apart faster. Planned obsolescence is the name of the game, an exciting race to see who can come up with the first thingamabob that'll self-destruct the instant it's unpacked!" The author goes on to issue a warning against signing warranty cards, on the grounds that by doing so consumers waive their legal right of protection in cases where goods have been compromised by planned obsolescence. "The law can't protect you, however, if you've signed a 'Warranty' like the one from Suckers-Only, which is really a promise that you won't ask Suckers-Only to obey the legal standards of 'Merchantibility.'"[34]

The temporality of credit, like that of the warranty, was similarly suspected of being tied to compromised product durability. "Let not the lure of credit / your innocent heart beguile / By the time the thing is paid for / It's worn out and out of style," we are warned in a light-hearted piece by Ralph Freeman of the *Los Angeles Times*.[35] In a 1967 article on Jimmy Hoffa, the infamous leader of the Teamsters union, a passing comment expresses a similar sentiment: "The final payment on the automobile will bring the sound of engine parts falling to the street in the dead of night."[36] Suspicion was also expressed that product service plans were part of the overall strategy of planned obsolescence. "In the world of planned obsolescence, the service contract plays a most vital role," wrote journalist Art Buchwald in the *Los Angeles Times* in 1971.[37] The concern was that intentionally faulty products would prompt consumers to buy lucrative service plans as insurance against premature failure.

At the same time, there was some suggestion in discussions about planned obsolescence that the pervasiveness of the practice had in a fundamental way

changed consumer expectations about what constitutes a "reasonable" duration of use in a commodity. In a 1967 newspaper article on everyday exchanges
that happened to pithily sum up the zeitgeist, a woman was described who,
overhearing someone boasting that some product had been working well
since 1965, responded with the comment: "Now that's barely two years but
to her its apparently endless eons . . . come on you ad writers, life may be
ephemeral—planned obsolescence and all—but not that ephemeral!"[38]

7. The Response of Business to Accusations of Planned Obsolescence

The intensity of the concerns about planned obsolescence meant that companies, as well as individuals working in business and marketing, felt some
pressure to address the issue. The response of business to planned obsolescence varied from sympathy, to puzzlement, to defensiveness, to leverag-
ing the issue through marketing campaigns in order to increase sales. How
business responded to the concerns about planned obsolescence sheds some
oblique light on the nature of public worries about the matter.

A significant number of people in business felt that the criticisms of
planned obsolescence were justified. This is indicated by a survey of 10,000
"business executives" about the matter conducted by the *Harvard Business
Review* in 1959. Of the 3,100 respondents, two-thirds agreed that "too large a
part of our present economy is based on superficial product obsolescence."[39]
Nonetheless, the gravity of the accusation that industry practiced planned
obsolescence prompted many businesses to formulate some kind of defen-
sive response. A number of different strategies were followed. One common
strategy on the part of business to the controversy was to argue that, without planned obsolescence, there would be a shortfall in effective demand,
which would damage the economy and therefore ultimately harm consumers
by putting their jobs in jeopardy. Top GM executives, interviewed in a 1960
New York Times article, admitted that annual model changes were "one of the
most highly controversial aspects of the automobile industry" but gave the
practice a positive spin by describing it as a manifestation of the "challenge of
change." They argued that model changes were ultimately justifiable because
of the supposed benefits of the practice for customers, workers, manufacturers, and the economy.[40] In a somewhat similar vein, rapid model changes were
portrayed by some business figures as necessary to achieve the economies of

scale that ultimately made consumer durables affordable. John F. Gordon, GM president and chief operating officer, defended his company's practice of annual model change by arguing that "little or no annual change [in style] would cut sales, and hence make each car more expensive," claiming that "the extra cost would be sufficient to offset any saving resulting from not changing models" (a view echoed by Herman F. Lehman, GM's vice-president in charge of the Frigidaire division).[41] If car owners did not "upgrade" their vehicles to new models every year, Gordon argued, they "would continue to use the same car as long as it gave satisfactory service. There would be no incentive to replace it. Obviously, this would cut our annual sales in half. . . . With volume reduced, each car would cost more to produce, and I am sure that this increased cost would more than offset any saving resulting from not changing models."[42] The reasoning here is quite strange. On one level it sets out quite clearly the high-volume logic of Fordist industrial production while making an association between what works best for the manufacturer with large capital investments (stable and high demand) and the interests of the consumer. Yet it is entirely unclear what the benefit to the consumer is supposed to be, for the argument is quite circular. The argument is that frequent model changes are required in order to make cars cheap enough for them to be replaced more frequently than is, from a strictly functional point of view (the view according to which the function of a car is to transport people safely and comfortably from point A to point B), necessary. So rather than having one entirely serviceable car over a six-year period, the consumer comes to own several cars over that period. What is also striking about GM's defense of its practice of frequent model changes is the conspicuous absence of the argument that value is a subjective matter—so if consumers want new cars, even though those that they own are still perfectly functional, that must be because there is genuine added value in newness. Rather, GM defended the practice of style obsolescence in terms of its role in stimulating real innovation, its importance in stabilizing the economy, and controlling price. GM's executives were then justifying a rapid product cycle in terms of its positive effect on social welfare. The social benefit argument was extended to include the role of planned obsolescence in facilitating a healthy secondhand market, which made durables available to socioeconomic groups that would not otherwise be able to afford them.

Perhaps this focus on the macroeconomic and social consequences of business practices was a hangover from the concerns of the Depression years.

Yet by the 1950s, thinking about consumption had to a significant extent moved beyond the collectivist mindset of the 1930s, instead becoming focused on a quasi-contractual relationship between producers and individual consumers. Even the "business executives" surveyed by the *Harvard Business Review* in 1959—many of whom surely had some vested interest in rationalizing planned obsolescence—were roughly equally divided for and against the view that planned obsolescence is a necessary evil to protect the economy.[43]

A second line of response to the controversy on the part of industry was simply to deny that the practice of planned obsolescence existed. For example, Harold W. Johnson, head of the vehicles and components research at Ford's Research and Engineering Center in Dearborn, in an interview with the *Los Angeles Times* about the auto industry, made a point of attacking the suggestion that nefarious forms of planned obsolescence were implemented by the industry: "Styling cycles are characteristic of American marketing in many, many products. Last year's car is no more obsolete than last year's coat or refrigerator. As for 'planned obsolescence', this is pure nonsense."[44] Likewise, when, in 1973, Gillette introduced a range of new disposable products and critics suggested that the new items represented "a sort of planned obsolescence," the company issued heated denials.[45]

A third line of response from a business perspective to public fears about planned obsolescence was to argue that consumers could not so easily be duped, asserting the primacy of consumer sovereignty in determining the shape of the marketplace. The financial weekly *Barron's* published a piece in 1961 defending business from accusations about planned obsolescence made by Packard and J. K. Galbraith: "Bureaucrats and best-selling authors to the contrary notwithstanding, the buying public, far from being the victim of ruthless manipulation, is actually the one that pulls the strings. Or, to hark back to an old saying which has lost none of its point, in the US the consumer is king. While his reign has been challenged time and again, often with a temporary measure of success, in the end he has tended to prevail. Let those who would challenge him now think twice."[46] Another financial weekly, *Fortune* magazine, in a 1963 editorial went so far as to blame the mini-recession of 1958, the sharpest economic downturn experienced in the United States during the boom years between 1945 and 1970, on "moralists" who objected to planned obsolescence: "Recall for a moment the auto industry's dark days in 1958. General Motor's net earnings were off 24.9 percent in that year; Ford was off 60.5 percent; Chrysler was suffering the worst season ever. Dealers had huge inventories and were closing up all over the country. The aesthetes were in rebellion over tail fins and chrome, and the moralists were lecturing against the 'planned obsolescence' of new models."[47] The opinion that there was a connection between the concern about planned obsolescence and the 1958 recession was not, however, shared by everyone in business. For example, Judson S. Sayre, head of Norge, the appliance-making division of the Borg Warner corporation, put the blame for the recession squarely on the practice of planned obsolescence itself, the effect of which was to cause "consumer confusion and self-induced business recession."[48] Perhaps in an effort to reduce "consumer confusion" about planned obsolescence, Maytag, another maker of appliances, made a decision in the late 1960s to provide the consumer with more information about the expected life span of its products. The objective was to counter "suggestions that manufacturers practice planned obsolescence by giving the consumer better notions of the life expectancy of his machines."[49]

The suggestion that there was a pervasive conspiracy to limit product durability stung industry and marketing enough to prompt public relations campaigns to debunk the notion. In 1964, Burson-Marsteller Inc., Chicago-based marketing and public relations firm, took out a series of full-page ads in the *Wall Street Journal* defending the activities of marketing firms against Packard's accusations.[50] The ad begins: "Some of our best friends are wastemakers. They waste the ordinary for the unique. They waste the possible for the impossible, the good for the better, the old for the new." The argument, often wheeled out in the back and forth over planned obsolescence, was that obsolescence is a result of progress. "Product innovation makes waste, say the critics of American marketing," the ad went on, "They say that innovation will shorten the life-span of a product, create dissatisfaction, and proliferate products. They are right, of course. But is it immoral to innovate?"[51] Herman F. Lehman, head of Frigidaire, likewise promoted the idea of planned obsolescence as the handmaiden of technical progress. He contrasted the technical dynamism encouraged by frequent product changes with the stasis implicit in the design philosophy championed by Ransom E. Olds, father of the Oldsmobile. Lehman noted disparagingly, and with the implication of naivety, that, in 1912, Olds had referred to his vehicle as "my farewell car" because, "I do not believe that a car materially better will ever be built" (Olds was expressing an attitude similar to Henry Ford's to the model T).[52]

In order to put a positive spin on the marketing and industrial strategies associated with planned obsolescence, the automobile industry adopted alternative names for the practice, using terms that imply that obsolescence is an inevitable byproduct of the march of progress. Planned obsolescence was referred to as "dynamic obsolescence," "progressive obsolescence," and "planned progress." John F. Gordon, GM head, in a 1960 statement on the issue put it as follows: "It is clear to me that new car buyers have benefited tremendously over the years from what has been termed planned obsolescence but which we think is more accurately called dynamic obsolescence."[53] James R. Roche, who succeeded Gordon as president of GM, echoed this defense of the auto industry against accusations of "wasteful planned obsolescence," describing yearly style changes as "planned improvements" and "planned creativity," which, he argued, "stimulates sales by offering improved quality, safety and performance" each year.[54] Robert F. Hurleigh, president of Mutual Broadcasting System Incorporated, averred that widespread planned obsolescence was a figment of the public's imagination, that the practice "is the exception, not the rule of industry" and that what was really being spoken about in most discussions about "planned obsolescence" was just progress, plain and simple. Writing in the MBS newsletter, *Of Mutual Interest*, Hurleigh contended that: "The great majority of American manufacturers do not 'plan' obsolescence. They plan progress," and that, "in the process of knocking 'planned obsolescence,' some authors have made enough money to 'obsolete' many of their own previous conceptions of how they would like to live."[55] Perhaps in response to the eagerness of industry to associate obsolescence with progress, the argument was made, in the late 1960s, that modern science itself—the supposed engine of progress—had been corrupted and co-opted by the industrial logic of planned obsolescence. The suggestion was that it was not that planned obsolescence served the forces of "progress" but rather the converse—that the forces of progress had come to serve planned obsolescence.[56]

Despite the efforts of business to defuse the issue, by the early 1960s planned obsolescence had become a matter of widespread concern, to the point that many prominent business and marketing figures, and some professional bodies, felt the need to publicly distance themselves from the practice. In 1962, the American Marketing Association became sufficiently concerned about the suggestion that its members were participants in a conspiracy to push planned obsolescence on the consuming public that it issued a broad call to arms to the profession, insisting that the matter needed to be forthrightly addressed. The argument the organization made was that what was needed in response to accusations about the marketing of planned obsolescence was a public relations campaign on behalf of marketing itself. D. Beryl Manischewitz and John A. Stuart, two prominent marketing executives, likewise drew attention, in an article published in the July issue of the *Journal of Marketing*, to the need for the advertising industry to take a more active stance in defending itself. They suggested that one way to accomplish this would be for marketers to preempt criticism by launching a systematic investigation into supposed practices of "planned obsolescence" and "administered prices" (Maniscewitz and Stuart 1960). The supposition was that the results of such an investigation would clear the industry of wrongdoing.[57] The authors accepted the moral logic on the basis of which planned obsolescence was regarded as an objectionable practice—the issue was not whether planned obsolescence is a bad thing or not, but rather whether or not the practice, as imagined by Packard and other critics, actually existed.

Anxiety about being implicated in planned obsolescence extended to members of various professions involved in industrial production. Henry Dreyfus, the prominent industrial designer, in 1968 contributed an op-ed piece to the *Wall Street Journal* defending his profession from any suggestion that it was involved in the conspiracy (the existence of which was taken as given) to compromise use value through planning obsolescence. "Although industrial designers are in the business of change," he comments, "we resent planned obsolescence. A change in technology, improved efficiency, additional safety or comfort, a new utility development, an improved method of fabrication, the introduction of new material—these warrant a new physical expression. But to put a 'new look' on an existing piece of merchandise—this, to us, constitutes the duping of an unsuspecting public."[58] Likewise, David M. Pesanelli, former designer for Ford automobiles, wrote an extended exposé for the *Washington Post* in which he described the practice of planned obsolescence; condemned it for violating the moral obligation to produce durable items, expressive of "the value system that considers that possessions are meant to be cherished for years"; and offered consumers practical advice on how to resist the associated marketing strategy: "Two factors limit the desirability span of any product. One is the precisely measured design life of product components. The other is faddish styling that causes that bluesy feeling when next year's model arrives. Either of these will get to you," he warned. The advice Pesanelli offered consumers, on the basis of which they would, he suggested, be empowered to resist the marketing sophistry of "new design," is to cultivate an eye for "timeless quality." He also advised them to make use of *Consumer Reports* test results to assess performance and reliability.[59] Similarly, in 1959 engineer and designer Jack Waldheim, penned a passionate denunciation of planned obsolescence and "death dating" in *Design News*: "Planned obsolescence is the deliberate attempt to have something break down or become outdated long before it has lost its usefulness—its utility—or its value. . . . Its danger to the customer is that it cheats him of his hard-earned money, though he may not realize it in the beginning."[60] The moral status of planned obsolescence was also addressed by engineers attempting to square their professional practice with their religious commitments. In October 1967, a Christian vocation seminar for engineers was held in Chicago specifically to discuss "ethical issues" arising from planned obsolescence. Taking a stronger position than these designers and engineers, perhaps because his profession was perceived as being more directly involved in the practice, Walter Henry Nelson, a repentant former ad man, went on the record about the pathologies of the American economic model, which he had spent his professional life promoting: "I've always been dismayed by the planned obsolescence and shoddy workmanship in all too many American cars. Too many American businessmen are more interested in seeming good than in being good."[61]

8. Marketing "Planned Durability"

The strongly negative opinions about planned obsolescence prompted some companies to make an effort to signal that their products were designed and constructed according to diametrically opposite principles. This was particularly true of the auto industry. In the 1960s a large number of ad campaigns were launched by corporations, the point of which was specifically to deny that they implemented planned obsolescence. "Borgward does not believe in 'planned obsolescence,'" went one advertisement, typical of those adopting this strategy, adding, "Improvements are made gradually—without outward changes."[62] Similarly, the copy in a Volkswagen ad from 1959 proclaims: "We do not believe in planned obsolescence. We don't change a car for the sake of change," continuing to note, like the Borgward advertisement, that while the company makes changes to its products every year, these changes constitute invisible improvements to function and durability rather than being merely stylistic.[63] One ad agency announced that its strategy was to take clients (in this case Volvo and the American Motor Company [AMC]) along a "value" route in promoting their products, in contradistinction to "planned obsolescence."[64] AMC issued a press release in 1960 proclaiming its resolute stance against planned obsolescence. According to one report, "American Motors Corporation announced it will open another attack on 'planned obsolescence' in automobiles in 1960. The company said it will introduce ceramic coated mufflers as standard equipment in its 1961 models in an effort to prove that cars don't have to start falling apart after three years or 70,000 miles of driving."[65] In the 1960s, at least eight major car manufacturers—Mercedes, Volkswagen, Peugeot, AMC, Volvo, BMW, Rover, Borgward, and Rolls Royce—in addition to several smaller brands (Checkers and Imperial, for example), launched advertising campaigns organized around the message that their cars were emphatically *not* produced according to the principle of planned obsolescence. A 1963 campaign launched for Checker Family Cars (an offshoot of Checker's taxi cabs) was built around the message "No Planned Obsolescence, Planned Permanence!"[66] Similarly, Imperial, Chrysler's luxury brand, went to great lengths in its 1961 advertising campaign to distinguish itself on the basis of being resistant to obsolescence. The lead copy of the ad was "Planned continuity is part of its elegance." It went on to note that "Imperial's design reflects planned continuity, not planned obsolescence. This magnificent automobile—except for many refinements—has remained unchanged for the past five model years. . . . Thus, Imperial's owners pay little penalty in money or satisfaction when the next Imperial model comes out." The ad makes an association between the absence of model changes and physical durability, describing the Imperial as "America's most carefully built car."[67]

Peugeot, another of the auto makers that pitched its cars as being made according to principles opposite to planned obsolescence—as "planned without obsolescence"—used the slogan "more car than you'll ever need" in one of its marketing campaigns. This prompts the question (most powerfully posed from the puzzled perspective of the value engineer) of why the consumer would ever want more car than she needs, especially given the likelihood of her having to pay for the excess. Another ad for the company claims that "it's common for a Peugeot to get 150,000 or even 200,000 miles."[68] Volvo struck a more ironic tone in its campaign, with a 1967 ad beginning: "The paper car. The next logical step of planned obsolescence." The ad contrasts that approach to car making with the one followed by Volvo, described as aiming to build cars that last longer "than a good suit," with an "average life" of eleven years.

Couched in a more straightforward and forthright rhetoric, a 1964 advertisement for Rover leads with the declaration: "No planned obsolescence, No calculated failure of material." In a 1967 ad campaign, Rover turned the logic of annual model changes on its head, pushing as a selling point for its cars their unchanging, even backward-looking, design: "Rover is proud to turn back the clock on another model year. The Rover 2000 Sports Sedans for 1968 are dead ringers for those we unveiled last year," one ad declares, adding, with pride, that "the Rover 2000 may become the longest running model car in history." The Rover campaign narrated the onward march of product change not as inexorable progress but rather as a decline and fall away from timeless "classic" design. In sticking with its "classic" models, and stubbornly resisting pressure for change, Rover presented itself as engaged in a heroic struggle to resist modern obsolescence.

The marketing strategy of promoting products by emphasizing that they are *not* produced according to principles of planned obsolescence was followed in industries beyond car making. Whirlpool, for example, a maker of appliances, in the late 1960s launched a television ad campaign that invoked the specter of a marketplace pervaded by planned product obsolescence representing its products as, by contrast, durable and dependable, offering consumers a safe haven from the creeping shoddiness of the age. A newspaper ad for KLH stereo equipment from 1967 begins by noting the ubiquity of "perishability" and "planned obsolescence," interpreted as "planned dissatisfaction," and then pitches its equipment as both durable and endowed with the aesthetic characteristics of a "classic" product—like a typewriter that "feels like a *real* typewriter."[69] Revco, maker of refrigerators, in a campaign from the early 1960s, made a point of emphasizing that its products are "not subjected to superficial changes resulting from 'planned obsolescence' as illustrated by conventional refrigeration."[70] Amana, a freezer manufacturer, poses a disturbing question to the reader of its ads: "Will it fall apart before the payments are made?" The ad notes that "with mass production has come the evil of inferior merchandise—of 'planned obsolescence,'" an evil steadfastly resisted by the "craftsmen" at Amana.[71] And in a 1971 advertisement for tiling, we are informed that "in this era of 'planned obsolescence,' and 'plastic imitations,' ceramic tile is still a trademark of quality and honesty."[72] Even swimming pool installers felt the need to reassure their customers that their equipment was free of planned obsolescence: "Sunset's progressive research and development program goes on continuously, to bring you the finest equipment possible. There is no 'planned obsolescence.'"[73] Like the auto makers, the advertising angle taken by these companies was not to make the clear and positive arguments about durability and value that Ford made in the 1920s but rather to mark their products by negation, as *not* made according to the principle of planned obsolescence.

Marketing campaigns and advertising content, it should be said, are by no means necessarily directly indicative of normative concerns characteristic of a particular kind of moral economy. But the prevalence in advertising copy, particularly in the auto industry, of the message that products were *not* produced according to the principle of planned obsolescence indicates how pervasive the concerns were about the practice.

9. Political Response to the Issue

By the mid-1960s, the concern over planned obsolescence had become sufficiently widespread and intense that it began to come to the attention of politicians and regulatory agencies. Representative Benjamin S. Rosenthal addressing a meeting in August 1969 on the topic of the rapid expansion of discount retailers commented that "today's typical consumer is tempted by the marketplace promises of product perfection. But the system that produces, promotes, sells, and services that product can more accurately be characterized by the reality of planned obsolescence and poor quality control."[74] A policy response to the "problem" of planned obsolescence was suggested in 1965 by Esther Peterson, special assistant to the president for consumer affairs. She argued that consumer education was the solution and ought to be incorporated into the high school curriculum. The overarching aim, as she put it, would be to produce a "consumer-led" economy, as opposed to a "consumption-led" economy. In the former, savvy and independent consumers are the chief actors, while in the latter, big business is in charge. Education was seen as a means to produce rational, sovereign consumers, who would secure the development of a virtuous and efficient consumer economy. Consumer sovereignty, on this account, is an ethical end to be accomplished, rather than, as some economists would have it, a given. Drawing attention to planned obsolescence as a central characteristic of the consumer economy, Peterson commented: "In a consumption oriented economy, anything would be permissible . . . planned obsolescence would be the rule rather than the exception to the rule."[75] Her sentiment did not meet with universal approval. The *Wall Street Journal* wryly commented in response that the "whole notion of indoctrinating the young in commercial conformity makes you wonder if the experts want a consumer directed economy or a flock of expert directed consumers."[76]

In a different vein, politicians made a connection, following Ralph Nader's groundbreaking work on automobile safety, between planned obsolescence and car accidents. Daniel Moynihan, then assistant secretary of labor, commented in 1966 that planned obsolescence might cause accidents, noting a correlation between accident rates and rates of profit of auto manufacturers, and speculated that planned obsolescence "itself may account for a fair number of vehicle failures"[77] (an association jokily riffed upon in a *Chicago Tribune* article, in 1966, about obsolescence in men's fashion, with the title "Unsafe in Any Tweed"[78]).

In the early 1970s, the issue of planned obsolescence came under the scrutiny of the Federal Trade Commission (FTC)—this despite the fact that there was by that time a growing consensus that the practice of annual model change was on the decline, at least in the auto industry.[79] The FTC began its investigations with an uncommitted position on the scale of the problem. Lawrence G. Meyer, the FTC's director of policy planning and evaluation issued a statement that he and his staff were trying to determine whether "we are dealing with a problem of mass proportions" while noting that the problem was "substantial from the consumer's viewpoint." At the same time, the General Counsel of the FTC, Joseph Martin, claimed that "cases of built-in obsolescence are common" and that "this planned obsolescence is accomplished by several ways—by failing to provide a source of spare parts for the reasonable life of the product, by making frequent style or nonfunctional changes so that the user feels he must turn in his old model for one which gives him better performance, and by including certain components made of materials which have a shorter life than the reasonable life expectancy of the product itself."

The FTC's investigation was a response to popular sentiment about the issue but also, more specifically, was in reaction to a well-publicized study on planned obsolescence, published in the *Yale Law Journal* by Bradford C.

Snell (1971). In his article Snell argued that annual model change in the auto industry constitutes an unfair trade practice, on the grounds that the yearly costs of retooling work as a barrier to market entry.[80] On Snell's estimate, in 1969 alone the "Big Three" auto manufacturers (GM, Ford, and Chrysler) spent $1.5 billion to change their tooling in order to produce new models. At the same time, Snell noted, the Bureau of Labor Statistics "reported a new reduction in performance improvements of $3 per 1969 automobile." The conclusion Snell drew from these figures was that the big three spent more than a billion and a half dollars to make their 1969 models seem "new and different" in appearance. In the process, they erected nigh impenetrable barriers to market entry: "In 1970, it would cost a company $779 million to enter the automobile industry. The costs of annual style change capability, it is estimated, account for fully $724 million, or more than 90 percent of this figure" (Snell 1971, p. 588). Snell further argued that the effect of planned obsolescence was to stifle "real" product improvements, by substituting superficial changes in design for genuine innovation. Snell's analysis is worth quoting at length, both because it proved quite influential and because Snell makes a connection not usually explicitly made between style and material obsolescence:

> It has been noted that the innovative characteristics of the industry began to decline shortly after annual restyling was introduced in the 1920s . . . by introducing a 'new' model each year, they provide the illusion of progress, and yet avoid the necessity of adopting technological improvements which would lower maintenance or initial purchase cost. It has been argued, for instance, that application of known metallurgical processes would permit doubling the life of an automobile for an additional cost of $36 per year. . . . These developments, however, would increase automobile durability and thereby reduce demand, price and profits on new car sales. It is suspected therefore, that the Big Three have repressed these cost-savings while offering consumers instead an annual restyling policy designed to bolster replacement demand through planned obsolescence. (Snell 1971, p. 59)

On Snell's reasoning, then, durability was sacrificed on the altar of style— not style as an independent source of utility, but rather style as a false sign of material progress, a substitute for the real thing. In this way, so the argument went, consumers are duped into buying new models, perhaps on the mistaken assumption that stylistic flourishes such as tail fins index substantive, functional improvements—and therein lies a deception. Ralph Nader joined Snell and the editors of the *Yale Law Journal* in petitioning the FTC to launch an investigation into planned obsolescence, and the FTC agreed to look into the matter. Significantly, the FTC, in responding to Snell and Nader's petition, made a distinction between material and style obsolescence. While evidence of material obsolescence was held to be actionable, style obsolescence was deemed to be an issue of taste and, therefore, not a proper matter for regulative intervention. Ultimately, however, nothing came of the FTC's investigation, because no evidence of intentional material obsolescence could be found.

The basis on which material obsolescence was considered by the FTC to be an illegitimate practice was that, in addition to possibly running afoul of federal antitrust laws, it short-changed the consumer. Planned obsolescence violated what were held to be reasonable, yet only vaguely defined, expectations about the durability and repairability of products. "The consumer is entitled," FTC director Meyers maintained, "to expect that replacement parts—particularly minor parts—will be available for the reasonably predicted useful life of the item in question. . . . Similarly, in my view, the commission is also concerned about durability obsolescence—the intentional inclusion by some manufacturers of an inferior part within a product where the usage of a better part would not add significantly to the cost of the final product."[81] The FTC's statement implies that a producer has a moral and legal obligation to make objects as durable as possible at a given price point—and that failure to do so, even under nonmonopoly conditions, warrants state regulation and possible sanctions.[82]

The response to the FTC investigation varied in quite predictable ways. Guenther Baumgart, president of the Association of Home Appliance Manufacturers, complained that the FTC was searching for something that did not exist: "We have no evidence of the deliberate planning of products to wear out prematurely." By contrast, Morris Kaplan, director of the Consumers Union, commented that "it is definitely possible to design products that will last a great deal longer than they do."[83] But all sides shared the assumption that there is some objectively "reasonable" (therefore fair) duration of use consumers should get out of the products they purchase.

10. Planned Obsolescence as Matter of Environmental Concern

By the early 1970s, the issue of planned obsolescence was beginning to be folded into growing concern about the environment. In 1970, the first Earth Day was organized by a coalition of some five thousand environmental groups. In publicity for the event, planned obsolescence featured prominently, listed alongside the other main causes of imminent environmental catastrophe, such as overpopulation, war, poverty, and pollution.[84] In the same year, design guru Viktor Papanek, in an interview in the *Chicago Tribune*, accused the big four auto makers of wasteful and environmentally irresponsible practices. He spoke in strong and provocative terms: "First they build the most perfect killing machine yet devised by man. As it runs, it pollutes the visual environment. Its offal pollutes the air. And when it expires at an early date, the result of planned obsolescence, its remains clutter up the landscape and waste space."[85]

This concern about the environmental consequences of planned obsolescence was relatively novel. Prior to the 1970s, environmental matters were not a significant presence in the discussions about the issue. In the 1940s, Alfred P. Sloan had offhandedly dismissed worries that planned obsolescence would lead to automobile graveyards "defiling the landscape," contemptuously characterizing such concerns as "a matter for women to deal with." By the mid-1970s, however, the opinion expressed, for example, by environmentally enlightened banker Louis B. Lundborg in the *Los Angeles Times* was not at all uncommon: "We have not reached this point of [incipient environmental catastrophe] entirely by accident: for a long time the concept of planned obsolescence has been accepted as a deliberate and admirable philosophy of management."[86] The essence of the environmental argument against planned obsolescence was that it is objectionable not because it is unfair to consumers but rather because of its material consequences—the production of ever-greater volumes of waste.

This emerging environmental framing of the problem with planned obsolescence had some precedent in worries expressed in the 1960s about solid waste disposal. Vance Packard, in *The Waste Makers*, makes reference to the growing problem of waste accumulation and resource depletion, although these issues are certainly not central to his critique. A number of pieces in newspapers, appearing in the second half of the 1960s and early 1970s, presented the growing problem of waste disposal as being a consequence of planned obsolescence.[87] Dr. Merril Eisenbud, head of New York City's EPA, attributed what he described as a "trash crisis" to the "built-in death dates and planned obsolescence of many of the commercial products we buy."[88] In a 1966 *New York Times* article, entitled "Help! The Junk Is Rising," the blame for the growing problem of solid waste disposal is put squarely on planned obsolescence. After a tirade against the practice, the piece concludes: "'Don't complain', someone will object, 'it's affluence.' And yet the junk is getting deeper. Surely it is written someplace that the country that lives by obsolescence shall perish of its own junk."[89] By the early 1970s, concern in government about the problem of solid waste disposal had been building for a number of years, and planned obsolescence was seen as the main source of the problem. Richard D. Vaughan, director of the U.S. Bureau of Solid Waste Management argued that the solution was to be found in a change in production, stressing the need to redesign "American consumer goods with repair in mind in order to move away from planned obsolescence."[90]

The rise of environmentalism led to calls for legislative and other government initiatives to regulate planned obsolescence. A nongovernmental organization of researchers and businessmen, the National Commission on Materials Policy, issued a report in 1973 suggesting the need for "counter-incentives to planned obsolescence," in order to combat environmental degradation.[91] In 1973, the Muskie bill (sponsored by Senator Edmund S. Muskie, a trailblazer for environmental legislation), which addressed the problem of solid waste disposal, incorporated a provision for the Environmental Protection Agency's Office of Solid Waste Disposal "to specify the useful life of such major items as tires, appliances and vehicles to discourage planned obsolescence."[92]

In the early 1970s, the energy crisis was added to the growing list of reasons for rejecting planned obsolescence. "The reasons for the profligate American use of energy are basic," wrote prominent public intellectual and journalist Anthony Lewis in a *New York Times* article: "They include the dominant place of automobiles in transportation, the suburban pattern of living, the emphasis on energy intensive rather than labor intensive industry and the economics of planned obsolescence."[93] Similarly, an article about the challenges facing the US economy against the backdrop of the oil shock leaves its readers with the following warning: "The policy of planned obsolescence which pervades manufacturing is another source of great waste. A slogan of 'make it do, wear it out, and do without' might help this situation. Our children are going to be left with many serious problems as a result of our profligate waste."[94]

The emergence of an environmental interpretation of the problem with planned obsolescence was accompanied by a shift in the center of gravity of perceived responsibility for the practice, away from business and toward consumers. While corporations were still targets for criticism, the environmental call to action was largely addressed to individual consumers. *Los Angeles Times* columnist Richard Buffman, writing in 1971, demanded that consumers "think before we consume. Think of the consequences and demand an end to planned obsolescence. Demand better engineered things, better crafted things and husband them carefully until they really wear out, not just until the style changes."[95] In summing up the new current of opinion, according to which waste is a byproduct of mercurial consumer taste, Mike Geist, of PR and marketing firm, *Geist and Geist*, commented that "planned obsolescence is just plain waste, and waste is no longer in fashion."[96]

The articulation of the issue of planned obsolescence to concerns about the environment could be interpreted as just reflecting growing consciousness about environmental issues. However, it is perhaps significant that the shift in criticism of planned obsolescence from the economic unfairness of the practice, to its environmental consequences, took place just as the Fordist framework of industrial capitalism was beginning to fall apart. Against the backdrop of the mid-century Fordism, planned obsolescence was seen as problematic primarily because it represented a reneging of obligations of business to consumers, in a corporatist context in which labor and business were locked in a loose compact to share the proceeds of economic growth. But, as historians have shown, the politics of consumption in America changed over the course of the twentieth century. Up until the mid-century period, consumption was thought about in terms that were closely tied to moral and political economy, involving the issue of the just and fair distribution of "purchasing power." As the century wore on, however, consumption increasingly became framed in terms of individual rights and preferences (L. Cohen 2003; Jacobs 2005). If this account is correct, the weakening grounds of the older moral economy opened up space for environmental concerns about obsolescence and consumer waste to move to the forefront, formulating a critique of planned obsolescence from a quite different angle. (I will return to this topic in the discussion section, at the end of this chapter.)

11. Obsolescence and Waste

The evolution of the debate about planned obsolescence is reflected in the way in which different conceptions of waste get expressed in discussions about the issue. The interpretation of product obsolescence as primarily an environmental concern rather than as a matter of fair exchange and economic justice, involved a shift between two distinct conceptions of waste: waste as the abstract product of calculations about fair or optimally efficient uses of resources and waste as an objectionable material byproduct.

In Stuart Chase's influential discussion of the economics of waste, written in the early part of the century, waste was conceived of as, in essence, inefficiency (Chase 1925). Chase, an engineer by training, and consumer advocate by vocation, thought of waste primarily as nonproductive labor and inefficient use of resources. He condemned as wasteful labor spent on wars, on the making of luxury goods, and the idle "manpower" of "both the idle rich and the wandering hobo." Waste was a result of the inefficient exploitation of natural resources and production not being sufficiently directed by "the technical arts." There was no nature-preserving environmentalism in Chase's account. He complained that that "for every reclaimed ton [of natural resources] a ton and more has been needlessly and irretrievably lost" (Chase 1925, p. 2). Within this framework, waste was not a useless or toxic byproduct but rather was a result of suboptimal use of resources. It could be figured counterfactually, by estimating how much more efficiently a given task could have been accomplished, and therefore how much could have been saved. The specific amount of wastefulness in any given goal-directed action can, on this view, be calculated by subtracting the resources required at optimal efficiency to accomplish the goal from those actually used. This concern with efficiency and waste encompassed not just production but also household consumption. The consumer movement, in which Chase was an important figure, was very much allied to the home economics movement in encouraging households to regiment themselves in an optimally efficient manner.

The understanding of waste as inefficiency informs the early attacks on planned obsolescence, only with squandered potential use value standing in for wasted resources as the object of the calculation. For example, "death dates" were regarded as wasteful to the extent that more durability, hence more use value, could have been designed into a product with no significant change in other product characteristics (including price). The counterfactual calculation of waste produced by planned material obsolescence thus measures a quantity of hypothetical use value illegitimately withheld from the consumer. The same is true for style obsolescence. When, under the nefarious influence of marketing, consumers replace perfectly functional products for seemingly superficial reasons, some amount of "true" use value is in effect being withheld from them. For rather than replacing a perfectly good product with a functionally equivalent new one, they could instead have acquired a product with use value along some new dimension. Planned obsolescence was thus wasteful of people's hard-earned wages and, therefore, of their labor.

But the moral outrage at the wastefulness of planned obsolescence in the 1950s and 1960s did not just reflect a general revulsion at inefficient use of resources but reflected also an interpretation of planned obsolescence as a concerted attack by big business on the purchasing power of the wage—causing wage earners to, in effect, get an insufficient return for their labor. The duty of business, in the mass consumer economy, to provide consumers with reasonable and fair durations of use in the commodities sold to them, was of a piece with the obligation of business to share the benefits of increasing productivity with its workforce. In reneging on its obligation to consumers, by employing planned obsolescence, and thereby in effect diminishing the purchasing power of the wage, big business reneged on its obligation to reward workers for their contribution to increasing productivity, by increasing *real* wages.

When, in the early 1970s, planned obsolescence was taken up in the context of concerns about the environment, waste changed from being the product of a counterfactual calculation—of how much more use value could have been realized in the design of a given product—to being an actual substance, a toxic excrescence of industrial society. Waste went from being an abstraction, based on unrealized potential use value, tied to the technocratic pursuit of optimal efficiency and to the ethics of fair economic exchange, to being a material effluence, a physical impinging of society on nature, and a collective sin for which every member of society bears some responsibility. Within the critical discourse about planned obsolescence, the objective of waste reduction therefore changed from the maximization of the use value in commodities to the minimization of environmentally damaging negative externalities.

12. Obsolescence Obsolete?

Just as the environmental critique of planned obsolescence was gathering force, the paradigmatic form of planned obsolescence—style obsolescence in the auto industry—began to wane. The move away from the rather rigid policy of annually revamping automobile models was driven in part by large-scale economic changes that caused a slow-down in the rate of productivity improvement, and a consequent squeeze on profit (Glyn 1991, 2006). The result was that less capital was available for the costly retooling required for yearly model changes. Special tooling costs were estimated to have amounted to $100 million dollars between 1964 and 1965 for Ford alone. By the early 1970s, yearly changes of model had become prohibitively expensive for car manufacturers.

The new situation did not go without comment in the press. "The trend seems clear," noted one reporter, "planned obsolescence in the domestic auto industry is dying—but it's dying slowly."[97] A *Los Angeles Times* piece in 1970 announced the death of the theretofore ubiquitous three-year product cycle in the auto industry. The dawning of a new, post-obsolescence era for auto manufacturers was also reported in *The Wall Street Journal*: "The most hallowed of Detroit traditions is planned obsolescence, which began at GM back in the 1920s and has been a cornerstone of automotive making ever since. Auto makers aren't planning to abandon the concept entirely under their new strategy, but they do plan to stretch out considerably the time between model changes."[98] Some auto makers chose to represent a necessity, imposed by unsustainably high retooling costs, as a virtue. "For those of you who are concerned about planned obsolescence," Ford announced in 1974, "the Maverick [one of its car models] next year will be unchanged."[99] But there was also some ambivalence about the decline of style obsolescence, because the practice of annual model change was associated with the postwar period of great affluence and growing productivity. One journalist lamented that "annual model change, which Detroit once held sacred to the good life, [is] fading away," suggesting that with it would go the stability of the industrial economy.[100]

In part this move away from the practice of planned obsolescence was in response to increasing competition from European car manufacturers, many of which still employed Ford's old design philosophy, centered on value and durability, only, at least so the advertising copy went, spruced up with a dash of "timeless" European style. Robert Anderson, a former top executive at Chrysler, commented on this cause of the decline of planned obsolescence: "You can buy a VW for $1700 and you are assured of being regarded as a sharp, brilliant, prudent guy for not spending money on an American car with planned obsolescence."[101] A 1970 article about trends in marketing noted a related change in advertising, which it characterized (in reference to a Volkswagen ad campaign) as the ascent of the theme of substance, or "steak," over style, or "sizzle."[102]

There also emerged a current of opinion in the early 1970s that consumers had, as a result of bitter experience, become much savvier, having over time developed a resistance to the marketing tricks of big business. In 1974, for example, Melville J. Ulmer, a marketing expert, reviewing a book about growing consumer resistance entitled *The Day the Pigs Refused to be Driven to Market*, opined that consumers had wised up to the mid-century marketing repertoire of selling techniques, including planned obsolescence. If this assessment is accurate, then the rather mechanical marketing ploy of changing models every year might have become too transparent as a ruse to continue to persuade consumers to trade in last year's model for a new one. Style changes, in order to do their marketing work, would consequently have to be more subtly indexical of added value, or else more organically connected to the drift of aesthetic taste. Perhaps the sense that people were becoming more knowledgeable and sophisticated presaged the turn in advertising to the use of irony, which presupposes a knowing consumer, wise to the ways of cruder sales pitches.

The waning of planned obsolescence did not, however, mean a return to the simple, functional principles of Fordist product design, exemplified by the model T. Systematic style obsolescence was now a permanent feature of the consumer economy, only implemented in a less regular and formulaic fashion than had been the case in the automobile industry. Moreover, technical obsolescence increased toward the end of the century, with consumer products ever more dependent on fast-changing technology. This produced, as Giles Slade (2006) chillingly charts, a problem of so-called e-waste of horrific and growing proportions. What did ebb, however, is the particular set of concerns about planned obsolescence that had been expressed in the middle years of the century. It is rare in the contemporary world to encounter the opinion, which was common in the 1950s and 1960s, that product changes per se exert an almost coercive effect on the consumer. Nor are rants about built-in product "death dates" to be found nearly as frequently in public discourse. The question arises, therefore, of why these concerns lost much of their force toward the end of the twentieth century. And, indeed, why did they emerge as and when they did earlier in the century?

In the next two chapter sections, drawing on matters discussed earlier in the book, I consider on a more general and theoretical level the significance of the controversy around planned obsolescence. The sections explore two distinct but related themes. The first, which has been touched on throughout this chapter, is the possible connections between the concern about planned obsolescence and the moral foundations of mid-century corporatist capitalism. The second is what the controversy reveals about the relationship between aesthetics and use value.

13. Planned Obsolescence and the Moral Economy of Mid-century Corporatist Capitalism

There are a number of plausible explanations for the decline in the concern about planned obsolescence from its peak in the 1960s. Although the auto industry backed away somewhat from the practice in the early 1970s, in the economy as a whole planned obsolescence, in the form of frequent model changes, had by that time become ubiquitous. Perhaps by the last quarter of the century the practices associated with planned obsolescence had become so widespread that they, in effect, dropped into the background, becoming part of the taken-for-granted framework of the consumer economy. Alternatively, Detroit's retreat from yearly model changes might have placated the current of opinion that fixed on that as the most egregious manifestation of planned obsolescence. Or maybe it was simply that any moral disturbance tends, in the absence of further provocations, or because of the intrusion of new ones of an entirely different sort, to run its course. Outrage, after all, takes some effort to sustain, and there are many competing demands on people's energy and attention in modern life. Another possible explanation for the fading of concerns about planned obsolescence is that consumer durables themselves changed in nature, becoming increasingly technological. Consumer durables, construed as technological artifacts, are inscribed in a narrative of inexorable product progress, according to which technical obsolescence is inevitable. And indeed, the rate of actual technical progress, demonstrated for example by the success of Moore's law at predicting the rate of increase of computer processor speed, must have made the "dynamic" or "progressive obsolescence" interpretation of the rapidity of the consumer product cycle seem more convincing. Perhaps people came to agree with Charles Babbage's (1832) contention that obsolescence is a natural process in an industrial economy.

All of these explanations probably have something to them. I want to suggest, however, that there is, in addition, a structural dimension to the rise and fall of the mid-century moral panic around planned obsolescence, which has to do with large scale changes in capitalism. Part of the explanation for the decline in worries about planned obsolescence, particularly as a matter concerning the morality of exchange, is that, from the later 1960s onward, the corporatist arrangements that undergirded the postwar Golden Age era of corporatist capitalism began to unravel. For reasons that are still the subject of much debate among social and economic historians, the relatively stable postwar order, in which economic growth was realized as increasing real wages as well as increasing profits, fell apart in the final decades of the century.[103] Real wages, which had been closely tied to productivity rates under collective bargaining arrangements institutionalized by the state, started to stagnate in the early 1970s and by the 1980s had almost flat-lined.

As discussed earlier in the book, there is a tendency among political economists to explain Fordism in terms of the balance of power between labor and capital, mediated by the state.[104] Mass production under Fordism, so the argument goes, entailed low unemployment, which made labor more powerful, and therefore better able to secure higher wages. The relative power of labor led to a diffusion of purchasing power, which increased aggregate effective demand, and so supported the Fordist system of high-volume mass production. When the balance of class power shifted decisively toward capital, one of the conditions that allowed for a stable system of macroeconomic regulation was thereby undermined. But while this account certainly seems plausible, it would be wrong to assert that the Fordist arrangement just reflected the power of wage earners to push for their interests, for Fordism also had a vital normative dimension. To explain Fordism in terms of a particular balance of class power, in conjunction with a functional model of the state (its function being to maintain economic, social, and political stability) does not account for the specific pattern of economic growth in the postwar years. It fails to account for why labor tended to press for, or at least be satisfied with, increased income rather than more free time. Therefore, it does not explain why productivity gains were converted into wage goods, rather than, as Keynes predicted, a progressively shorter working week. It was the tendency for increases in productivity to lead to increases in real wages that facilitated the emergence of a mass consumption to complement mass production. And that tendency rested in part on an underlying moral framework, centered on the imperative of securing "fair" compensation for labor.

The stability of the postwar configuration thus reflected not just a balance of economic power but also a degree of consensus on a vision of what a just and fair economy looks like, the roots of which can be at least proximately traced back to the politics and institutional innovations of the New Deal period. There were two sides to the mid-century Fordist moral economy. On the production side, a linking of wages to increasing productivity; on the consumption side, the right to what was regarded as a "reasonable" (therefore fair) amount of use-value in the consumer commodities received in exchange for the wage. It is important to emphasize here that the picture of economic fairness as commensurate exchange of use values was, by the middle part of the century, not just a feature of a union-bound workerist mind-set, contained therefore within the labor movement narrowly conceived. Rather, it underpinned a very widely held opinion that work should be commensurately compensated—a view summed up in the maxim, "a fair day's work for a fair day's wage" (which was adopted by the American Federation of Labor as its motto). The mid-century moral and political economy focused on the importance of purchasing power—the capacity of a wage to capture use values—as an evaluative category in economic life. A given amount of labor power is fairly exchanged when it is compensated by an amount of purchasing power deemed to be its equivalent. And the magnitude of the purchasing power of a wage is grounded in the use power (and, therefore, the notional use value) of the commodities it affords.

The high point of the politics of purchasing power came in the 1930s and 1940s. It was in those decades that increasing the purchasing power of the mass of the American population became an explicit political agenda, an active project of organized labor, the state, and significant parts of civil society, especially the consumer movement (which, roughly speaking, represented middle-class sentiment), working in concert. By the later 1940s, the alliance that had been forged between middle-class consumer advocates, the New Deal state, and labor unions had begun to fray somewhat. The interests of labor, seeking higher wages, diverged from those of the middle classes, which were more concerned about the inflation that had begun to increase after the removal of wartime price controls (Jacobs 2005). But the general concern with the buying power of the wage, and its centrality to a corporatist vision of capitalism, continued well into the postwar period. So, too, did the New Deal institutional framework designed to facilitate the maintenance and expansion of buying power—most importantly, collective bargaining arrangements supported by the state, and Keynesian macroeconomic policy. A concatenation of developments—the falling rate of profit, increased international competition, technological change in production, compounded by the oil shocks of the 1970s—led to the dissolution of the postwar corporatist compromise in the last quarter of the century.

With the collapse of the corporatism of the mid-century period, the last two decades of the twentieth century witnessed the rise in influence of neoliberal ideology. This affirmed the view that wages should be determined solely by market forces, rather than through corporatist notions of objectively fair exchange. At the same time, in the new ideological climate, the consumer was increasingly taken to be by nature a sovereign, self-making agent. The "manipulationist" narrative about the role of marketing in cultivating false needs consequently became increasingly marginalized.

What does this history have to do with planned obsolescence? As I noted, insofar as the term refers to a high rate of consumer product turnover caused by rapid technological change, planned obsolescence did not, in fact, dwindle toward the end of the century. But the idea of planned obsolescence as a ruse of business to swindle consumers out of their hard-earned wages became increasingly sidelined by the newly ascendant neoliberal narrative, according to which the consumer is sovereign and consequently knows best.[105] The pointed concern with planned obsolescence, construed as an act of business, directed against the consumer, is then a peculiarly mid-century phenomenon, which has much to do with Fordism as a particular kind of moral order.

I would suggest that the timing of the emergence of the concern over planned obsolescence, as well as the timing of its decline, makes sense, therefore, when put in the context of these changes in the broader character of capitalism. The disquiet about the specter of planned obsolescence coincided with the coalescing of the postwar industrial order—the so-called Golden Age. In that period of the history of capitalism, labor entered into a relatively stable (although often fractious) agreement with business, and the legitimacy of capitalism in general became hinged on the notion that increases in productivity would be shared with workers through increasing real wages, supported by conventions of collective bargaining in industry. This compact between wage earners and their employers was not an easy one, and consumers, who were almost always also wage workers, suspected that the value of the real wage—the purchasing power they received in exchange for their labor—was being eroded by big business employing strategies of planned obsolescence to deprive them of the full use power of the things they bought. In this sense, worries about planned obsolescence were of a piece with worries about inflation eroding the buying power of wages. Much of the energy behind the moral panic about planned obsolescence derived from the suspicion that what capital gives to wage earners with one hand (an increasing nominal wage) is, through planned obsolescence, surreptitiously taken away by the other, through shoddily produced products, or as psychological tricks were deployed to prompt consumers to needlessly replace perfectly good repositories of use value.[106] At the root of the concern about planned obsolescence during the "Golden Age" were worries that the labor given at work would not be commensurately compensated. The standardized goods afforded by the wage were suspected of being deliberately deprived of adequate amounts of potential use value, and would, therefore, fail to measure up to the free activity lost through labor. The very strong reaction against the specter of planned obsolescence thus reflected the moral economy, centered on wage labor commensuration, that organized postwar economic life. And when the socioeconomic conditions underlying that moral economy began to fall apart in the last quarter of the century, its normative force became attenuated, and consequently the concern about planned obsolescence faded.

14. Use Value and Aesthetics

That style obsolescence should have been seen as so problematic is, as noted at the outset of the chapter, on reflection, somewhat perplexing. For why should aesthetics be excluded from considerations of usefulness? If, for example, a consumer chooses to upgrade her car after three years (as was typical for automobiles), then it would be reasonable to assume that the aesthetic benefits of owning the new model justifies its price. That is certainly how an economist would typically explain the consumer's behavior. And indeed, as we have seen, industry spokespersons often took that interpretation as self-evident and were incredulous that anyone could find objectionable yearly model changes for which there seemed to be genuine demand. And yet the attacks on planned "style" or "psychological" obsolescence presupposed a categorical distinction between the aesthetic and functional properties of products, with "real value" accruing to consumers only from the latter. The normative force of that distinction is reflected in the strategy followed by industry to justify frequent model changes by claiming that they entailed substantive (that is, functional) improvements, as opposed to "superficial," merely aesthetic changes.

Of course, the distinction between plain, functional, useful properties and fanciful and superfluous aesthetics is not just found in twentieth-century industrial societies. It is present in and is probably in part a legacy of a complex of cultural currents, including Protestant asceticism, Victorian utilitarianism, as well as modernist minimalism. Perhaps therefore, the distinction is just one element of the general process of rationalization supposedly underlying all of these. Yet to approach the concern about style obsolescence as just a manifestation of a modern imperative to subordinate form to function does not explain why the practice of frequent model changes was portrayed as a kind of fraud, in which the consumer gets cheated out of something. More sense can be made of the value-laden distinction between the aesthetic properties of commodities and their narrowly functional properties when it is interpreted in terms of the theory of consumption as wage-labor commensuration set out in Chapter 4.[107] If this theory is right, it would follow that the functional properties of commodities—those seen as securing some duration of use—would be differentiated from properties seen as peripheral to use (narrowly construed), such as aesthetic characteristics. So for example, a car's material properties endow it with a certain amount of durability and with certain technical capacities. Owning that car then gives the consumer access to a concrete reserve of potential activity (use power), which is similar in kind to the activity given up as labor in exchange for the wage. The aesthetic characteristics of the car, however, are by comparison much more difficult to make commensurable with labor power. This is because it is hard to construe the aesthetic properties of objects, as opposed to their functional, use-conferring properties, as *objectively* commensurable with labor. There are two reasons why this is so. First, the aesthetic characteristics of products are less clearly linked to a temporal span of activity than their functional characteristics. This makes it more difficult to think of aesthetic properties as commensurable with the *duration* of activity given up as labor. Second, aesthetic value is typically regarded as at least somewhat *subjective* in nature. If beauty is in the eye of the beholder, then how can the aesthetic dimension of commodities serve as a criterion for establishing the *objective* fairness of a given wage? It is difficult to see how the quite subjective aesthetic side of the commodities afforded by the wage could serve as an objective measure of purchasing power.

If, therefore, wage earners are encouraged to exchange their labor (by way of spending the wage) for functionally redundant product features, such as the latest model year's styling on an automobile, then that labor is, in effect, not being sufficiently (that is, commensurately) compensated.[108] In replacing a perfectly good commodity with a new version that differs only aesthetically from the one it replaces, wage earning consumers are effectively exchanging labor for a characteristic of an object that adds no substantive, functional (therefore commensurable) value. So they are exchanging the use value of their labor, abstracted in the wage, for an essentially insubstantial return. This interpretation of the objection to style obsolescence would explain why there was a strong current of opinion in society that consumers were duped and defrauded by the practice.

Of course, none of this is to say that there were not countervailing psychological motivations and cultural forces in play. If concerns about status, neophilia, and the dialectics of fashion (as, for example, theorized by Simmel), were not also powerful influences on consumer behavior, then the whole strategy of style obsolescence would not have become successful in the first place.[109] However, the strong reaction against the success of the strategy suggests that it ran in some tension with the normative framework underpinning the consensus that wage labor is a potentially objectively fair exchange of commensurable substances. Thus, even the very distinction between style and material obsolescence expresses the fear that, when proper commensuration is sabotaged, the free activity lost to labor is unrecoverable.

In this chapter, and in the four that precede it, I examined various developments in US history that fit with the theory of mass consumption as wage-labor commensuration. The set of developments I considered is by no means exhaustive. The development of chain stores and the transformation of retail, for example, could be interpreted in a similar fashion (Rosenberg 2017). The empirical analysis of those chapters could also be supplemented by a much more detailed historical ethnography of attitudes toward the connection between work and consumption, along the lines of the brief account given in Chapter 5. But, as mentioned in the introduction, the point of the historical analysis is not to develop a comprehensive picture of one context but rather to serve as a heuristic, to "flesh out," the argument and think through the theory in a historically grounded fashion. The objective was to construct through historical analysis a quite general explanation for the relation between mass production and mass consumption under industrial capitalism. The next chapter, which concludes the book, comprises a summation of the argument and some ruminations on the general character of economic normativity under advanced industrial capitalism.

TEN

Conclusion: Capitalism, Commensuration, and the Normativity of Economic Action

Underlying the argument of this book is a claim that the peculiarity of capitalism has something to do with the kind of normativity that governs its economic activity. More specifically, the claim is that economic normativity under capitalism has features that go some way toward explaining the dynamic, yet irrational and treadmill-like character of the system.[1] One side of the dynamism of capitalism, much discussed in social theory, is the imperative on the side of production to accumulate exchange value. The other side, the focus of this book, is the open-ended character of aggregate demand, which is rooted in patterns of consumer behavior. A normative feature of industrial capitalism that helps explain the character of consumer demand is the assumption that a wage ideally ought to be *commensurate* with the labor given in exchange for it. This assumption is expressed in the idea that, at least in theory, there is a fair level of wages for any given amount of labor. But for labor to be commensurate with its wages, the two must first be *commensurable*. The presupposition that wage and labor are commensurable helps explain the behavior underlying the demand side of the dynamic of capitalism.

To recap in some more detail, I argued that the materialistic orientation of capitalism—specifically, the tendency for increasing productivity to be turned into unending commodity accumulation, as opposed to the expansion of free time—is a consequence of the rise to prominence of the notion that wage-labor exchange can, at least potentially, be objectively fair. As noted in Chapter 4, what makes an exchange *objectively* fair cannot just be a matter of convention, so that an exchange is fair just because it accords with some norm or custom. Rather, the notion of an objectively fair exchange entails that fairness is grounded in facts about the substances being exchanged. I suggested that the idea that labor can be commensurately compensated by its wage leads to a tendency for usefulness to be construed in quite abstract, yet at the same time also narrowly materialistic terms, as a function of the properties of wage goods. This is because the only way for labor to seem commensurate with its wage is for wage goods to become *qualitatively equivalent* to the labor that is given (and, therefore, free activity that is given up) in exchange for them. In effect, wage goods come to represent quantities of free activity, roughly measured by the duration of useful activity those goods, in theory, could facilitate. The legitimacy accorded to the exchange of labor for a wage thus both depends on, and in turn encourages, the ongoing accumulation by wage earners of stores of potential activity, reified in the form of wage goods. For by accumulating consumer commodities, wage earners accumulate a store of hypothetical "activity power" that, as such, is roughly equivalent in kind to the free activity given up through selling their labor power. The notional equivalence established between increasingly standardized consumer commodities and standardized labor was an essential part of what I described as the Fordist moral economy, which contributed to the stabilization of advanced industrial economies in the middle decades of the twentieth century.

While the notional equivalence between standardized consumer commodities and standardized labor makes sense of the work-time regime in advanced industrial capitalism, the open-endedness of consumer demand might nonetheless remain puzzling. For the commensurability between wage and labor by virtue of the activity power of commodities would not in itself preclude the possibility of reaching the state of satiation predicted by Keynes (thus ending the dynamic form of demand manifested in mass consumption). Considering this directs attention to the criteriological uncertainty of wage labor commensuration, which was discussed in Chapter 4. The criteria defining fair exchange of wage for labor are deeply ambiguous, because there are in fact no objective grounds on which to establish just when a given amount of labor has been commensurately compensated (if there were, then it would be much easier to resolve disagreements about how much a given amount of work should be paid). Even where wages are turned into goods that represent hypothetical free activity, thus establishing a notional equivalence between labor and its wage (the free activity indexed by wage goods being equivalent to the free activity given up in order to work), the exchange of work for commodities remains fundamentally problematic. This is because work and commodities— activity and things—are ultimately different in kind and *have no obvious natural common measure*. Indeed, as noted earlier in the book, it is not even clear how labor could be an alienable commodity in the first place. The norm of objectively fair exchange, thus, in practice, lacks criteria of satisfaction— criteria by virtue of which a fair exchange can be judged to have self-evidently occurred (or not). The imperative to obtain "fair" compensation for work (a wage able to command a quantity of wage goods that is, in some sense, objectively equivalent to the labor given in exchange for it) demands something that is impossible to accomplish—an equal exchange ungrounded by common measure, therefore without an obvious criterion for determining parity between the exchanged substances. The lack of *inherent* common measure between work and its wage means that any commensurability between the two can only be a pseudocommensurability.

Furthermore, the commensuration of wage and labor by virtue of the time signified by wage goods will always be uncertain because there is a basic difference between these two forms of time. Time given up in work is real time. On the other hand, time *indexed* by wage goods is hypothetical, in the sense that using those goods is conditional on having *actual* free time (as well as enough energy, complementary resources and access to an appropriate setting). Workers, at least in affluent countries, where wage levels are well above absolute subsistence levels, thus give up chunks of their lives in exchange for a store of potential free activity represented by a set of wage goods. However, it is unclear how the merely potential activity indexed by consumer commodities could serve as adequate compensation for the real time and energy spent at work. The commodities accumulated by spending the wage amount to a kind of promissory note (much like the warranty), to the effect that commensuration will be achieved at some point in the indefinite future through using those commodities in free activities. But the perturbing question remains of whether that will in fact come to pass.

In the absence of clear, objective criteria for determining a fair rate of exchange between labor and its wage, action oriented by the norm of fair wage exchange becomes open-ended. It becomes guided by an end that is presupposed as being achievable but, at the same time, lacks criteria for establishing whether or not it has been achieved.[2] In the public realm, this leads to unending debates about what constitutes a fair wage, with different competing conceptions of the conditions under which wage labor is fairly compensated. In industrial relations, it leads to a tendency for labor to push for ever more purchasing power (as opposed to shorter hours, for reasons set out in Chapter 3), at least in part on the assumption that at *some* level of real wages, commensuration with work will be self-evidently achieved. To the individual wage-earning consumer, however, it will be ambiguous whether the failure of any given amount of wages to seem like objectively commensurate compensation for the work given in exchange for it, is the result of an inadequate wage or simply spending the wage on the wrong set of goods.

Here we encounter another kind of normative vagueness under capitalism, one not discussed at length in the book. While the hypothetical utility of a commodity in one way objectively subsists in its material properties, whether that utility will "work" for a given person is a matter of that person's preferences, made clear to her by way of introspection. Yet the criteria determining whether a given set of goods counts as the right one for a given consumer are, like the criteria determining fair wages, quite obscure. There is some sense that the consumer ought to "optimize" over a set of choices but, because the different options are themselves often incommensurable, it is not at all clear what that might mean. The problem is compounded by the fact that preferences are uncertain and mercurial, and can always be subjected to skeptical interrogation. Indeed, the entire cultural machinery around consumption under capitalism encourages second-guessing about preferences. There is some tension between the notion that fair compensation for work is an objective matter, rooted in measurable substances, on the one hand, and the normatively subjective, evanescent character of individual preferences in consumption, on the other. Consumption by individuals is then at least to some degree driven by the urge to find the right set of choices to satisfy internal and external criteria that are ill-defined, unstable, and potentially contradictory.

Moreover, according to an influential norm concerning consumption under capitalism, rooted in the notion of consumer sovereignty, the subjective preferences of a given individual are supposed to constitute a kind of private knowledge. The normatively private character of individual preferences works against judgments about value being informed by public, intersubjective checks. Such checks can bring social knowledge to bear on assessments made by individuals about matters of usefulness. An example would be knowledge within a community about the contextual constraints on making use of commodities. But the asocial, private character of final consumption insulates thinking about consumption (and by extension also production) from social knowledge of that kind.

The normative force behind the idea of a fair wage, in conjunction with the uncertainty about the criteria that define fair compensation for labor and the notional privacy of individual preferences in consumption can lead wage-earners into a restless quest for some set of wage goods commensurate with the labor they have sold. The objective is to find a kind of mapping between those goods and life lost to labor, such that some quantity of the former becomes equivalent to the latter. To the extent that attention focuses on that objective (which, in its most general form, involves the purchasing power of the wage) larger questions about the form of economic life realized under capitalism (including its work-time regime) will tend to fall by the wayside.

This emphasis on the normativity of economic action leads to a different understanding of capitalism from that given by many political economists.[3] Rather than conceiving of capitalism as a particular manifestation of timeless motives and forces, we can embed it in the development of a peculiar set of norms governing action in the economic realm. These norms seem to indicate how economic action should proceed yet have the effect of impeding the normatively scripted, and socially achieved, closure of action that makes other economic systems, by comparison, quite nondynamic.[4] According to the argument of this book, consumer behavior in fully developed capitalist economies is to a significant extent guided by an imperative to make the wage objectively commensurate with the labor exchanged for it, in the absence of any criteria establishing when commensuration between the two has been achieved. Against that background, the criticism that the continuous sacrifice of free time to work is fundamentally wrongheaded and self-defeating will not get much traction. Consequently, the material expansion of capitalism, entailing the production of ever more commodities and the contraction of time available for making use of each of them, will be facilitated by an open-ended form of demand.

All of this suggests an answer to the question posed at the beginning of this book: Why did Keynes's 1930 prediction about the future of industrial capitalism fail to come true? Keynes thought that following a necessary diversion into a growth-driven economy under capitalism, the economy would eventually enter into a stationary state, in which material wants would be satiated. But Keynes was presupposing that economic action is organized by ends the satisfaction of which would, when met, be quite apparent. If, however, consumer (and wage earner) behavior under capitalism is influenced to a significant degree by very general norms that stand without clear criteria of satisfaction, then consumption would, as a result, become unbounded. Keynes's envisioned state would never come about.[5] Thus, the peculiar pattern of *accumulative consumption* characteristic of mass consumer society, and the corresponding inelasticity of work time to increasing productivity and hourly wages, is at least in part a consequence of the open-endedness of economic norms under capitalism

As noted earlier in the book, the focus on norms (those concerning commensurability, commensuration, fairness, and utility) in my account brings it close to Weber's approach to capitalism. For Weber also saw a normative imperative as lying at the root of modern industrial capitalism. But while Weber provides a coherent account of the origins of the normative framework that motivated capitalist production, he pays much less attention to the normative dimension of the mode of consumption that is required for the material expansion of capitalism (and for the realization of profit against the background of rising productivity).[6] As noted throughout the book, the conditions of possibility for the inexorable expansion of the industrial economy include not just the instrumental pursuit of profit by capitalists but also ever-increasing consumer demand. And the dynamism of consumer demand, which is so crucial to industrial capitalism, rests on peculiar aspects of capitalism's normative structure—namely, the notion of the possibility of objective commensuration between wage and work, and the privacy of the criterion that determines whether or not consumers have ultimately made the two commensurate through their particular spending decisions. These features make the normativity around wage-labor exchange, economic value, and consumption indeterminate, with the effect of encouraging behavioral tendencies that in the aggregate produce a mass consumption capable of absorbing the output of capitalist mass production. This form of consumption represents, in Marxian terms, the endless pursuit not of "exchange value" but of a peculiarly decontextualized form of "use value," contained in commodities, yet disconnected from actual activity, hence often unrealized. If, as Marx argues, capital pursues fetishized exchange value, then labor, in a mirror image, pursues a fetishized form of use value—a merely indexical use value, signified by dead things rather than animated through activity. The normative indeterminateness of wage-labor commensuration and consumption thus contributes to capitalism's expansionary tendency, which is impervious to considerations about what its consequences are for human welfare. Once consumption, like production, is untethered in this way, the growth machine can then grind inexorably onward—at least until some ultimate limit in nature is reached.

But what would a different arrangement look like—one in which attitudes to consumption and work time are no longer influenced by an imperative to make labor and its wage commensurable, and therefore potentially commensurate? What would need to be in place for patterns of work, free time, and consumption to be more attuned to human welfare? Part of the answer surely has to do with making consumption and work matters of explicit *public* deliberation, about alternatives that are very often incommensurable. What is required is the cultivation of a thoroughly conversational and contextual approach to the ends toward which economic activity ought to be directed. A dialogic procedure, focused on the concrete realities of everyday life, would stand in for isolated individual introspection, or an abstract quest for the objective ground of value (by virtue of which all things can be made commensurable), as the method for deciding questions about economic value. Public deliberation about economic value would bring to the fore the communal practices that make up a form of life—practices that provide a horizon or condition of possibility for the very coherence of norms and therefore for meaningful action of any sort (Wittgenstein 1953).[7] To make usefulness and utility matters of public deliberation would thus bring them within a social frame of reference. Within this frame of reference, the conditions under which practices actually take place, including constraints of time and energy, could be brought to bear more systematically on thinking about the human consequences of commodity production and consumption.

Making consumption, work, and use value thoroughly explicit, public matters would therefore involve a kind of reembedding of the economy in political and social life. It would, more specifically, involve resolving questions about economic value through a democratic politics comprehensively extended to the economic sphere. How choices are made between incommensurable alternatives, and how economic priorities should be established, would then emerge contingently from an ongoing conversation about the nature of the good life—a conversation grounded in collective experience and knowledge. Utility, instead of being a rarefied abstraction—"a metaphysical concept of impregnable circularity," as the prominent economist Joan Robinson (1962) put it—or being reified in decontextualized material objects, would be substantively defined through public deliberation. Usefulness and utility would thus no longer be phantasms in the mind of abstracted individuals or fetishized properties of commodities. They would be concrete and contextual, assuming their natural form as emergent features in the social life of communities. The result of this regrounding of utility would be to make possible the state of affairs Keynes optimistically envisioned for the future during the dark early years of the Depression.

APPENDIX 1

Value in billions of 1998 dollars of fixed residential assets and consumer durables
between 1925 and 1998 (source of data: US Department of Commerce)

Year	Residential Assets	Residential assets measured using chain-type quantity index.	Consumer Durables	Consumer durables measured using chain-type quantity index
1925	100.5	17.23	32.0	5.08
1926	104.9	17.98	33.5	5.36
1927	108.3	18.67	34.6	5.60
1928	114.5	19.29	35.7	5.83
1929	118.5	19.69	36.5	6.16
1930	112.8	19.83	34.4	6.27
1931	97.4	19.90	30.1	6.19
1932	86.3	19.81	26.5	5.92
1933	90.1	19.70	25.8	5.66
1934	94.0	19.64	25.7	5.50
1935	95.7	19.66	25.7	5.47
1936	103.6	19.75	27.1	5.62
1937	111.3	19.87	28.7	5.82
1938	114.2	19.99	28.5	5.84
1939	118.5	20.26	29.5	6.02
1940	128.3	20.60	32.3	6.32
1941	141.0	20.97	37.2	6.54
1942	152.0	21.04	41.6	6.49
1943	164.2	20.99	45.2	6.32

TABLE 1

Value in billions of 1998 dollars of fixed residential assets and consumer durables between 1925 and 1998 (source of data: US Department of Commerce)

Year	Residential Assets	Residential assets measured using chain-type quantity index.	Consumer Durables	Consumer durables measured using chain-type quantity index
1944	176.7	20.92	47.2	6.11
1945	190.3	20.86	47.9	6.04
1946	224.7	21.42	55.6	6.70
1947	265.8	22.23	66.9	7.63
1948	290.8	23.20	76.5	8.50
1949	307.4	24.07	85.5	9.37
1950	339.5	25.34	101.0	10.69
1951	370.0	26.33	113.1	11.56
1952	390.0	27.29	120.0	11.74
1953	406.2	28.26	128.3	12.44
1954	427.2	29.34	132.1	13.32
1955	457.2	30.62	141.6	14.55
1956	481.6	31.74	152.6	15.46
1957	496.3	32.75	162.0	16.03
1958	512.0	33.76	165.6	16.22
1959	534.5	35.12	171.5	16.70
1969	555.6	36.33	176.8	17.24
1961	576.0	37.53	179.9	17.56
1962	597.5	38.87	186.2	18.25
1963	612.7	40.42	196.5	19.17
1964	661.9	42.06	207.0	20.30
1965	703.6	43.60	218.6	21.86
1966	760.7	44.92	239.0	23.61
1967	811.1	46.14	261.4	25.16
1968	897.1	47.61	290.4	27.08
1969	960.5	49.12	317.1	28.81
1970	1,015.7	50.47	340.6	30.02
1971	1,140.8	52.36	362.4	31.64
1972	1,278.9	54.64	392.5	33.79

TABLE 1

Value in billions of 1998 dollars of fixed residential assets and consumer durables
between 1925 and 1998 (source of data: US Department of Commerce)

Year	Residential Assets	Residential assets measured using chain-type quantity index.	Consumer Durables	Consumer durables measured using chain-type quantity index
1973	1,467.8	56.90	434.2	36.38
1974	1,667.7	58.47	500.0	37.97
1975	1,805.1	59.69	550.1	39.36
1976	2,003.4	61.38	602.3	41.49
1977	2,338.5	63.61	668.4	44.07
1978	2,700.2	66.01	754.1	46.77
1979	3,137.3	68.24	847.3	49.04
1980	3,536.8	69.75	934.0	50.09
1981	3,804.0	71.03	1,003.7	51.20
1982	3,973.4	71.86	1,047.2	52.43
1983	4,134.8	73.47	1,115.1	55.18
1984	4,368.9	75.48	1,201.9	58.87
1985	4,601.3	77.48	1,291.5	62.95
1986	4,967.8	79.86	1,420.3	67.95
1987	5,283.3	82.22	1,534.0	72.42
1988	5,606.1	84.50	1,661.6	77.09
1989	5,912.2	86.63	1,768.5	81.15
1990	6,137.7	88.47	1,852.9	84.05
1991	6,261.0	89.82	1,894.7	84.95
1992	6,595.8	91.46	1,933.5	86.50
1993	6,991.0	93.47	2,014.1	89.12
1994	7,472.2	95.62	2,110.7	92.57
1995	7,784.2	97.66	2,188.7	96.14
1996	8,195.3	100.00	2,259.2	100.00
1997	8,618.5	102.35	2,324.5	104.29
1998	9,193.0	105.01	2,418.8	110.13

APPENDIX 2

TABLE 2

OECD savings rates, as a percent of disposable household income, 1985–2009

	1985	1990	1995	2000	2005	2009
United Kingdom	6.9	5.6	6.7	1.2	1.2	1.2
United States	8.5	6.7	5.7	3.0	1.5	6.2
Australia	12.1	6.7	6.3	2.6	0.4	—
Canada	16.0	13.3	9.4	4.8	2.2	4.7
France	10.2	9.2	12.7	11.8	11.4	12.5
Germany	12.1	13.7	11.0	9.2	10.5	11.1
Italy	21.5	21.7	17.0	8.4	9.9	7.1
Japan	16.5	13.9	11.9	8.8	3.9	5.0
Switzerland	—	9.6	12.7	11.7	10.1	—
Austria	10.5	10.3	11.8	9.2	9.7	11.1
Belgium	11.1	9.5	16.4	12.3	10.2	13.5
Netherlands	5.6	18.2	14.3	6.9	6.4	6.8
Sweden	3.2	3.4	8.3	4.3	5.5	12.9

Data source: Sheldon Garon, *Beyond Our Means* (Princeton, NJ: Princeton University Press, 2012), Appendix.

Notes

CHAPTER 1: INTRODUCTION

1. The first version of Keynes's paper was presented at Winchester public school in 1928, before the financial crash of the following year. Keynes continued to work on the paper, which he presented a second time before an audience in Madrid, in 1930. In the second version, he added some thoughts about the economic crisis then ongoing. The paper was eventually published in a 1931 collection (Skidelsky 1992). As Lorenzo Pecchi and Gustavo Piga (2008) note in their introduction, it is reasonable to suppose that, when writing the first version in 1928, Keynes's concerns reflected broader anxieties, quite common in the 1920s, about waste and inefficiency in the industrial economy.

2. Keynes (1931, p. 24) ridiculed the figure of the purposive man in the following, whimsical fashion: "The purposive man is always trying to secure a spurious and delusive immortality for his acts by pushing his interest in them forward into time. He does not love his cat, but his kittens; nor in truth his kittens, but only his kittens' kittens, and so on forward forever to the end of catdom. For him jam is not jam unless it is a case of jam tomorrow and never jam today. Thus, by pushing his jam always forward into the future, he strives to secure for his act of boiling it an immortality."

3. Zilibotti examined population weighted real per capita GDP growth for the world, on a purchasing power parity basis, and calculated the average growth rate between 1950 and 2000.

4. Thereafter OECD growth slowed to a still healthy 2.3 percent, while non-OECD growth increased to 3.1 percent.

5. Avner Offer (2006, p. 298) notes that in the United States, "families with children had a combined 53-hour week working for pay in 1968, and a 64-hour working week in 2000."

6. Robert Solow (2008) makes the valid point that Keynes ignores distributional issues in his analysis. Keynes just assumes that as the ratio of capital to labor increases (capital deepening), so real wages will rise. But, Solow observes, there is no reason why that should necessarily be the case. After all, in a fully robotic capitalist economy all income would flow to those who own capital. That the benefits of growth were distributed relatively evenly in the

advanced capitalist world during the postwar years was not just a natural outcome of increasing productivity. It was, rather, contingent on complex historical conditions, political agreements, and institutional arrangements, most importantly the welfare state, the disruption of which, in the 1970s, led to stagnation in real wage levels and increasing inequality (Piketty 2014). But although Solow's observation is cogent, it still leaves in place the puzzle of why the gains of increasing productivity were devoted so exclusively during the Golden Age of capitalism to increasing consumption rather than reducing work time. Solow's point also fails to address the issue of why, in the absence of continuing increases in real wages, consumers toward the end of the twentieth century made use of credit to make up the difference between their expectation that standards of living should continue to increase and the economic reality of static real wages. The resort to credit suggests that the rate of increase of consumer demand had, by the late twentieth century, become quite entrenched—that is, relatively inelastic to changes in the rate at which real incomes were increasing.

7. In *The Protestant Ethic and the Spirit of Capitalism*, Weber ([1930] 1992) famously argues that the Calvinist doctrine of predestination created an unbearable uncertainty in early Protestants about whether or not they were among the elect. To assuage that uncertainty, Protestants sought to regiment their lives in such a way as to be as economically productive as possible—"testifying to their belief" through their conduct. Economic productivity then served as a sign of true belief, as well as an indication of God's favor, thereby providing reassurance to the individual that she was a member of the elect.

8. Knight (1921) argued that leisure is a commodity that workers will be increasingly inclined to "buy back" as their hourly wages increase: "In so far as men act rationally—i.e., from fixed motives subject to the law of diminishing utility—they will at a higher rate divide their time between wage earning and non-industrial uses in such a way as to earn more money but to work fewer hours" (pp. 117–18). Pigou (1932) argued that when income decreases (as a result of increased taxation, for example), workers will be willing to expend more effort up until the point at which marginal disutility of effort equals the marginal utility of income. This is simply because the marginal disutility of effort does not decrease when income decreases. It follows that for Pigou, the value of leisure decreases in relative terms as income declines, so prompting the worker to increase her effort (and reduce her leisure). In theoretical terms, Pigou's argument proceeds from the same ground as Knight's, only looking in the other direction, as it were—as increments of income are lost (rather than gained), the associated loss of utility per increment increases. Conversely, it follows that Pigou, like Knight, holds that as income increases, workers will reduce their effort, cutting hours. It should be mentioned that the prominent economist Lionel Robbins, who had strongly subjectivist leanings with respect to value, disagreed with both Knight and Pigou on this, arguing that it is not possible to know a priori what the consequences of changes in income will be on the demand for work or leisure. Robbins pointed out that even if we accept as a law that returns to income tend to diminish at the margin, there is no way of knowing at what rate they will diminish and hence no way to predict what effect a change in income will have on the supply of labor. The consequences of an increase in the wage rate then depends, according to Robbins, entirely on the income elasticity of demand for wage goods and leisure. "It is all a matter of elasticities," as he put it (Robbins 1930, p. 128).

Although Robbins's point is, within the framework of economics, theoretically sound, the fact that the use of increasing productivity in industrial economies over the course of the twentieth century has been so skewed in the direction of increasing income, as opposed to free time, is nonetheless quite puzzling. It seems odd that the demand for free time, under conditions of increasing affluence, should have become so inelastic.

9. Conversely, if income drops, the relative value of leisure should also decline, leading to increased effort on the part of workers.

10. *Abduction* refers to the logic involved in the generation of hypotheses, as well as to how explanations are justified. The concept has roots in the philosophy of science of Charles Sander Pierce. For Peirce, abduction was one part of what he described as a "logical triad" in scientific method, the other two being deduction and induction. Abduction generates a hypothesis, and deduction derives some testable logical entailment from the hypothesis, which is then inductively tested through experimentation. Abduction, deduction, and induction thus make up the three phases of the process of scientific investigation. While philosophers of science have generally agreed on the importance of deduction and induction, and have put much effort into their explication, less attention has been given to how hypotheses are generated.

Peirce (1931) held that "all the ideas of science come to it by the way of Abduction" (p. 5:145). By contrast, the other two phases of scientific reasoning, deduction and induction, while being crucial parts of scientific method, are unable to produce new knowledge. On Peirce's account, the urge to make a theory begins when we encounter a state of affairs that surprises us. We theorize by thinking about what would have to be true of the world in order for the surprising state of affairs to follow as a matter of course—coming up with a hypothesis which, if true, would remove the grounds for our surprise at the world being thus and so. The form of inference in abduction, according to Peirce (1931), is:

> The surprising fact, C, is observed;
> But if A were true, C would be a matter of course,
> Hence, there is reason to suspect that A is true. (p. 5:189)

How exactly to cash this out when there are a number of possible candidates for A is not entirely clear, as philosophers have observed (Frankfurt 1958; Achinstein 1970, 1971, 1987). However, broadly put, the procedure is to compare members of a set of plausible candidates for A and pick the one that seems least problematic. This is the strategy I follow in Chapters 3 and 4, where I examine other possible explanations for the pattern of work time and consumption and then show how the theory I develop has advantages over those other explanations.

CHAPTER 2: THE PUZZLE

1. According to the classical doctrine posited in Say's law, supply must be met with an equivalent volume of effective demand. The argument is that since producers must pay for production, they create the purchasing power required for their goods to be sold. Keynes pointed out in *The General Theory* that while Say's law might hold in the long run, the fact

that money mediates exchange under capitalism means that there is potential for liquidity to become trapped (as a result of money hoarding), leading to short-turn deficits of effective demand, which can in turn lead to a vicious recessive cycle.

2. The roots of this insight can be traced to Bernoulli's ([1738] 1954) solution to the St. Petersburg paradox, which, he argued, is the declining marginal utility of money. As mentioned in the introduction, economists Frank Knight and Arthur Pigou subscribed to some version of the theory. The doctrine also seems implicit in Keynes's contention that, all things being equal, the propensity to consume added increments of real income should be less than unity, and increasingly so with growing affluence.

3. Sen conceives of welfare as an irreducibly complex basket of incommensurable goods. Commodities are valuable insofar as they can produce capabilities to achieve certain "functionings" ("doings and beings"). Although Sen holds that the value attached to different functionings should be a matter left for democratic deliberation, at the same time he thinks that there are certain basic functionings—those facilitated by access to shelter, nutrition, health, and education—the importance of which is not in dispute. This suggests that money spent achieving these basic functionings will generally obtain a higher return in welfare than money spent in order to achieve more specialized ones. The underlying assumptions are then not so very different from Maslow's hierarchy of needs.

4. Layard and Mayraz (2008) examined data on subjective happiness from fifty countries between 1972 and 2005 to estimate the average rate of declining marginal utility of income and found the rate of decline to be steeper than economists tend to assume.

5. As noted in Chapter 1, in this book I employ *use value* to mean the value attached to the activities made possible by a commodity. *Utility* is a broader term, meaning roughly actual satisfaction. Utility does not necessarily entail the use of commodities. Use value by contrast, is always tied to things—it is, in the Marxian tradition, a property of commodities.

6. Simon (1971, pp. 40–41) comments: "in an information-rich world, the wealth of information means a dearth of something else: a scarcity of whatever it is that information consumes. What information consumes is rather obvious: it consumes the attention of its recipients. Hence a wealth of information creates a poverty of attention and a need to allocate that attention efficiently among the overabundance of information sources that might consume it."

7. Attention economics dovetails with work in psychology, which has shown that when consumers are faced with more than eight choices, they experience cognitive overload and, consequently, discomfort (Schwartz 2004). Contemplating consumers become overwhelmed with information, making the decision at hand very difficult, with detrimental consequences for their psychological well-being. Yet even after they are owned, commodities call on our attention and demand choices. There is no reason to suppose that the choice about which item in a set of owned items to make use of at a given point in time should be less uncomfortably distracting than the choice about which commodities should be acquired in the first place. The cognitive difficulty of managing a set of owned commodities (potential sources of utility) is perhaps reflected in the sentiment commonly expressed by people that their material possessions feel burdensome—and in the sense of lightness and clarity that often follows a purging of stuff.

8. According to a chain-quantity index measure, which best approximates actual quantity of things produced, per capita output of consumer durables in the United States increased by nine times between 1925 and 1998 (Sherby 2000).

9. The literature on the measurement of happiness and well-being is now vast. See Weimann, Knabe, and Schob (2015) for an overview.

10. Sen ([1985] 1999, p. 3) points out the complexities involved in measuring happiness utility as follows: "You could be well-off without being well. You could be well without being able to lead the life you want to lead. You could have the life you wanted, without being happy. You could be happy, without having much freedom. You could have a great deal of freedom, without achieving much. We can go on."

11. In an attempt to replace the monetary measure of well-being represented by per capita gross national income, some countries, most famously Bhutan, have begun to use the recent research on happiness as the basis for a more sophisticated measure of economic development—something like gross national happiness.

12. See also Layard (2005) on the failure in America of indices of happiness to increase with increasing productivity, income, and wealth.

13. Blanchflower and Oswald found a similar insensitivity of happiness to increases in income in the case of Britain over the same period.

14. Offer suggests that this offers support for the "hedonic treadmill" hypothesis, according to which people increase their expectations, but not their levels of satisfaction, as income rises.

15. Easterlin analyzed survey data from seventeen Latin American countries between 1994 and 2006.

16. Reports of "life evaluation" were, however, to a greater extent correlated with income. The relation between income and well-being thus differed depending on whether subjects were asked to report on their affective states or to evaluate their lives. I would suggest that questions that ask about life evaluation incline respondents to take a third-person viewpoint on their lives, assessing how their lives might look to others. This third-person perspective might well prompt subjects to place themselves in an "objective" status hierarchy and evaluate their lives according to their relative position within that hierarchy. That hierarchy need not just be internal to a country—it can also be a perceived global hierarchy encompassing people in other countries. For instance, a Turkish person, asked to evaluate her life, might think about how it objectively compares with that of an imagined middle-class American or German, on the one hand, and, say, an Egyptian on the other. Moreover, the concept of life *evaluation* immediately evokes quantitative assessment—a number that measures how much a life is valued. I suspect that income—the most immediately accessible quantitative measure of the worth of a life—would quite naturally come to mind as a rough proxy for a quantitative rating of life evaluation. Self-assessment of emotional well-being, by comparison, seems better insulated from tendency for money to serve in that way as a stand-in and, therefore, arguably provides a better gauge of welfare. Also, research by Pew, as part of its global attitudes project, shows that in measures of life satisfaction (roughly the same measure as life evaluation), emerging economies have converged on the advanced economies, even as the prospects of economic development converging

between the emerging and advanced world have diminished (Pew Research Center 2014). In 2014, 54 percent of respondents in rich countries rated themselves between 7 and 10 on a 10-point scale measuring life satisfaction, while 51 percent of those in emerging economies did so. This suggests that for life satisfaction, as well as subjective well-being, income matters most up to the point at which basic needs are met, after which it begins to lose relevance.

17. In part this is because such studies tend to compare countries, and comparative data on hours of work are not good.

18. Perhaps part of what keeps people attached to the current work regime are the opportunities work provides for social interaction. That would mean that for the switch to noncommodified productive activities to capture the same set of benefits as paid work, people would have to shift in concert away from paid work—so that they could be productive *with* other people in noncommodified ways. I discuss this issue in more detail in the following chapter.

19. There is some evidence, from a German study, that while being unemployed is associated with a low overall assessment of life satisfaction, when the unemployed are asked to report on their moment-to-moment emotional state, their overall level of happiness is about the same as that of employed persons (Knabe et al. 2010). The authors of the study suggest that their findings indicate that the control that the unemployed have over their time produces enough happiness to cancel out the "saddening effect" of unemployment. For a given activity, the employed experience more happiness than the unemployed. But the fact that the unemployed are more able than the employed to steer their time toward those activities that produce relatively more happiness for them means that they can make up for the happiness deficit they experience for any given activity. This is a surprising finding given the stigma attached to being unemployed in modern capitalist societies and the tendency of the unemployed to become socially isolated.

20. In the 1990s, Robert Brenner criticized the sanguine view of post-Fordist work expounded by Piore and Sabel and, to a lesser extent, by the regulation theorists, according to which work, after the demise of the mass production paradigm, became reskilled and increasingly democratized. Brenner noted that the new work regime involves a combination of the micromanagement of workers, so that their productivity comes to be measured by the number of seconds worked per minute, and the use of a superficially horizontal work team organizational structure to make workers responsible for quality control. As he and Glick argue in a 1991 paper: "Whatever else it offers, 'lean' production does nothing to increase the level of the workers' skill, let alone make them into craftspeople. Indeed, far from the anti-Taylorian revolution that Regulation theorist Alain Lipietz envisions, the foundation for the productivity gains secured on the shop floor is hyper-Taylorization—the super-deskilling of jobs by means of their breakdown into their simplest possible components" (p. 118). The authors go on to argue that insofar as workers under the new regime gain any initiative, it is solely in the matter of "helping the company further identify slack and waste in the system" (Brenner and Glick 1991, p. 119).

21. Tony Schwartz and Christine Porath, "Why You Hate Work," *New York Times*, May 30, 2014, SR1. Research indicating the discontents of work is not a new thing. Investigations by industrial sociologists in the middle decades of the twentieth century, for example,

likewise discovered widespread dissatisfaction with work (Watson 1940; Walker and Guest 1952; Chinoy 1955).

22. The deflating take on this reaction is that it reflects a culturally and historically specific sensibility that is hostile to materialism—a legacy of some combination of value-systems such as Victorian sobriety, Protestant asceticism, monastic self-abnegation, or perhaps even (reaching more deeply into the past) classical Stoicism. On this view, the question of overconsumption is not a real question at all but rather is just an expression of value judgments made within a particular culture. I want to resist this kind of argument, insisting instead that we take seriously our puzzlement about modern patterns of consumption. After all, any question, scientific or otherwise, can be explained as a product of the culture or history within which it is formulated. To interpret the surprise we feel and questions we have about the world as *merely* expressive of the violation of normative expectations that are essentially arbitrary is, in effect, a species of skepticism (what some philosophers call "genealogical skepticism")—according to which our normative responses to the world are questionable because they are held to be nothing more than contingent consequences of culture, historical forces, society, and so on. But of course, to assume that position raises the question of the status of the skeptical claim itself, since skeptical arguments can (and indeed should, for the sake of consistency) be made against skeptical positions. After all, skepticism is no less contingent on culture and history than any other position. So why should the skeptical stance be the only valid one? In taking seriously the question of consumption and free time under conditions of affluence, as I have construed it, I am admittedly assuming to some degree a normative position with respect to economic life. In doing so I follow the tradition—with origins in Aristotle and most powerfully represented in modern times by Marx, although also supported by economists such as Amartya Sen—that seeks to ground theories of economic behavior in a general account of our social and ethical makeup. See Scott Meikle (1985, 1992, 2000) for an excellent discussion and defense of this tradition.

23. On the Marxian view, commodities must have some use value. Yet use value is ultimately only realized through final consumption. Capital goods can of course have use value in the production process, but the usefulness of that process is in turn tied to the production of consumer goods. For that reason, in order for the capital goods produced in Department I to realize a profit, they must be connected to the consumption of final goods produced by Department II. Capital goods must be used to facilitate the production of consumer goods. Those consumer goods must in turn be sold, or else the demand for capital goods will eventually collapse. If the means of production are not used to facilitate final consumption, they are ultimately useless.

24. It is possible in the short run for irrational collective optimism about the future prospects of Department I to manufacture economic booms. But, as Magdoff and Sweezy (2013) note, "sooner or later—many factors, technological as well historical in a broader sense, affect the length of time—the weak growth of final demand for consumption goods works its way through the system and brings the boom to an end." Demand for consumer goods works in this way as an ultimate limit for demand for capital goods.

25. The idea that the capitalist economy faces a structural contradiction of underconsumption is quite controversial within the Marxist tradition. Marx in general wanted to

locate the central contradiction of capitalism on the side of production, in the tension between the tendency of the organic composition of capital to increase over time and the constitution of value by labor time. Nonetheless there has been a persistent current of Marxian theorizing that has drawn attention to systemic problems of aggregate effective demand and profit realization created by the downward pressure on real wages relative to productive capacity.

26. The other condition described by Aglietta was that the working classes be separated from the means of consumption. One of the structural imbalances in early industrial capitalism was that while a workforce was created by concentration of ownership of the means of production, households still created their own means of consumption. In order for the productive capacity of industry to be absorbed by commensurate levels of demand, domestic production of consumer goods for the use of the household had to be halted.

27. Aglietta could argue that fewer hours would mean a further increase in the intensity of the labor process, in order to increase the rate of relative surplus value creation. But there are limits to the extent to which that is possible as production becomes increasingly capital intensive, and improvements in productivity increasingly come from technological change rather than more "sweating" of labor.

28. "When the capitalist class is 'too strong' it shifts the income distribution in its favor, reducing the ratio of working-class consumption to national income and rendering the economy prone to crises of under-consumption or—in more contemporary Keynesian terms—a failure of aggregate demand" (Weisskopf, Bowles, and Gordon 1985, p. 226).

29. This relative lack of attention to the question of the sources of demand, as opposed to the conditions under which given demand becomes effective, is odd given the importance attached by SSA and regulation theory to custom and habit as forming the environment within which the capitalist system functions. Surely the kind of contextual and embedded approach to the workings of the capitalist economy sought by these theorists should give an account of that which gives rise to a dynamic, materialist form of demand?

30. Keynes took the propensity to consume to be a given. The argument of this book, however, is that we can explain the behavior that underpins the propensity to consume under industrial capitalism in a way that makes it endogenous to the cultural and social organization of capitalism—specifically, it can be explained as a consequence of the grounds on which wage labor became construable as a legitimate form of economic exchange.

31. Piore and Sabel argue that the Depression only took hold in 1931, following a withdrawal of capital from investment. The importance of the initial financial crash of 1929 was more psychological than substantive.

32. Piore and Sabel follow historian David Brody (1993) in arguing that welfare capitalism was instituted because big industrial capitalists realized that finding a market for their products depended on the expansion of effective demand. The most famous example of welfare capitalism in the 1920s was Henry Ford's decision to pay his workers five dollars per day.

33. Piore and Sabel's account of the nature of these difficulties is the most perspicuous of these. On their account, Fordist mass production demanded very large fixed capital

investments upfront, in order to get factories up and running. Given these large capital investments, in order for those factories to be profitable they needed to be run quite close to maximum capacity. The result of this was that the Fordist economy was very vulnerable to demand shocks.

34. Indifference would lead to passive acceptance of businesses' preference to avoid cuts in work time.

35. This discussion to some extent rehearses the points made in the previous chapter, in which I introduced the puzzle.

36. Economists tend to claim that they don't have much to say about preferences. People want utility because, rather tautologically, utility is, by definition, something that is wanted. What gives rise to utility is not supposed to be a question for investigation within economics. However, there is a tendency among economists to assume that utility is most accurately and conveniently measured by money.

37. Marx likewise made the content of use value exogenous to his theory—a product of collective self-discovery through history. There are exceptions to this generalization about the neoclassical exogenization of tastes. Becker and Stigler (1977, p. 76), for example, infamously argued that preferences are endogenous, claiming "that tastes neither change capriciously nor differ importantly between people."

38. Joseph Stiglitz (2010), considering the question of why Keynes's prediction of falling work time failed to come to pass, expresses skepticism about the standard economic explanation. He notes that the capacity of economic theory to explain *anything* is reason enough to be suspicious of the theory. Stiglitz also points out that the research on happiness casts doubt on the invocation of utility maximizing consumer choice as an explanation for why Keynes's prediction failed. If subjective well-being is any measure of utility, then it seems not to be the case that consumption under conditions of affluence continued to increase because by doing so it increased utility. Part of the difficulty economic approaches to consumption have when confronted with apparently substantively suboptimal patterns of the kind under investigation in this book is the tremendous emphasis they put on choice. As Amartya Sen (1985, p. 12) points out, choice is very limited as a gauge of welfare because "it confounds choosing with benefiting." The emphasis on choice as the key index of valuation in economics suits the positivist inclinations of the discipline because choices can easily be observed. Yet any theory of welfare must rest on more substantive grounds.

39. The usual response given by neoclassical economists when presented with their often quite implausible assumptions, for example about the degree to which instrumental rationality can be precisely operationalized, is that their models seek parsimony and so must be as simple as possible.

40. The point of saving might be to buy time later on in life (by, say, early retirement) or as insurance against unforeseen eventualities, as a form of risk control. It is not obvious, theoretically, which of the two—leisure or savings—should increase. As noted, Frank Knight thought that the demand for leisure would increase with income. Keynes, by contrast (and somewhat in tension with his argument in *The Economic Possibilities for Our Grandchildren*), argued in *The General Theory* that in the short run, the savings rate would increase.

41. Savings rates obviously vary considerably across different capitalist economies. To the extent that this is so, arguably the argument of this book best fits a specific variety of capitalism—Fordist mass consumption–driven capitalism rather than, for example, the export-driven capitalism of newly industrializing countries. However, the pattern of accumulative consumption could conceivably be a condition on a capitalist economy developing a largely internally driven market (in which domestic effective demand is sufficient to support mass production). Export-led growth tends to be seen as a stage on the way to developing a mature economy, led by endogenous aggregate demand. Note the importance attached, for example, in contemporary China on transitioning from an export-led economy to one driven by an internal market for consumer goods.

42. The time-utility intensive (as opposed to extensive) dimension of the utility conferred by objects can be framed in a quite abstract and prospective way. One could use a concept similar in spirit to a measure dear to health economists—the quality-adjusted life year, or QALY—to capture the idea that increments of free time vary in value according to how productive they are of utility (Pliskin, Shepard, and Weinstein 1980). Thus, we could speak of quality-adjusted leisure time units (QALTUs). As commodities become more efficient at generating utility, the value of each QALTU increases.

43. This is not an exhaustive list of approaches to consumption. It does not include Bataille's (1988) theory of consumption as sacrifice, which has been influential on anthropologists of consumption such as Daniel Miller (1998). I also leave out Colin Campbell's (1987) neo-Weberian account of modern consumerism. The discussion does cover what I take to be the main paradigms researchers on consumption have worked within. It should be mentioned in passing that both Miller and Campbell fail to provide adequate explanations for the materialistic bias underpinning modern mass consumption. While Miller might account for the role of shopping in the ritual reproduction of the family as a transcendent value in modern life, his theory cannot explain the historical pattern under investigation in this book. Campbell's approach is more historical than Miller's, yet his theory does not explain why hedonic expectation should fix on things, rather than practices, as foci for exercises of the imagination. More is said about this in Chapter 4 of this book.

44. My discussion of the behavioral economics literature, which is large, diverse, and fast growing, is by necessity extremely truncated and selective. The aim is simply to give some sense of the general orientation of the approach where consumer behavior is concerned.

45. This assumes that interest payments are compensation for delayed gratification. Since interest is paid at an exponential rate, this suggests that the discount function is also exponential.

46. Ainslie suggests, interestingly, that the two modes of behavior, exponential and hyperbolic discounting, can be mapped onto Freud's distinction between the reality principle (concerned with long-term outcomes) and the pleasure principle (concerned with immediate gratification).

47. Kahneman (2011) has set out a very general account of this kind of view of the architecture of the human brain.

48. Status is what economists call a positional good, competition for which is a zero-sum game—for a given person to improve their position in a status hierarchy, the status of others

must decline. This means that the status value of goods is also positional. As increasing wealth broadens access to a given good, its status value will decline.

49. This point is made by Avner Offer (2006, p. 279), who notes that "widely diffused consumer goods confer distinction only temporarily if at all" and that "only at the more costly end of cars and housing is consumption a prime means of signaling status." Offer notes, as an aside, that Vance Packard's hugely influential 1959 jeremiad against status competition, *The Status Seekers*, contains only one brief chapter, out of twenty-four, about conspicuous consumption.

50. Samual Bowles and Yongjin Park, in a 2005 paper, claim, on the basis of analysis of data on work hours in ten countries between 1963 and 1998, that work hours are predicted by the degree of inequality. They interpret the correlation between inequality and work hours as evidence for a "Veblen effect." Their argument is that higher inequality means that the material trappings of the wealthy are further removed from the mass of the population, and this leads to increased willingness to work, so as to earn more income and "catch up" with the consumption of the emulated class. I find their argument unconvincing because they use quite historically limited data as a basis for a very general claim about economic behavior. As we have seen, the supply curve of labor in the late nineteenth century (ironically, more or less at the time Veblen was writing *Theory of the Leisure Class*) was backward curving. And yet that period in American history was one of extreme inequality. Why, then, were late nineteenth-century American workers not willing to work more hours to fund pecuniary emulation? Moreover, there are many alternative explanations for why inequality should be correlated with higher hours. For example, higher inequality generally indicates a situation in which capital is more powerful than labor. Since capitalists tend to prefer longer hours, the correlation between hours and inequality could just indicate the degree to which capitalists are able to enforce their will.

51. De Certeau (1984, p. 31) sets up the opposition between consumption and production in the following terms: "In reality, a rationalized, expansionist, centralized, spectacular, and clamorous production is confronted by an entirely different kind of production, called 'consumption', and characterized by its ruses, its fragmentation . . . its poaching, its clandestine nature, its tireless but quiet activity, in short by its quasi-invisibility, since it shows itself not in its own products . . . but in an art of using those imposed upon them."

52. Desublimation, according to Herbert Marcuse (1964), is the reversal of the Freudian process of sublimation, by which desire, under early capitalism, became channeled into work. To facilitate mass industrial production under capitalism, desire first had to be "unleashed" and then attached to commodity objects.

53. Economists have argued that advertising simply serves to provide consumers with information and has little effect on tastes (Nelson 1974, 1975).

54. It is possible, however, that advertising has the aggregate effect of biasing people toward material accumulation rather than reducing work time.

55. The preference for stable work hours is a contingent matter. It made some sense for mid-century businesses engaged in industrial mass production, as plants had to be in continual operation to cover their expenses (Piore and Sabel, 1986). Under current postindustrial conditions, however, businesses have shifted toward flexible hours. It should be noted

that the flexibility demanded by the "gig economy" reflects the preferences of business rather than of workers.

1. Becker (1965, p. 507), in any case, does at least admit that "the productivity of working time has probably advanced more than that of consumption time, if only because of familiar reasons associated with the division of labor and economies of scale." But if this is so—if it takes increasingly less time to produce the equipment used to generate utility, while the time it takes to use that equipment to generate that utility has grown relatively more slowly—why then does work time not fall at a rate closer to the rate at which productivity is increasing?

2. There are efforts to incorporate changing product quality in measures of productivity by coming up with hedonic price indexes, for example to register the added value of faster processors in ICT. However, there are serious difficulties with operationalizing hedonic pricing (Block 1990).

3. Multifactor productivity (MFP) is productivity net of changes in labor and capital inputs. The idea behind MFP is to isolate that part of productivity that is *not* accounted for by increasing capital per worker ("capital deepening") or by changes in the composition of the labor force (which affects its average quality). MFP is calculated, roughly speaking, by subtracting percent changes in inputs of labor and capital from percent changes in output. If the calculation yields a residual, this is taken to represent the contribution of technical improvements to productivity.

4. Angus Maddison (2001) breaks down annual improvements in per hour output (combined across all economic activities) in the long twentieth century as follows: 1870–1913, 1.92 percent; 1913–1950, 2.48 percent; 1950–1973, 2.77 percent; 1973–1998, 1.74 percent. The project of this book is to inquire into what was done with increasing productivity regardless of whether its source is capital accumulation, compositional change in the labor force, or exogenous factors such as technical improvements to the production process. My question is: Given ongoing improvements over the course of the twentieth century in productivity per hour of labor from whatever source, why have work hours not been reduced to a greater extent than has been the case? For the purposes of answering this question, the blunter measure of labor productivity is more relevant than multifactor productivity, and the most relevant sector is manufacturing, since it was organized workers in that sector who pressed hard up until the Second World War for reductions in the working week and largely let the issue drop in the postwar period.

5. According to the "Baumol thesis," services are intrinsically less amenable to improvements in productivity, and this accounts for the lag in services productivity compared to manufacturing productivity. However, Zvi Griliches argues that the difference between productivity rates in these two sectors is largely explained by measurement issues (Baumol and Bowen 1966; Griliches 1992).

6. The shift in the labor force toward services to some degree accounts for the apparent slowdown in productivity growth in the last third of the twentieth century.

7. The roughness of this estimate indicates how challenging it is to come up with precise figures measuring this expanded concept of productivity. However, DeLong argues that most economists who have studied the issue agree that the true increase in productivity figure lies somewhere in that range.

8. Per capita income in 1900 was $4,200 in 1999 dollars, while in 1999 it was $33,700, an eightfold increase (Fisk 2001).

9. On the assumption that average marginal productivity of the workforce declines with added units of labor, all other things being equal, shedding labor would also increase productivity.

10. A recent Gallup poll about work time found that people worked forty-seven hours each week, with only one in ten people working the official forty-hour week (Saad 2014).

11. The exact numbers vary according to which source is used. The census of manufacturing shows a drop in hours from 59.6 in 1900 to 51.2 in 1919. Ethel Jones (1963) found that hours in manufacturing dropped from 55.5 in 1900 to 46 in 1919. John Owen's (1976, 1988) analysis of hours for nonstudent males over the same period finds a decrease from 58.5 hours in 1900 to 50 hours in 1919.

12. For a very critical assessment of Schor's argument, see Lebergott (1996). However, research by the Bureau of Labor Statistics (1997) indicates that workers did put in more hours on average over the last quarter of the twentieth century. Total hours worked per year, for those who worked at all between 1976 and 1993, increased from 1,805 to 1,905 for men and from 1,293 to 1,526 for women.

13. The current population survey of work time is based on how many hours of work people do in total each week, so numbers of jobs is controlled for.

14. Annual work hours in the United States were 1,983 in 1950 and 1,764 in 2014, while productivity increased from $18.24 per hour in 1950 to $63.35 in 2014 (Roser 2018).

15. 433/10 = 43. A 43 percent increase in productivity multiplies person hour output by 1.43. Forgoing that increase in output, the person could produce the same output as she did before the increase in productivity in about two-thirds of the time. So, had this portion of increasing productivity since 1929 been used to reduce work time, the working week would by 2007 have been reduced by about one-third (48 hours in 1929/1.43 = 29.3 hours). Applying the same calculation, converting 20 percent of the 433 percent increase in productivity between 1929 and 2007 into less work time, at the cost of lower output, would reduce working time in 2007 compared to 1929 by about one half—so workers would put in a 24-hour workweek, rather than a 39-hour week. Of course, a 24-hour week would result in 2007 output dropping by close to 40 percent, a very substantial reduction and obviously one that people in 2007 would be not likely to countenance. However, the decision to take some of the benefits of increasing productivity in the form of fewer work hours at the same level of income would have been made incrementally over time.

16. Interestingly, Hobsbawm (1964) notes that this did not always militate against the interests of the employers. Customary rates also applied to compensation, so if the profits of an enterprise increased, workers would not demand an increased share of revenues.

17. Costa's explanation for the growth of female part-time work is that it was a response on the part of firms to a decline in the female workforce, caused by lower age at marriage,

the baby boom, and increasing college attendance by women. By offering flexible, part-time work, businesses hoped to entice women back into the workforce.

18. The most recent (2011) labor force statistics from the current population survey indicate that average hours at work, including those who work part-time, are 38.3, while for full-time workers the figure is 42.4.

19. Moreover, casual work tends not to be unionized and so was not part of the collective bargaining arrangements of the middle part of the twentieth century. For this reason, arguably full-time hours give a better measure of the work time regime than do aggregate hours worked.

20. Offer's findings have recently been echoed by a National Bureau of Labor (2015) report on combined hours of married couples. In 1969, married couples between twenty-five and fifty-four worked a combined average of fifty-six hours per week. By 2000, this had increased to sixty-seven hours.

21. This is a much-debated topic. For a study of more recent trends in domestic labor, along with an overview of the debate, see Bianchi et al. (2000). Their finding is that housework hours have declined significantly since 1965, in part because families became smaller and marriage occurred later and in part because households made greater use of services in place of domestic work. It is hard to get clarity on this issue because time use surveys are subject to misreporting.

22. Robinson and Godbey also note that most of the increase in free time went to older people. Moreover, the additional free time was broken up into very small increments, making it more difficult to make use of it in a satisfying manner.

23. Time use surveys also have very patchy coverage over the course of the century. The most recent annual American Time Use Survey, conducted by the Bureau of Labor Statistics, for example, only stretches as far back as 2003. Time use surveys are also in their nature quite unreliable since they rely on self-reporting.

24. Wage compression between high hourly earners and low hourly earners mostly took place in the 1920s. Costa suggests that this was at least in part a response to electrification, which allowed for shift work, and hours legislation.

25. Labor historian David Brody (1993) estimates that between 1939 and 1945, union membership increased from 9 to 15 million.

26. Compared with 7.3 percent of private sector workers in 2013 (Desilver 2014).

27. I tracked reports about strikes for shorter hours in newspapers between 1869 and 2015, using a database of historical newspapers to search abstracts of articles using the terms *strike* and *working hours*. The results certainly corroborate Hunnicutt's (1988) narrative. There are 294 newspaper reports about strikes where reducing hours was cited as an objective. Of these, 273 took place between 1870 and 1945 (with the majority of strikes occurring between 1880 and 1920), while only 21 took place between 1945 and 2015 (significantly, most of the strikes post-1945 were of salaried workers rather than those paid on hourly rates). Press coverage greatly increased over the time period, as did the size of the workforce. With increasing numbers of workers and more newspaper coverage, if the concern with reducing hours had remained constant, there should have been a greater number of reports of strikes about work time in the later period. While industrial action declined after about 1980, between 1940 and 1980 there were a great many strikes—on average around 300 large (1,000-plus employees)

strikes each year. Similarly, while reports on all strikes become less common in the 1990s, they do not vary in number by that much over the preceding decades. So, at least until the last decade or two of the century, the dramatic decline in the number of reports about strikes over hours cannot easily be explained just by a general reduction in industrial action. Now it could be that union leaders post-1945 simply ignored the preference of rank-and-file members for fewer hours. Yet it seems very improbable that, had concerns about hours been as intense in the postwar period as in the first fifth of the century, so few strikes would have taken place about the issue after 1945. Union leaders are, after all, elected officials.

28. The stabilization of work hours in the postwar period was partly encouraged by the state because of concerns about maintaining production during the Cold War. Fear of a return to depression also played a role, particularly with respect to union attitudes. Since the received narrative about the Depression was that it was caused by inadequate effective demand, pushing for higher wages rather than shorter hours seemed like a way to secure jobs. For a rich synthetic discussion of the political economy of this period of US history, see James Sparrow (2011).

29. Something akin to what Hochschild describes—the embrace of work as an alternative to the discontents of family life—certainly seems to have been a big factor in in the decision of women in the middle decades of the twentieth century to enter the workforce. Indeed, the trade-off between leisure and work was (and probably still is) different for women than for men, as not being at work for women meant being constrained by traditional gender roles (Friedan 1963). To the extent that work was an alternative to the shackles of domesticity, it is not surprising that many women threw themselves into paid labor.

30. Indeed, the fact that from the mid-century onward pay and conditions were set by collective bargaining meant that it would have been easier to coordinate a general move to a new work-time regime.

31. As philosopher Elizabeth Anderson (2000) has noted, the idea of unpopular norms, kept in play because of intersubjective ignorance about real preferences, does not give a good account of how such norms take hold in the first place. The theory of unpopular norms presupposes that people are quite passive with respect to the making of norms, following them purely in order to avoid the consequences of violating them. Yet for any norm to get up and running, some significant part of the population must be willing to sanction those who fail to follow the norm. Especially in the early stages of the development of a norm, people's motivation for sanctioning others for failing to follow the norm cannot be reduced to fear of others sanctioning them for failing to do so. While a norm could conceivably live on even after everyone has ceased to believe in it, that state of affairs is, as Anderson observes, likely to be highly unstable.

32. The social security safety net, which began to be extended with the Social Security Act of 1935, arguably lessened the urgency of saving for life after retirement—yet this still leaves the question of why not having to save led people to spend more rather than work less.

33. Another possible argument that adduces life expectancy as a variable to explain people's preference for more income over more free time during their working lives is that income and life expectancy are correlated such that at higher incomes, life spans are longer. While there is certainly an empirical relation between income and life span, this is, I think,

nonetheless a rather weak argument. At the aggregate level, higher average incomes do not necessarily mean longer life spans. For example, Costa Rica has a higher life expectancy than the United States, even though its per capita GDP is only 12 percent of that of the United States (Offer 2006). So, it is certainly possible for a society to have a high life expectancy at quite modest levels of income. Moreover, under conditions of affluence, the correlation between income and life expectancy is mediated by the correlation between income and lifestyle. It is possible, once a certain minimum standard of living has been achieved, for people on relatively modest incomes to live in a healthy manner, increasing longevity. In addition, work is itself often a source of profound physical and psychological stress, which tends to reduce life expectancy. It might well be the case that working less, given the right background conditions, would decrease stress to a degree that would make up for the life span increasing effect of income.

34. Parfit has an answer, but it has nothing to do with rational self-interest. Rather, he thinks that we should be concerned about the well-being of our future selves in order to follow the general moral principle that we should always be concerned about the consequences of our actions for others.

35. For a good—and surprisingly positive, given the assessment quoted earlier—overview of the history of the life cycle hypothesis, see Angus Deaton (2005).

36. The pattern reported by Deaton also casts doubt on the suggestion that people choose earnings over free time in order to leave a legacy to their heirs.

37. Carter 2006, Table Bc523–536: Enrollment in institutions of higher education, by sex, enrollment status, and type of institution: 1869–1995.

38. Interestingly, in contrast to the recessions of the 1970s and 1980s, the downturns of the early 1990s and late 2000s did not produce an equivalent spike in savings.

39. Angus Maddison (1992) observes that the pattern in the United States for savings rates not to increase as incomes go up is unique among developed capitalist economies. Keynes's prediction about the relation between income and saving is more accurate with respect to other advanced economies.

40. On page 31 of *The General Theory*, Keynes (1935) states that "the marginal propensity to consume [is] weaker in a wealthy community" and that "with the growth in wealth [comes] the diminishing marginal propensity to consume."

41. Those savings could either add to aggregate effective demand, as investment, or be hoarded. Keynes thought that ensuring the former outcome should be the primary goal of macroeconomic management in modern money economies.

42. The first was Diners card in 1949.

43. Offer here is explicitly making a Ulysses and the Sirens–type argument, in which taking on credit works as a self-binding mechanism (Elster 1979).

44. The notable exceptions were the Depression years of the 1930s, during which consumption declined and savings increased somewhat, and, to a much lesser extent, the period of recession in the mid-1970s.

45. The whole idea that flexible production has advantages over mass production, for example, is that capital investments and capital stocks are kept lower in the former than in the latter, which facilitates greater flexibility in an unpredictable world.

46. Moreover, the great majority of cars were bought using credit, which would have been risky under conditions of uncertain employment (Olney 1991).

47. The value of private residential assets in 1998 dollars increased from $100.5 billion in 1925 to $9,183 billion in 1998. Measuring the change using a chain-type quantity index indicates a more moderate, yet still very significant increase from 17.23 to 105.01 (see the table in Appendix 1).

48. The 1913 reforms made all interest payments tax deductible. According to Prasad it was in the 1930s that promoting homeownership became an active project for the state.

49. Data collected by the National Association of Realtors indicates that the median length of tenure for sellers in the United States between 1985 and 2008 was just six years (Riggs 2016).

50. According to Eurostat data, full-time workers in France have since 2006 consistently worked more than forty hours per week despite the thirty-five-hour law. So even though the Aubry laws established a thirty-five-hour workweek, French workers chose to work more than that in order to increase their wages. As the thirty-five-hour week established a limit beyond which overtime must be paid, the obvious interpretation of the failure of full-time work hours to fall is that French workers preferred increasing their earnings (by working more overtime) to increasing their free time. In the EU, full-time work hours since 2006 have on average exceeded forty-one hours (Eurostat 2017).

51. John D. Owen (1988), in an earlier analysis suggests that higher marginal income tax rates in Europe might account for some of the difference in hours between Europe and America.

52. Austria, Belgium, Denmark, Finland, France, Germany, Greece, Ireland, Italy, Luxembourg, the Netherlands, Portugal, Spain, Sweden, and the United Kingdom.

53. Angus Maddison estimates total annual manufacturing work hours per employee for 1987 in the United Kingdom, the United States, and Germany to be, respectively, 1,763, 1,909, and 1,630. For the whole economy (and this would include many more part-time employees), the numbers are 1,557 for the United Kingdom, 1,608 for the United States, and 1,620 for Germany. So in manufacturing, German workers work 15 percent fewer hours than in the United States, while across the whole economy hours per year were actually higher in Germany than in America (Maddison 1991).

54. *Workers* are those who in a given year have worked at all, so the term would exclude the unemployed but include the underemployed.

55. The total amount changed over time, but, somewhat oddly, the aggregate numbers in Europe and the United States tracked one another (Burda, Hammermesh, and Weil 2006).

56. The Burda study, which was based on data from time-use diaries, indicates that the amount of recorded leisure time in the sample of European countries and in the United States differed very little.

57. In survey research conducted at the turn of the twenty-first century, European workers expressed a preference for higher income at constant hours over constant income at reduced hours (Bell and Freeman 2001).

58. Keynes's 1930 prediction was based on a projection into the future of the 30 percent reduction in work hours that had occurred over the previous fifty years in both the United

States and Europe. Although in Europe work hours continued to decrease through the end of the twentieth century to a greater extent than they did in the United States, the rate of decrease was substantially less than that experienced between 1870 and 1930. So, as with the United States, with increasing affluence, the rate at which hours declined in Europe *decreased.*

CHAPTER 4: A THEORY OF MASS CONSUMPTION AS WAGE-LABOR COMMENSURATION

1. A growing body of work in the social and historical sciences has drawn attention to the importance of processes of measurement and commensuration in the making of modern society. Wendy Esperland and Mitchell Stevens (1998) give a useful overview of the issue from a sociological point of view.

2. The literature on this topic is a vast one, including much of the social history and historical sociology stemming from the work of E. P. Thompson, and other historians. My account here is extremely schematic and abbreviated. The point here is to give a very broad overview of the contours of the history of labor under capitalism to adequately motivate the ensuing theory. A more fully fleshed out, although still brief, summary of this historiography will appear in the next chapter.

3. See E. P. Thompson (1966, 1993). One could, in the spirit of David Lewis (2002), make the argument that conventions and customs represent equilibrium solutions to coordination problems or, following Elinor Ostrom (1990), that they are solutions to collective action problems such as the tragedy of the commons. Part of what establishes consent to a given custom might then be that it represents a compromise between a fair distribution of goods and the pragmatic exigencies of a situation—the need, for example, to ensure that common goods are not depleted to the point of exhaustion. This would entail a contractual view of convention and custom. But explaining customs in such a fashion involves a good deal of projection. To interpret traditions and customs as rational solutions to problems of collective action risks falling into what E. P. Thompson (1966) famously described as the "condescension of posterity."

4. Gareth Stedman-Jones (1984, p. 85) notes that historians of medieval law have discovered that the phrase "since time immemorial" in practice could refer to customs in existence for as few as twenty-one years. The important point, however, is that practices were regarded as legitimate to the extent that they were supported by established norms rather than because they were appraised as being fair on an objective basis.

5. Along with the idea of a fair wage, there were also a variety of ideas about what constitutes a decent or minimally acceptable wage. These would include the notion of a "living wage" and the "family wage." But note that these concepts stipulated a bare minimum standard for what wages should afford—essentially, providing for a decent living standard (whatever that might be thought to entail). They do not set out criteria for what makes a wage a fair one, once that minimum standard had been met. Although the ideas of a living wage and family wage had great rhetorical power, they provide no guidance about what should happen when productivity increases—whether and to what degree increasing wealth

should be returned to labor. The conception of fairness in economic exchange underlying the notion of the living wage is continuous with earlier notions about the right to subsistence, with roots in the preindustrial moral economy (Thompson 1991). Perhaps for this reason it works very imperfectly as a normative guide to distribution in the context of the very dynamic growth conditions, characterized by a strong trend for the productivity of labor to increase, created by capitalism.

6. In addition, if a set of different goods and services is offered by one party, the contents of that set must be aggregated, and for that to be possible they must be made commensurable.

7. This is not to say that the objective conception of fairness is not in a very general sense itself also conventional—the proposition that fairness obtains where there is an equal exchange of commensurable substances is clearly not self-evidently true but rather amounts to a normative claim. But the convention of objectively fair exchange—according to which fairness is a function of the objective properties of the sets of things being exchanged—is neutral with regard to the social identities of exchanging parties in a way that is not the case in the example of economic exchanges between feudal lord and various dependents. In feudal exchange, for instance, the dependent is fairly treated where the lord does what is expected of him according to custom, given their respective social identities.

8. This is a basic Euclidian mathematical principle.

9. The economic consequences of that notion of fair pay have been explored by George Akerlof and Janet Yellen (Akerlof and Yellen 1990).

10. I use the term *wage earners* (as opposed to the more loaded word *workers*) to mean, quite literally, all those who exchange labor for a wage. This includes service workers and middle-class salaried workers in addition to members of the traditional working class.

11. Mandel's account of the roots of mass consumption is that the commodification of working-class culture deprived communities of the capacity to spend free time in cultivated ways. Traditional practices and pastimes were replaced by a very passive and object-oriented style of consumption, well-suited to the needs of advanced industrial capitalism. Yet it is not clear, if indeed Mandel's account is correct, why working-class communities should have proven so pliable. As discussed in Chapter 2, M. Aglietta (2000) gives a different account of how consumption norms and mass production are connected. He follows Marx in arguing that after limits were placed on the length of the working week, constraining the accumulation of *absolute* surplus value, businesses intensified the labor process in order to extract *relative* surplus value. This intensification of work then made greater demands on workers, who consequently had to consume more in order to reproduce their capacity to provide labor power. The rather reductive assumption in Aglietta's model is that consumption is driven by the need to reproduce the capacity to labor. In effect this takes consumption to be equivalent to the *actual realization* of use value. However, it is difficult to make sense of the pattern sketched in the last chapter with that very limited account of consumption. Nor, indeed, does Aglietta explain why labor acquiesced in fixing the working week at around forty hours rather than fighting for further increases in productivity to be used to cut working time, at constant levels of intensity of the labor process, and at constant real wages.

12. There is some suggestion in Keynes that animal spirits, and the associated optimistic outlook, to some extent generate a self-fulfilling prophecy. Yet it is not clear why that should be the case.

13. Keynes's preoccupation in *The General Theory* with demand shocks of the sort that led to the Great Depression perhaps distracted him from the crucial role that positive projections about latent consumer demand, made on a rational, inductive basis, play in inducing productive investment of profits.

14. The difficulty is compounded by the tendency for norms of economic action under capitalism to be specified in private terms, as rules the satisfaction of which is a matter for individuals to discern, based on introspection about things like preferences. When commensuration is understood in utilitarian terms, for example, as the disutility of work being offset by the utility of consumption, each individual must come to his or her own judgment about what amount of consumption provides commensurate compensation. I discuss this issue in the conclusion.

15. The latter two are connected, insofar as the importance of securing the purchasing power of the wage became a matter of widespread concern. But it would be wrong to reduce supply-side changes in products and distribution to changes in the moral economy linking work and consumption.

16. The development of consumer society and the history of the institution of wage labor are related such that the two are, on the one hand, sufficiently independent to have discrete identities, but nonetheless, are interdependent to the degree that change in the historical trajectory of one is highly likely to cause a change in the other and, further, that the point of contact between the two is such that the contradictions and tensions internal to one tend to get expressed in changes of form in the other. Note that the claim here is not that one line of historical development supervenes upon the other, such that there cannot be a difference in that line of development without there being also a difference in the other (Davidson 1980). Rather the two are ontologically distinct, yet systemically highly embedded in one another.

17. Although Campbell is a historicist, his ideas are in some ways similar to psychoanalytic theories according to which desire primarily seeks to sustain itself—such that desire desires desire rather than its closure, achieved through consummation. For Campbell, the point of modern consumer desire is anticipation rather than actual consumption. Yet if the object of desire is the state of anticipation, why should people ever end that state by actually acquiring what it is that they want?

18. In Aristotle's original formulation, which Marx both developed and criticized in chapter 1 of the first volume of *Capital*, the exchange circuit C-M-C has the telos of acquiring goods in order to put them to use in qualitatively distinct ways. Objects serve as means to particular ends attached to kinds of activity, which are entirely *incommensurable* with one another. Although Marx disagreed with what he took to be Aristotle's contention that the exchange ratio between different Cs is set by a combination of exigency and convention ("a makeshift for practical purposes," Marx 1981 [1867] p.40), holding that there must be some underlying substance that determines the ratio at which different commodities exchange, he agreed with Aristotle's argument that C-M-C is regulated by demand for

use values that meet real wants and needs. However, the puzzling patterns identified in Chapter 2 and Chapter 3 cast some doubt on the idea that, at least under capitalism, the C-M-C circuit is regulated by real needs for actual use values, realized in actual activity (Aristotle 1981; Marx [1867] 1981; Meikle 1992, 2000; Booth 1991).

19. For Marx subsistence standards—understood as the minimal level of wages that induces potential workers to sell their labor power—are historically variable and so can change over time. But I would suggest that a distinction can be made between a wage level that allows for brute biological reproduction of labor power, and one that allows for a material standard of living sufficient to secure a willing and quiescent labor force. For capitalism, ensuring the latter is a structural necessity. For labor, securing the former is existentially necessary. But as we move further up a hierarchy of wants and needs, consumption levels become, from the point of view of labor, increasingly negotiable, and so the question of the trade-off between real income and free time becomes more salient.

20. It might well also be that some nonwage sources of income are equally or even more likely to get spent on goods than wage earnings—windfalls such as unexpected inheritances or gambling winnings for example. In her ethnographic study of gambling, anthropologist Natasha Schull found that the unearned character of money obtained as winnings induces gamblers to gamble it away, continuing to play until their winnings are entirely depleted. Maybe the motive is to return the money whence it came, rather than withdrawing it and using it for other purposes, in order to restore a kind of moral equilibrium to the pecuniary universe (Schull 2012).

21. Indeed, this is the idea behind Zip cars, civic bike loan schemes, and similar enterprises.

22. As society becomes progressively segmented, so cultural codes become differentiated along those segmented lines. In a complex and fragmented society, people have to negotiate code-switching between what Anne Mische and Harrison White (1998) have characterized as the discrete "netdoms" that constitute the structure of social space. One consequence of differentiation is, therefore, increasing need for semiotic flexibility. If goods have quite local semiotic value, then being able to change them rapidly, as is the case where they are rented, enables greater ease of movement across social space.

23. The question has particular force if one conceives of households, as does Gary Becker, as analogous to firms, deploying durables as firms make use of capital equipment, in order to, as far as is possible, generate optimal levels of an output—household utility—much as capital is used to produce goods with the aim of maximizing returns to investment. Since tastes are complex and mercurial, it would seem rational for consumers not to sink too much capital into fixed means of satisfying them and, therefore, to rent goods as need and desire dictates rather than own them. If the analogy between household and firm has anything to it, why, therefore, is the market for rented consumer durables relatively small compared to the market for purchasing goods outright?

24. As noted in Chapter 2, the on average quite short period of property ownership between moves, in conjunction with high transaction costs of buying and selling homes, suggests that for most people owning is not primarily about securing good returns to an investment. Rather, owning a home seems to be, to a significant extent, an end in itself.

25. Indeed, housing, construed as a consumer durable, is one very prominent exception to the marginal position of the market for rented goods—although renting housing is less common in the United States, it is the norm in many parts of continental Europe.

26. Esping-Andersen uses the term *decomodification* rather than *commodification* because all of the countries he analyzes are capitalist, so the default state is for labor to be commodified. The action of different welfare state regimes to differing degrees *decommodifies* this antecedent state of affairs.

27. The liberal group is Australia, the United States, the United Kingdom, New Zealand, Canada, and Ireland; the corporatist group is Italy, Japan, France, Germany, Finland, and Switzerland; and the social democratic group is Austria, Belgium, the Netherlands, Denmark, Norway, and Sweden.

28. The OECD countries in the corporatist group consist of France, Germany, Italy, Japan, and Switzerland; the OECD social democrat group, of Austria, Belgium, Netherlands, and Sweden; and the OECD liberal group, of the United States, the United Kingdom, Australia, and Canada.

29. At the same time the countries of continental Europe have shorter working weeks, and renting homes, as opposed to homeownership is more common than in the liberal states.

30. For De Vries the direction of causality between wage labor and consumer demand is the reverse of the argument of this book—the desire to consume prompted an "industrious revolution," the result of which was greater participation in labor markets.

31. And indeed, there is at least a loose correlation between early periods of capitalism, in which the putting out system predominated and what many historians have referred to as a "traditional," or "customary" attitude to work and time existed, in which the inclination to work was either relatively insensitive to changes in pay rates or else declined as hourly pay rates increased (Thompson 1991; Hobsbawm 1964; Gutman 1973).

32. According to this theory, humans are endowed with two different thought systems, system 1 and system 2, which developed at different points in our evolutionary history. System 1 is fast and makes use of heuristics, while system 2 is slow and involves reasoning (Kahneman 2011).

33. As philosopher John Rawls (1999, p. 293), expressing the intuition underlying the normative objection to hyperbolic discounting from the point of view of rationality, puts it: "Rationality requires an impartial concern for all parts of our life. The mere difference of location in time, of some things being earlier or later, is not a rational ground for having more or less regard for it."

34. On the other hand, perhaps the prospective ratio of what Frank Knight (1921) calls risk and uncertainty changes over future time in a quite nonlinear fashion. In Knight's definition, risk involves measurable probabilities, like the chance of getting a six on a role of a die. Uncertainty, on the other hand, refers to situations in which we have no measurable probabilities. Perhaps in the short term, risk predominates, but, at a certain point in the future, an epistemic horizon is reached, making it impossible to assign probabilities on a rational basis. At that point the world switches quite abruptly from being risky to being uncertain. If any two given days more than, say, a year in the future will be equally

dominated by uncertainty, then there would not be a good reason to distinguish between them. They would be equally "unknown unknowns."

35. More on this point follows, in the discussion of possible objections to the theory.

36. Note that the finding is not that the young do not borrow but rather that they do not borrow *enough* to fund discretionary consumption at levels that would smooth consumption over the life course.

37. A sense of urgency to turn money into things, in order to make it commensurable with labor, perhaps explains the feeling, and consequent pattern of behavior, described in the adage that "money burns a hole in one's pocket" (the earliest origins of this adage, according to the *Oxford English Dictionary*, can be found in the eighteenth century "My tyme lyes heavy on my hands, and my money burns in my pocket" G. Farquhar [1702], *Inconstant* v.iii 77 [OED]). What burns is the memory of a deficit, constituted by free activity sold as work. Spending money, then, is an attempt to fill this deficit and turn what might well have been experienced as an exploitative relationship into one retrospectively becalmed by the projection of an aura of equal exchange. The saying "work hard, play hard" is also suggestive with respect to the commensuration theory, as it evokes an equivalence between work and leisure—that the two need to be in some sense of equal intensity for them to be in a balanced relationship.

38. It is perhaps not surprising that the struggle over hours took place mainly in an era before wage labor had become fully legitimate, a quasi-naturalized fact about social life.

39. In acquiring things, people generally do not acquire more free time. But there are two possible exceptions to this. The first is certain labor-saving devices. However, as we saw in the last chapter, the empirical evidence suggests that the deployment of such devices has not freed up much more discretionary time (Cowan 1983; Robinson and Godbey 1999). The second exception is artifacts that *increase* life span. To be sure, warm clothes and adequate heat and nutrition can increase the life spans of the poor. But once affluent conditions prevail, it is not clear that further increments of consumption lead to further increases in life span. What of consumption directed to health care? An argument could certainly be made that spending on health care increases life span. Life-prolonging devices such as pacemakers clearly add time to lives, and it might well be the case that some part of the preference for higher wages over less work time is explained by increasing health care costs, at least in the United States. But it is doubtful that the general pattern described in the last chapter can be explained away in that way. The postwar pattern for real incomes to increase and for decreases in work time to slow to a crawl was also experienced in other advanced industrial capitalist nations. For example, it is also evident in the United Kingdom, which, from 1945 onward, has had a national health care system that makes access to health care independent of income. Furthermore, a very significant determinant of life expectancy in advanced industrial countries is lifestyle. Stress, lack of sleep, not having time to exercise, and eating badly all have a pronounced negative impact on life expectancy, and all are associated working conditions under capitalism. Given those correlations, working less at constant levels of income, if it leads to decreased levels of stress, might well yield a health and longevity dividend that more than offsets the added longevity yielded by more health care at the expense of a longer work week.

40. Perhaps this hypothetical plenitude of use value underlies the mistake of conflating increasing wealth with increasing well-being. The accumulation of material wealth entails

(the service economy notwithstanding) the accumulation of commodity objects. But wealth is plausibly construable as a measure of well-being only if it can reasonably be expected that the useful powers subsisting within it will be deployed to improve lives. Otherwise, wealth remains inert, unused, and therefore useless. To see wealth as a gauge of well-being is to forget this basic point. Amartya Sen (1988) has repeatedly pointed out the perversity of this way of thinking, and the awful consequences it has for human welfare—yet this raises the question of why such odd habits of thought should have become so deeply entrenched.

41. The shift to services was to some degree facilitated by globalization, as industrial production moved elsewhere in the world. Although the proportion of workers in manufacturing might have gone down in the West, it increased dramatically elsewhere in the world, as people moved from agriculture to industry. Likewise, although the United States, for example, produces relatively fewer material commodities than used to be the case, the rate at which consumer commodities are accumulated in the United States has remained as high as ever. The only difference is that many of those commodities are now imported.

42. The general tendency to hoard then might be explained by aversion to loss of goods that are inscribed with the sacrifice involved in the labor exchanged for the money used to buy them. David Lord Smail (2014) has suggested that hoarding has both a neurological and a cultural-historical basis and that the study of the epigenetics of the behavior might be a fruitful way to bring the two together.

CHAPTER 5: ECONOMIC FAIRNESS AND THE WAGE LABOR
BACKGROUND

1. Some psychologists, especially those inclined toward evolutionary explanations, hold fairness in a very general sense to be a transhistorical category, perhaps even extending beyond the boundaries of the human species (Humphries 2006). These analysts draw on experimental evidence that indicates that fairness plays a major role in social behaviors to support the claim that "it is in the nature of human beings to value objective fairness" (Mack 2006). The suggestion is that a sense of fairness is part human nature, a component of a "moral instinct" that is inscribed in our genes. Be this as it may, the diversity of cultural conceptions of fairness evident across time and space suggests that if there is an invariant substrate to the instinct to be fair, it is rudimentary and underdetermining. As evolutionary game theorist Ken Binmore (1994) has observed, even if it is the case that people have a "fairness gene," how it gets expressed is clearly mediated by, and therefore contingent on, historical and cultural context.

2. This is not to say that the idea of objective equal exchange itself was new with modernity. Aristotle (1982), in book five of the *Nichomachean Ethics*, considers the question of fair exchange at length. But Aristotle's philosophical inquiries were not the basis of an ideology governing economic activity in the ancient Greek world.

3. For example, in the feudal system lords would grant land to vassals in exchange for military service, while peasants gave labor services in exchange for protection and the right to work the land (Bloch 1961).

4. As I argued in the last chapter, one can make a distinction between the *internal* legitimacy of an institution such as feudalism—which is a matter of the degree to which the institution in practice lives up to its normative ideals—and the legitimacy of a normative system itself, which can be challenged on the *external* grounds that it violates other norms and customs, or is in tension with changing expectations.

5. Here I'm invoking the distinction made by Karl Polanyi (1968) in his analysis of market society.

6. Wierzbicka argues that there is no word in other European languages exactly equivalent to the English term *fair*. Insofar as it was in an English-speaking country that industrial capitalism first developed, her findings are consistent with the argument that the modern concept of fairness had something to do with the emergence of capitalism. Moreover, Wierzbicka admits that this concept is nowadays widespread in modern capitalist societies. It should be noted that other linguists have disputed Wierzbicka's suggestion that the modern, ethical sense of the English word *fair* cannot be found in other languages.

7. As Wierzbicka comments (2006, p. 152): "values like 'equity' and 'equal distribution of goods' have become so important for many people that they have come to see them as the essence of 'fairness,' and when they try to define fairness, many people do so along the lines of 'equity.'"

8. The matter is complicated, however, by the degree to which a given exchange is seen as taking place under coercive conditions. If a given exchange were unequal, yet both parties agreed to its terms under completely noncoercive conditions, would it be regarded as unfair? The question raises complicated issues. Objectively unequal exchanges that are knowingly and noncoercively entered into might not be categorized as a narrowly economic exchange—the kind that occurs in markets—and instead fall into something like charity or gifting. On the other hand, some theorists subsume gifting under an expanded concept of formal economic exchange (Akerlof 1982).

9. The list of historians whose research has shown the degree to which legitimacy was not accorded to the institution of wage labor in the early years of capitalism is extremely long. It would include E. P. Thompson, Eric Hobsbawm, and other luminaries of British social history, as well as pioneers of American social and labor history such as David Montgomery, Sean Wilentz, David Roediger, Eric and Philip Foner, and Herbert Gutman.

10. It was only in the last quarter of the nineteenth century that wage earners in America finally came to outnumber the self-employed.

11. In part, this was because employers often specified very stringent terms in their labor contracts. For example, Stanley notes that the so-called ironclad contracts drawn up by employers, which forbade collective bargaining, were a cause of much ire among workers. The rise of the written labor contract laid bare class divisions and conflicts of interest, became a focal point for industrial action, and so propelled the "labor question" into national consciousness.

12. The phrase *wage slavery* was not unique to America—it was also used by the Chartists in Britain and by Friedrich Engels, in his journalism.

13. Indeed, the Adkins ruling was in effect overturned with the passage of the Fair Labor Standards Act of 1938.

14. In the 1930s, the issue of work time was more about reducing unemployment by redistributing work hours than curtailing subjection to wage slavery. During the Depression years, the state also sought to limit the length of the working week or, at least, to ensure that overtime rates were paid for time at work in excess of forty hours, which would have a similar effect. This objective lay behind the Fair Labor Standards Act of 1938. But the goal of ensuring overtime pay and, at the same time, limiting work time had for the New Deal state a macroeconomic rationale. At one and the same time, it boosted the purchasing power of labor, stimulating demand, and spread employment more evenly across the population. Following the same logic, during the Depression the AFL pushed for a thirty-hour work week, in order to redistribute scarce work and provide relief for the unemployed.

15. Although Cutler suggests that the issue of hours remained of great importance for workers in the postwar period, it should be noted that his study rests heavily on inconclusive evidence from just one factory, so provides a very limited basis for generalization. As noted in Chapter 3, note 27, after 1945 there is a dramatic decline in shorter hours as a reported reason for strikes.

16. Of course, absolute conceptions of decent living standards—those deserved in exchange for labor—were very vague. What exactly is it for a home to be "comfortably furnished"? What does it mean to "maintain" a family?

17. The general historical pattern in the United States, from debate over the legitimacy of wage labor and struggles over the length of the working week, to a corporatist industrial politics based on purchasing power, is evident elsewhere in the industrial capitalist world.

18. The broader influence of autoworkers' attitudes was mediated by well-publicized industrial negotiations.

19. Status-centered accounts of consumption, such as Thorsten Veblen's, arguably assimilate all social positions to that of the Weberian capitalist. Conspicuous consumption involves the semiotic conversion of commodity objects back into their money value. The value of those objects is then read as indexical of the value of their owner, by virtue of what ownership of the objects demonstrates about the owner's capacity to generate money.

20. According to an automobile finance officer interviewed by the Lynds (1929, p. 255), between 75 percent and 90 percent of cars were purchased on an installment plan.

21. The fascination with cars among the industrial workers studied by the Lynds and Chinoy might in addition reflect a dialectic between the subjection of industrial workers to the discipline of the machine during the labor process (on a production line), which made workers into mere appendages of technology, and an urge to invert this relation by becoming masters of technology in leisure. If that is right, then as production becomes ever more technological, and as humans become ever more subjected to technology in the workplace, then the desire to dominate machines—to use them to express agency—in consumption should increase. The consumption of technological objects then counterbalances subjection of human beings to technology in the workplace.

22. The relatively more prominent place given by Chinoy's informants to accumulation as justification for work, when compared to Lynds' workers, is all the more surprising because the American working classes in the postwar years were significantly more affluent than in the interwar period.

23. Note that Chinoy's workers' comments on the satisfactions (or lack thereof) of work echo more recent research on the sources of happiness discussed in the introduction of this book.

24. The Lynds (1933, pp. 467–68) write: "This illustrates Veblen's point of the paramount importance of 'conspicuous consumption' as an identifying device in a community grown too large for more subtle means of appraisal. This would suggest a tendency, as a community grows, for its citizens to put more of their possessions 'on their backs,' into cars and other seeable goods."

CHAPTER 6: STANDARDIZATION OF CONSUMPTION, WORK, AND WAGES

1. Standardization, understood on a very general level as a means by which rationalization is achieved, is a feature of almost every domain of modern society. For a general overview of different forms of standardization see Timmermans and Epstein (2010).

2. Busch has a very broad concept of what a standard is, stretching the idea even to cover conventional forms of language usage.

3. That the word should first have appeared in the context of science, only later taking on its economic sense is not at all surprising given that standardization of production was largely a matter of applying of scientific methods to industrial processes (Noble 1977).

4. Analysis of article titles in which the term *standardization* appears in major US newspapers shows the following distribution over time: 1800–1899: 0; 1900–1909: 54; 1909–1919: 268; 1920–1929: 348; 1930–1939: 178; 1940–1949: 149; 1950–1959: 77; 1960–1969: 29; 1970–1979: 28; 1980–1989: 40; 1990–1999: 194. The term *standard*, which obviously has a broader range of meanings than does *standardization*, is distributed as follows: 1800–1849: 9; 1850–1859: 46; 1860–1869: 126; 1870–1879: 772; 1880–1889: 2,043; 1890–1899: 5,018; 1900–1909: 9,535; 1910–1919: 11,495; 1920–1929: 17,968; 1930–1939: 15,619; 1940–1949: 8,176; 1950–1959: 9,903; 1960–1969: 10,962; 1970–1979: 8,175; 1980–1989: 6,216; 1990–1999: 2,818. So, even though *standard* can be used in ways that have little to do with the late nineteenth-century neologism *standardization*, the pattern of distribution of the two words is quite similar. The terms are either absent, or else have relatively little presence, for most of the nineteenth century but begin to appear with increasing frequency around the turn of the century. Both terms peak between 1920 and 1929 and decline thereafter in a fairly steady fashion (the newspapers surveyed include the *New York Times, Chicago Tribune, Baltimore Sun Times, Los Angeles Times, Wall Street Journal, Washington Post, Chicago Sun Times, New York Post, Pittsburgh Courier, New York Amsterdam Times, Los Angeles Sentinel,* and *Atlanta Daily World*).

5. For example, the discussion about standardization in a 1928 issue of the *American Annals of the American Academy of Political and Social Science* (Lansburgh 1928) portrayed standardization as one end of pole at the other end of which lies variation and individualism. Both principles, "sameness and variation," are described, in a manner reminiscent of Simmel, as "essential," both in nature and for civilization (Whitney, 1928, p. 33). Too much of one demands a corrective rebalancing toward the opposite pole.

6. The fact that talk about standards and standardization picked up again at the end of the twentieth century can be explained by the so-called third industrial revolution—the rise of information technology.

7. "Standardization Work Nearly Complete," *Wall Street Journal*, March 3, 1910, p. 6.

8. Albert W. Whitney, "The Faults and Virtues of Standardization," *New York Times*, September 2, 1923, p. XX10.

9. "Standardization," *Chicago Defender*, March 29, 1913, p. 2.

10. The example of a charismatic religious movement seeking to revive its flagging flock by finding more standardized methods of conversion would give Weber food for thought.

11. "Urges Standardization of Evangelism Methods," *Boston Daily Globe*, January 8, 1918, p. 6.

12. "Standardization of Everything," *San Francisco Chronicle*, May 30, 1920, p. W2.

13. The AESC coordinated the standardizing activities of government, industry, and professional organizations, in effect serving as a national clearing house for standards.

14. "What Others Think about It: Problems in Standardization," *Los Angeles Times*, October 9, 1930, p. A4.

15. "Standardization and Improvement," *San Francisco Chronicle*, November 7, 1906, p. 6.

16. "Says Nation Suffers from Scientific Fads: Standardization Is Killing Common Sense and Individuality," *New York Times*, October 19, 1924, p. 21; William S. Packer, "Declares Standardization Bedevils Our Life," *Boston Daily Globe*, January 26, 1931, p. 13; "Fleming Asks Originality in Architecture: Expert Deplores Trend to Standardization as Foe of Beauty," *Washington Post*, July 22, 1934, p. R6. For ironic comment, see "Let Standardization Thrive!," *New York Times*, January 17, 1922, p. 13.

17. "Standardization," *Los Angeles Times*, January 22, 1922, p. V3.

18. Llewelyn Powys, "Dark Age of the Literary Essay," *New York Times*, June 1, 1924, p. BR7.

19. John Barry, "Clever Men Are the Aids of Curley at the State House," *Boston Daily Globe*, February 24, 1935, p. A30.

20. "The Blight of Standardization," *Washington Post*, June 7, 1925, p. E1.

21. Thomas L. Masson, "Life as It Is: Standardization," *Boston Daily Globe*, December 26, 1923, p. 13.

22. James R. Beniger takes the Chandler argument a step further. Taking his cue from a cybernetic theory, Beniger (1986) sees standardization as one element of a broad effort to mobilize *information* to control the disastrous consequences of an unprecedented speed up of production and distribution caused by new technologies that appeared in the nineteenth century in transportation and manufacturing.

23. The Bureau of Standards was created by act of Congress on March 3, 1901. Prior to 1901, a bureau of standards had existed, but in a very specialized capacity, as a small branch of the coast and geodetic survey, which dealt exclusively with fixing standards of length, mass, and time. The new, enlarged bureau was initially set up as a part of the Treasury Department (the Treasury had previously housed the Office of Weights and Measurements, founded in 1832, which was superseded by the new bureau). It was moved to the Department of Commerce and Labor when that department was created in 1904 and stayed a part of the Commerce Department when the Department of Labor was created in 1913. The bureau had two branches, one that undertook scientific and technical research and conducted product testing, the other concerned with commercial standardization. In addition to its testing

activities, the research branch of the bureau invented entirely new products and manufacturing processes. For example, it created a radio-beacon system to guide aircraft, developed a new process for chromium plating, created stronger paper for use in currency and improved the design and construction of tires (Cochrane 1966; Silbur 1983; N. D. Katz 1977; see also Milton E. Ailes, "National Bureau of Standards," *Washington Post*, January 10, 1921, p. 7).

24. "Predicts Adoption of Standardization: Cars Built by This Method Will Supersede Manufactured Types" *New York Times*, January 26, 1913, p. X14.

25. The American Standards Association was a voluntary industry group, founded in 1919, to promote standardization across the economy.

26. "Standardization Reduces Costly Waste," *New York Times*, May 10, 1925, p. X13.

27. "Industrial Standardization," *Wall Street Journal*, December 2, 1932, p. 2.

28. "Activity Is Greater for Standardization," *New York Times*, January 2, 1923, p. 27.

29. "Standardization Reduces Costly Waste," *New York Times*, May 10, 1925, p. X13.

30. "Engineers Are to Be Praised," *Los Angeles Times*, January 25, 1920, p. VI6.

31. Voluntary industry standardization, primarily guided by the American Engineering Standards Committee (later the American Standards Association), increasingly came to supplant the regulatory efforts of the National Bureau of Standards (Olshan 1993)

32. "Big Banquet of Engineers: Plan for Permanent Home Discussed. George Westinghouse Is One of Well-Known Guests: Advocates a Bureau of Standardization," *Boston Daily Globe*, January 22, 1910, p. 16.

33. "Good Progress Being Made: Motor Engineers Are Doing Things. Standardization Is the Keynote of Their Society," *Boston Daily Globe*, April 2, 1911, p. 67.

34. John W. Worthing, "Work of S.A.E. Fills 25 Years," *New York Times*, May 25, 1930, p. 140.

35. "Industries Agree on Standardization," *New York Times*, June 16, 1930, p. 4.

36. John W. Leavitt, "Standardization and Big Output Make Possible the Cheap Car," *San Francisco Chronicle*, December 31, 1911, p. 102.

37. "Standardization Is the Life of Business," *Los Angeles Times*, June 17, 1922, p. I7.

38. "Many Styles Cause Waste: Hoover Leads Movement for Standardization," *Los Angeles Times*, July 26, 1925, p. 10.

39. "Finds Art a Factor in Modern Industry: E. T. Pickard Tells Textile Men," *New York Times*, September 16, 1927, p. 38.

40. Harold Whitling Slauson, "Debt to Standardization: It Has Brought Order Out of Chaos in the Machinery World and Helped Materially in the Winning of the War," *New York Times*, May 18, 1919, p. 62.

41. "Upholds Standardization: Federal Trade Body Denies Opposing Commodity Simplification," *New York Times*, April 17, 1931, p. 39.

42. "The Secret of Big Auto Production in U.S. Is Standardization," *Washington Post*, Apr 27, 1924, p. A9.

43. "Many Styles Cause Waste: Hoover Leads Movement for Standardization," *Los Angeles Times*, July 26, 1925, p. 10.

44. "Age of Opportunity Is Seen by Hoover," *New York Times*, December 9, 1931, p. 28.

45. "Urges a Campaign for Standardization," *New York Times*, Jun 28, 1931, p. N2.

46. "Standards Bureau Facilitating Plant," *Washington Post*, December 31, 1931, p. DC3.

47. Max Gertz, "Standardization in Informative Selling—1940 Outlook," *Journal of Home Economics* 32, no. 8 (October 1940): pp. 520–25, p. 522.

48. George Burgess, "Bureau Helps Lower Costs," *Washington Post*, December 31, 1931, p. DC18.

49. "U.S. Standards Declared Vital to NRA Codes," *Washington Post*, October 20, 1933, p. 5.

50. James Sullivan, "Why Automobiles Are Much Cheaper Now Comparatively: Standardization and Pooling of Patents Brought Better Cars, Thereby Saving Consumers Millions," *Boston Daily Globe*, June 15, 1930, p. B56.

51. Stuart Chase and F. J. Schlink, "A Few Billions for Consumers," *New Republic*, December 20, 1925, pp. 153–55.

52. "Cars Must Be Built to Last," *San Francisco Chronicle*, June 22, 1908, p. 9.

53. "Standardization Is a Factor in the Life of a Car: Cadillac Manager Declares a Good Auto Should Last Several Years," *San Francisco Chronicle*, November 6, 1910, p. 36. Not one to rest with a point clearly made, later that year Leland reiterated it once more. Standardization, he said, resulted in "less wear on the parts, and in a correctly designed car they mean long life, the elimination of many so-called automobile troubles, together with greatest economy in operation and maintenance" ("Standardization Facts: An Important Feature of Motor Construction Not Realized by All," *Boston Daily Globe*, April 3, 1910, p. 53).

54. "Standardization in Costs Is Worked Out," *Los Angeles Times*, July 27, 1924, p. F13.

55. F. E. Moskovics, "Expert Gives Selden Boost: Says That All Will Benefit Finally: Standardization Is Now the Great Keynote," *Los Angeles Times*, February 20, 1910, p. VII8.

56. "Thoroughly Standardized: Perfectly Balanced High-Grade Car for $1500," *San Francisco Chronicle*, May 28, 1911, p. 47.

57. "Trend toward Standardization," *Chicago Daily Tribune*, February 6, 1910, p. I6.

58. "Standardization Aim of Builders: Maxwell Official Says It Is Only Fair to Motorists to Make Cars Uniform," *San Francisco Chronicle*, July 16, 1916, p. 46.

59. "Standardization Affects Buying of Automobiles," *Los Angeles Times*, February 27, 1927, p. G18.

60. "Upholds Merit of Assembled Autos: Value of Specialization and Standardization Pointed Out by Motor Builder" *New York Times*, May 18, 1913, p. XX13.

61. "Anthony Saw the Big Show," *Los Angeles Times*, January 30, 1910, p. VII3.

62. John F. Sinclair, "Standardization Idea Hit," *Los Angeles Times*, June 19, 1931, p. 16.

63. "For a 'Pure Textile Law': Women's Clubs Should Work for the Standardization of Fabrics," *Washington Post*, October 29, 1910, p. 6.

64. "Bill Proposes Standardization of Cotton Duck," *Los Angeles Times*, February 28, 1925, p. 16.

65. "For New Auto Laws: Owners of Cars Plan Crusade for Uniformity," *Washington Post*, January 17, 1910, p. 1.

66. The 1909 standard for candlepower was an international agreement, reached by the National Bureau of Standards, Laboratoire Central de l'Electricite of France, the National

Physical Laboratory of the United Kingdom, and Germany's Physikalische Technische Reichsanstalt.

67. "Government Standardization: Important Work for Benefit of Consumers," *Los Angeles Times*, November 17, 1912, p. VI14.

68. Coker F. Clarkson, "Standardization the Keynote of Recent Auto Development," *New York Times*, October 18, 1908, p. AS3.

69. "Urges Motor Truck Rating: Standardization of Practice One of Industrial Needs," *Chicago Daily Tribune*, February 5, 1911, p. I3.

70. "Uncle Sam on the Trail of the Cheaters," *Washington Post*, November 2, 1924, p. SM3. The Bureau of Standards also investigated weights and measures in the meat packing industry: "Shrinkage of Meat Cited at Weight Meeting," *Washington Post*, May 28, 1927, p. 22.

71. "Textile Color Card Association of the United States Presses for Standardization of Color," *New York Times*, February 21, 1922, p. 26; "Retail Packaging Studied: Dry Goods Group to Recommend Standardization Plan," *New York Times*, October 28, 1934, p. N15.

72. "Color Standards Praised by Reyburn," *New York Times*, February 27, 1926, p. 27.

73. "Trade Cooperation Urged: Michael Schaap Emphasizes Need for Homeware Standardization," *New York Times*, November 7, 1935, p. 34. Although it is not at all clear what benefit standardized colors represent for consumers—unless items are being purchased sight unseen from a catalog, which would not be the case in a department store.

74. "Macy's Testing Bureau to Observe 25th Anniversary Today," *New York Times*, August 22, 1952, p. 25.

75. "Standards Bureau Launched by Hearn," *New York Times*, November 4, 1937, p. 36.

76. "Yarn Mills Asked to Identify Clothes," *New York Times*, September 22, 1937, p. 49.

77. That Ford's policy was not simple paternalism is made quite clear by the text of a pamphlet explaining the new policy to workers at the Ford plant: "The Ford Motor Company does not believe in giving without a fair return. So to acquire the right to participate in the profits [the new wage scheme] a man must be willing to pay in increased efficiency" (quoted in Gartman 1986, p. 205).

78. "Need Standardized Wages: Necessary as a War Measure, Gompers Tells Senate Committee," *New York Times*, February 12, 1918, p. 13.

79. Calls for the standardization of wages by organized labor were not unique to the United States. In 1916, British miners launched a "wage standardization" campaign "wage standardization campaign" launched by miners in the UK ("Future of the Mines," *Manchester Guardian*, October 9, 1919, p. 5).

80. Plans to push for standardized wages were first formulated by the railway workers union in 1907 but were delayed because of the economic panic of that year. The plans were eventually put into action in 1909, with industrial action aimed in the first instance at the Baltimore and Ohio railway company, but soon thereafter targeting other East Coast and Midwest lines. The federal government stepped in to arbitrate, invoking the Erdman Act, and imposed a settlement on the New York Central and then extended it to other lines (Cunningham 1910).

81. "Trainmen Ask Advance: Standardization of Conductor's Pay Sought on Roads East of Mississippi," *New York Times*, December 21, 1909, p. 1.

82. "Pennsylvania Vote Not Likely to End in Walkout," *Wall Street Journal*, July 6, 1910, p. 2; "Pennsylvania's Wage Offer Not Likely to Be Accepted," *Wall Street Journal*, March 31, 1910, p. 6.

83. "Many Railroad Rates Have Tripled since 1915: Standardization of Scales the Country over Leads to Inequalities and Disregard of Local Conditions," *Wall Street Journal*, April 4, 1921, p. 13.

84. "Ask Prompt Aid for New England Lines," *Boston Daily Globe*, November 30, 1920, p. 7.

85. "Engineers Wage Demands Place Roads in Serious Situation: Standardization of Wages in Eastern Territory Will Put Heavy Burden on Many of the Smaller lines," *Wall Street Journal*, February 20, 1912, p. 1.

86. "New England Roads Wish Wage Reduction," *Wall Street Journal*, December 28, 1921, p. 13.

87. R. Gill Smith, "Standardization of Wages to Regulate Cost of Living," *Wall Street Journal*, November 19, 1912, p. 2.

88. "Fact Commission Sends Coal: Questionnaire Asks Miners and Operators for Data on Wages and Profits," *New York Times*, October 27, 1922, p. 34.

89. "Industry Warned on Wage Classing," *New York Times*, November 11, 1938, p. 38.

90. "Ford Warns Men of 'Wage Dictator,'" *New York Times*, July 1, 1937, p. 2; "Ford Blames 'Pay Dictators' in Union Drive," *Washington Post*, July 1, 1937, p. 15. Ford's condemnation of standardized wages might also reflect his bitterness about the failure of his own experiment with high wage paternalism, which, in Meyer's (1981, p. 195) analysis, failed "to achieve its principal objective—the control of workers."

91. "Women Urged to Seek Equal Federal Wages: Party Leaders Asked to Demand Standardization on Equality with Men," *Los Angeles Times*, January 13, 1920, p. I3.

92. "Says Railroads Are Hiring More Women: Miss Goldmark Heard by Wage Commission," *Boston Daily Globe*, March 1, 1918, p. 9.

93. "Classification of All City Posts: Council Adopts Measures for Standardization," *Los Angeles Times*, March 14, 1916, p. II12; "City Workers' Wages to Be Standardized," *Los Angeles Times*, May 29, 1918, p. II7.

94. "Budget Is to Be Completed Today," *Los Angeles Times*, July 7, 1917, p. II2.

95. "City Salary Cut Seen as a Victim: Points to Men of Long Service and Much Ability Reduced to a Laborer's Pay," *New York Times*, October 17, 1915, p. XX7.

96. "Urge $1,500,000 Cut in State Payroll," *New York Times*, March 20, 1916, p. 7.

97. "City Salaries as Before," *New York Times*, July 19, 1915, p. 7.

98. "City Salaries as Before," *New York Times*, July 19, 1915, p. 7.

99. "Boyle Urges Bureau to Fix City Salaries" *San Francisco Chronicle*, April 5, 1918, p. 11.

100. "Standardization of State Pay Discussed," *Boston Daily Globe*, September 13, 1916, p. 16; Gladys H. Kelsey, "Detroit Debates Civil Service Pay," *New York Times*, August 12, 1934, p. E7.

101. For Karpik, economic singularities require special explanation precisely because they are not homogeneous. They form a set of unique goods and services, characterized by being multidimensional, incommensurable, and of uncertain quality (Karpik 2010).

CHAPTER 7: STANDARDIZING UTILITY

1. Although there were changes to trademark law in 1870 and throughout the 1880s, the most important legal change occurred in 1905. Earlier trademark statutes had been overturned by the Supreme Court, which ruled in 1870 and 1876, in accordance with common law tradition, that property rights only applied to physical things. However, legal thinking on the issue gradually changed, in part under the influence of energetic lobbying from business, and trademark legislation was finally passed and kept on the statute books in 1905. The 1905 trademark laws provided the definition of a brand that has carried through to the present day: a brand is defined as "a name, term or design—or a combination of these elements that is intended to clearly identify and differentiate a seller's product from a competitor's product" (quoted in Twitchell, 2004, p. 18).

2. Although it should be noted that it is not clear that branding per se was responsible for the increase in value of those companies, despite the Lynds' suggestion to that effect.

3. George Burton Hotchkiss, "Prestige of Advertised Brands Aids Marketing," *Washington Post*, September 6, 1925, S2.

4. Margaret Dana, "Continuity of Quality Is Hallmark of Brand Name," *Los Angeles Times*, May 14, 1967, p. N20.

5. The notion that attaching a brand name to a product ensures its quality underlies the argument often made by pharmaceutical companies that name-brand drugs are more reliable than their generic versions, even though the two are in theory identical. See for example the arguments made before Congress by a spokesperson for the pharmaceutical industry, as reported by John Jacobs in "Drug Spokesman Defends Emphasis on Brand Names," *Washington Post*, November 17, 1977, p. B15. And indeed the continued success of over-the-counter name-brand drugs such as Bayer, Excedrin, and Tylenol, despite the fact that they cost significantly more than generic versions sold on the same shelf, suggests that consumers buy this reasoning.

6. *Consumer Research Bulletin*, November 1949.

7. "Names on Cigar Boxes: Explanation of Terms Most Commonly Used," *Boston Daily Globe*, June 2, 1889, p. 20; "Names of Cigars," *Washington Post*, June 23, 1889, p. 13; "The Raisin Crower," *San Francisco Chronicle*, April 23, 1893, p. 13.

8. "Americans Brand, Quality Conscious," *Los Angeles Sentinel*, January 11, 1962, p. C5.

9. "Brand Lines Found Favored by Stores," *New York Times*, January 20, 1945, p. 17.

10. "Sears Own Brand Names Recognized as Standards of Quality and Value," *Los Angeles Times*, November 10, 1938, p. 8.

11. "Preaching National Brands," *Literary Digest*, March 7, 1931, p. 4.

12. "Town Plugs National Brands," *Business Week*, November 1, 1947, pp. 42–48.

13. "Buyers Want National Brands," *Business Week*, July 5, 1947, pp. 65–66. The analysis given of the experiment's result by the writer of the *Business Week* article was that the shift in retail toward self-service had amplified the power of advertising. The absence of "thicker" interactions within stores between salespersons and consumers meant that only advertising was left to "do the talking" (p. 66).

14. "Marketing: Brands on the Way Up Again," *Business Week*, April 1954, p. 83.

15. This is very much in line with the analysis given in the contemporary economics literature. Economists interpret brands as information conveying devices, the function of which is to reduce uncertainty for the consumer. The predominance of branded goods in the marketplace reduces the variance of product quality, as producers have an interest in "defending" their brands.

16. Although as Katz points out, this conception of brands was not shared by the pre-World War II consumer movement. Early consumer activists saw branding as obfuscation by producers (N. D. Katz 1977, p. 278).

17. "Fair Trade Protection of Name Brand Integrity," *Los Angeles Sentinel*, October 18, 1951, p. A10.

18. Carter 2006, Table De482–515, Advertising Expenditures.

19. See also Belk and Pollay (1985).

20. Pollay controlled for the influence of changes in the product mix by restricting his analysis to advertisements for manufactured goods and found a similar pattern. Pollay's findings cast some doubt on the Thorsten Veblen thesis. If, as Veblen and his followers suggest, increasing accumulation of products was driven *primarily* by status competition, this was *not* reflected in the degree of prominence of status as a theme in advertising content.

21. In some states, express warranties negate implied warranties, while in others the implied warranty holds over and above the express warranty.

22. Express warranties apply to *any* statement made by a company about the performance of a product. So if during a television commercial a manufacturer promises 100,000 hours of use for a light bulb, this can count as an express warranty, even if the written warranty is limited to thirty days. The legal implications of the express warranty then forces companies to be circumspect about claims made about their products, because they can be held accountable for the failure of their products to perform as described.

23. "The Free Sewing Machine," *Boston Globe*, July 11, 1920, p. 4.

24. Sheaffer "Lifetime" advertisement, *Chicago Daily Tribune*, November 24, 1924, p. 5.

25. "Sell on Quality, Not on Price—Says Pen Head," *Wall Street Journal*, January 29, 1935, p. 3; "Small Town Jeweler's Acumen Guided Sheaffer Pen to the Top," *Chicago Daily Tribune*, September 5, 1959, p. 5.

26. David and Mark Shepherd *Parker "51*, Surrenden Pens Limited, 2004; Dr. S. S. L. Hettiarachchi, "The Most Wanted Pen in History," *Sunday Times of Sri Lanka*. There is still a very active secondhand market for Parker 51s and "Lifetime" Sheaffer pens, not just as collector's items but as everyday working pens. Some of these pens are now over seventy years old and are still used as everyday writers.

27. The durable and reusable fountain pen, which reigned supreme through the first two-thirds of the twentieth century, eventually became superseded by the disposable ball point pen, the most famous example of which was introduced into the American market by Marcel Bich (later shortened to Bic) in 1959.

28. "Manufacturers Make Progressive Strides in General Standardization Work," *New York Times*, June 9, 1912, p. X15.

29. "The Roosevelt Policies—In the President's Own Words" *New York Times*, March 4, 1934, p. XX3. In the 1930s, Roosevelt was, in theory at least, quite sympathetic to the cause of

the consumer movement. He gave it an institutional voice through the creation of the Consumers Advisory Board (CAB) as part of the National Recovery Administration. However, as Lizabeth Cohen (2003) and Glickman (2006) note, in practice the influence of the CAB was quite limited.

30. "We Buy Dollars with Merchandise," *Chain Store Magazine* 3, no. 6 (July 1931): pp. 3–9.

31. Although Hamilton's essay was written over eighty years ago, it remains the most widely cited historical analysis of the development of the legal principle of caveat emptor prior to the twentieth century.

32. At the same time, many states outlawed "as is" clause exceptions.

33. During the war, enormous levels of public spending required to fuel the military effort resulted in high inflation. The OPA then had the role of intervening to set prices at levels deemed reasonable.

34. Max Freedman, "Mr. Kennedy Champions the Consumer," *The Guardian*, March 16, 1962, p. 13; Joseph A. Loftus, "Kennedy Submits Broad Program to Aid Consumer," special to *New York Times*, March 16, 1962, p. 1.

CHAPTER 8: PRODUCT TESTING AND PRODUCT REGULARIZATION

1. Although, given how vague normative notions of satisfactory product quality were, it is not at all clear what it would take for expectations to be met.

2. Of course, product testing was not just about ensuring product quality. It was also an important part of the process of the standardization of products, to ensure that products met specifications. As we have seen, standardization was the application of science to production, and clearly product testing was a manifestation of this (Noble 1977).

3. The insurance industry was heavily involved in the early movement to use testing as a basis for standardized products. Underwriters Laboratories, an organization that promoted standards and conducted research on behalf of the insurance industry, sought to make construction more insurable by applying labels to wires and fixtures certifying their resistance to fire (Silbur 1983). Other independent testing laboratories also emerged in the early part of the twentieth century to serve firms too small to be able to afford their own facilities.

4. *Good Housekeeping* established a prototype laboratory, named the "Experimental Station" in 1900.

5. "Sign of the Times," *Journal of Home Economics* 29, no. 4 (April 1937): p. 248.

6. Editorial, *Journal of Home Economics* 19, no. 4 (April 1927): p. 207.

7. "Plan to Cut Cost of Sales to Nation," *New York Times*, November 19, 1922, p. 44.

8. Stuart Chase and F. J. Schlink, "A Few Billion for Consumers," *New Republic*, December 30, 1925, pp. 153–55.

9. Ibid.

10. "Standards Bureau to Curtail Testing," *Washington Post*, November 16, 1924, p. EF7.

11. "Standards Bureau Tests Are Doubled," *Washington Post*, November 22, 1927, p. 12.

12. "Inferior Goods Meet Obstacle," *Los Angeles Times*, December 26, 1928, p. 15.

13. "Standards Bureau Facilitating Plant," *Washington Post*, December 31, 1931, p. DC3.

14. "$35,000 More Urged for Federal Work on Auto Problems," *Washington Post*, December 23, 1923, p. 55.

15. "Motor Body Asks for Funds to Aid Standards Bureau: Experiments Save Motorists a Huge Sum Every Year," *Chicago Daily Tribune*, January 13, 1924, p. A6.

16. Henry Litchfield West, "Standards Bureau Driving Machine Is Used at Columbia," *Washington Post*, March 28, 1924, p. S3.

17. Katz notes that one index of the change was a change in nomenclature from "members" of CU to "subscribers."

18. *Consumer Reports* 20, no. 2 (Feb 1955): p. 56.

19. *Consumer Reports*, 1, no. 3 (July 1936), p. 2.

20. *Consumer Reports*, 1, no. 1 (May 1936), p. 24.

21. Ibid.

22. Although, as Jacobs (2005) shows, in the postwar period control of inflation then became as important an issue as wage levels—and once inflation became politicized in this way, it was a short step to labor itself becoming divided, as one part blamed another (the more heavily unionized part) for causing inflation by pushing wage demands.

23. The shift from perishables to durables also reflects change in orientation of the Consumers Union. In its early years, CU was very much concerned with encouraging rational utility-maximizing consumption and discouraging conspicuous consumption of the kind described by Veblen. For that reason, CU deliberately avoided paying attention to goods it categorized as "luxuries" (N. D. Katz 1977, p. 280). At the same time, it was very difficult to draw the line between "necessities" and "luxuries," especially as new products were continually appearing in the marketplace.

24. *Consumer Reports*, 1, no. 1 (May 1936), p. 24.

25. The test-focused turn of the organization was not uncontroversial with some of its members. It was CU's narrow emphasis on product testing, at the expense of consumer advocacy and activism, that prompted Ralph Nader in 1975 to depart from the board of directors of the organization "Notes on People: Nader Quits Consumers Union," *New York Times*, August 23, 1975, p. 10.

26. Harry Braverman (1974) describes this as the separation of conception and execution in the labor process. Increasingly simplified and divided labor on the factory floor was accompanied by the emergence of specialized engineers, product designers, and management, who planned and orchestrated production. Modern, Taylorist techniques of production thus greatly narrowed the perspective workers had on the making of whole products. This deskilling in the workplace had the effect of reducing the level of knowledge and understanding people had about products. Product testing then evolved to fill this knowledge gap.

27. Marshall (2013, p. 103) introduced the concept as follows: "We have already seen that the price which a person pays for a thing can never exceed, and seldom comes up to that which he would be willing to pay rather than go without it: so that the satisfaction which he gets from its purchase generally exceeds that which he gives up in paying away its price; and he thus derives from the purchase a surplus of satisfaction. The excess of the price which he would be willing to pay rather than go without the thing, over that which he actually does pay, is the economic measure of this surplus satisfaction. It may be called consumer's

surplus." Although Marshall coined the term, the idea of the consumer surplus has deeper historical origins. The consensus is that it was first thought up by French engineer Jules Depuit in 1844. See R. W. Houghton (1958).

28. Becker could perhaps evade this difficulty by invoking his conception of preferences as definite, ordered, and fixed. In his theory, economic agents, including households, have, in essence, constant tastes and variable means to satisfy those tastes. According to Becker, "tastes neither change capriciously, nor differ importantly between people," and therefore, all differences in behavior can be accounted for in terms of variation in income and price—while conversely, holding price and income constant, all households should behave the same way (Becker and Stigler 1977, p. 76). But what this amounts to is the position that the economic behavior of households is (along with all other economic behavior) rational by definition—which clearly involves very questionable assumptions.

CHAPTER 9: MORAL PANIC ABOUT UTILITY

1. Searching through the Proquest database of nineteenth-century newspapers, for example, turns up over eleven thousand pieces in which some mention is made of the issue of adulteration.

2. Note however that in applications where a substantial margin of safety is required, and safety is a function of material robustness, overengineering can be desirable.

3. Slade's (2006) suggestion that material obsolescence is just the application of science to the traditional practice of adulteration ignores the alternative interpretation of that form of obsolescence as "value engineering." While it is entirely unclear how, in the paradigmatic case of adulteration, adding gravel to bread to reduce cost while also reducing calorific and nutritional content could possibly be seen as increasing efficiency (even in the unlikely scenario in which price is reduced to match the cheaper costs entailed), one can entertain a plausible story about the efficiencies gained by only building into an item as much durability as is required for a given pattern of predicted use.

4. *Business Review*, April 1958, Federal Reserve Bank of Philadelphia. Economists have argued more recently that style obsolescence under monopoly conditions produces a suboptimal social welfare outcome, since firms do not have to internalize the loss of value of older models consequent on the release of updated versions, and so produce more models than would otherwise be the case. See Waldman (2001).

5. Of course, the suggestion could be that what is objectionable is savvy marketing manipulating the consumer into desiring the latest version of a product. But as we shall see, in the discussions about style obsolescence, the main issue is just the fact that models are changed, rather than the exact means used to promote new models.

6. A lexical search of Google Books using NGram Viewer shows up a slightly different pattern—the term takes off in the mid-1950s, becoming increasingly common until reaching a peak in 1974, at 0.0000079877 percent of all bigrams.

7. According to Giles Slade the term "progressive obsolescence" was first coined by Christine Frederick's husband, Justus George Frederick, an ad man, in a 1928 article in the trade journal *Advertising and Selling* (Slade 2006).

8. Frederick wrote: "Just as old George F. Baker, the greatest living banker, discovered that the way to relieve panics was for banks to unhesitatingly *pay out their resources instead of hoarding them*, when stringency arrived, so we have learned that the way to break the vicious deadlock of a low standard of living is to spend freely, and even to waste creatively" (Frederick 1929, p. 81).

9. In 1956, Burke wrote an essay in *The Nation* in which he expresses surprise that an idea he had intended as satire had now become standard business practice. He commented: "In my original article . . . I thought I was making much sport of the trick psychological devices whereby a customer with a perfectly serviceable car was persuaded that he should get rid of it because there was a newer model available. In particular, I guyed the doctrine of 'obsolescence' that was implied in such high pressure selling tactics. But now I find *Business Week* referring quite respectfully to the way in which General Motors 'adopted the annual model change, helping to establish the auto-industry's renowned principle of 'planned obsolescence.' I had mistakenly thought that the principle was a joke; by now it has become 'renowned'" (Burke 1956, p. 211).

10. Oddly, Gregory also noted that a condition of possibility for the new policy of obsolescence was the presence of oligopoly market conditions in the automobile industry. The question of why oligopoly should lead to psychological obsolescence was left unanswered.

11. Malvina Lindsay, "Outmoding the Mode: Joneses' New Pace," *Washington Post*, February 5, 1948, p. 10.

12. "Vance Packard: Specialist in Touching Raw Nerves," *Chicago Tribune*, March 15, 1964, p. K3.

13. George Melloan, "The American Way: UK Auto Maker Hires Ex-Ford Man in a Bid to Learn from Detroit," *Wall Street Journal*. November 7, 1967, p. 1.

14. "Problems in Review: Planned Obsolescence," *Harvard Business Review* 37, no. 5 (September–October 1959): pp. 14–31, p. 14 [henceforth *HBR*].

15. Ibid., p. 14.

16. Genevieve Flavin, "Voice of Youth," *Chicago Tribune*, March 14, 1971, p. S7.

17. Charles V. Neal Jr., "Family Finance: Newest and Best Eyed," *Los Angeles Times*, June 22, 1958, p. D13.

18. Marylou Luther, "Consumer Panel: They Test for the Best," *Los Angeles Times*, August 12, 1960, p. A1.

19. "Consumer Problems: 'Planned Obsolescence,'" WBAI-FM: 9:30–10:30, July 2, 1962.

20. "Set in S. M. Garage: Satire Aims Barbs at Horsepower Addicts," reviewed by Ripton Ray, *Los Angeles Times*, December 26, 1968, p. WS4.

21. "Save the Old Federal Building," *Chicago Tribune*, February 3, 1965, p. 16.

22. Roger Verhulst, "The Game Room: Ask the Man Who Owns One—And Stand Back!," *Chicago Tribune*, April 13, 1973, p. B3.

23. Philip H. Dougherty, "Angry Consumers," *New York Time*, June 20, 1972, p. 60.

24. Louise Tanner, "Review: The Catalogue of Catalogues: The Complete Guide to World-Wide Shopping by Mail," *New York Times*, December 10, 1972, p. BR50.

25. Don Heckman, "The Return of the Hi-Fi Spectacular," *New York Times*, September 24, 1972, p. HF8.

26. Robert F. Mathieson, "Redoubtable Samuelson: The Redoubtable Samuelson Writes Again," *New York Times*, July 29, 1973, p. F1.

27. William Curry, "Researchers and Developers Are Taking Their Lumps," *Washington Post*, December 27, 1970, p. 9.

28. "Times Series to Eye Housewife Dilemma," *Los Angeles Times*, November 20, 1960, p. H1.

29. Walter Sullivan, "Can We Control Aging?," *New York Times*, July 7, 1968, p. E12. Although interpreted as an evolutionary adaptation to prevent cancerous mutation, cell apoptosis might in fact be thought of as a literal case of planned obsolescence!

30. Sue Cronk, "The Role of Organized Resistance Is the Consumer's Best Defense: It Is Partly Your Fault," *Washington Post*, February 14, 1964, p. C2.

31. "Happiness Is Well Planned Obsolescence—That Fails!," *Los Angeles Times*, February 23, 1966.

32. "A Complaint about Planned Obsolescence: Room Dividers Anne's Reader Exchange," *Washington Post*, October 19, 1969, p. 150. She also provides, in an aside, evidence for the "Diderot effect" posited by consumer theorist Grant McCracken (1988b), by noting that replacing one element of the kitchen entails that one must replace all the other elements also.

33. Although, as discussed in Chapter 6, the precise meaning of these warranties—which could be measured by the lifetime of the original owner, a lifetime of product use "under reasonable conditions" or, tautologically, by the lifetime of the product itself—was often, and perhaps deliberately, left ambiguous.

34. "Falling Apart Is the Name of the Game," *Chicago Tribune*, August 11, 1973, p. B24.

35. "Those Pushy Occupants Are Still Busy Social Climbing," *Los Angeles Times*, February 23, 1967, p. A6.

36. Russell Baker, "Observer: With Hoffa Jailed, Losers Lose Again," *New York Times*, March 9, 1967, p. 38.

37. "This Item Is Guaranteed . . . to Need Some Repairs Soon," *Los Angeles Times*, March 25, 1971, p. C7.

38. "Cup of Good Will Can't Be Priced Out of the Market," *Los Angeles Times*, January 25, 1967, p. ab.

39. The precise wording of the question was: "Do you feel that, for the long-term benefit of the United States, too large a part of our present economy is based on superficial product obsolescence, inducing people to buy new models before their old models are worn out?" To which the answer was yes: 64.2 percent; no: 33.3 percent; no answer 2.5 percent (*HBR*, p. 24).

40. "Auto Men Restyle Motive of Change: GM Official View Problem as 'Challenge,'" *New York Times*, November 6, 1960, p. F1.

41. Ibid.

42. "GM to Raise '61 Capital Spending to $1,250,000,000," *Wall Street Journal*, November 1, 1960, p. 2.

43. The full statement respondents were asked about is: "If we were to abandon our policies of forced product obsolescence the economy simply couldn't stand the shock of the drop in consumer spending that would result" (*HBR*, p. 24).

44. Bob Thomas, "Automotive: Dream Car Here Now—For Price," *Los Angeles Times*, August 9, 1964, p. G11.

45. George Lazarus, "Marketing: Gillette Sharpens New Trac for Competition," *Chicago Tribune*, Jun 25, 1973, p. C10.

46. *Barrons*, October 2, 1961.

47. *Fortune*, January 1963.

48. "Industries' Ills Blamed on Gimmicks: Sayre Hits Aping of Fashion Field," *Chicago Daily Tribune*, November 18, 1958, p. C7.

49. Elisabeth Shelton, "Tags Tell Washer's Life," *Washington Post;* Feb 25, 1970; pg. C2.

50. The company also represented GM in the wake of the publication of Ralph Nader's *Unsafe at any Speed.*

51. The ad ran in the *Wall Street Journal* throughout 1964.

52. Joseph C. Ingraham, "Auto Men Restyle Motive of Change: GM Officials View Problem as 'Challenge,'" *New York Times*, November 6, 1960, p. F1.

53. "GM to Raise '61 Capital Spending to $1,250,000,000," *Wall Street Journal*, November 1, 1960.

54. *Wall Street Journal*, January 13, 1966, p. 2.

55. Peter Bart, "Advertising: Donahue & Co Acquires Rival," *New York Times*, July 24, 1961, p. 31.

56. "Science Criticized for Serving Industry's Planned Obsolescence," *Chicago Tribune*, December 29, 1969, p. 5.

57. Reported in *New York Times*, July 6, 1962.

58. Op-ed, *Wall Street Journal*, January 8, 1968, p. 14.

59. David M. Pesanelli, "Life Style," *Washington Post*, January 12, 1969, p. 29.

60. Quoted in Slade (2006), p. 169.

61. "Author Assails Cut Rate Sales: Ex-Ad Man, Is Curious about Life in America," *New York Times*, July 12, 1965, p. 39.

62. Borgward ad, *New York Times*, January 10, 1960, p. S8.

63. Volkswagen ad, *Los Angeles Times*, October 4, 1959, p. 35.

64. Philip H. Dougherty, "Advertising: Car Campaigns Getting Tough," *New York Times*, September 13, 1967, p. 58.

65. "Automative Views: Rate '60 Good Car Export Year," *Chicago Daily Tribune*, June 19, 1960, p. A10.

66. *New York Times*, October 2, 1963, p. 33.

67. *Wall Street Journal*, March 24, 1961, p. 11.

68. *Washington Post*, June 14, 1968.

69. *New York Times*, October 9, 1967, p. 54.

70. *Washington Post*, July 15, 1963.

71. *New York Times*, March 15, 1962.

72. *Los Angeles Time*, July 18, 1971, p. 030.

73. *Los Angeles Times*, September 25, 1966, p. K86.

74. Isadore Barmash, "Discount Stores Find Pace Torrid: Industry Delegates Assess Programs of Expansion," *New York Times*, April 22, 1969, p. 59.

75. John D. Pomfrets, "Consumer Course Urged in Schools: Presidential Aide Describes Classes in High School," *New York Times*, May 18, 1965, p. 41.

76. "The Directed Consumer," *Wall Street Journal*, May 25, 1965, p. 18.

77. "Moynihan Assails Industry," *New York Times*, May 13, 1966, p. 27.

78. "Unsafe in Any Tweed," *Chicago Tribune*, June 12, 1966, p. H22.

79. "Washington Wire: A Special Weekly Report from the Wall Street Journal's Capital Bureau," *Wall Street Journal*, March 19, 1971, p. 1.

80. Review of *America, Inc. Who Owns and Operates the United States*, Morton Mintz and Jerry S. Cohen, Robert C. Townsend, *New York Times*, May 30, 1971. P. BR1.

81. John D. Morris, "FTC Eyes 'Planned' Obsolescence," *New York Times*, March 28, 1971, p. 40.

82. As mentioned earlier in the chapter, the response an economist would give to this suggestion is that under market competition, given equal pricing, inferior goods will be driven out by superior ones—such that in effect the market itself does the regulating. And indeed, as mentioned, economic analysis of planned obsolescence maintains that the practice is possible only under monopoly market conditions.

83. John D. Morris, "FTC Eyes 'Planned' Obsolescence," *New York Times*, March 28, 1971, p. 40.

84. *New York Times*, May 3, 1970, p. 17.

85. "Design and the New Environment," *Chicago Tribune*, Willis Thomas, April 12, 1970, p. I62.

86. Louis B. Lundborg, "A Banker's Rejection of Our Rapacious Economy: Slowdown Urged," *Los Angeles Times*, July 14, 1974, p. F1.

87. For example, John Carroll, "Down in the Dumps," *New York Times*, April 22, 1972, p. 33.

88. Martin Gansberg, "Crash Efforts Urged on Refuse: Eisenbud Predicts Outlay of $50 Million in Decade," *New York Times*, May 7, 1968, p. 93.

89. Russell Baker, "Help! The Junk Is Rising!" *New York Times*, September 18, 1966, p. 212.

90. Jim Mann, "Trash Crisis Continues as Cities Seek Relief," *Washington Post*, February 23, 1970, p. A1.

91. "Researchers Urge Nation to Cut Use of Raw Materials: Equalizing Incomes," *New York Times*, February 18, 1973, p. 54.

92. E. W. Kenworthy, "Bills by Nixon and Muskie on Waste Differ Sharply," *New York Times*, February 5, 1973, p. 39.

93. "Waking Up: Abroad at Home," *New York Times*, January 3, 1974, p. 35.

94. Walter F. Hoeppner, "Energy Saving Urged," *Chicago Tribune*, November 14, 1973, p. 20.

95. "Influence Effluence," *Los Angeles Times*, January 17, 1971, p. OC1.

96. MaryLou Luther, "The Designer as Behavioral Scientist," *Los Angeles Times*, September 27, 1973, p. E1.

97. Dan Fisher, "Costs Making Auto Industry's Planned Obsolescence Obsolete: Obsolete Autos," *Los Angeles Times*, April 26, 1970, p. H1.

98. Charles B. Camp and Laurence G. O'Donnell, "New Age for Autos: With Profits Dwindling, Detroit Launches Drive to Hold Down Its Costs," *Wall Street Journal*, June 22, 1971, p. 1.

99. "Business Bulletin: A Special Background Report on Trends in Industry and Finance," *Wall Street Journal*, February 21, 1974, p. 1.

100. Jerry M. Flint, "Styling Changes in Autos Wane," *New York Times*, August 26, 1969, p. 1.

101. "Detroit in Uphill Fight with Small Car Imports," *Washington Post*, November 27, 1969, p. H7.

102. Jaklich Allen, "Advertising Marketing: Auto Makers Selling 'Steak,'" *Chicago Tribune*, July 20, 1970, p. C7.

103. Some, for example Robert Brenner (2006), stress the role of increasing competition. Others, such as Andrew Glyn (2006), give a more class-based explanation.

104. The argument is as follows. The cost of job loss was low in the postwar period because under conditions of near full employment, workers could be reasonably assured that should they choose to leave their jobs, other options would be readily available. This meant that labor had a strong bargaining position, and the result was increasing real wages. From the point of view of capital, this was acceptable and sustainable *if* productivity rates continued to increase sufficiently. But for a complex and still somewhat opaque set of reasons, in the 1960s productivity began to slow down. Between this slowdown and ongoing wage demands, profits were squeezed. In response, the stable collective bargaining arrangements began to come under attack, resulting, for example, in the political sidelining of the National Labor Relations Board in the early 1970s. For extensive discussion see Marglin and Schor (1991) and Glyn (2006). Note that Glyn presents data that suggest a similar historical pattern across the advanced industrial capitalist world.

105. As we have seen, it also became displaced by the new environmentalism (which largely agreed with neoliberalism that the locus of economic action is the consumer yet disagreed that she necessarily knows best and so focused on the project of consciousness-raising), and by the increasingly prevalent current of opinion that obsolescence is a natural corollary of technological progress.

106. In this sense, the concern about the erosion of use value is continuous with postwar concerns about inflation, which also threatened the value of the real wage. Jacobs (2005) notes how fear of inflation became a very significant political concern in the postwar era (which was in fact not a period of very high inflation by the standards of the century).

107. To give a brief review, the hypothesis is that that mass consumption, particularly in the Golden Age of industrial capitalism, is to a significant extent motivated by and rationalized in terms of the commensuration of labor and its wage. The wage is commensurable with labor only insofar as it gets turned into a set of commodities the use value of which is seen as roughly equivalent to the free time and energy sacrificed as work. Since labor itself is some duration of life activity used by the employer, it is properly compensated by something equivalent to it—by wage goods that index a duration of free life activity. When construed as repositories of durations of potential free activity, commodities thus serve as rough equivalents to the activity sold as labor. The accumulation of commodities then to some degree negates the loss of life to work.

108. Where "function" is a temporal concept—that which bestows some notional quantity of use or, in the case of time-saving devices, saves some quantity of time.

109. Simmel [1904] 1957. See Campbell (1992) for an account of the place of neophilia in consumerism.

CHAPTER 10: CONCLUSION

1. By normativity I mean the "ought-ness" produced by norms—how people think they ought to proceed in order to follow a norm, and what criteria establish whether a course of action counts as satisfactorily following that norm.

2. It is true that ad hoc decisions can always be made about what constitutes fair and reasonable exchange. Explicitly conventional systems of commensuration are, of course, certainly possible, and sociologists have charted the ways in which actors and institutions go about *making* things commensurable (Esperland and Stevens 1998). But to resort to pragmatic rules of thumb to provide a provisional solution to the problem of commensuration goes against the principle that exchange be objectively fair. The tension between any given conventional scheme for commensuration and the broad ideal that exchange should proceed according to some "natural" (that is, nonconventional and self-evident) and objective principle makes such schemes eminently contestable and therefore very unstable. That said, clearly ad hoc agreements about fair wage rates are possible, for a while at least—for example, the postwar convergence, discussed throughout this book, on a formula for determining wages, according to which wages should keep up with the cost of living while increasing (in real terms) in line with improvements in productivity. It is much less clear, for reasons briefly set out this conclusion, how individuals could arrive, even provisionally, at some objective sense of having been fairly compensated for their labor.

3. While the focus on normativity also makes my account different in emphasis from orthodox Marxist political economy, at the same time the approach is quite compatible with Marxism. There are certainly historical conditions of a kind that Marxist analysis tends to focus on—a balance of class power, for example, and certain technical conditions in production—that form background conditions to the emergence of the peculiar forms of economic normativity of capitalism. And the idea of capitalism as involving perverse forms of normativity is similar in spirit to the kind of analysis given by the theorists of the Frankfurt School.

4. Here I have in mind systems in which demand is anchored to ritual exchanges, expressing social relations of obligation and reciprocity. Feudal exchange would be one example and, also, from the classical anthropological literature, systems such as the potlach and Kula ring (Malinowski 1920; Mauss [1950] 1990; Polanyi 1957). In describing such economic systems as comparatively nondynamic, I do not mean that they are unchanging or unchangeable. Rather, economic action in such systems is, by comparison with capitalism, more immanently regulated by explicit, socially endorsed scripts. Those systems can, of course, change with time, yet do so in a way that is, in Polyanian terms, more fully embedded in, and therefore guided by, the social than is the case with capitalism.

5. Unless wage labor itself withers away, replaced by fully automated production. Under those circumstances, it is possible to imagine a leisured population, subsisting on some sort of basic income.

6. Also, while Weber focuses on the content of norms, I'm putting more emphasis on the effects of their form—specifically, whether they have clear criteria of satisfaction and whether those criteria are public or private.

7. For Wittgenstein, rules and norms must be public things. As Wittgenstein comments: "To obey a rule, make a report, to give an order, to play a game of chess are *customs* (uses, institutions)" (Wittgenstein 1953, PI 199). To follow a rule, to use a particular norm as guide to action, is, therefore, for Wittgenstein, to go on as *we* do. Rules and norms are not, and cannot be, private and abstract—exhaustive instructions available for internal consultation by way of reflection—but rather are open, social, public, interactional phenomena, embedded within histories and traditions of practice. On this understanding, a norm is correctly followed when it yields behavior that conforms to the public standards of a given community. In order for a rule or norm to be public whether or not it has been followed must, in theory, be subject to external, public checks. Rules and rule following thus rest on a concordance of practice within a community, and correct comportment is secured by way of external checks. Seen from this perspective, the degree to which economic normativity under capitalism is insulated from public ratification and characterized by notionally private conditions of satisfaction, suggests that it amounts to a kind of pseudonormativity, failing therefore to work as a stable guide to practice.

References

Abbott, Lawrence (1957). "Old Hats and New." *Challenge* 5, no. 9/10 (June–July): pp. 32–36.

Achinstein, P. (1970). "Inference to Scientific Laws." In *Historical and Philosophical Perspectives of Science*, edited by R. H. Stuewer, pp. 87–111. Minneapolis: University of Minnesota Press.

Achinstein, P. (1971). *Law and Explanation: An Essay in the Philosophy of Science.* Oxford: Clarendon Press.

Achinstein, P. (1987). "Scientific Discovery and Maxwell's Kinetic Theory." *Philosophy of Science* 54, no. 3: pp. 409–34.

Adamson, Glenn (2003). *Industrial Strength Design: How Brooks Stevens Shaped Your World* Cambridge, MA: MIT Press.

Adorno, Theodore, and Max Horkheimer (1976). *Dialectic of Enlightenment.* New York: Seabury Press.

Aglietta, Michel ([1977] 2000). *A Theory of Capitalist Regulation.* New ed. London: Verso Press.

Aglietta, Michel (2008). "Into a New Growth Regime" *New Left Review* 54: pp. 61–74.

Agnew, P. G. (1934). "The Movement for Standards for Consumer Goods." *The Annals of the American Academy of Political and Social Science* 173 (May): pp. 60–69.

Ainslie, George (1992). *Picoeconomics.* Cambridge: Cambridge University Press.

Ainslie, George (2001). *Breakdown of Will.* Cambridge: Cambridge University Press.

Akerlof, George A. (1970). "The Market for 'Lemons': Quality, Uncertainty and the Market Mechanism." *Quarterly Journal of Economics* 84, no. 3: pp. 488–500.

Akerlof, George A. (1982). "Labor Contracts as Partial Gift Exchanges." *Quarterly Journal of Economics* 97, no. 4: pp. 543–689.

Akerlof, George, and Janet Yellen (1990). "The Fair Wage-Effort Hypothesis and Unemployment." *Quarterly Journal of Economics* 105, no. 2: pp. 255–83.

Anderson, Elizabeth (2000). "Beyond Homo-Economicus: New Developments in Theories of Social Norms." *Philosophy and Public Affairs* 29, no. 2: pp. 170–200.

Aristotle (1981). *The Politics*. Edited by Trevor Sanders. Translated by T. A. Sinclair. London: Penguin.

Aristotle (1982). *The Nicomachean Ethics*. Translated by H. Rackham. Cambridge: Harvard University Press.

Ayres, Edith (1934). "Private Organizations Working for the Consumer." *The Annals of the American Academy of Political and Social Science* 193 (May): pp. 158–65.

Babbage, Charles (1832). *On the Economy of Machines and Manufactures*. London: Charles Knight.

The Barnhart Dictionary of New English since 1963 (1974). New York: Harper Row.

Bataille, Georges (1988). *The Accursed Share: An Essay on General Economy*. Vol. 1, *Consumption*. New York: Zone Books.

Baudrillard (1996). *The System of Objects*. London: Verso.

Baumol, William, and William Bowen (1966). *Performing Arts, The Economic Dilemma: A Study of Problems Common to Theater, Opera, Music, and Dance*. New York: Twentieth Century Fund.

Becker, Gary (1965). "A Theory of the Allocation of Time." *Economic Journal* 75, no. 299: pp. 493–517.

Becker, Gary (1981). *A Treatise on the Family*. Cambridge, MA: Harvard University Press.

Becker, Gary, and George Stigler (1977). "De gustibus non est disputandum." *American Economic Review* 67, no. 2: pp. 76–90.

Belk, Russel W., and Richard W. Pollay (1985). "Materialism and Magazine Advertising during the Twentieth Century." *Advances in Consumer Research* 12: pp. 394–98.

Bell, L., and R. Freeman (2001). "The Incentive for Working Hard: Explaining Hours Worked Differences in the US and Germany." *Labour Economics* 8, no. 2: pp. 181–202.

Beniger, James R (1986). *Control Society: Technological and Economic Origins of the Information Society*. Cambridge, MA: Harvard University Press.

Beracha, Eli, Alexandre Skiba, and Ken H. Johnson (2017). "A Revision of the American Dream of Home Ownership." *Journal of Housing Research* 26, no.1: pp. 1–25.

Berger, Bennet ([1961] 1970). *Working Class Suburb: A Study of Autoworkers in Suburbia*. Berkeley: University of California Press.

Bernoulli, Daniel ([1738] 1954). "Exposition of a New Theory on the Measurement of Risk." *Econometrica* 22, no. 1: pp. 23–36.

Bianchi, Suzanne M., Melissa A. Milkie, Liana C. Sayer, and John P. Robinson (2000). "Is Anyone Doing the Housework? U.S. Trends and Gender Differentials in Domestic Labor." *Social Forces* 79, no. 1: pp. 191–228.

Biernacki, R. (1995). *The Fabrication of Labor: Germany and Britain, 1640–1914*. Berkeley: University of California Press, 1995.

Binmore, Ken (1994). *Game Theory and Social Contract*. Vol. 1, *Playing Fair*. Cambridge, MA: MIT Press.

Blanchard, Olivier (2004). "The Economic Future of Europe." National Bureau of Economic Research (NBER) working paper no. 10310. Cambridge, MA: National Bureau of Economic Research.

Blanchflower, David G., and Andrew J. Oswald (2004). "Well-Being over Time in Britain and the USA." *Journal of Public Economics* 88, no. 7–8: pp. 1359–86.

Bliss, William (1897). *The Encyclopedia of Social Reform*. New York: Funk and Wagnall Company.

Bloch, Marc (1961). *Feudal Society*. 2 vols. Chicago: University of Chicago Press.

Block, Fred (1990). *Postindustrial Possibilities: A Critique of Economic Discourse*. Berkeley: University of California Press.

Bok, Derek (2010). *The Politics of Happiness: What Government Can Learn from the New Research on Wellbeing*. Princeton, NJ: Princeton University Press.

Booth, William James (1991). "The New Household Economy." *American Political Science Review* 85, no. 1: pp. 59–75.

Bourdieu, Pierre (1984). *Distinction: A Social Critique of the Judgment of Taste*. Cambridge, MA: Harvard University Press.

Bowden, Sue, and Avner Offer (1994). "Household Appliances and the Use of Time: The United States and Britain since the 1920s." *Economic History Review*, n.s., 47, no. 4: pp. 725–48.

Bowles, Samuel, and Yongjin Park (2005). "Emulation, Inequality, and Work Hours: Was Thorstein Veblen Right?" *Economic Journal* 115 (November): pp. F397–F412.

Boyer, R. (1988) "Wage/Labour Relations, Growth, and Crisis:A Hidden Dialectic." In *The Search for Labour Market Flexibility: The European Economies in Transition,* edited by R. Boyer, pp. 3–22. Oxford: Clarendon.

Boyer, R. (1990). *The Regulation School: A Critical Introduction*. New York: Columbia University Press.

Boyer, R., and Yves Saillard (2002). *Regulation Theory: The State of the Art*. London: Routledge.

Braverman, Harry (1974). *Labor and Monopoly Capital*. New York: Monthly Review Press.

Brenner, Robert (2006). *The Economics of Global Turbulence: The Advanced Capitalist Economies from Long Boom to Long Downturn, 1945–2005*. New York: Verso.

Brenner, Robert, and Mark Glick (1991). "The Regulation Approach: Theory and History." *New Left Review* 1/188 (July / August): pp. 45–119.

Brick, Howard (2006). *Transcending Capitalism: Visions of a New Society in Modern American Thought*. Ithaca, NY: Cornell University Press.

Briggs, Lyman (1934). "Services of the National Bureau of Standards to Consumers." *The Annals of the American Academy of Political and Social Science* 173 (May): pp. 153–57.

Brody, David (1993). *Workers in Industrial America: Essays on the Twentieth-Century Struggle*. New York: Oxford University Press.

Bulow, Jeremy (1986). "An Economic Theory of Planned Obsolescence." *Quarterly Journal of Economics* 101, no. 4. (November): pp. 729–50.

Burda, Michael, Daniel S. Hammermesh, and Phillipe Weil (2006). "The Distribution of Total Work in the EU and US." IZA Institute of Labor Economics, discussion paper no. 2270. Bonn: Institute for the Study of Labor.

Bureau of Labor Statistics (1997). "Workers Are on the Job More Hours over the Course of the Year." *Issues in Labor Statistics*, Summary 1997/3, February. www.bls.gov/opub/ils/pdf /opbils10.pdf.

Bureau of the Census (1960). *Historical Statistics of the United States, Colonial Times to 1957.* Washington, DC: US Department of Commerce.

Burke, Kenneth (1930). "Waste, or the Future of Prosperity." *New Republic* 63 (July): pp. 228–31.

Burke, Kenneth (1956) "Recipe for Prosperity: 'Borrow, Buy, Waste, Want.'" *Nation* 183 (September 8): pp. 191–93.

Busch, Lawrence (2011). *Standards: Recipes for Reality.* Cambridge, MA: MIT Press.

Campbell, Colin (1987). *The Romantic Ethic and the Spirit of Modern Consumerism.* Oxford: Blackwell.

Campbell, Colin (1992). "The Desire for the New: Its Nature and Social Location as Presented in Theories of Fashion and Modern Consumerism." In *Consuming Technologies: Media and Information in Domestic Spaces,* edited by Roger Silverman and Eric Hirsch, pp. 26–34. London: Routledge, 1992.

Carter, Susan B., ed. (2006). *Historical Statistics of the United States.* 5 vols. Millennial ed. Edited by Scott S. Gartner, Michael R. Haines, Alan L. Olmstead, Richard Sutch, and Gavin Wright. New York: Cambridge University Press.

Carver, T. N. (1917). "Standardization in Marketing." *Quarterly Journal of Economics* 1, no. 2 (February): pp. 341–44.

Centola, Damon, Robb Willer, and Michael W. Macy (2005). "The Emperor's Dilemma: A Computational Model of Self-Enforcing Norms." *American Journal of Sociology* 110: pp. 1009–40.

Chandler, Alfred D. (1977). *The Visible Hand.* Cambridge, MA: Harvard University Press.

Chase, Stuart (1925). *The Tragedy of Waste.* New York: Macmillan.

Chase, Stuart, and Frederick Schlink (1927). *Your Money's Worth: A Study in the Waste of the Consumer's Dollar.* New York: Macmillan.

Chinoy, Ely (1955). *The Autoworker and the American Dream.* Urbana-Champaign: University of Illinois Press.

Cobet, Aaron E., and Gregory A. Wilson (2002). "Comparing 50 Years of Productivity in the US and Foreign Manufacturing." Bureau of Labor Statistics, *Monthly Labor Review,* June.

Cochrane, Rexmond (1966). *Measures for Progress: A History of the National Bureau of Standards.* Washington, DC: US Department of Commerce.

Cohen, G. A. (2000). *Karl Marx's Theory of History: A Defense.* Princeton, NJ: Princeton University Press.

Cohen, Lizabeth (2003). *A Consumers' Republic: The Politics of Mass Consumption in Postwar America.* New York: Vintage Press.

Cook, Rosalind (1927). "Standardization or Taking the Guesswork Out of Buying." *Journal of Home Economics* 19 (January): pp. 164–75.

Costa, Dora (1998a). "The Unequal Work Day: A Long Term View." Papers and Proceedings of the Hundred and Tenth Annual Meeting of the American Economic Association. *American Economic Review* 88, no. 2 (May): pp. 330–34.

Costa, Dora (1998b). *The Evolution of Retirement: An American Economic History, 1880–1999.* Chicago: University of Chicago Press.

Costa, Dora (2000a). "The Wage and the Length of the Work Day: From the 1890s to 1991." *Journal of Labor Economics* 18, no. 1 (January): pp. 156–81.

Costa, Dora (2000b). "From Mill Town to Board Room: The Rise of Women's Paid Labor." *Journal of Economic Perspectives* 14, no. 4 (Fall): pp. 101–22.

Courant, Paul, Edward Gramlich, and John Laitner (1986). "A Dynamic Micro Estimate of the Life Cycle Model." In *Retirement and Economic Behavior*, edited by Henry J. Aaron and Gary Burtless, pp. 279–314. Washington, DC: Brookings Institution.

Cowan, Ruth (1983). *More Work for Mother: The Ironies of Household Technology from the Open Hearth to the Microwave.* New York: Basic Books.

Creighton, Lucy Black (1976). *Pretenders to the Throne: The Consumers Movement in the United States.* Lexington, MA: Lexington Books.

Cross, Gary (2000). *An All-Consuming Century: Why Commercialism Won in Modern America.* New York: Columbia University Press.

Cunningham, William J. (1910). "Standardizing the Wages of Railroad Trainmen." *Quarterly Journal of Economics* 25, no. 1: pp. 139–60.

Cutler, Jonathan C. (2004). *Labor's Time: Shorter Hours, the UAW, and the Struggle for American Unionism.* Philadelphia: Temple University Press.

Davenport, T. H., and J. C. Beck (2001). *The Attention Economy: Understanding the New Currency of Business.* Cambridge, MA: Harvard Business School Press.

Davidson, Donald (1980). *Essays on Actions and Events.* Oxford: Clarendon Press.

Deaton, Angus (1992). *Understanding Consumption.* Oxford: Clarendon Press.

Deaton, Angus (2005). "Franco Modigliani and the Life Cycle Theory of Consumption." Unpublished paper presented at the Research Program in Development Studies and Center for Health and Wellbeing, Princeton, March.

De Certeau, Michel (1984). *The Practice of Everyday Life.* Berkeley: University of California Press.

DeLong, Bradford (2002). *Macroeconomics.* New York: McGraw Hill.

DeSilver, Drew (2014). "American Unions Membership Declines as Public Support Fluctuates." Pew Research Center, February 20. www.pewresearch.org/fact-tank/2014/02/20/for-american-unions-membership-trails-far-behind-public-support/.

De Vries, Jan (2008). *The Industrious Revolution: Consumer Behavior and the Household Economy, 1650 to the Present.* Cambridge: Cambridge University Press.

Diener, E. (1984). "Subjective Wellbeing." *Psychological Bulletin* 125, no. 2: pp. 276–303.

Diener, E., W. Ng, J. Harter, and R. Arora (2010). "Wealth and Happiness across the World: Material Prosperity Predicts Life Evaluation, whereas Psychosocial Prosperity Predicts Positive Feeling." *Journal of Personality and Social Psychology* 99, no. 1: pp. 52–61.

Dunaway, J. A. (1916). "Standardization and Inspection." *American Political Science Review* vol. 10, no. 2 (May): pp. 315–19.

Easterlin, Richard (1974). "Does Economic Growth Improve the Human Lot?" In *Nations and Households in Economic Growth: Essays in Honor of Moses Abramovitz*, edited by P. A. David and M. W. Reder, pp. 89–127. New York: Academic Press.

Easterlin, R. (2003). "Explaining Happiness." *Proceedings of the National Academy of Sciences of the United States of America* 100, no. 19: pp. 11176–83.

Eckman P., R. Davidson, and W. Friesen (1990). "The Duchenne Smile: Emotional Expression and Brain Psychology II." *Journal of Personality and Social Psychology* 58: pp. 342–53.

Elster, Jon (1979). *Ulysses and the Sirens*. Cambridge: Cambridge University Press.

Erskine, Lillian, and John Roach (1917). "The Standardization of Work Essentials." *The Annals of the American Academy of Political and Social Science* 71, "Stabilizing Industrial Employment. Reducing the Labor Turnover" (May): pp. 82–95.

Esperland, Wendy, and Mitchell Stevens (1998). "Commensuration as Social Process." *Annual Review of Sociology* 24: pp. 312–43.

Esping-Andersen, Gøsta (1990). *The Three Worlds of Welfare Capitalism*. Princeton, NJ, Princeton University Press.

Eurostat (2017). "Hours Worked per Week of Full-Time Employment." Retrieved from http://ec.europa.eu/eurostat/web/products-datasets/-/tps00071.

Ewen S. (1976). *Captains of Consciousness: Advertising and the Social Roots of the Consumer Culture*. New York: McGraw-Hill.

Fisk, Donald M. (2001). "American Labor in the Twentieth Century." *Compensation and Working Conditions*. Bureau of Labor Statistics, Fall.

Fogel, Robert (2000). *The Fourth Great Awakening and the Future of Egalitarianism*. Chicago: University of Chicago Press.

Foner, Eric (1995). *Free Soil, Free Labor, Free Men: The Ideology of the Republican Party before the Civil War*. New York: Oxford University Press.

Foner, Philip, and David Roediger (1987). *Our Own Time: A History of American Labor and the Working Day*. London: Verso Press.

Frank, Dana (1994). *Purchasing Power: Consumer Organizing, Gender, and the Seattle Labor Movement, 1919–1929*. New York: Cambridge University Press.

Frankfurt, Harry G. (1958). "Peirce's Notion of Abduction." *Journal of Philosophy* 55, no. 14 (July 3): pp. 593–97.

Frederick, Christine (1929). *Selling Mrs. Consumer*. New York: Business Bourse.

Frey, Bruno S., and Alois Stutzer (2002). "What Can Economists Learn from Happiness Research?" *Journal of Economic Literature* 40, no. 2 (June): pp. 402–35.

Friedan, Betty (1963). *The Feminine Mystique*. New York: Norton.

Friedman, Milton (1957). *A Theory of the Consumption Function*. Princeton, NJ: Princeton University Press.

Frost, Randy O. (2010). "Introduction." *Cognitive and Behavioral Practice* 17: pp. 401–3.

Frost, Randy O. (2013). "From Dante to DSM-V: A Short History of Hoarding." htpp://www.ocfoundation.org/hoarding/dante-to-dsm-v.aspx.

Frost, Randy, and Gail Steketee (2011). *Stuff: Compulsive Hoarding and the Meaning of Things.* New York: Mariner Books.

Gallup (2013). *State of the American Workplace: Employee Engagement Insights for U.S. Business Leaders.* New York: Gallup.

Garon, Sheldon (2012). *Beyond Our Means.* Princeton, NJ: Princeton University Press.

Gartman, David (1986). *Auto-Slavery: The Labor Process in the American Automobile Industry, 1897–1950.* New Brunswick, NJ: Rutgers University Press.

Gershuny, Jonathan, and Ian Miles (1983). *New Service Economy: The Transformation of Employment in Industrial Societies.* London: Continuum Press.

Getz, Max (1940). "Standardization in Informative Selling." *Journal of Home Economics* 32, no. 8 (October): pp. 520–25.

Glickman, Lawrence (1997). *A Living Wage: American Workers and the Making of Consumer Society.* Ithaca, NY: Cornell University Press.

Glickman, Lawrence (2009). *Buying Power: A History of Consumer Activism in America.* Chicago: University of Chicago Press.

Glyn, Andrew (1991). *Capitalism since 1945.* New York: Blackwell's.

Glyn, Andrew (2006). *Capitalism Unleashed.* Oxford: Oxford University Press.

Goldin, Claudia (1986). "The Female Labor Force and American Economic Growth: 1890 to 1980." In *Long-Term Factors in American Economic Growth,* Conference on Income and Wealth, vol. 51, edited by Stanley Engerman and Robert Gallman, pp. 557–604. Chicago: University of Chicago Press.

Goldin, Claudia (1998). "America's Graduation from High School: The Evolution and Spread of Secondary Schooling in the Twentieth Century." *Journal of Economic History* 58 (June): pp. 345–74.

Goldin, Claudia (1999) "A Brief History of Education in the United States." NBER Working Paper No. h0119.

Goldin, Claudia (2000). 'Labor Markets in the Twentieth Century." In *Cambridge Economic History of the United States,* vol. 3, *The Twentieth Century,* edited by Stanley Engerman and Robert Gallman, pp. 549–624. New York: Cambridge University Press.

Goldstein, Carolyn M. (1997). "Part of the Package: Home Economics in the Consumer Products Industry, 1920–1940." In *Rethinking Home Economics: Women and the History of a Profession,* edited by Sarah Stage and Virginia B. Vincenti, pp. 271–96. Ithaca, NY: Cornell University Press.

Gordon, David M., Richard Edwards, and Michael Reich (1982). *Segmented Work, Divided Workers: The Historical Transformation of Labor in the United States.* Cambridge: Cambridge University Press.

Gordon, David M., Thomas E. Weisskopf, and Samuel Bowles (1996). "Power, Accumulation, and Crisis: The Demise of the Postwar Social Structure of Accumulation." In *The Imperiled Economy: Macroeconomics from a Left Perspective,* edited by R. Cherry, pp. 43–57. New York: Union for Radical Political Economists.

Gordon, Robert J. (1999). "U.S. Economic Growth since 1870: One Big Wave?" *American Economic Review* 89 (May): pp. 123–28.

Gordon, Robert J. (2004). "Two Centuries of Economic Growth: Europe Chasing the American Frontier." *National Bureau of Economic Research Working Paper Series*, paper no. 10662, Cambridge, MA.

Gordon, Robert J. (2010). "Revisiting U.S Productivity Growth over the Past Century with a View of the Future." *National Bureau of Economic Research Working Paper Series*, paper no. 15834, Cambridge, MA.

Gregory, Paul M. (1947) "A Theory of Purposeful Obsolescence." *Southern Economic Journal* 14, no. 1 (July): pp. 24–25.

Griliches, Zvi, ed. (1992). *Output Measurement in the Services Sector*. National Bureau of Economic Research, Studies in Income and Wealth, vol. 56. Chicago: University of Chicago Press.

Guest, Robert (1954). "Work Careers and Aspirations of Automobile Workers." *American Journal of Sociology* 19, no. 2 (April): pp. 155–63.

Guiltinan, Joseph H. (2009). "Creative Destruction and Destructive Creations: Environmental Ethics and Planned Obsolescence." *Journal of Business Ethics* 89: pp. 19–28.

Gullickson, William, and Michael J. Harper (1987). "Multifactor Productivity in US Manufacturing 1949–1983." Bureau of Labor Statistics.

Gutman, Herbert (1973). "Work, Culture, and Society in Industrializing America, 1815–1919." *American Historical Review* 78, no. 3 (June): pp. 531–88.

Hackney, James R. (1995). "The Intellectual Origins of American Strict Product Liability: A Case Study in American Pragmatism." *American Journal of Legal History* 39, no. 4 (October): pp. 443–509.

Hamilton, Walton H. (1931). "The Ancient Maxim, Caveat Emptor." *Yale Law Journal* 40, no. 8 (June): pp. 1133–87.

Hammermesh, David S., Harley Frazis, and Jay Stewart (2005). "Data Watch: The American Time Use Survey." *Journal of Economic Perspectives* 19, no. 1 (Winter): pp. 221–32.

Hawken, Paul, Amory Josin, and L. Hunter Lovins (1999). *Natural Capitalism: Creating the Next Industrial Revolution*. New York: Little, Brown & Co.

Heskett, John (2003). "The Desire for the New: The Context of Brook Stevens's Career." In Glenn Adamson (2003), pp. 1–9.

Hirsch, Fred (1977). *The Social Limits to Growth*. London: Routledge.

Hobsbawm, Eric (1964). *Labouring Men: Studies in the History of Labour*. London: Weidenfeld and Nicolson.

Hochschild, Arlie (1997). *The Time Bind*. New York: Metropolitan Books.

Holmes, Wendell (2010). *The Mind and Faith of Justice Holmes: His Speeches, Essays, Letters, and Judicial Opinions*. Edited by Max Lerner. New York: Transaction Press.

Horowitz, David (1994). *Vance Packard and American Social Criticism*. Chapel Hill: University of North Carolina Press.

Houghton, R. W. (1958). "A Note on the Early History of Consumers' Surplus." *Economica*, n.s., 25, no. 97 (February): pp. 49–57.

Hoyt, Homer (1919). "Industrial Combination and the Standardization of Production." *Journal of Political Economy* 27, no. 2 (February): pp. 95–104.

Humphries, Nicholas (2006). "Science Looks at Fairness." *Social Research*, special issue "Fairness: Its Role in Our Lives," 73, no. 2 (Summer): pp. 345–47.

Hunnicutt, B. K. (1984). "The End of Shorter Hours." *Labor History* 25 (Summer): pp. 373–404.

Hunnicutt, B. K. (1988). *Work without End: Abandoning Shorter Hours for the Right to Work.* Philadelphia: Temple University Press.

Hunnicutt, Benjamin Kline (1996). *Kellogg's Six Hour Day.* Philadelphia: Temple University Press.

Isaacs, Nathan (1934). "The Consumer at Law." *The Annals of the American Academy of Political and Social Science* 173 (May): pp. 177–87.

Jacobs, Meg (2005). *Pocketbook Politics: Economic Citizenship in Twentieth Century America* Princeton, NJ: Princeton University Press.

Jones, Ethel (1963). "New Estimates of Hours of Work per Week and Hourly Earnings, 1900–1957." *Review of Economics and Statistics* 45, no. 4: pp. 374–85.

Kahneman, Daniel (2011). *Thinking Fast and Thinking Slow.* New York: Farrar, Straus and Giraux.

Kahneman, Daniel, and Angus Deaton (2010). "High Income Improves Evaluation of Life but Not Emotional Well-Being." *Proceedings of the National Academy of Sciences of the United States of America* 107, no. 38 (September 21): pp. 16489–93.

Kahneman, Daniel, Jack L. Knetsch, and Richard Thaler (1990). "Experimental Tests of the Endowment Effect and the Coase Theorem." *Journal of Political Economy* 98, no. 6, (December): pp. 1325–48.

Kahneman, Daniel, Jack L. Knetsch, and Richard Thaler (1991). "Anomalies: The Endowment Effect, Loss Aversion and Status Quo Bias." *Journal of Economic Perspectives* 5, no. 1: pp. 193–206.

Kahneman, Daniel, Alan B. Krueger, David Schkade, Norbert Schwarz, and Arthur Stone. (2004). "Toward National Well-Being Accounts." *American Economic Review* 94, no. 2: pp. 429–34.

Karpik, Lucien (2010). *Valuing the Unique: The Economics of Singularities.* Princeton, NJ: Princeton University Press.

Katz, Harry (1985). *Shifting Gears: Changing Labor Relations in the US Auto Industry* Cambridge, MA: MIT Press.

Katz, Norman David (1977). *The Consumers Movement: The Movement and the Magazine, 1936–1957.* PhD diss., Rutgers University.

Keynes, J. M. (1930). "Economic Possibilities for Our grandchildren." In *Essays in Persuasion*, pp. 358–73. New York: W.W. Norton.

Keynes, John M. (1936). *The General Theory Employment, Interest and Money*. London: Macmillan.

Kimeldorf, Howard (1999). *The Battle for American Labor: Wobblies, Craft Workers, and the Making of the Union Movement*. Berkeley: University of California Press.

Knabe, Andreas, S. Ratzel, R. Schob, and J. Weimann (2010). "Dissatisfied with Life but Having a Good Day: Time Use and Well-Being of the Unemployed." *Economic Journal* 120, no. 547 (September): pp. 887–89.

Knetsch, Jack L. (1989). "The Endowment Effect and Evidence of Nonreversible Indifference Curves." *American Economic Review* 79, no. 5: pp. 1277–84.

Knight, Frank (1921). *Risk, Uncertainty, and Profit*. Boston, MA: Hart, Schaffer & Marx; Houghton Mifflin Co.

Lancaster, Kelvin (1966a). "Change and Innovation in the Technology of Consumption." *American Economic Review* 56, no. 1 / 2 (March 1): pp. 14–23.

Lancaster, Kelvin (1966b). "A New Approach to Consumer Theory." *Journal of Political Economy* 74, no. 2 (April): pp. 132–57.

Lansburgh, Richard H., ed. (1928). "Standards in Industry." *The Annals of the American Academy of Political and Social Science* 137, no. 226 (May).

Larson, John Lauritz (2009). *The Market Revolution in America: Liberty, Ambition, and the Eclipse of the Common Good*. Cambridge: Cambridge University Press.

Lawrence Mishel, and Heidi Shierholz (2011). "The Sad but True Story of Wages in America." *Economic Policy Institute Brief*, no. 297 (March 14).

Layard, Richard (2005). *Happiness, Lessons from a New Science*. New York: Penguin Press.

Layard, R., S. Nickell, G. Mayraz (2008). "The Marginal Utility of Income." *Journal of Public Economics* 92: pp. 1846–57.

Lears, Jackson (1994). *Fables of Abundance: A Cultural History of Advertising in America*. New York: Basic Books.

Lebergott, Stanley (1996). *Pursuing Happiness: American Consumers in the Twentieth Century*. Princeton: Princeton University Press.

Lebhar, Godfrey M. (1932). *Chain Store: Boon or Bane?* New York: Harper Torch Books.

Levinson, Marc (2011). *The Great A&P and the Struggle for Small Business in America*. New York: Hill and Wang.

Lewis, David (2002). *Convention: A Philosophical Study*. Oxford: Blackwell Press.

London, Bernard (1932). *Ending the Depression by Means of Planned Obsolescence*. New York: n.p.

Longstreth, Richard (1997). *City Center to Regional Mall: Architecture, the Automobile, and Retailing in Los Angeles, 1920–1950*. Cambridge, MA: MIT Press.

Longstreth, Richard (1999). *The Drive-In, the Supermarket, and the Transformation of Commercial Space in Los Angeles, 1914–1941*. Cambridge, MA: MIT Press.

Longstreth, Richard (2007). "Bringing 'Downtown' to the Neighborhoods: Wiebolt's, Goldblatt's, and the Creation of the Department Store Chains in Chicago." *Buildings and Landscapes: Journal of the Vernacular Architecture Forum* 14 (Fall): pp. 13–49.

Low, George S., and Ronald A. Fullerton (1994). "Brands, Brand Management, and the Brand Manager System." *Journal of Marketing Research* 31, no. 2 (May): pp. 173–90.

Lury, Celia (1996). *Consumer Culture*. Cambridge: Polity.

Lury, Celia (2004). *Brands: The Logos of the Global Economy*. London: Routledge.

Lynd, Robert Straughton (1933). "The People as Consumers." In *Recent Social Trends in the United States: Report of the President's Research Committee on Social Trends*, vol. 2, pp. 857–911. New York: McGraw-Hill.

Lynd, Robert S. (1934). "The Consumer Becomes a Problem." *The Annals of the American Academy of Social and Political Science* 173 (May): pp. 1–6.

Lynd, Robert Straughton, and Helen Lynd (1929). *Middletown: A Study in Contemporary American Culture*. New York: Harcourt, Brace, and Company.

Lynd, Robert Straughton, and Helen Lynd (1937). *Middletown in Transition*. New York: Harcourt, Brace, and Company.

Mack, Adrian (2006). "Introduction." *Social Research*, special issue, "Fairness: Its Role in Our Lives," 73, no. 2 (Summer): pp. v–vi.

Mack, Pauline B. (1934) "Clothing and Household Goods for the Consumer." *The Annals of the American Academy of Social and Political Science*. Vol. 173 (May): pp. 35–42.

MacPherson, C. B. (1962). *The Political Theory of Possessive Individualism: Hobbes to Locke* Oxford: Clarendon Press.

Maddison, Angus (1991). *Dynamic Forces in Capitalist Development*. Oxford, OUP.

Maddison, Angus (1992). "A Long Run Perspective on Saving." *Journal of Scandinavian Economics* 94, no. 2 (June): pp. 181–96.

Maddison, Angus (2001). *The World Economy: A Millennial Perspective*. Development Centre of the Organisation for Economic Co-Operation and Development.

Malinowski, Bronislaw (1920). *Argonauts of the Western Pacific: An Account of Native Enterprise and Adventure in the Archipelagos of Melanesian New Guinea*. London: Routledge & Kegan Paul.

Mandel, Ernst (1999). *Late Capitalism*. London: Verso Press.

Maniscewitz, D. Beryl, and J. Stuart (1960). "Marketing under Attack." *Journal of Marketing* 26, no. 3 (July): pp. 1–6.

Marcuse, Herbert (1964). *One Dimensional Man: Studies in the Ideology of Advanced Industrial Society*. Boston: Beacon Press.

Marglin, Stephen A., and Juliet Schor, eds. (1991). *The Golden Age of Capitalism*. Oxford University Press, Oxford.

Marshall, Alfred (2013). *Principles of Economics: Unabridged Eight Edition*. New York: Palgrave Macmillan.

Marx, Karl ([1867] 1981). *Capital: A Critique of Political Economy*. Vol. 1. London: Penguin Books in association with New Left Review.

Marx, Karl ([1893] 1993). *Capital: A Critique of Political Economy*. Vol. 2. London: Penguin Books in association with New Left Review.

Maslow, A. H. (1943). "A Theory of Human Motivation." *Psychological Review* 50, no. 4: pp. 370–96.

Mauss, Marcel ([1950] 1990). *The Gift: The Form and Reason for Exchange in Archaic Societies.* London: Routledge.

McConnell, D. W. (1934). "The Bureau of Standards and the Ultimate Consumer." *The Annals of the American Academy of Social and Political Science* 173 (May): pp. 146–52.

McCracken, Grant, ed. (1988a). *Culture and Consumption: New Approaches to the Symbolic Character of Consumer Goods and Activities.* Bloomington: Indiana University Press.

McCracken, Grant (1988b). "Diderot Unities and Diderot Effects." In McCracken (1988a), pp. 118–29.

McCraw, Thomas, ed. (1998). *Creating Modern Capitalism: How Entrepreneurs, Companies, and Countries Triumphed in Three Industrial Revolutions.* Cambridge: Harvard University Press.

McCraw, Thomas, and Richard Tedlow (1998). "Henry Ford, Alfred Sloan, and the Three Phases of Marketing." In McCraw (1998), pp. 264–301.

McKendrick, Neil, John Brewer, and J. H. Plumb, eds. (1984). *The Birth of a Consumer Society: The Commercialization of Eighteenth-Century England.* New York: HarperCollins.

McLuhan, Marshall (1951). *The Mechanical Bride: Folklore of Industrial Man.* New York, Beacon Press.

Meikle, Scott (1985). *Essentialism in the Thought of Karl Marx.* London: Duckworth.

Meikle, Scott (1992). *Aristotle's Economic Thought.* Oxford: Clarendon Press.

Meikle, Scott (2000). "Quality and Quantity in Economics: The Metaphysical Construction of the Economic Realm." *New Literary History* 31, no. 2 (Spring): pp. 247–68.

Mertes, John E. (1949). "The Shopping Center: A New Trend in Retailing." *Journal of Marketing* 13, no. 3 (January): pp. 374–79.

Meyer Stephen (1981). *The Five Dollar Day: Labor Management and Social Control in the Ford Motor Company, 1908–1921.* Albany: State University of New York Press.

Miller, Daniel (1998). *A Theory of Shopping.* Ithaca, NY: Cornell University Press.

Mische, Anne, and Harrison White (1998). "Between Conversation and Situation: Public Switching across Network Domains." *Social Research* 65, no. 3 (Fall): pp. 695–724.

Modigliani, Franco (1970). "The Life-Cycle Hypothesis and Intercountry Differences in the Saving Ratio." In *Induction, Growth, and Trade: Essays in Honour of Sir Roy Harrod,* edited by W. A. Eltis, M. F G. Scott, and J. N. Wolfe, pp. 197–225. Oxford. Oxford University Press.

Moehrle, Thomas G (2001). "The Evolution of Compensation in a Changing Economy." Bureau of Labor Statistics, Fall issue of *Compensation and Working Conditions.*

Mokyr, Joel (2003). *Oxford Encyclopedia of Economic History.* Oxford, Oxford University Press.

Montgomery, David (1980). "Strikes in Nineteenth-Century America." *Social Science History* 4, no. 1 (Winter): pp. 81–104.

Montgomery, David (1987). *The Fall of the House of Labor: The Workplace, the State, and American Labor Activism, 1865–1925.* New York: Press Syndicate of the University of Cambridge.

Moore, Karl, and Susan Reid (2008). "The Birth of Brand: 4000 Years of Branding History." *Business History* 50, no. 4 (July): pp. 419–32.

National Bureau of Labor Statistics (2015). "Working in the 21st Century." http://www.bls.gov /opub/working/page17b.htm.

National Bureau of Labor Statistics Report (2006). "100 Years of Consumer Spending: Data for the Nation, New York City, and Boston." US Department of Labor, Bureau of Labor Statistics.

National Bureau of Standards (1915). *Measurements for the Household: Circular No. 55.*

National Bureau of Standards (1917). *Materials for the Household: Circular No. 70.*

Nelson, Phillip (1974). "Advertising as information." *Journal of Political Economy*, July / August, pp. 729–54.

Nelson, Phillip (1975). "The Economic Consequences of Advertising." *Journal of Business* 48: pp. 213–41.

Noble, David (1977). *America by Design.* Oxford: Oxford University Press.

Offer, Avner (2006). *The Challenge of Affluence: Self Control and Well-Being in the United States and Britain since 1950.* Oxford: Oxford University Press.

Olney, Martha L. (1989). "Credit as a Production Smoothing Device: The Case of Automobiles, 1913–1938." *Journal of Economic History* 49 (June): pp. 377–99.

Olney, Martha L. (1990). "Consumer Durables in the Interwar Years: New Estimates, New Patterns." *Research in Economic History* 27 (June): pp. 322–49.

Olney, Martha L. (1991). *Buy Now Pay Later: Advertising, Credit and Consumer Durables in the 1920s.* Chapel Hill: University of North Carolina Press.

Olney, Martha L. (1998). "Demand for Durable Goods in Twentieth Century America." *Explorations in Economic History* 58 (June): pp. 408–31.

Olshan, M. A. (1993). "Standards-Making Organizations and the Rationalization of American Life." *Sociological Quarterly* 34: pp. 319–35.

Ostrom, Elinor (1990). *Governing the Commons: The Evolution of Institutions for Collective Action.* Cambridge: Cambridge University Press.

Owen, John (1976). "Workweeks and Leisure: An Analysis of Trends, 1948–1975." *Monthly Labor Review* 99, pp. 3–8.

Owen, John (1988). "Work-Time Reduction in the United States and Western Europe." *Monthly Labor Review* 111, pp. 41–45.

Packard, Vance (1957). *The Hidden Persuaders.* New York: McKay.

Packard, Vance (1959). The Status Seekers. New York: McKay.

Packard, Vance (1960). *The Waste Makers.* New York: McKay.

Panzar, John C., and Robert D. Willig (1981). "Economies of Scope." *American Economic Review* 71, no. 2: pp. 268–72.

Parfit, Derek (1984). *Reasons and Persons.* Oxford: Oxford University Press.

Pecchi, Lorenzo, and Gustavo Piga, eds. (2008). *Revisiting Keynes "Economic Possibilities for our Grandchildren."* Cambridge, MA: MIT Press.

Peirce, C. S. ([1903] 1997). *Pragmatism as a Principle and Method of Right Thinking: The 1903 Lectures on Pragmatism*. Albany: State University of New York Press.

Peirce, Charles S. (1931). *Collected Papers*. 6 vols. Edited by C. Hartshorne and P. Weiss. Cambridge: Harvard University Press.

Penzer, Jonathan, Harry Magdoff, and Paul Sweezy (2013). "Capitalism and the Fallacy of Crude Under-Consumptionism." *Monthly Review* 64, no. 8 (January): pp. 45–48.

Perlman, Selig (1928). *A Theory of the Labor Movement*. New York: Macmillan.

Pew Research Center (2014). "People in Emerging Markets Catch Up to Advanced Economies in Life Satisfaction." (October).

Pigou, Arthur C. (1932). *The Economics of Welfare*. 4th ed. London: Macmillan and Co.

Piketty, Thomas (2014). *Capital in the Twenty-First Century*. Cambridge, MA: Harvard University Press.

Piore, Michael, and Charles Sabel (1986). *The Second Industrial Divide: Possibilities for Prosperity*. New York: Basic Books.

Pliskin, J. S., D. S. Shepard, and M. C. Weinstein (1980). "Utility Functions for Life Years and Health Status." *Operations Research* 28: pp. 206–24.

Polanyi, Karl (1968). *Primitive, Archaic, and Modern Economies: Essays of Karl Polanyi*. Edited by Charles Dalton. Garden City, NY: Anchor Books.

Polanyi, Karl (2000). *The Great Transformation*. Boston: Beacon Press.

Pollay, Richard W. (1985). "The Subsiding Sizzle: History of Print Advertising 1900–1980." *Journal of Marketing* 49, no. 3 (Summer): pp. 24–37.

Pound, Roscoe (1911a). "The Scope and Purpose of Sociological Jurisprudence I." *Harvard Law Review* 24, no. 8 (June): pp. 591–619.

Pound, Roscoe (1911b). "The Scope and Purpose of Sociological Jurisprudence II." *Harvard Law Review* 25, no. 2 (December): pp. 140–68.

Pound, Roscoe (1912). "The Scope and Purpose of Sociological Jurisprudence III." *Harvard Law Review* 25, no. 6 (April): pp. 489–516.

Prasad, Monica (2012). *The Land of Too Much: American Abundance and the Paradox of Poverty*. Cambridge, MA: Harvard University Press.

Prescott, E. (2004). "Why Do Americans Work So Much More Than Europeans." *Federal Reserve Bank of Minneapolis Quarterly Review* 28: pp. 2–14.

President's Research Committee on Social Trends [Chairman: Wesley C. Mitchell] (1933). *Recent Social Trends: Report of the President's Research Committee on Social Trends*. 2 vols. New York: McGraw-Hill.

Raff, M. G. (1988). "Wage Determination Theory and the Five-Dollar Day at Ford." *Journal of Economic History* 48, no. 2 (January): pp. 387–99.

Rawls, John (2009). *A Theory of Justice*. Cambridge, MA: Belknap Press (Harvard University Press).

Reid, Margaret (1938). *Consumers and the Market*. New York: F. S. Crofts.

Riesman, David, and Howard Roseborough (1955). "Careers and Consumer Behavior." In *Consumer Behavior II*, edited by Lincoln Clark, pp. 1–18. New York: New York University Press.

Riggs, Amanda (2016). "Tenure in Home Has Steadily Increased in last 30 Years." Economists' Outlook. October 13. http://economistsoutlook.blogs.realtor.org/2016/10/13/tenure-in-home-has-steadily-increased-in-last-30-years/.

Robbins, Lionel (1930). "On the Elasticity of Demand for Income in Terms of Effort." *Economica*, no. 29 (June): pp. 123–29.

Robinson, Joan (1962). *Economic Philosophy*. London: Penguin Books.

Robinson, John P., and Geoffrey Godbey (1999). *Time for Life: The Surprising Way Americans Use their Time*. University Park: Pennsylvania State University Press.

Roediger, David (1986). "Ira Steward and the Antislavery Origins of American Eight-Hour Theory." *Labor History* 27 (Summer): pp. 410–26.

Rosenberg, Stephen (2017). "The Rise of the Chain-Store, the Decontextualization of Utility, and the Origins of Mass Consumer Capitalism." Unpublished manuscript.

Rosenzweig, Roy (1985). *Eight Hours for What We Will: Work and Leisure in an Industrial City, 1870–1920*. Cambridge: Cambridge University Press.

Roser, Max (2018). "Working Hours." Published online at OurWorldInData.org. Retrieved from: https://ourworldindata.org/working-hours.

Russell, Andrew Lawrence (2008). "'Industrial Legislatures': Consensus Standardization in the Second and Third Industrial Revolutions." PhD diss., Johns Hopkins University, Department of History.

Ryff, C. D., B. H. Singer, and G. D. Love (2004). "Positive Health: Connecting Wellbeing with Biology." *Philosophical Transactions of the Royal Society* 359, no. 1449 (September): pp. 1383–94.

Saad, Lydia (2014). "The '40-Hour Workweek' Is Actually Longer—by 7 Hours." http://www.gallup.com/poll/175286/hour-workweek-actually-longer-seven-hours.aspx.

Samuelson, P. (1938). "A Note on the Pure Theory of Consumers' Behavior." *Economica* 5: pp. 61–71.

Samuelson, P. (1976). *Economics*. 10th ed. New York: McGraw-Hill.

Sargent, Hugh Williams (1958). *The Influence of Consumer-Product Testing and Reporting Services on Consumer Buying Behavior*. PhD diss., Department of Communications, University of Illinois at Urbana Champaign.

Schlink, F. J. (1934). "What Government Does and Might Do for the Consumer." *The Annals of the American Academy of Social and Political Science* 173 (May): pp. 125–43.

Schor, Juliet (1991). *The Overworked American: The Unexpected Decline of Leisure*. New York: Basic Books.

Schudson, Michael (1986). *Advertising: The Uneasy Persuasion; Its Dubious Impact on American Society*. New York: Basic Books.

Schull, Natasha (2012). *Addiction by Design: Machine Gambling in Las Vegas*. Princeton, NJ: Princeton University Press.

Schwartz, Barry (2004). *The Paradox of Choice: Why More Is Less*. New York: Harper Perennial.

Scitovsky, Tibor (1992). *The Joyless Economy: The Psychology of Human Satisfaction*. Oxford: Oxford University Press.

Sen, Amartya (1988). *The Standard of Living.* Cambridge: Cambridge University Press.

Sen, Amartya ([1985] 1999). *Commodities and Capabilities.* New Delhi: Oxford University Press.

Shank, Susan (1986). "Preferred Hours of Work and Corresponding Earnings." Bureau of Labor Statistics.

Shepherd, David, and Mark Shepherd (2004). *Parker 51.* Brighton: Surrenden Pens.

Sherby, Herman (2000). "Fixed Assets and Consumer Durables." *Survey of Current Business,* April 2000, Bureau of Economic Analysis. Washington: US Department of Commerce.

Shergold, Peter (1982). *Working Class Life: The "American Standard" in Comparative Perspective.* Pittsburgh: University of Pittsburgh Press.

Silbur, Norman (1983). *Test and Protest: The Influence of Consumers Union.* New York: Holmes and Milbauer.

Simmel, Georg ([1904] 1957). "Fashion." *American Journal of Sociology* 62, no. 6 (May): pp. 541–58.

Simon, Herbert (1971). "Designing Organizations for an Information-Rich World." In *Computers, Communication, and the Public Interest,* edited by Martin Greenberger, pp. 38–72. Baltimore: Johns Hopkins Press.

Skidelsky, Robert (1992). *John Maynard Keynes.* Vol. 2, *The Economist as Savior.* London: Macmillan.

Slade, Giles (2006). *Made to Break: Technology and Obsolescence in America.* Cambridge: Harvard University Press.

Smail, David Lord (2014). "Neurohistory in Action: Hoarding and the Human Past." *Isis* 105, no. 1 (March): pp. 110–22.

Snell, Bradford C. (1971). "Annual Style Change in the Automobile Industry as an Unfair Method of Competition." *Yale Law Journal* 80, no. 3 (June): pp. 567–613.

Solow, Robert (2008). "Whose Grandchildren?" In Pecchi and Piga (2008).

Sombart, Werner (1967). *Luxury and Capitalism.* Ann Arbor: University of Michigan Press.

Sparrow, James T. (2011). *Warfare State: World War II Americans and the Age of Big Government.* New York: Oxford University Press, 2011.

Stanley, Amy Dru (1998). *From Bondage to Contract: Wage Labor, Marriage and the Market in the Age of Slave Emancipation.* Cambridge: Cambridge University Press.

Stedman-Jones, Gareth (1984). *Languages of Class: Studies in English Working Class History, 1832–1982.* Cambridge: Cambridge University Press.

Steptoe A., J. Wardle, and M. Marmot (2005). "Positive Affect and Health-Related Neuroendocrine, Cardiovascular, and Inflammatory Processes." *Proceedings of the National Academy of Science* 102, no. 18: pp. 6508–12.

Stevenson, B., and J. Wolfers (2008). "Economic Growth and Subjective Well-Being: Reassessing the Easterlin Paradox." *Brookings Papers on Economic Activity,* Spring, pp. 1–87.

Stiglitz, Joseph (2008). "Toward a General Theory of Consumerism: Reflections on Keynes's 'Economic Possibilities for Our Grandchildren.'" In Pecchi and Piga (2008).

Strasser, Susan (1989). *Satisfaction Guaranteed: The Making of the American Mass Market.* New York: Pantheon.

Students for a Democratic Society (1964). *Port Huron Statement*. New York: Students for a Democratic Society.

Summers, Lawrence, and Chris Carroll (1987). "Why Is the U.S. Saving Rate So Low?" *Brookings Papers on Economic Activity* 2, pp. 607–35.

Sundstrom William A. (2006). "Hours and Working Conditions." In *Historical Statistics of the United States Millennial Edition*, vol. 2, edited by Susan B. Carter et. al., pp. 301–55. Cambridge: Cambridge University Press.

Sweezy, Paul (1942). *The Theory of Capitalist Development*. Oxford: Oxford University Press.

Swiencicki, Mark (1998). "Consuming Brotherhood: Men's Culture, Style and Recreation as Consumer Culture, 1880–1930. *Journal of Social History* 31, no. 4: pp. 773–808.

Tate, Jay (2001). "National Varieties of Standardization." In *Varieties of Capitalism: The Institutional Basis of Comparative Advantage*, edited by Peter A. Hall and David Soskice, pp. 442–73. Oxford: Oxford University Press.

Tedlow, Richard (1981). "From Competitor to Consumer: The Changing Focus of Federal Regulation of Advertising, 1914–1938." *Business History Review* 55, no. 1 (Spring): pp. 33–58.

Thaler, Richard (1980). "Towards a Positive Theory of Consumer Choice." *Journal of Economic Behavior & Organization* 1, no. 1: pp. 39–60.

Thaler, Richard H. (1990). "Anomalies: Saving, Fungibility, and Mental Accounts." *Journal of Economic Perspectives* 4, no. 1 (Winter): pp. 193–205.

Thompson, E. P. (1966). *The Making of the English Working Class*. London: Penguin Press.

Thompson, E. P. (1967). "Time, Work-Discipline, and Industrial Capitalism." *Past & Present*, no. 38 (December): pp. 56–97.

Thompson, E. P. (1991). *Customs in Common*. London: New Press.

Thompson, George V. (1954). "Inter-Company Technical Standardization in the Early American Automobile Industry." *Journal of Economic History* 14, no. 1 (Winter): pp. 1–20.

Timmermans, S., and S. Epstein (2010). "A World of Standards, but Not a Standard World: Toward a Sociology of Standards and Standardization." *Annual Review of Sociology* 36: pp. 69–89.

Toph, Olla Perkins (1898). "The Nazarene and Labor," *American Federationist* 5, no. 7 (September): pp. 29–30.

Twitchell, James B. (2004). *Branded Nation*. New York: Simon & Schuster.

Van Boven, L. (2005) "Experientialism, Materialism, and the Pursuit of Happiness." *Review of General Psychology* 9: pp. 132–42.

Van Boven, L., and T. Gilovich (2003). "To Do or to Have? That Is the Question." *Journal of Personality and Social Psychology* 85: pp. 1193–202.

Veblen, Thorstein (1994). *The Theory of the Leisure Class*. New York: Dover Publications.

Voss, Kim (1993). *The Making of American Exceptionalism: The Knights of Labor and Class Formation in the Nineteenth Century*. Ithaca, NY: Cornell University Press.

Waldman, Michael (2001). "A New Perspective on Planned Obsolescence." *Quarterly Journal of Economics*, February, pp. 273–83.

Walker, Charles R., and Robert H. Guest (1952). *The Man on the Assembly Line*. Cambridge MA: Harvard University Press.

Watson, Goodwin (1940). "Work Satisfaction." In *Industrial Conflict: A Psychological Interpretation*, edited by G. W. Hartman and T. Newcomb, pp. 114–25. Oxford: Cordon.

Weber, Max ([1930] 1992). *The Protestant Ethic and the Spirit of Capitalism*. London: Routledge.

Weber, Max (2013). *Economy and Society*. 2 vols.. Edited by Guenther Roth and Claus Wittich. Berkeley: University Of California Press.

Weimann, J., A. Knabe, and R. Schob (2015). *Measuring Happiness: The Economics of Wellbeing*. Cambridge, MA: MIT Press.

Weisskopf, Thomas E., Samuel Bowles, and David M. Gordon (1985). "Two Views of Capitalist Stagnation: Underconsumption and Challenges to Capitalist Control." *Science and Society* 49, no. 3 (Fall): pp. 259–86.

Whaples, Robert (2001). "Hours of Work in U.S. History." Economic History.Net Encyclopedia. http://eh.net/encyclopedia/hours-of-work-in-u-s-history/.

Whitney, Alvert W. (1928). "The Place of Standardization in Modern Life." *The Annals of the American Academy of Political and Social Science* 137, "Standards in Industry," (May): pp. 32–37.

Whyte, William (1954). "The Consumer in the New Suburbia." In *Consumer Behavior: The Dynamics of Consumer Reaction*, edited by Lincoln Clark, pp. 1–14. New York: New York University Press.

Wierzbicka, Anna (2006). *English: Meaning and Culture*. Oxford: Oxford University Press.

Wilcox, Clair (1934). "Brand Names, Quality, and Price." *The Annals of the American Academy of Social and Political Science* 173 (May): pp. 80–85.

Wilentz, Sean (1984). *Chants Democratic: New York City and the Rise of the American Working Class*. Oxford: Oxford University Press.

Willer, Rob, Ko Kuwabara, and Michael W. Macy (2009). "The False Enforcement of Unpopular Norms." *American Journal of Sociology* 115: pp. 451–90.

Wittgenstein, Ludwig (1953). *Philosophical Investigations*. New York: Macmillan.

Wood, Andy (1997). "The Place of Custom in English Political Culture: England 1550–1800." *Social History* 22, no. 1: pp. 46–60.

Wright Mills, C. (2008). *The Politics of Truth: Selected Writings of C Wright Mills*. Edited by John H. Summers. Oxford: Oxford University Press.

Wyland, Charles (1937). *The Economics of Consumption*. New York: Macmillan.

Zeitlin, Jonathan (1987). "From Labour History to the History of Industrial Relations." *Economic History Review*, 2nd ser., 40, no. 2: pp. 59–84.

Zelizer, Viviana (1989). "The Social Meaning of Money: 'Special Monies.'" *American Journal of Sociology* 95, no. 2 (September): pp. 342–77.

Zelizer, Viviana (1994). *The Social Meaning of Money*. New York: Basic Books.

Zilibotti, Fabrizio (2008). "Economic Possibilities 75 Years After: A Global Perspective." In Pecchi and Piga (2008), pp. 27–40.

Acknowledgments

Heartfelt thanks, first, to Andy Abbott, for his moral and practical support, his enthusiasm, and his always penetrating and helpful comments. Andy's capacious, imaginative, and deeply historical approach to social science has been an inspiration to me (indeed, to an entire generation of sociologists). Thanks also to Bill Sewell, for his constructive comments on this project when it was at an early stage. The combination of historical inquiry and social theory characteristic of Bill's work has provided something of a model for my own. Bill's example, as well as Andy's, is what I had in mind when I talk about doing social theory by thinking about history. Thanks, too, to Karin Knorr Cetina, in whose graduate classes on economic sociology I first began to ruminate on the questions at the center of this book. Karin's measured and rigorous inquiries in economic sociology piqued my interest in the field. James Brandt, my editor at Harvard University Press, has my deep gratitude for his very helpful and thoughtful comments on the book, which led me to think hard about how to sharpen its argument. Thanks also to James for being patient and encouraging during the quite protracted gestation of the book. The anonymous reviewers of the manuscript have my gratitude for providing helpful feedback.

Monica Prasad and Andres Villarreal have been close friends and intellectual comrades for many years now. Monica read several drafts of the book, challenging me with trenchant criticism that was well balanced by encouraging comments. Andres has been a stalwart friend and constant source of moral support. Thanks also to a host of others for their friendship over the years: they include Peter Van Der Poorten, Natasha Schull, Guy Leavitt, Saul Thomas, Simeon Thornton, Hamza Yilmaz, and Francis Archer.

Marsaura Shukla, my partner, whose emotional and intellectual companionship has been invaluable, has my endless gratitude. She read pretty much the entire book and, despite it being on a topic far-removed from her own scholarly concerns, offered always intelligent advice about how to clarify its argument. Our children, Jonah and Phoebe, have put up with an often quite distracted dad with good cheer and have provided a delightful backdrop to the writing of the book. Lastly, deep thanks to my mother for her love and support. This book is dedicated to her, as well as to the memory of my father, who would have been thrilled at its completion.

Index